A History of
MEDICINE

FROM PREHISTORY TO THE YEAR 2020

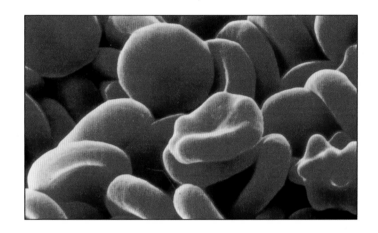

For Dorothy and Edgar Duin;
and for Geoffrey Sutcliffe and Mish

A *History of*
MEDICINE

FROM PREHISTORY TO THE YEAR 2020

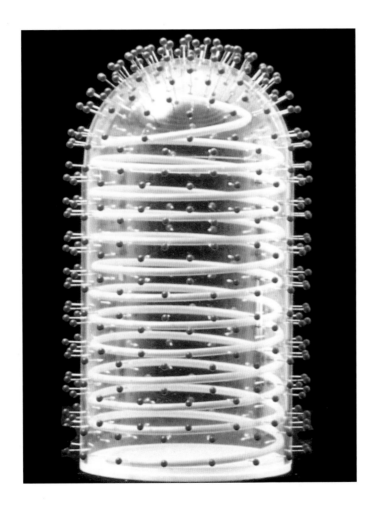

FOREWORD BY

PROFESSOR DR HERO VAN URK

NANCY DUIN
DR JENNY SUTCLIFFE

BARNES
&NOBLE
BOOKS
NEW YORK

Published in the United States of America by:
Barnes & Noble Inc.
1992 Barnes & Noble Books

ISBN 0-88029-927-4

This book was conceived, edited, designed and produced by
Morgan Samuel Editions,
11 Uxbridge Street,
London W8 7TQ

Typeset in Perpetua at 10pt on 11pt by Blackjacks, London.
Separated, printed and bound by Toppan Printing Co (HK) Ltd, Hong Kong.

FOR MORGAN SAMUEL EDITIONS:
Additional writers: Mike Groushko; Bonnie Estridge; Dr Richard Hawkins;
Mal Sainsbury; Mary Ingoldby
Managing Editor: Pip Morgan
Editorial: Rob Saunders, Jenny Barling
Editorial assistants: Nisha Jani; Louise Francis
Editorial research: Beverley Cook; Mary Ingoldby; Paul Worth; Nicholas Haining:
Zad Rogers; Tamsin Marshal
Picture research: Beverley Cook; Colin Humphrey; Jan Croot
Design: Jonathan Baker & Jack Buchan of Blackjacks
Cover design: Tony Paine, Atkinson Duckett Consultants
Indexer: Michèle Clarke
Publisher: Nigel Perryman

This book is intended solely as a work of reference on the history and possible future of
medicine. It should not be referred to for advice or guidance on the diagnosis, treatment
or prognosis of any medical condition. In case of illness, consult your doctor.

CONTENTS

FOREWORD

LIVING AND WORKING, as I do, at the end of the 20th century, and waiting with a sense of expectancy for the 21st, it may be difficult to understand why I should welcome a new history of medicine. After all, I spend my life part-submerged by a sea of learned medical journals, ponderous textbooks and exotic medical atlases. So why should I – a pragmatic surgeon – wish to look over my shoulder at the history of medicine, or take time to nod to the innovators of former ages?

The simple answer is that history is important, and that when I gulp for air to escape the deluge of up-to-the-minute information, it is the air of historical perspective that I seek. In fact, this is indispensable if we want to try to understand the present and anticipate trends for the future – just as politicians have to learn the lessons of ancient and recent wars if they want to avoid future conflict. The analogy is accurate, for humanity has been fighting disease for centuries – winning some battles, but losing others, too. In my view, the stories of such battles, of the frustrations of researchers, the perseverance of individual physicians and the victories and defeats of the whole medical profession, should be told – and taught – again and again.

But what I find most attractive about this book is that it works on several different levels. It gives the facts to those of us in medicine who are looking for historical perspective; but it also provides excellent entertainment for the general as well as for the medical reader in a way that has never, to my knowledge, been attempted before. The authors take you on a fascinating tour through ages and continents, with stories of superstition, bravery, eccentricity, extraordinary characters, perseverance against the odds, persecution and inspiration: from East to West; from quacks to humble scientists and then to Nobel prize-winners; from witch doctors to royal surgeons.

You will read in these pages of the horrors and the unexpected successes of the medicine of ancient Greece and Rome and the Dark Ages; of how the bubonic plague decimated populations in the Middle Ages; and of the triumphs of anaesthesia, antisepsis, vaccination and antibiotics. But it is not just the stories of triumphs and failures and of great men and women that shaped the outlines of medical history: the compelling adventure that has been the development of medicine has also encompassed phenomena such as dogmatism, based on religious or political power, plagiarism and betrayal of the truth for personal ends.

Another attractive and unique feature of this book is revealed in its sub-title "From Prehistory to the Year 2020". This is no idle boast. Eminent scientists, doctors and surgeons have produced a fascinating account of the way that they see the science and practice of medicine developing over the next 30-odd years, each in their chosen field. This is of particular interest to me, covering as it does the implications of gene mapping, aging populations, and so on.

You have already been attracted by the concept of A HISTORY OF MEDICINE, and by the carefully chosen illustrations that complement the text so well. Now read on – for sheer pleasure and fun.

Hero van Urk

Hero van Urk MD
Professor of Surgery,
Head of the Department of Vascular Surgery,
Erasmus University, Rotterdam.
Secretary of the European Vascular Surgery Society.

Morgan Samuel Editions would like to thank all those who have contributed to the production of this book: they are acknowledged in detail on page 256. In particular, though, they would like to thank the eminent medical historian Professor Sir John Dewhurst, for his many helpful and constructive comments about the text.

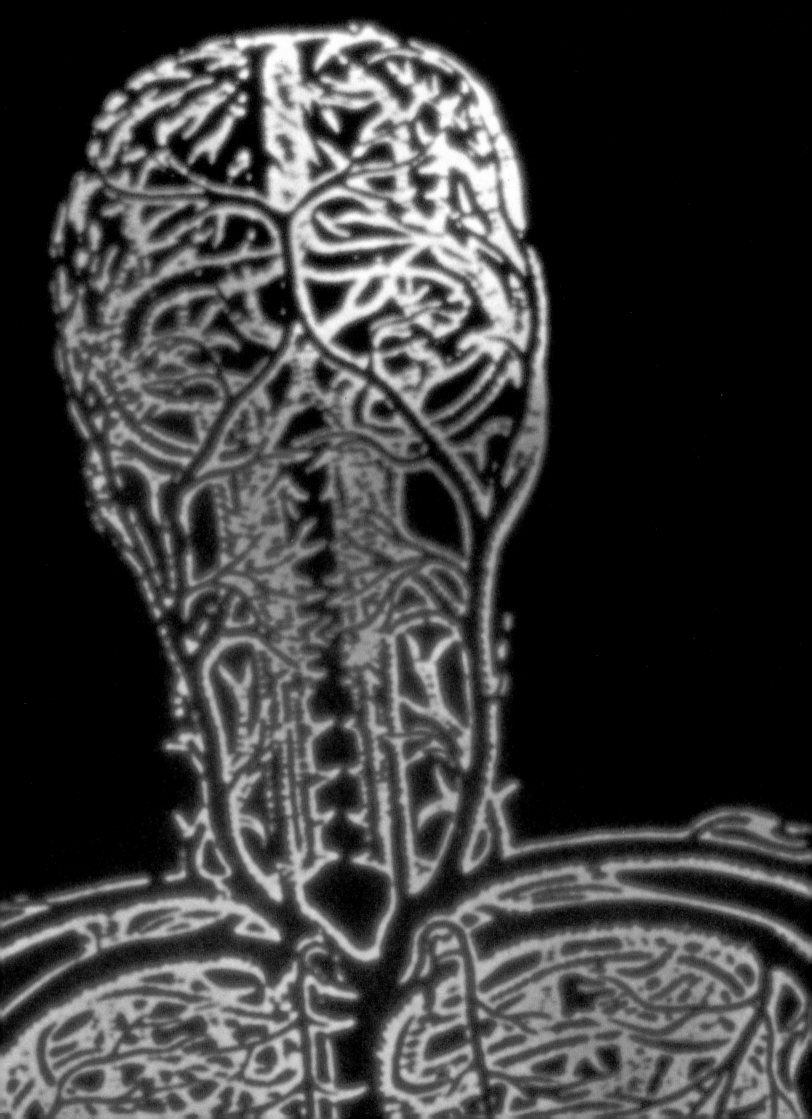

1

The Earliest Medicine

The story of medicine opens with a struggle — both for survival and for understanding of a world that seemed, to its first human inhabitants, to operate by the whim of powerful forces. So, for millennia, humanity practised primitive preventive medicine – for this was all it could do – by appeasing the gods through ritual and sacrifice.

Gradually, a body of knowledge built up, based on chance observation and trial and error. To people who believed that disease was caused by evil spirits, was it not logical to drill the skull of a person suffering from a blinding headache, in order to release them? Unconcerned that this might also relieve intra-cranial pressure, they were simply content the procedure sometimes worked.

And slowly, in measured steps over thousands of years, the body of medical information acquired more flesh, as civilization gathered pace. First, the ancient Egyptians mixed magic spells with psychotherapy, while using animal fat and dung as their drugs of choice; then

Hammurabi of Babylon codified medical practice, primitive and brutal though it was; next, Judaic law laid down dietary and hygienic proscriptions.

But the first, tentative attempts to treat medicine as a science developed at more or less the same time in Greece, India and China. Doctors – for we may now call them so – were often wrong, but their approach to the body and disease was based on logic, each in their own tradition.

It was a golden age, soon to be torn apart by the fall of Rome, by barbarian hordes, and by the destruction of the great storehouse of ancient learning in Alexandria: in short, the Dark Ages of medicine.

As the shadow of superstition fell once more on Europe, the beam of knowledge was kept alight in the Muslim world of the Middle East. Long-forgotten truths returned, embellished, to Europe as the Moors occupied Spain and the Crusaders fought for the Holy Land. But this re-awakening was cruelly shattered as the medieval world was torn apart by the Black Death.

ABOVE *Egyptian priest-doctors from* The Book of the Dead of Hunefer, *c.1310 BC.*

PREHISTORIC HEALTH

A STRUGGLE FOR SURVIVAL

Women survived to 30, but men lived five years longer

BECOMING HUMAN WAS a distinct advantage to our prehistoric ancestors. While animals lost up to 80 per cent of their offspring at or shortly after birth, human beings were able to raise 70-80 per cent of their children. Human beings were also occasionally able to live beyond their reproductive years – a very unusual occurrence in animals – and this lengthening of life proved a human adaptative change of major importance.

Our primitive forebears probably suffered fewer diseases than we in modern industrialized societies do. However, early hunter-gatherers were prone to chronic diseases, caused by organisms that can survive within individuals and be passed (through touch, sneezing and breathing or through infected food) to other members of a group – the types of illness afflicting apes and other primates today. Top of the list are various bacterial infections and invasions of intestinal protozoa (including some causing dysentery). A number of viruses, herpes among them, are also considered causes of ancient human infections, as are intestinal worms.

'Accidental' infections from organisms that normally complete their life cycles in animal hosts were picked up by handling wild animals, butchering and eating them. Hunters were exposed to rabies, toxoplasmosis, anthrax, tetanus, trichinosis and many other illnesses. The environment was also hazardous: the African trypanosomiasis parasite carried by tsetse flies gave sleeping sickness; ticks passed on viral diseases; anaerobic bacteria in the soil caused, among other things, gangrene and botulism.

Because organisms responsible for chronic diseases were continually present in the body, human beings gradually developed immunity and their effects became relatively mild. Accidental infections – which only occasionally afflicted human beings who, thus, were unable to develop immunity – could, though, be quite devastating.

From the evidence, it seems unlikely that diseases unknown today affected these early societies. However, some illnesses that are now quite mild may have been extremely virulent.

A HARD AND VIOLENT LIFE

The earliest nomadic tribes were, however, surprisingly healthy – tall and with good teeth. Men lived on average to 35, while women died about five years earlier. This difference was due not only to stresses of pregnancy and

Lacking understanding of the processes governing life, birth and death, prehistoric humans turned instead to ritual symbols, such as fertility goddesses ABOVE and hunting imagery BELOW.

dangers of childbirth, but also to women's probable responsibility for shifting camp, carrying burdens, collecting food and cooking.

Endemic diseases do not account for the short lifespans of these people, only their hard nomadic life, the climate and warfare. At one site on the Nile, the archaeological evidence of projectile wounds suggests that almost half the population died violently.

In the Mesolithic period (c.8000 BC), as these early peoples began the transition to more settled communities, humans seem to have become shorter. The reason may have been a less nourishing diet, but it is also probable that new endemic diseases were beginning to have an impact, especially those causing anaemia, such as malaria and hookworm. It is also from this time that the first evidence of thalassaemia is found – an inherited adaptation of the red blood cells that acts as a protection against malaria.

SETTLING DOWN

By about 5000 BC, many wandering nomads had settled into communities. Initially, this promoted health and longevity, especially among women, as the stresses of migration were reduced, and it was far easier to care for the sick. There was a more certain food supply, too, and people were increasingly able to develop immunity to common infections.

However, settling also had major health disadvantages. Increased trade brought more diseases. Permanent houses made their spread more likely, as did the accumulation of human waste and the closeness of domesticated animals. Rats and other disease-carrying animals were attracted to refuse; and people staying in one place were constantly reinfected by parasites, such as the blood flukes responsible for schistosomiasis (bilharzia).

As land was cleared for agriculture, non-human primates lost their habitats. These animals were the primary hosts of mosquitoes, and the malarial parasites and yellow fever viruses they carried. All these now preyed on humans, who often chose to settle near marshes and streams where mosquitoes breed. Malaria, in particular, had an immense influence on the future growth of societies and cultures.

Neolithic and early Bronze Age farmers were still not as tall as their Paleolithic ancestors had been – indeed, only today, and then only in well-off Western societies, has the human frame returned to the stature of that time. Nutrition was not particularly good – the Neolithic diet consisted mainly of cereals, and people ate only 10-20 per cent as much protein as their forebears had.

As settlements became more densely populated after 2000 BC, epidemics of childhood diseases became possible. Living cheek by jowl also undoubtedly led to personality clashes and depression – the first signs of modern stress.

A HOLE IN THE HEAD

Prehistoric people believed that pain and disease originated outside the body – not only from injuries but also from evil spirits. Witch doctors and shamans were employed to exorcise malevolent beings, but if they failed, there was an operation that might do the trick.

Trepannation – one of the very few prehistoric medical practices for which we have archaeological evidence – involved cutting a small hole in the skull, often with an instrument resembling a carpenter's bit with a handle. The procedure was used to treat headaches, skull fractures, epilepsy and some forms of mental illness, and it was employed around the world – in Neolithic Gaul and

Bohemia, North Africa, Asia, Tahiti, New Zealand and South America.

It was particularly popular in ancient Peru, where sharp knives of obsidian, stone and bronze were used. Skulls have been found with as many as five trepanned holes. Those who survived the operation (and some did, as healed skulls attest) had their wounds covered with a piece of gourd, stone, shell or even silver and gold. In Europe, the excised rounds of skull bone were worn as amulets.

Trepannation lasted well into the Middle Ages, and even today has been taken up by a few adventurous souls who swear by its ability to expand consciousness.

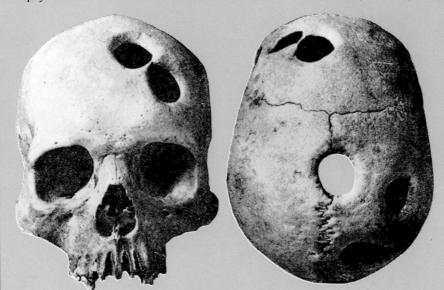

A male cranium from Patallacta, Peru, shows four trepanned holes – experts believe all the wounds had healed eventually.

EGYPTIAN MEDICINE

MAGIC SPELLS AS PSYCHOTHERAPY

They fought disease with lettuce, onions and positive thinking

THE PEOPLE WHO SETTLED the Nile Valley believed that disease came from evil spirits that entered the body through the mouth, nose or ears and devoured the victim's vital substance.

To combat these spirits, a magician uttered spells over the afflicted person and applied ritual remedies. In the case of burns, he swabbed the wound with the milk of a mother of a baby boy, and appealed to the goddess Isis by repeating words that, according to legend, she had used to rescue her son Horus from being burned: "There is water in my mouth and a Nile between my legs; I come to quench the fire".

FROM SPELLS TO DIAGNOSES

As magicians noticed connections between various treatments and the course of certain diseases, they began to compile their observations on papyri. Fragments of these exist today – for example, the Ebers Papyrus, dating from 1550 BC. These papyri – the first systematic classification of medicine – give 'recipes' for the treatment of certain diseases and symptoms. For instance, the Ebers Papyrus lists 21 ways to treat coughs, and it and others deal with at least 15 diseases of the abdomen, 29 of the eyes and 18 of the skin.

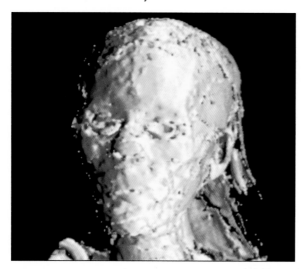

ABOVE *Ta-bes, a mummified Egyptian singer from around 900 BC, was recreated in 3D by computer tomography in an attempt to assess her medical condition at the time of death.*

The medical profession gradually evolved into three different but interacting branches. First, physicians attempted cures by means of internal and external remedies. They used a vast number of substances medicinally, ranging from lettuce and onions, to alum, hippopotamus fat and human excreta. Physicians became specialized, each concentrating on one area of the body.

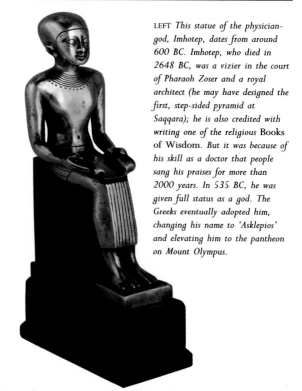

LEFT *This statue of the physician-god, Imhotep, dates from around 600 BC. Imhotep, who died in 2648 BC, was a vizier in the court of Pharaoh Zoser and a royal architect (he may have designed the first, step-sided pyramid at Saqqara); he is also credited with writing one of the religious* Books of Wisdom. *But it was because of his skill as a doctor that people sang his praises for more than 2000 years. In 535 BC, he was given full status as a god. The Greeks eventually adopted him, changing his name to 'Asklepios' and elevating him to the pantheon on Mount Olympus.*

Second were the surgeons ('the goddess Sachmet's priests' in the Ebers Papyrus) who primarily treated external wounds and injuries, such as fractures and dislocations. They never opened the abdomen, but performed operations on the outside of the body, such as circumcision, lancing boils and cutting out cysts, using delicate scalpels, knives, forceps and probes. They also employed red-hot irons to cauterize wounds.

MIND OVER MATTER

The third branch of Egyptian medicine comprised sorcerers or exorcists, who fought evil with incantations and amulets.

Physicians, surgeons and sorcerers alike divided diseases into three categories: "It is an ailment I will treat", implying confidence in a cure; "It is an ailment I will contend with", recognising that a cure would be difficult; and "An untreatable ailment". Diseases in the last two categories, especially the third, were held to benefit most from supernatural intervention. For some diseases the instruction was "Thou shalt not put thy hand to such a thing". In such cases, a soothing remedy and an incantation were prescribed instead of an operation or an active medicament – the remedy so that the patient had at least some treatment, and the incantation to give a little solace. The evidence is that Egyptian doctors (and their sorcerer colleagues) were aware of the power of positive thinking.

CURES FROM THE DEAD

The practice of mummification gave the early Egyptians less knowledge of anatomy than might be supposed. They removed the contents of the abdomen and chest (except the heart, which was usually left in place), so they could distinguish a great many internal organs. But because the procedure was carried out crudely, they did not notice their placement. And although they realized the importance of the heart — considering it the seat of intelligence and of life itself — they did not understand the circulation of the blood.

Mummification did have a profound, if more indirect effect on the growth of medical science. It made the Egyptians familiar with the idea of cutting up corpses, and so encouraged an atmosphere of research. Eventually, the Ptolomaic rulers of Egypt (320-30 BC) gave their Greek physicians permission to study the human body systematically by dissection (see p.19).

Many centuries later, an Alexandrian Jew named Elmagar is said to have treated both Crusaders and Saracens with 'mummy' — a powder made from ground-up portions of embalmed cadavers. This 'therapy' was also used by Guy de Chauliac (see p.31), surgeon to Pope Clement VI, in the 14th century. 'Mummy' was still highly regarded in the early 16th century. François I of France used to carry a little packet of it, mixed with powdered rhubarb, in case of accident since it was thought to be good for bruises and wounds, although it was also taken internally for various ailments. The efficacy of the powder purporting to come from mummies but actually derived from the corpses of recently deceased convicts, stuffed with asphalt and sun dried, is not known.

Mummification occurred sporadically over the centuries, some of the Egyptians' techniques being used to preserve the bodies of Henri IV and Louis XIV of France. It reached its apotheosis in 1852, with the embalming of Alexander, Tenth Duke of Hamilton. An 'Egyptian' ceremony was carried out, with T. J. Pettigrew, the first Professor of Anatomy at Charing Cross Hospital, London, as embalmer and chief ritualist, and the body was laid to rest in an ancient Egyptian sarcophagus that had originally been intended for the British Museum.

Today, Egypt's mummies tell us much about the ancient Egyptians themselves. Modern palaeopathologists have discovered that they suffered from bladder and kidney stones, gallstones, schistosomiasis (bilharzia), arterial disease, gout, appendicitis, mastoid disease and a great many afflictions of the eye. Rheumatoid arthritis was so common that virtually all skeletons show evidence of it; but dental decay was rare, usually only appearing in the wealthy. So far no evidence of such diseases as rickets or syphilis has been found.

BELOW The three-stage process of mummification began with the removal of the body's internal organs. The heart and kidneys would be replaced while the viscera were embalmed and sealed in canopic jars (TOP, MIDDLE). The disembowelled body was placed in a mound of dry natron, a natural compound rich in common salt, and, more importantly for preservation, sodium bicarbonate. The natron soaked up the fluids of the body before it was cleaned and bandaged. Bandaging was extensive and elaborate — hundreds of strips of linen were tightly wrapped around joints, limbs and eventually the whole body. Later, though, the priests found that too much bandaging in fact speeded decomposition, and so discontinued the practice.

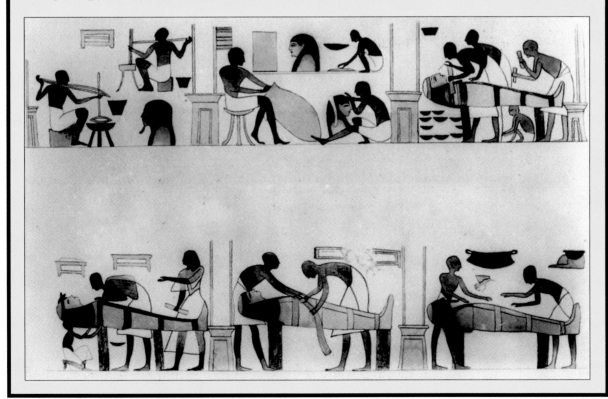

THE FERTILE CRESCENT

MEDICINE REGULATED BY LAW

If the patient died through surgery … the surgeon lost a hand

LONG BEFORE THE EGYPTIANS' ancestors arrived at the Nile, the 'Fertile Crescent' – modern Iran, Iraq, Syria, Lebanon and Israel – had seen the rise and fall of numerous civilizations. The 'land between the rivers' (the Tigris and Euphrates), known as Mesopotamia, was particularly prized, and there, in turn, the Sumerians, Amorites, Babylonians, Elamites and Assyrians held sway.

What we know of their medicine comes almost exclusively from wedge-shaped cuneiform writing on clay tablets. Most of the medical ones were once part of the library of Assurbanipal, the ruthless king of Assyria who reigned from 668 to about 627 BC. Among the 20,000 recovered in 1853 from the site of Nineveh (near Mosul, Iraq) were some 660 of a medical nature, many containing texts at least 1000 years old when the tablets were made.

ABOVE *Relief on a palace wall at Nineveh depicts Assurbanipal killing a wounded lion by stabbing it in the heart with a sword.*

Like the Egyptian papyri, the Mesopotamian tablets list conditions, remedies and prognoses. Some genuine diseases are mentioned, such as jaundice, and occasionally relationships between disease and method of transmission are given – for example, sexually transmitted diseases and sexual intercourse. However, the ancient Mesopotamians generally approached illness with one eye on the gods, placing significance on such esoteric findings as the number of nipple openings in pregnancy: five or six were bad, seven to ten were good. The Babylonians were also excellent astronomers and based much of their religious and medical practice on astrology and the influence of the heavens.

The medical profession consisted of sorcerers (*ashipu*) and physicians (*asu*). The sorcerers, employing charms and incantations, worked closely with the physicians, who were primarily involved in primitive first aid, the giving of drugs, and surgery, being skilled (according to a tablet quoting Assurbanipal) in "the way of operating with the brass knife". With the exception of the Hammurabi Code (*see below*), there is almost no evidence of what this surgery comprised.

We do know – from the world's oldest medical record, a Sumerian clay tablet of about 2150 BC – that the physicians washed wounds (unlike the Egyptians), made poultices and used bandages. Wounds were bathed in beer and hot water; poultices were made from materials such as pounded pine, prunes, wine dregs and lizard dung – a list of about 230 such 'drugs' was found in the remains of an Assyrian pharmacy. They also knew the process of distillation, once thought to be a much later invention, and used it to make 'essence' of cedar and other volatile oils.

Babylonian medicine combined ritual incantations, herbal remedies and physical therapy. Illness demons, often personified by statues, RIGHT, had to be identified and then driven from the afflicted body.

THE HAMMURABI CODE

The Babylonians were possibly the first to regulate medicine by law. In 1901, labourers at an excavation at Susa (in Iran) uncovered three large fragments of polished black diorite, which, when joined together, formed a pillar over 7ft, (2.1m) high, covered in cuneiform script. Archaeologists soon realized it was Babylonian.

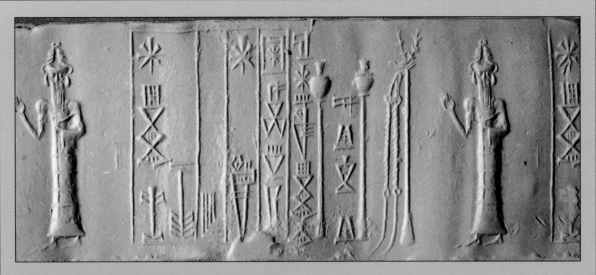

OLD TESTAMENT MEDICINE

ABOVE *This 4000-year-old Sumerian cylinder seal depicts the deity, Gir, an assistant to women in childbirth.*

From the Old Testament (the Hebrew Bible) – written between the 8th and 3rd centuries BC, but recording much earlier events – it is clear that the ancient Hebrews believed disease resulted from displeasing God, and that only priests could help.

Although there were midwives, circumcisions, first aid and fracture treatments, Hebrew medicine excelled in the area of public health. The priests acted as primitive medical officers of health, and were keen to prevent the transmission of disease from one person to another.

They were fanatical about cleanliness, and demanded that hands always be washed after handling dead bodies or impure substances and before eating – a remarkable rule for a desert people, and perhaps borrowed from Egyptian priests during their days under the pharaohs.

The priests also insisted that refuse be burned outside camps and excreta buried.

If leprosy or plague was suspected, patients' clothing was washed or burned and their houses destroyed or disinfected (even to the point of scraping the walls). Patients were isolated for 40 days, a rule taken up by medieval European Gentiles trying to deal with the Black Death (see p.30); the Italian word for 40 is **quaranta**, *from which we get the modern word 'quarantine'.*

Perhaps the best-known tenets of Hebrew medicine are those found in the Book of Leviticus in the Bible that deal with hygiene – for example, the prohibitions against eating unclean animals such as pigs. However, the advantages for health were incidental by-products of what were basically religious rituals.

The upper part of the pillar shows King Hammurabi (*c.*1695 BC) receiving the commission to write his laws from Shamash, the Babylonian sun god and god of justice. Below this are 282 laws dealing with social structure, economic conditions, industries, family life – and medical practitioners. Seventeen tell what a physician should be paid for certain types of work and what his responsibilities were. For example, the Hammurabi Code specifies that: "If a physician has performed a major operation on a lord with a bronze lancet and has saved the lord's life ... he shall receive ten shekels of silver".

The work was well paid: ten shekels equalled a carpenter's income for 450 working days. (Saving the life of a commoner was only worth five shekels, and that of a slave, two.) However, there were high risks:

"If a physician performed a major operation on a lord ... and has caused the lord's death ... they shall cut off his hand." These laws only dealt with surgery; bad results from drugs or incantations were not subject to penalty. This was in keeping with Babylonian beliefs: if people became ill, it was their own fault, because they had sinned or had allowed a bad spirit to invade them; but if a physician made a deliberate surgical wound and the outcome was death, that was the physician's responsibility.

The following spell for 'fever sickness', from R. Campbell Thompson's Devils and Evil Spirits of Babylonia *(1905), would have been one of a battery used by the sorcerers:*

Fever hath blown the man as the windblast,
It hath smitten this man, and humbled his pride ...
His mouth it hath turned to gall So that the moisture therein
hath no sweetness ...
Take a white kid of Tammuz,
Lay it down facing the sick man and
Take out its heart and
Place it in the hand of that man ...
Invoke the great gods
That the evil Spirit, the evil Demon, evil Ghost, Hag-demon,
Ghoul, Fever, or heavy Sickness
Which is in the body of the man,
May be removed and go forth from the house! ...
O evil Spirit! O evil Demon! O evil Ghost!
Hag-demon! O Ghoul! O Sickness of the heart!
O Heartache! O Headache! O Toothache!
O Pestilence! O grievous Fever!
By Heaven and Earth may ye be exorcised!

MEDICINE OF THE EAST

AN ALTERNATIVE TRADITION

Pulverized seahorses to treat goitre; elephant skins for sores

THE SYSTEMS OF MEDICINE developed in ancient China and India survive today virtually unchanged. They differ greatly from those of other ancient cultures, which can be seen as steps along the way to modern Western medicine.

ANCIENT CHINA

By 400 BC, Chinese medicine had separated from religion and magic, and was in the hands of professionals. These were organized in a state system and graded according to achievement. Lowest were the surgeons, a small group of what the Chinese called 'third-rate graduates'.

Chinese physicians attempted to cure disease by restoring harmony and balance, between the five basic elements – earth, water, fire, wood and metal – of which they believed everything was made; and also between two opposing, yet complementary, forces: *yin* and *yang*. YIN was the dark, moist, female aspect; YANG, the bright, dry, masculine. The Chinese belief that one cannot exist without the other can be seen in the original meanings of the words: *yin* meant 'shady side of a hill'; *yang* meant 'sunny side of a hill'.

Much of what we know about early Chinese medicine is contained in the *Nei Ching* (loosely translated as *Manual of Physic*), believed to have been compiled between 479 and 300 BC. It takes the form of a conversation between the 'golden emperor' Huang Ti, who is supposed to have lived between 2629 and 2598 BC, and his prime minister Ch'i Po. It deals almost exclusively with acupuncture: treating disease by allowing energy (*chi*) to enter or leave the body at one of 365 points (or 600, according to some schools) along meridians, by the insertion of fine needles. The meridians are vertical pathways through which *chi* flows, each related to an organ. They do not correspond to the body's nervous system – human dissection was strictly forbidden in ancient China, and physicians knew very little about anatomy – but some seem to follow known paths of referred pain, such as gallstone pain in the right shoulder blade.

The *Nei Ching* also describes the 12 pulses to be palpated by the physician, six in each wrist. The multitude of qualities that each one could have are poetically described – for example, 'smooth as a flowing stream', 'dead as a rock', 'like water dripping through the roof', 'light as flicking the skin with a plume' – and the whole procedure could take many hours.

Chinese physicians also used 'moxibustion'. A cone of moxa – powdered leaves of the mugwort plant – was placed on a particular acupuncture point and set alight. The warmth and resulting blister supposedly increased yang; they certainly masked any pain caused by disease by creating a new one.

The Chinese also had an extensive pharmacy of some 2000 items and 16,000 remedies, not all herbal; many of them seem strange and even repulsive from the Western viewpoint. Patients were given pulverized seahorses for goitre, snakemeat for eye ailments, octopus ink mixed with vinegar for heart disease and elephant skin for persistent sores.

THE SURGEON AND THE GENERAL

Ancient China produced only one surgeon of sufficient prominence that his name has come down to us over the centuries: Hua T'o, who is thought to have lived some 1800 years ago. One of his patients was the warlord Kuan Yun. When Kuan's arm was pierced by a poisoned arrow, Hua cut and scraped out the wound down to the bone – while the warlord played chess and drank cups of wine. This may have been taking **sang-froid** *to extremes but history does not record whether he had the benefit of any acupuncture anaesthesia.*

Foolishly, Hua believed himself above politics. When Kuan's bitterest enemy, Tsao Tsao, came to him with a bad headache, Hua decided to treat it by trepannation (see p.11). Just as he was about to begin, Tsao suddenly got the notion that Hua might have been bribed by Kuan to murder him and had the unfortunate surgeon executed on the spot.

RIGHT *Ancient Chinese surgeon, Hua T'o, operates on Kuan Yun's arm while his warlord patient drinks wine and plays chess. Hua's ultimate reward for this service was execution.*

ABOVE *A page from the* Nei Ching (Manual of Physic), *recording detailed conversations* *about acupuncture treatments between the Emperor and the Prime Minister of China.*

ANCIENT INDIA

It is impossible to date the origins of the Indian system of medicine now known as the Ayurveda (literally, 'knowledge, or science, of life'). Few written records survive. The four *Vedas*, sacred Sanskrit books that were passed down orally through the ages, are all that is left.

Ayurvedic medicine is based on two treatises supplementing the *Atharva Veda* and supposedly composed by the men named in their titles: the *Charaka Samhita*, mainly medical; and the *Sushruta Samhita*, which deals with surgery. No one knows when they were written down, but researchers have claimed that Sushruta could have lived at any time between 1000 BC and AD 1000.

Unlike Chinese medicine, Ayurvedic medicine was wrapped up in religion. Doctors used incantations and watched for portents as often as they administered drugs and operated. However, like the Chinese, they identified a variety of points on the body (107 in all) considered crucial to health, called *marmas*. If a person were wounded in one of these *marmas*, the outcome was likely to be fatal – some of them correspond to major arteries, nerves and tendons.

Indian physicians also believed that disturbances in the levels of various substances – in this case, wind (*vayu*), bile (*pitta*), phlegm (*kapha*) and blood (*rakta*) – were responsible for disease. It is likely that this theory, picked up by travellers and transplanted to Greece, was the origin of the idea of the 'four humours' *(see p.18)*.

The Indians excelled in surgery. Nowhere else in the ancient world were operations, both inside and outside the body, so extensive. They had 121 different steel instruments – scalpels, probes, trocars, catheters and even magnets to remove metal objects – to carry out a multiplicity of procedures: cauterizing fistulae, sewing up wounds, draining fluid, treating cataracts, removing bladder and kidney stones and, most remarkable of all, repairing noses and earlobes with plastic surgery.

Trainee doctors had to memorize the two *Samhitas* and other Vedic works, and they practised their surgical skills on inanimate objects: making incisions on pickles, lancing leather bags filled with slime, cauterizing pieces of meat. The *Sushruta Samhita* required certain other qualities of these young men – as well as purity of mind and a retentive memory, they had to have a thin tongue, lips and teeth, a straight nose and large, honest, intelligent eyes.

THE FIRST NOSE JOBS

The amputation of body parts was a common punishment in ancient India, and quite often it was the culprit's nose that was singled out for attention. With plenty of opportunities for practice and experiment – probably based on trial and error – the Ayurvedic doctors came up with a new technique: this led to the earliest recorded nose restorations.

They would cut a leaf-shaped flap of skin from the forehead, making sure that the end nearest the bridge of the nose remained attached. The flap would be brought down over where the nose should be; then it would be twisted skin-side-out and sewn into place. Finally, to keep the air passages open during healing, two polished wooden tubes would be inserted into the 'nostrils'. A similar procedure, rhinoplasty, is still carried out by plastic surgeons today.

BELOW *This picture of an Indian bullock driver, whose nose has been successfully restored after punitive mutilation, completely* *astonished the British sahibs and memsahibs when they saw it in the October 1794 issue of the* Gentleman's Magazine of Calcutta.

ANCIENT GREECE

THE START OF THE HIPPOCRATIC TRADITION

"I will prescribe treatment to the best of my ability and judgment ..."

WITH THE RISE OF GREEK CIVILIZATION, physical ills in the West were no longer blamed on the gods or sin, but on imbalance within the body itself.

The theory of the four humours was the basis of much medical practice. Like the Chinese and the Indians, the Greeks believed in balance. Indeed, the whole of their civilization could be seen as a search for symmetry. When the balance between the four humours was disturbed, said the Greeks, the result was disease.

THE FOUR HUMOURS

The Greeks believed in the existence of four fluids, or humours, within the body, the balance of which was vital for health. The humours corresponded to the four elements, and had the same qualities; they were also associated with particular parts of the body.

HUMOUR	ELEMENT	QUALITIES	BODY PART
Blood	*Air*	*Hot and wet*	*Blood*
Phlegm	*Water*	*Cold and wet*	*Brain (pituitary)*
Yellow bile	*Fire*	*Hot and dry*	*Liver*
Black bile	*Earth*	*Cold and dry*	*Spleen*

PRACTITIONERS AND TREATMENT

Doctors were usually itinerant – their travels, curiously enough, being known as epidemics – but some had offices in towns. Owning no land, they had no high social standing, although they were clearly men of some importance.

They stressed cleanliness, and examined wounds only with probes. Questioning their patients closely about their symptoms, they looked for things within people's lives and surroundings that might have a bearing on their health. They dressed wounds with herbal/mineral mixtures (*enhemes*) and with vinegar and wine, all of which had antiseptic qualities. They also employed tourniquets and auscultation (pressing an ear against the chest) – techniques that, with the passing of classical Greek civilization, were lost until the 15th century. Perhaps most important was the doctors' belief that they were not disinterested arbiters between the gods and humanity, but servants of the sick.

Some of their practices were, however, unfortunate. Wounds were bandaged extremely tightly, and suppuration (the formation of pus) was considered an excellent way to eliminate phlegm (any colourless or white secretion other than semen or breastmilk.) Even if patients were haemorrhaging, doctors might start bleeding them elsewhere,

---

THE HIPPOCRATIC OATH

One of the bases of modern medical ethics, the Hippocratic oath was probably sworn by those admitted to the school and guild of Cos. It is unlikely that it was written by Hippocrates himself.

"I swear by Apollo the physician, and by Asklepios, Hygeia and Panacea, and all the gods and goddesses, and call them to witness that ... I will prescribe treatment to the best of my ability and judgment for the good of the sick, and never for a harmful or illicit purpose. I will give no poisonous drug, even if asked to, nor make any such suggestion; and likewise I will give no woman a pessary to cause abortion. I will both live and work in purity and godliness ... I will ... refrain from all deliberate harm or corruption, especially from sexual relations with women or men, free or slave. Anything I see or hear about people, whether in the course of my practice or outside it, that should not be made public, I will keep to myself and treat as an inviolable secret ....

ABOVE *This engraving of a bust by Flemish painter, Peter Rubens, profiles Hippocrates, who did more than anyone else to dispel the* notion that disease and ill-health were caused by direct interference from the gods, whose interventions were unpredictable.

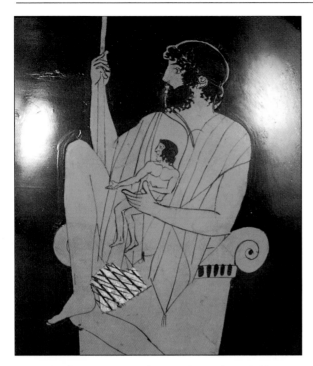

ABOVE *This illustration on a Greek*
vase depicts Telethos with a thigh
wound wrapped in a double spica
bandage – a type still used today.

to remove any excess of the humour, blood. Similarly they
would probably prescribe a purgative, to induce vomiting or
diarrhoea; some of these, such as hellebore, could be lethal.
Finally, an extremely restricted diet would be recommended –
to prevent an increase in humours.

The belief in the four humours, and the use of
suppuration and blood-letting, persisted for another 2000
years, until the causes and transmission of disease, and the
nature of infection, were understood.

HIPPOCRATES

The greatest of all the doctors of ancient Greece was
Hippocrates (*c*.400 BC). A physician and surgeon (although
performing only such minor procedures as haemorrhoid and
polyp removal), he became the leader of a medical school
and guild on the Aegean island of Cos. His works, and those
of his followers, are contained in the *Hippocratic Corpus,* over
70 volumes that range from detailed case histories to
thoughts on the practice of medicine, the role of environment in health, epilepsy (commonly known as the 'sacred
disease') and prognoses.

It was the Hippocratic school's concentration on this last
that made it different from others of the time. While non-
Hippocratic doctors would elicit symptoms and make
diagnoses, the Cos physicians would go one step further and
try to predict the outcome for their patients – a technique
that was both brave and reassuring to those in their care.

TEMPLE MEDICINE

The Greek doctors recognized the spiritual side of healing:
when all else failed, they were quite happy for their patients
to attend one of the many *asklepieia* – temples to the patron
god of physicians, Asklepios (Aesculapius to the Romans and
really Imhotep [*see p.12*] in Greek dress), and his daughters
Hygeia (health) and Panacea (healing). Asklepios would often
be accompanied by a snake, the drakon – hence the medical
symbol of a snake wound round a staff.

Pilgrims to the temples relaxed among beautiful
surroundings and read inscriptions on marble pillars that told
of the miraculous cures performed by the god. Then they
would bed down for the night in the sacred hall, where
Asklepios would supposedly appear as they slept, to give
them a 'dream drug' or even to perform 'dream surgery'.

BELOW *Asklepios, the patron god of*   *staff to hand as a Greek physician*
physicians, watches with his serpent   *examines the body of a patient.*

ANCIENT ROME

CONTINUING THE GREEK TRADITION

Gravestones reported: "It was the crowd of physicians that killed me"

IN THE EARLY DAYS OF THE CITY, Roman medicine consisted of little more than propitiating the gods and reliance on traditional folk remedies. Then, in 293 BC, according to the historian Livy, a plague ravaged Rome and the city sought help from the Greek god Asklepios (the Roman Aesculapius). A ship was sent to Greece, and the god came aboard in the form of his snake. Approaching Rome, the snake swam to an island in the Tiber. A temple was erected there and the plague disappeared (a hospital has been on this site ever since). This marked the beginning of Greek influence on Roman medicine; eventually, healing came to be almost entirely in Greek hands and remained so for centuries.

Asclepiades of Bithynia, a man of great natural shrewdness, was the first Greek doctor to succeed in Rome, in the 1st century BC. He avoided preaching Greek theories and rejected many of the extreme treatments prevalent in Rome, his motto being '*cito tuto jucunde*' ('swiftly, safely, sweetly'). This moderate approach – and, possibly, his habit of prescribing wine in liberal doses – smoothed the acceptance of other Greek doctors.

The Greeks established schools of medicine in Rome, all influenced by the Hippocratic Corpus. There were three main groups: the dogmatists, who were keen to understand disease and approved of dissection, but most of whose medicine was theoretical; the empiricists, who relied on experience and observation to discover effective remedies; and the methodists, who believed that doctors should follow only a few simple rules, which could be learned in about six months – thus rejecting at a stroke both complicated theories and long experience.

THE STATUS OF DOCTORS

In 46 BC, Julius Caesar granted citizenship to all foreigners teaching a liberal art in Rome. This included doctors, most of whom were slaves or freed men. When Antonius Musa, once Mark Antony's slave, cured Emperor Augustus of a serious illness in 23 BC by cold hydrotherapy, he was richly rewarded and won immunity from taxation for all doctors.

During the reign of Vespasian (AD 69–79), physicians were also freed from military service. This, combined with freedom from taxation, caused such a boom in the medical profession that, in AD 160, the emperor Antoninus Pius restricted the number of *archiatri*, or 'public physicians'.

Doctors belonged to one of three groups: independent practitioners; physicians attached to a particular family or the emperor; and *archiatri*, who were paid by a town to look after its citizens. Until AD 200, when medical licensing was introduced, anyone, man or woman, could declare themselves a doctor. Training was difficult to obtain, apprentices being dependent for learning on doctors to whom they were attached. Hospitals and infirmaries –

valetudinaria – were only for wounded soldiers and found on the empire's frontiers, or for slaves and found on farms. Only the well-off could afford to travel to different medical centres such as Alexandria and Ephesus to obtain a well-rounded education, and medical texts were expensive or inaccessible. However, guilds often purchased texts for the benefit of members, and medical books were also sent to all military forts. In this way, medical knowledge spread to every corner of the empire.

Social rank depended on wealth and ownership of land. Most doctors had neither, though well-educated physicians in the households of aristocrats achieved high status. However, some were famous more for their wealth than for their medical skill. There were far more *medici*, poor physicians working out of small side-street shops (*tabernae medicae*).

In the view of the common people, doctors spent their time theorizing and arguing among themselves, sometimes killing their patients with promised cures and then asking for payment from relatives. Medicine's bad image was reflected in literature – for example, the historian Pliny wrote:

"There is no doubt that all these [physicians], in their hunt for popularity by means of some novelty, do not hesitate to buy it with our lives .... Hence too that gloomy inscription on monuments: 'It was the crowd of physicians that killed me'."

ABOVE *Seated at his desk, a Graeco-Roman physician reads a manuscript in his office in Rome. The scene, carved in relief on a* sarcophagus *dated around AD 100, also includes the physician's medical cabinet with a case of surgical instruments.*

WOMEN AND MEDICINE

Women doctors (*medicae*) concentrated, though not exclusively, on female diseases: one inscription refers to a *medica a mammis* – a female specialist in breast disorders. Midwives (*obstetrices*) were of enormous help and influence before, during and after childbirth. Most were probably simple village women who learned their craft by experience, but others studied treatises on gynaecology and obstetrics, and a few became eminent authorities.

ABOVE *The castor oil plant* (Ricinus communis) *supplied the ingredients for one of the hundreds of remedies that the Roman physician Dioscorides prepared. His* De Materia Medica *established him as the undisputed authority on plant medicines – his position was not to be seriously challenged for more than 1500 years.*

However, the best-known writer on gynaecology was a man: Soranus of Ephesus, who lived around AD 100. Much of what he wrote in his great work *Gynaecology* is applicable today. He rejected the Greek idea that the uterus moved erratically around a woman's body, causing pain. However, he and his contemporaries did believe that it was responsible for certain mental problems. This idea persisted, and 'hysteria' (from the Greek *hustera*, 'uterus') became the province of women.

MEDICAL AMMUNITION

All doctors used herbal drugs, and a thriving trade developed in rarities, such as 'balsam of Mecca' and 'Indian lycium'. There was a huge market, too, for theriac, a compound of over 60 ingredients, including viper meat and opium, which was used as a universal panacea.

The Romans compiled a number of lists of medicinal plants, or herbals. The greatest of them (which continued to be published well into the Renaissance) was Dioscorides' five-volume *De Materia Medica* (*c*.AD 64). It contains some 600 remedies, of which only about 20 per cent would now be thought to have any medical benefit.

However, striking advances were made in surgery and public health: as many as 200 different medical instruments were known, including the vaginal speculum, one of which was found at Pompeii. Unfortunately, the Romans' technical competence in surgery was hampered by a limited knowledge of the anatomy of the body.

Hygiene and public health progressed with the development of sophisticated latrines in military forts and wealthy homes. Clean water reached the populace via impressive aqueducts, some in use today; and magnificent public baths became increasingly common.

Concern for hygiene even extended to draining marshes. The scholar Marcus Terentius Varro (116–28 BC) anticipated the germ theory of disease, advising caution near swamps – where malarial mosquitoes breed – "because there are bred certain minute creatures which cannot be seen by the eyes, which float through the air and enter the body through the mouth and the nose and there cause serious disease".

CELSUS

A work educated doctors might have consulted was **De Medicina (On Medicine)**, *written by the encyclopaedist Cornelius Celsus during the reign of Tiberius (AD 14–37). This eight-volume work, which has survived from antiquity in its entirety, reveals an enormous amount about Roman medical thought and practice.*

Celsus knew the difference between fresh wounds and ulcers that are slow to heal; and he knew about clamping veins to prevent haemorrhage (a number of Roman forceps have been found to prove it). He describes complex surgical operations, including goitre and cataract removal, and refers to plastic surgery, which probably reached Rome (and Celsus) from India (see p.17). Most important of all, Celsus was the first to record the definition of acute inflammation: **'rubor et tumor cum calore et dolore'** *('redness and swelling with heat and pain').*

RIGHT *The Roman rectal speculum (*LEFT*) bears close comparison with the modern version (*RIGHT*).*

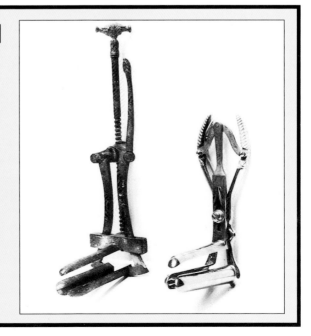

GALEN

*The prodigy who wrote three books by the age of 13
but held medicine back for 1000 years*

THE DOCTOR WHO WOULD INFLUENCE medicine for nearly 15 centuries was born in the once-Greek city of Pergamum (now Bergama, Turkey) around AD 129. Galen was a prodigy, writing three books by the age of 13. Later, after becoming accomplished in mathematics, architecture, astronomy, agriculture and philosophy, he turned to medicine and, for 12 years (an astonishingly long period for that time), studied in his home city and at Smyrna, Corinth and, most important, Alexandria. Back in Pergamum, he spent three years as 'physician to the gladiators', using wounds as 'windows' into the body, to learn anatomy.

In AD 162, the 33-year-old Galen arrived in Rome. To make a name for himself, he gave public demonstrations of his anatomical and surgical skill, often before some of the greatest men of the empire. One of his specialities was to dissect the nerves in the neck of a live pig. As these were severed, one by one, the pig continued to squeal; however, when Galen cut one of the laryngeal nerves (now also called 'Galen's nerves'), the squealing stopped, to the awe of the crowd. Little did they know that, with this snip, Galen was disproving the Aristotelian belief that mental faculties resided in the heart; it was obviously the brain, reached via the nerves, that was in charge. Many other animals came under Galen's knife — even two elephants — but only two known human corpses.

As Galen's reputation grew, so did his clientele, until it included the emperor Marcus Aurelius. Galen also became exceedingly wealthy — he once charged the consul Boethus 400 gold pieces (about 15 times the going rate) to make a night call on his wife.

THE UNITY OF MEDICINE

Through his anatomical studies, Galen added immeasurably to medical knowledge, even though his concentration on animals meant that some detail was incorrect when applied to human beings. As well as his work on nerves, he understood the role of blood in tissue nutrition, showed that arteries as well as veins carried blood and demonstrated the effects of injuries at different levels of the spinal cord. He did not hesitate to disagree with the rival schools of medicine in Rome. Perhaps most important, he constantly stressed the unity of medicine — head and hand, physician and surgeon, logic and experience.

Galen was an arrogant and unpleasant man, who used his learning and his verbal skills to bludgeon opponents into submission. When he left Rome abruptly in AD 166 to spend three years in Pergamum, he claimed it was because he feared assassination by his rivals. He may have written as many as 600 books, but none of those that survive makes any mention of friends and, as far as is known, not one statue was erected to this great medical talent — perhaps not surprising when one remembers that he said: "Whoever seeks fame need only become familiar with all that I have achieved". Oddly enough, it was Galen's contempt for such illustrious forebears as Herophilus and especially Erasistratus (*see p.19*), whom he despised for the Alexandrian's disbelief in the four humours, that led him to write at length about these medical patriarchs, so that they have been able to take their rightful places in medical history.

But this part of Galen's writings, and his revolutionary work on anatomy, did not reach the world until the late Middle Ages. Unfortunately, the same cannot be said of the rest. Galen elevated the Greek theory of the four humours

BELOW *Two 16th-century versions of Galen's corrective treatment for disorders of the spinal joints echo more the scenes in a torture chamber than the routine of orthopaedic surgery.*

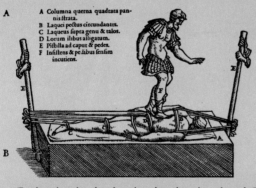

A Columna querna quadrata pannis ftrata.
B Laquei pectus circundantes.
C Laqueus fupra genu & talos.
D Lorum ilibus alligatum.
E Piftilla ad caput & pedes.
F Infiftens & pedibus fenfim incutiens.

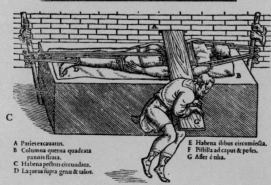

A Paries excauatus.
B Columna querna quadrata pannis ftrata.
C Habena pectori circundata.
D Laqueus fupra genu & talos.
E Habena ilibus circumiecta.
F Piftilla ad caput & pedes.
G Affer è tiha.

(*see p.18*) to such a position that it became the medical equivalent of holy writ; indeed, it later became part of Church dogma. His massive pharmaceutical works – the remedies, none particularly effective, often being translated into garbled Latin from the original Greek – continued to be used for reference for centuries; and his championing of blood-letting and what came to be called 'laudable pus' was responsible for much ill health and many deaths through the ages. But, perhaps most destructive of all, Galen believed

that everything was part of a grand plan, one that only he could recognize. Unfortunately, if the evidence did not fit that plan, he ignored it or tried to explain it away; even if he had no evidence, he would state as fact impossible assumptions. This grand plan was seized upon by the early Christians, who added the concept of human suffering to the mix. In the centuries that followed, critics of the plan, and so the four humours, risked severe penalties. As a result, medical progress was held back for well over a millennium.

One of the methods employed by virtually all Roman doctors was 'cupping'. A piece of lint would be lit and placed inside a bell-shaped vessel, usually metal, which would then be applied to the skin. The burning would use up the oxygen inside the cup, creating a partial vacuum, and the resulting suction would extract the 'vicious humour'. There were two different approaches to 'cupping': in 'wet cupping', the cup was placed over a wound or a deliberate cut so that blood could be drawn; in 'dry cupping', it was believed that the suction on the skin would be enough.

THE MIDDLE AGES

FROM MONASTERIES TO MEDICAL SCHOOLS

Physicians checked urine, while barber-surgeons advertised with blood

WHEN ROME FELL to Germanic tribes in the 5th century AD, the centre of Western learning shifted to Constantinople (now Istanbul), the capital of the Byzantine empire, which had been Christian for more than 150 years. The Church swiftly gained converts – and power – throughout western Europe, and Galen's less plausible tenets were embraced with fervour. The flame of scientific inquiry was extinguished.

Suffering was seen as part of the human condition: as people became obsessed with their souls, they neglected their bodies; medicine became a matter of faith, and prescriptions became prayers.

CHRISTIAN CHARITY

Although the Church decreed that sickness was a consequence of sin, caring for the sick was an act of Christian charity, and this was the impetus behind the foundation of many hospitals. Fabiola (*d*.AD 399), a wealthy

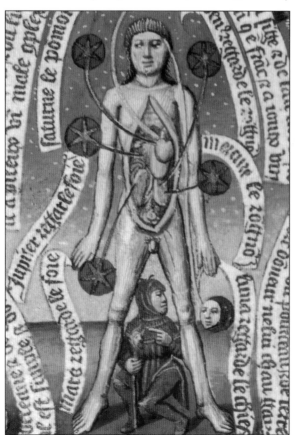

ABOVE *In medieval times, the body and health were linked inextricably with the cosmos – parts of the body and internal organs were governed by particular planets and signs of the astrological zodiac.*

Roman woman, created one of the first, which was followed by several hospitals in Byzantium – one, in Constantinople, could accommodate 7000 patients. Religious institutions were established to care for the sick, and in the 1280s, one of these built the large Santa Maria Nuova hospital in Florence, Italy, which by the 15th century had 300 beds and employed nine doctors. There were, in addition, the various military hospital orders founded during the Crusades: the Knights Hospitallers of St John; the Teutonic Knights; and the Order of Lazarus.

By the 13th century, there were about 19,000 hospitals in western Europe, for the most part simply providing food, shelter and prayer for pilgrims, the old and the poor as well as for the sick.

PRESERVING ANCIENT LEARNING

Many monasteries became healing centres, but their medical importance lies in their preservation, copying and study of secular medical books from the past. Initially, these were mainly the works of Galen, but only some of them survived and then often in abridged versions, so that his insights into anatomy, his belief in experimentation and much of the rationale behind his ringing statements of fact were missing.

Later, the work of scholars in the Middle East and Spain (*see p.28*) trickled into the West, and medical writers busily translated and absorbed the technical literature of ancients previously unknown to them. They expanded on this, identifying major themes, enlarging the medical vocabulary and combining physiological theory with what they now knew about logic and natural philosophy. This would be the basis for the revolutionary work of the Renaissance.

REGULATION AND TRAINING

With the fall of Rome, Roman medical regulations disappeared. Occasionally, new secular authorities instituted their own: Theodoric the Great, the Ostrogothic king of Italy (*c*.474–526), appointed an official to supervise physicians; and Visigothic Spain established regulations in the 7th century. However, regulation, like medical care, was generally taken over by the Church. Despite this, a few secular physicians remained, as well as practitioners of folk medicine or magic, who were probably the most serious competitors to the physician-monks.

Western European society changed rapidly between 1050 and 1225. As populations, cities and economies grew, more sophisticated forms of government were created. Literacy rates went up, and so did the number of secular healers. As medicine became increasingly commercial, religious leaders took steps to prevent this 'infection' spreading to the cloisters. In 1163, at the Council of Tours, monks were forbidden to practise medicine "for the sake of temporal gain". Then, in 1215, the Fourth Lateran Council prevented clergy in the major orders from performing cautery and making surgical incisions. Four years later, in 1219, a papal decree forbade non-monastic clergy to absent themselves from their ecclesiastical duties to study medicine.

Secular regulation was again found necessary. Roger II of Sicily (1095–1154), one of the most powerful kings in the Mediterranean, ordered those desiring to practise medicine to be examined by royal officials. His grandson, the Holy Roman Emperor Frederick II (1194–1250), then entrusted the responsibility for those examinations to the 'masters' of

Salerno (see p.27). Frederick also set fixed fees for medical treatment (the poor were seen free), and forbade doctors from colluding with apothecaries to fleece their clients by prescribing expensive medicaments.

Similar ordinances were passed in Spain in 1283, and in Germany in 1347. By ensuring that doctors were well trained, and restraining their more disreputable practices, these regulations did much to elevate physicians' status.

From its beginnings in 10th-century Salerno, European medical education grew rapidly. In 1220, Pope Honorius appointed Cardinal Conrad to supervise medical teaching at Montpellier in France. His decree that no one could be considered a student there who did not receive instruction from an approved master established the faculty of medicine in Western medical education. Soon, there were prestigious schools in Paris and Montpellier in France, Parma, Bologna, Padua and Ferrara in Italy, and Tubingen in Germany, all with medical courses lasting four to five years.

DIAGNOSIS AND TREATMENT

The Greek concept of the four humours – as revised by Galen – was the basis of all diagnosis and treatment. However, it had by now evolved into a theory of 'complexion', or temperament, which accounted for psychological and social as well as physical characteristics. An excess of blood, phlegm, yellow bile or black bile made a person, respectively, sanguine, phlegmatic, choleric or melancholy, and the cold and moist 'complexion' of women explained their timidity as well as their menstruation.

LEFT *An illuminated manuscript depicts a medieval doctor administering a potion to his patient.*

BELOW *A page from* Boccaccio's Decameron *shows the use of leeches in the Middle Ages.*

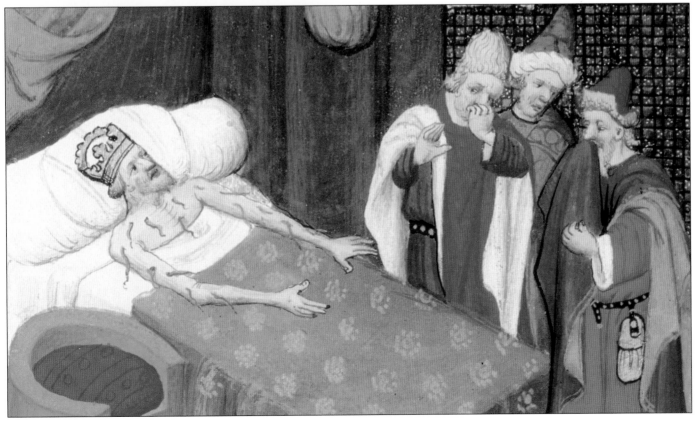

On first visiting patients, doctors noted their appearance, listened to their stories, felt their pulses and examined their urine. Urine inspection was the most common method of diagnosis – there were 29 observations to be made – and the urine flask became the symbol of the doctor. Contracts between towns and doctors often stipulated that the urine of all residents would be inspected on demand.

Many medieval treatments – cupping, blood-letting, medications and diet – were Roman, but more elaborate, with ritual added to cupping and blood-letting, and most prescriptions involving a multiplicity of ingredients.

ABOVE *Patients in 13th-century Europe queue up to describe their ills and receive medicine from their itinerant physician, who travelled from town to town attempting to cure the sick.*

SURGEONS VERSUS PHYSICIANS

For most of the medieval period, all forms of treatment were carried out by physicians. However, from the 13th century, incisions, heat treatments and physical manipulation (setting fractures, for example) were increasingly relegated to a separate craft-oriented hierarchy of barbers, barber-surgeons and surgeons, the last group primarily receiving their training not from universities, but from a system of apprenticeship regulated by guilds. The division of labour was not clear-cut, since physicians also carried out cupping with heated instruments and blood-letting.

Only a few surgeons undertook complicated operations and then only for life-threatening or extremely painful conditions, such as bladder stones, urinary obstruction and toothache. There were attempts at anaesthesia to reduce pain: sponges were impregnated with opium or mandragora and placed in the mouth or nose. However, it is unlikely that these worked very well, since contemporary illustrations show that it was necessary to restrain patients physically during operations.

Surgical training improved as Muslim works on surgery were translated, first into Latin for the few and then, from the 14th century, into the vernacular for the many. Medieval surgeons also produced new textbooks, the first being Roger Frugard of Parma, whose *Surgery* (c.1180) was immensely influential. These works culminated in Guy de Chauliac's massive *Great Surgery* of 1363, a systematic overview of the discipline, which, significantly, made use of Galen's work on anatomical physiology – the first time this had happened since the 3rd century.

However, despite this progress the split between surgeons and physicians widened. Most barbers and many barber-surgeons (who received some form of medical training) were illiterate, but all were keen to carry out the more lucrative medical procedures to supplement their income from shaving and cutting hair. In London in 1307, barbers were criticised for advertising their medical services – tactlessly, one may think – by displaying buckets of blood and hanging bloody rags on poles outside their shops. The University of Paris refused to admit students to its medical school until they had sworn never to perform surgery.

SALERNO: THE FIRST EUROPEAN MEDICAL SCHOOL

By the 10th century, the Italian city of Salerno was already famous as a centre of medical healing, and two centuries later it had developed into the first medical school. Legend has it that Salerno's medical school was begun by a Jew, an Arab, a Greek and a Roman, but although there is no evidence for this, its position south of Naples brought it into contact with both the Greek- and the Arab-speaking worlds, and it was only some 70 miles from the Benedictine monastery of Monte Cassino, where Arabic medical works were translated.

At first, Salerno carried on the tradition of practical healing rather than bookish learning. It was also co-educational in the mid-11th century, one of its finest practitioners being a woman, Trotula, who became immortalized in folk tales as 'Dame Trot'. Both men and women sought her advice, and she wrote about the medical conditions of both sexes. However, her most famous work was on gynaecology and obstetrics – **De Mulierum Passionibus**: *"Wherefore I, Trotula, pitying the calamities of women and at the urgent request of certain ones, began to write this book on the diseases which affect their sex".*

Salerno was at its peak in the 12th and 13th centuries – the title 'doctor', meaning physician, was first used legally there in 1180. For the first time, a curriculum based on medical textbooks was established. The school's most famous publication was the **Regimen Sanitatis Salernitanum**, *generally credited to Arnold of Villanova (1234–1311). Eight hundred and forty-two lines of verse helped doctors (who could not afford to buy books) remember the advice given. For example:*

> *"If thou to health and vigour wouldst attain,*
> *Shun weighty cares – all anger deem profane,*
> *From heavy suppers and much wine abstain".*

After Salerno was sacked in the summer of 1194 by the Holy Roman Emperor, Henry VI, its finest medical minds gradually left to establish other faculties. The Salerno medical school continued to train doctors until the early 19th century, when it was closed on Napoleon's orders.

BELOW *Roger of Salerno attends to a patient with a plainly visible abscess from a diseased tooth* (LEFT) *and administers a herbal remedy to a patient with an eye complaint* (RIGHT).

ANCIENT MEDICINE REVIVED

FROM PERSIA TO SPAIN

He described measles and smallpox, then was blinded by his own book

MANY OF THE MEDICAL WORKS of the ancient Greeks and Galen reached western Europe by a roundabout route that took centuries to complete.

In AD 431, the Church banished Nestorius, the heretical patriarch of Constantinople, with his followers. Their descendants fled to Persia where, at Jundi Shapur, they made the university and its medical school and hospital a leading intellectual centre. There the Nestorians translated into Syriac all the Greek books they could find, including the *Hippocratic Corpus* and the works of Galen.

With the rise of Islam in the 7th century, medical schools spread. In the Eastern Caliphate of Baghdad, Muslim scholars and physicians continued to translate Greek works, adding their own commentaries.

THE LEARNING OF ISLAM

Rhazes (*d.*925), drawing on his own experience, wrote the first accurate descriptions of measles and smallpox, and realized that fever could be a defence against disease. *Continens Liber*, one of his 200 or so treatises, gained him fame, but also made him blind: he offended a mullah, who demanded he be beaten on the head with his own book until one of them broke; the doctor's head broke first.

Rhazes was followed by Avicenna (980–1037) – also known as Ibn Sina – whose breadth of learning matched Galen's. His *Canon Medicina*, one million words long, became a medical bible, supplanting Galen's work first in the Arab-speaking world and then in western Europe until the 17th century. He recognized the contagious nature of tuberculosis and the dissemination of diseases by water and soil; he also recommended the use of cautery instead of the knife, and so perpetuated the Arab disinclination to dissect, which had originated in horror at the prospect.

Islam spread through North Africa and into Spain and south-west France, until it was stopped by the Christians at the Battle of Tours in AD 732. The Western Caliphate was centred on the Spanish city of Cordoba, which had 50 hospitals, 70 public libraries and the most renowned university of the 10th century.

Albucasis (936–1013) was possibly the greatest surgeon of the Middle Ages. Born in Cordoba, he wrote *al-Tasrif*, the first illustrated book of surgery, which describes procedures for opening abscesses, eye surgery and manipulation of spinal deformities. It also contains the earliest description of haemophilia. From Seville came the intensely practical Avenzoar (*d.*1162), who taught how to carry out tracheotomies and remove cataracts and kidney stones.

In 1148, the 13-year-old Maimonides (born Moses ben Maimon), scion of a family of Jewish scholars, fled from Cordoba to Fez in Morocco as the fanatical Muslim sect, the Almohades, completed their takeover of Spain. Moving to Cairo, he became physician to the Saracen sultan, Saladin, whose Crusader foe, Richard Coeur de Lion of England, tried in vain to secure the Jewish doctor's services. Maimonides studied the patient, not the disease; he also rejected astrology and attempted to separate medicine from religion. He wrote: "Teach thy tongue to say 'I know not,' and thou wilt progress".

Some of the works of these men were first translated into Latin by the mysterious Constantinus Africanus (*c.*1020-87).

THE ONLY DOCTOR TO BECOME POPE

Despite the Church's attempts to dissuade them, many non-monastic clergy became doctors. One was Petrus Hispanus – Peter of Spain (although Portuguese) – who studied at Paris and later taught at Siena. In the mid-13th century, he compiled **A Treasury of Poor Men,** *a medical compendium in which he recommended lettuce leaves for toothache, lettuce seed to reduce sex drive and the application of pig dung to stop nose-bleeds.*

Following his appointment as physician to the Vatican, popes Gregory X (1271-6), Innocent V (1276) and Adrian V (1276) all died in quick succession. Despite this the cardinals elected Petrus as pontiff, perhaps hoping that his medical skills would keep him healthy. However, within a year of his elevation, in 1276, the roof of a palace he had ordered to be built fell in and killed him. His death came as a relief to orthodox clerics who believed he was the anti-Christ.

WOMEN DOCTORS IN THE DOCK

Although formal medical education and practice spread from Salerno – where Trotula had flourished – its liberal attitudes did not. In England, France and the rest of northern Europe, women were forbidden to study at university, and were refused licences to practise medicine, although they were permitted to continue working as midwives and 'wise women'.

In Paris in 1322, five women stood trial for practising medicine without a licence. One was Jacqueline Felicie de Almania: "The said Jacqueline visited the sick folk", the charge read, "... examining their urine, touching, feeling and holding their pulses, body and limbs .... She was wont to say to the sick folk, 'I will cure you by God's will, if you will trust in me,' making a compact with them and receiving money from them".

The main witness against her was the surgeon John of Padua. As women could not practise as lawyers, he stated that it was even more important that they not practise medicine, since losing a life was more serious than losing a law suit. Eight of De Almania's patients testified on her behalf, saying that she had been able to cure them when male doctors had failed.

De Almania argued that women would receive better treatment from a female physician since she could examine their "breasts, belly and feet" and a male doctor could not.

The Court of Justice was not convinced, stating that "it is certain that a man approved in the aforesaid art could cure the sick better than any woman". The five women were all found guilty and received a most severe penalty: excommunication from the Church.

He had studied medicine and magic in Babylon and Tunisia and turned up at Salerno in 1072, bringing with him a great collection of Arabian manuscripts. He later became a monk at Monte Cassino, where he translated from the Arabic the works of Arabian, Jewish and Graeco-Roman physicians, especially those of Galen. This work of translation was continued in the 12th century by Gerard of Cremona and his pupils in Spain, and by Burgundio of Pisa, who translated the works of Galen from Greek – the beginning of the Western rediscovery of the original ancient texts which was continued by the humanists of the Renaissance.

BELOW *The 17th-century illustration on the front binding board of Avicenna's monumental* Canon Medicina, *which became a medical bible, shows the great physician conducting an* al fresco *examination.*

THE ABBOT & THE DOCTORS

In the winter of 1150/1, Peter the Venerable, Abbot of Cluny, was taken ill with a congested chest and headaches. Because of pressure of work, he had postponed his bi-monthly blood-letting, and now that he was ill with "the disease called catarrh", he felt it would be too dangerous. However, after four months of suffering he twice allowed large amounts of blood to be drawn off. His fears were realized: he lost his voice, could no longer preach, and his congestion was as bad as ever.

The Cluny doctors reckoned that the blood-letting had cooled his blood and left "sluggish phlegm diffused through the veins and vital channels". They advised heating and moistening medicines, such as hyssop, cumin, licorice and figs steeped in wine. Peter was not happy. He wrote to another doctor, Bartholomeus, for advice:

"There were many and varied discussions about my case among the medical practitioners in attendance. And although what they were saying did not seem very reasonable to me, I gave in to them. I have used the diet and medicines they recommended for almost three months already, but up to now I feel very little, indeed scarcely at all, better."

In his reply, Bartholomeus agreed with the Cluny doctors, but took care not to contradict his important patient overtly. He suggested cupping for the abbot's headaches, hot baths, medicated steam inhalations, chest poultices, mouth lozenges and gargles for his laryngitis and chest infection – and a laxative for good measure.

THE BLACK DEATH

"... the cruelty of heaven and to a great degree of man"

I N THE LATE 1320s, plague erupted in the Gobi desert of Mongolia. Within a generation, it had spread east to China where, in 1351, chroniclers claimed that it had killed two thirds of the population. It was also carried by Mongol nomads along the trade routes west.

According to sailors' stories reported by the notary Gabriele de Mussi, merchants from the Italian city of Genoa came under siege from the Tartar army of a Kipchak khan called Janibeg. At the Black Sea port of Caffa (now Feodosiya) in the Crimea in 1346, plague broke out among the Tartars, and Janibeg ordered the survivors to load their comrades' corpses on to catapults and toss them over Caffa's walls. As the horrific rain of cadavers fell, the plague entered Caffa. When the Genoese fled, they carried with them into Europe what came to be called the Black Death.

Along the circuitous trade routes of the 14th century, the plague cut short the lives of millions. In Constantinople in 1347, it struck down thousands of Byzantines, including Andronicus, son of Emperor John Cantacuzene. In Cairo in 1348, up to two fifths of the population died. In the Nile Delta village of Bilbais, corpses were piled so high along the roads that bandits took to hiding behind them during ambushes. Aswan, Antioch, Damascus, Jerusalem, Tunis and even Mecca followed – by 1349, one third of the Islamic world had perished.

Death marched into Italy via Genoa – with the returning merchants – and Pisa in late 1347, and ravaged its crowded cities. At Siena, one chronicler wrote:

"They died by the hundreds, both day and night, and all were thrown in ... ditches and covered with earth. And as soon as those ditches were filled, more were dug. And I, Agnolo di Tura ... buried my five children with my own hands ... And so many died that all believed it was the end of the world."

The humanist Giovanni Boccaccio witnessed the Black Death in Florence, and told of what he had seen in the introduction to his *Decameron*:

"Such was the cruelty of heaven and to a great degree of man that between March [1348] and the following July it is estimated that more than 100,000 human beings lost their lives within the walls of Florence, what with the ravages attendant on the plague and the barbarity of the survivors towards the sick."

The pestilence spread to France. At Marseilles, 50-60 per cent died; at Montpellier, only seven of 140 Dominican

RIGHT *The martyrdom of St Sebastian, portrayed here by Andrea Mantegna, became symbolic of the plague. His* *adoption as the patron saint of plague sufferers echoed a traditional association between arrows and attacks of the plague.*

friars survived. At Avignon, the great surgeon Guy de Chauliac advised Pope Clement VI to flee, but stayed himself and caught the disease, amazingly recovering after six weeks. In 1350, the army of Alfonso XI of Castile was besieging Gibraltar when the Black Death struck both sides; Alfonso refused to leave his troops and died – the only crowned head of Europe to succumb to the plague.

The Black Death arrived in England, at Weymouth, in June 1348, and quickly spread north to devastate London. The countryside was also harshly affected. In all, about two million British people perished, half the population. The plague reached Germany in June 1349, Scandinavia and northern Scotland the following December and Russia at the end of 1350. Then, having killed perhaps one third or more of the people of Europe, for some inexplicable reason the pandemic halted.

MAKING SENSE OF IT ALL

According to the Church, the Black Death was God's punishment for the sinfulness of humankind. Medieval doctors, however, tended to blame a 'pestilential atmosphere' caused either by a planetary conjunction or by earthquakes and volcanic eruptions that had occurred before the disease appeared.

Doctors tried every possible cure and preventive. Gentilis of Foligno wrote that huge fires of aromatic woods should be lit to purify the atmosphere. The University of Paris medical faculty agreed, and stressed that "olive oil, as an article of food, is fatal …. Bathing is injurious. Men must preserve chastity as they value their lives". Others believed that the air had become 'stiff' and had to be broken up by loud noises. So bells were rung, guns were fired and birds were released to fly around rooms.

Eventually, doctors came to recognize the principle of contagion, or at least to act upon it. In Milan, they advised the reigning Viscontis to wall up houses in which victims were found, even if they also immured healthy family members. This drastic measure seems to have paid off: Milan lost less than 15 per cent of its population, the lowest death-rate in Italy.

Fleeing the Black Death simply spread it further, and doctors ran away like everyone else. In Venice, this led to surgeons being allowed to practise like physicians, to make up the numbers. But physicians and surgeons alike found that nothing they did made any difference. As Guy de Chauliac was to write: "The disease was most humiliating for the physicians, who were unable to render any assistance".

THE TRUTH REVEALED

Only in 1894, during an epidemic in Hong Kong, was the plague bacillus *Pasteurella pestis* identified and found to be a disease of black rats and other rodents, spread by their fleas. When all the rats died, the fleas would look for new hosts: human beings. The plague bacillus is extremely virulent: laboratory mice die after being infected with three bacilli – and fleas can disgorge up to 24,000 in one bite.

There are three human types of the disease. Bubonic plague, the most common, is characterized by 'buboes', large, inflamed and painful swellings in the groin and armpit; in septicaemic plague, the bacilli enter the bloodstream. Both are caused directly by flea bites. Pneumonic plague is highly contagious, especially in crowded, poorly ventilated buildings: severe pneumonia occurs and the bacilli are present in coughs. Death occurs quickly with pneumonic plague – within three or four days – and even faster with the septicaemic variety: 24 hours. In all three types, internal bleeding causes large bruises to appear on the skin – hence the name, the Black Death.

In 1932, with sulphonamide drugs (*see p.107*), there was finally an effective treatment for the plague. Yet within 50 years there were reports – persistent, though unconfirmed – that a strain of plague bacillus resistant to all medicinal and control measures had been developed for bacteriological warfare by the US army.

FLAGELLANTS AND JEWS

Mass hysteria was also a characteristic of the Black Death. In 1348, the 'Brotherhood of the Flagellants' – whose aim was to induce God to stop punishing the world with the plague – sprang up; ominously, this bizarre sect was particularly common in Germany. Large groups would march from town to town, stripped to the waist and whipping themselves with metal-tipped scourges – frequently, though, carrying the infection with them.

Much more serious was the persecution of the Jews. Claims that they had started the plague by poisoning wells were fuelled by the confessions, at a trial in the Swiss town of Chillon in September 1348, of Jews who had been tortured. In Basle, all Jews were penned up in a wooden building and burned alive – a practice that also found favour in Germany, although simple slaughter also sufficed: at least 2000 Jews were murdered in Strasbourg; 12,000 in Mainz; 600 in Brussels. In July 1349, the Flagellants led the people of Frankfurt to the Jewish quarter for a wholesale massacre. Not until the appalling Holocaust of World War II would the Jews again suffer such persecution.

BELOW *A woodcut from the Nuremberg Chronicle, published in 1493, depicts the tragic scene in Cologne, Germany, where thousands of Jews were burned alive after claims that they had started the plague.*

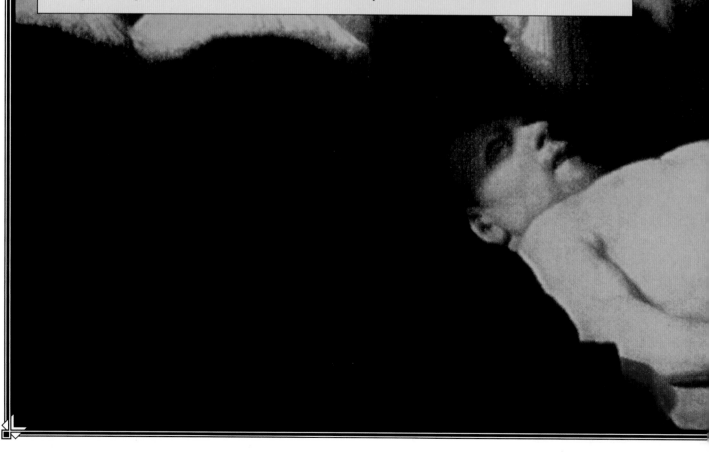

2

The Renaissance and the Enlightenment

s the Black Death swept through Italy in 1347 and 1348, taking its terrible toll, the pretensions of the physicians and barber-surgeons were stripped bare. But within 75 years or so, there was an new air of enquiry in medicine as the Renaissance began. This remarkable explosion of creative energy, in which classical texts were analyzed and reassessed, and humanist thought began to replace dogma, soon spread throughout Europe, helped by the invention of printing.

In Italy, Leonardo da Vinci, among others, spearheaded the new interest in anatomy; while on the battlefields of Europe surgeons learned better how to cope with savage wounds. Medicine's new sense of science was matched by a new appreciation of the status of the profession, as royal colleges were formed and charters given.

And so, on this more solid base, medicine grew into the age of Enlightenment — two centuries that saw Britain's Glorious Revolution of 1688, America's Declaration of Independence of 1776 and the French Revolution of 1789. But these events did not occur in a vacuum. They were reflections of an attitude of mind: a rejection of social and religious constraints; a belief that progress in science and technology would lead to a utopian existence; and, as far as medicine was concerned, a determination that one day all diseases would be conquered — or so they were convinced.

Scientific and technological progress certainly played its part in medicine, as Galen's erroneous theories were finally overthrown, the circulation of the blood was understood, microbes were revealed by the microscope, and smallpox vaccination was introduced.

But this confidence in future health led to some extraordinary and bizarre twists in the story of medicine. For the 18th century was also the century of naïveté, when quacks and charlatans made fortunes.

ABOVE *Rembrandt's* The Anatomical Lesson, *of 1632.*

THE RENAISSANCE

DISCOVERING THE FABRIC OF THE BODY

Night-time dissections and battlefield injuries led to new insights

THE 15TH- AND 16TH-CENTURY 'REBIRTH', or renaissance, in medicine as in the arts and other branches of learning centred on the rediscovery of ancient Greek and Roman works in their original form. Some were known, but others had never been seen before, in particular those on medical philosophy, anatomy and classical surgery. The invention of printing, around 1455, led to an explosion in the publication and distribution of these works, and of other relatively inexpensive medical books.

REDISCOVERING THE BODY

By the late Middle Ages, medical schools were again carrying out human dissection (with ecclesiastical permission), but only rarely – and in circumstances hardly conducive to learning. The professor, in long robes, sat on high in a great chair reading his anatomy lecture, with the cadaver on a table below him. A junior colleague – the *ostensor* – pointed out the line of incision, and a third – the menial *demonstrator* – did the actual cutting.

This procedure was radically changed by Mondino de' Luzzi (*c.*1275–1326), who taught at the University of Bologna and acted as his own *demonstrator*. His anatomy textbook, the *Anathomia,* is considered the first modern work on the subject, but despite his 'hands on' experience, it is full of inaccuracies passed down from Galen and Avicenna. His teaching methods were, however, a major advance, and soon spread to other medical schools.

It was that complete 'Renaissance man', Leonardo da Vinci (1452–1519), who first reproduced exactly what he saw, in 750 anatomical drawings. Dissecting at night (and possibly in secret), he drew the uterus as a single cavity with the foetus in its true position, showed the actual curvature of the spine, carried out extensive work on the heart and the movement of blood, and made the first cross-sectional drawings of the body. Unfortunately, his pioneering work remained hidden for more than 300 years, and others had to forge on without knowledge of his discoveries.

In 1543, Andreas Vesalius, the cantankerous 29-year-old Flemish Professor of Anatomy at Padua, published *De Humani Corporis Fabrica* (*The Fabric of the Human Body*). Like Mondini, he dissected personally, and his great work showed for the first time how nerves penetrated muscles, the nutrition of bone, the true relationship of the abdominal organs and the structure of the brain.

Two of Vesalius's assistants also made major findings. Gabriel Fallopio described the internal workings of the ear, the anatomy of bones and muscles, and the sex organs: the tubes leading from the ovaries to the uterus are named after him. Bartolommeo Eustachio studied the kidneys and the head, describing the anatomy of the teeth and, in particular, the 'Eustachian tubes' from the throat to the middle ear.

The true circulation of the blood continued to elude these pioneers. However, in 1546, a former Professor of Anatomy at Paris, the Spanish-born Michael Servetus, completed a theological work entitled *The Restoration of Christianity*, which rather surprisingly, included the first description of the circulation of the blood in the lungs. Then another Italian (known chiefly as a botanist), Andrea Cesalpino (1519–1603), stumbled across not only the pulmonary circulation but the systemic circulation as well. He may not have realized the importance of what he had discovered, and his work met with very little response.

RIGHT *A dissected torso from the 5th Book of* De Humani Corporis Fabrica *by Andreas Vesalius, one of a series commissioned by the Flemish anatomist. The torso, falsely coloured using modern techniques, shows the liver, stomach and intestines in their true positions.*

GUNSHOT WOUNDS AND SURGERY

During the Renaissance, surgery made great progress, while medicine remained the province of book-oriented physicians, or 'leeches', so called because of the blood-sucking worms they attached to patients to bleed them. Many fine surgeons of the Middle Ages had gained experience and knowledge on the battlefield – for example, the British surgeon John Arderne (1307–*c.*1390), who served in the Hundred Years' War – and dealt not only with slashes and punctures from sword and lance but also with gaping, dirt-filled wounds caused by bullets from the newly invented guns and artillery. Surgeons initially believed such wounds were poisoned, for the majority became septic, and to get rid of the poison (and stop bleeding), boiling oil was poured on to the shattered flesh – an agonizing experience that many soldiers did not survive. The barber-surgeon Ambroise Paré (1510–90) changed all that. In 1536, at the siege of Turin, his supply of boiling oil ran out, so, instead he used a concoction of egg yolk, rose oil and turpentine to dress wounds. He later wrote in his *Method of Treating Wounds* (1545) that injuries so treated were less painful, free of swelling and less inflamed than those cauterized with boiling oil – "I dressed him and God healed him", he said modestly. Paré also developed a method of ligature (tying off blood vessels) that made amputations far more successful; however, thigh amputations required skilled assistants to tie the required 53 ligatures, and these were not generally available. Soldiers also had the German surgeon Fabricius Hildanus (1560–1634) to thank for improved treatment of gangrene and burns.

THE PHYSICIANS ORGANIZE

Perhaps as a result of the doctors' failure to get to grips with the Black Death, 'physic' became increasingly concerned with *practica* (the particulars of diseases and treatment). However, little new was discovered, and the reputation of physicians among common folk was low. Small wonder that Shakespeare wrote – in *Timon of Athens* (1607) – "Trust not the physician;/His antidotes are poison".

To bolster their status, physicians created professional structures for themselves, in order to prevent anyone not properly trained (and, in effect, women and Jews) from practising. In England, in 1423, they joined briefly with the

BELOW *The 'miracle of the black leg'. According to legend, Saints Cosmas and Damian, doctor-brothers martyred in the 4th century, returned centuries later to amputate the ulcerated leg of a Christian and replace it with the undiseased leg of a dead Moor.*

surgeons to keep the untrained out of both professions. Then, nearly a century later, in 1518, six physicians, including Henry VIII's doctor Thomas Linacre, and Cardinal Wolsey, then at the height of his power, were granted a charter by the King to form the Royal College of Physicians: it could license doctors, and prosecute, fine and imprison unlicensed practitioners.

THE ILL-FATED QUEEN

The execution of Mary Queen of Scots by Elizabeth I in 1587 was not only politically inept but hardly necessary, as both her Scottish and English physicians knew she was dying.

Before she was 18, Mary had had the 'prevailing flux', dysentery, malaria, smallpox and the 'green sickness' (probably iron-deficiency anaemia). While Queen of France (1559–60), she first showed signs of recurring illness, with abdominal pain, vomiting and bouts of hysteria, that was to last until the end of her life. Some historians now believe that these were symptoms of porphyria (the 'Royal disease'), an hereditary condition from which several of her descendants suffered, most notably George III.

Its effects on Mary's ability to rule were disastrous and she often appeared close to death. In 1566, her courtiers ordered mourning dress, as their queen lay seemingly dead at Jedburgh, but her surgeon, Arnault, revived her by bandaging her big toes, legs and arms tightly, pouring wine into her mouth and giving her a 'clyster' (an enema). After her husband Lord Darnley's murder in 1567, Mary had a complete mental and physical breakdown, during which she married the Earl of Bothwell. Her army deserted her, Bothwell fled, and she was imprisoned in Loch Leven castle, where she had a miscarriage of twins. Later, as a state prisoner of the English, she was prescribed cinnamon water, unicorn's horn and bathing in wine (Elizabeth complained of the cost), and allowed to 'take the waters' at Buxton Spa.

Despite her illnesses, Mary retained her charm and proved very dangerous for two of her doctors, Edward Atslowe and James Good. Implicated in plots to free the Scottish queen, Atslowe was twice tortured on the rack in the Tower, and Good was imprisoned.

When she was beheaded in 1587, the 44-year-old Mary was almost permanently lame and had to be helped to the scaffold. She also had oedema of the legs (dropsy) and possibly chronic nephritis.

RIGHT *Mary Queen of Scots is portrayed in widow's attire after the death of her husband, François II, in 1560, when he was 16 years old.*

PARACELSUS

"Medicine ... deals with the processes of life"

RENAISSANCE REBEL Philipp Auroelus Theophrastus Bombastus von Hohenheim – later appropriately, but erroneously, linked with the origins of the word 'bombastic' – was born near Zurich in 1493. Before he died 48 years later, he had styled himself 'Paracelsus' – implying that he was greater than the great Roman encyclopaedist Celsus – and had earned his niche in medical history as standard bearer for freedom of scientific inquiry and the central position of the patient in medicine.

Paracelsus's medical studies led him to a surprising conclusion: "When I saw that nothing resulted from [doctors'] practice but killing and laming, that they deemed most complaints incurable ... I determined to abandon such a miserable art and seek truth elsewhere".

He travelled all over western Europe, the Middle East, Russia and Turkey, and to virtually all the major medical centres of the time, making friends and enemies in equal measure (Paracelsus was a difficult young man, egotistical and dogmatic, as well as kind and generous), and talking to doctors, barber-surgeons, gypsies, vagabonds, witches and midwives in his search for 'truth'.

Paracelsus returned to Europe ten years later, setting up practice in Strasbourg. His reputation grew. In 1527, he accepted the post of town physician in Basle, his duties to include lecturing to local medical students and supervising

apothecaries. He lasted one year – this was hardly surprising, considering his unorthodox behaviour.

Paracelsus harked back to the simplicity of Hippocrates and Celsus and hated the elaborations of Galen and Avicenna, as well as much current medical practice. This was reflected in his lectures: "The best of our popular physicians

ABOVE *The Flemish painter, Quentin Massys, painted this portrait of the iconoclastic Swiss physician Paracelsus, who* vehemently attacked the teachings of Galen and Avicenna, and tried to return to the simplicity of Hippocratic medicine.

BELOW *A woodcut from Paracelsus's master work* Opus Chyrurgicum, *published in 1565,* shows a surgeon removing a bladder stone during a well-attended operation.

are the ones who do the least harm. But unfortunately some poison their patients with mercury, and others purge or bleed them to death. There are some who have learned so much that their learning has driven out all their common sense, and there are others who care a great deal more for their own profit than for the health of their patients". To

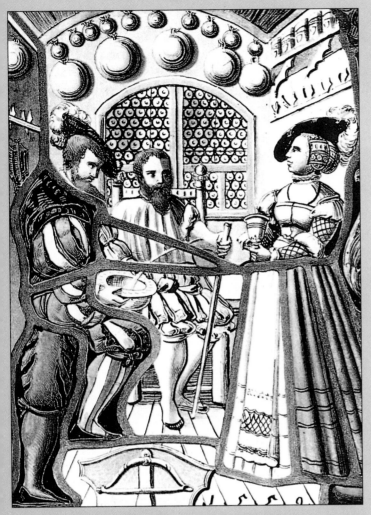

LEFT *After puncturing the forearm of his patient, a barber-surgeon collects the resulting spout of blood. Although the common practice of such blood-letting did some harm, it was thought to lower the patient's temperature and create a calm state of mind.*

In fairness, lest this all seems too good to be true, it must be added that Paracelsus, in many ways ahead of his time, also had a theory of the universe based in part on supernatural creatures, sylphs, nymphs and gnomes from the folklore of the mountain villages he visited. He also believed that toothache could be transferred to a tree, and that wounds could be cured by rubbing a special ointment on the weapons that had caused them.

After Paracelsus's death, his reputation reached new heights. Shakespeare linked him with Galen in *All's Well That Ends Well* (which must have made the Swiss-born rebel turn in his grave); in 1835, Robert Browning's career took off with the publication of his dramatic poem *Paracelsus*.

And in 1982, the heir to the British throne, Prince Charles, said in a lecture to the British Medical Association:

"We could do worse than to look … at the principles he so desperately believed in, for they have a message for our time: a time in which science has tended to become estranged from nature — and that is the moment when we should remember Paracelsus".

emphasize his point, he pitched the books of Galen, Avicenna and other masters of medieval medicine on to a bonfire in a public square.

His students were afraid of the effect that this wild man would have on their careers; the apothecaries were alarmed when he stated: "[Medicine] does not consist of compounding pills and plasters and drugs of all kinds, but it deals with the processes of life, which must be understood before they can be guided".

So in 1528, Paracelsus was off on his travels again. He spent time in mining communities, and was the first to link an occupation with certain diseases; he also noticed the connection between the incidence of chronic goitre and congenital mental handicap.

Next, Paracelsus experimented with chemicals, rejecting the approach then current, in which five or more dilute medicines would be tried in case one worked, in favour of more concentrated drugs given one at a time (even if these sometimes caused violent side-effects and occasionally death). In this, he was the forerunner of pharmaceutical chemistry.

Above all, Paracelsus believed in the power of nature and the imagination to cure the body and the mind. The patient had to be treated as a whole; diet, surroundings, the behaviour of doctor and carers — all these and more could have a profound effect on recovery.

THE STARS AND THE DOCTORS

From the time of the Babylonians, astrology had a place in medicine. Doctors took into account such things as the conjunction of planets when deciding the time for gathering medicinal plants, giving medicine or performing blood-letting.

In the 14th century, innumerable tracts explained the Black Death pandemic by means of the state of the heavens. Even the great medieval surgeon Guy de Chauliac linked prognoses with constellations — for example, believing a neck wound received when the moon was in Taurus to be particularly dangerous.

In 1424, an Englishman, William Forest, sued three surgeons for maiming his right hand during treatment. The verdict went against him:

"William Forest, plaintiff, when the moon was dark and in a bloody sign, namely under the very malevolent constellation Aquarius, was seriously hurt in the said muscles. We further declare that any defect of the aforesaid right hand is due to the aforesaid constellation".

Astrology probably played an even greater part in medicine in the 15th and 16th centuries, with the invention of printing. One of the earliest printed documents is a calendar published in Mainz, in 1462, showing the best astrological times for blood-letting. Small medical almanacs and calendars such as this were common, some displaying the signs controlling parts of the body, from Aries at the head to Pisces at the feet. Many volvelles were also printed — these were revolving concentric discs from which constellation and zodiac calibrations could be worked out.

THE ENLIGHTENMENT

THE OVERTHROW OF GALEN

He could remove a bladder stone in 45 seconds – without pain relief

I N 1603, THE BRITISH DOCTOR William Harvey jotted down: "The movement of the blood occurs constantly in a circular manner and is the result of the beating of the heart". However, this momentous insight – which overthrew Galen's theory that the body daily manufactures and eliminates large quantities of blood – did not reach the outside world until 1628, when Harvey published his masterpiece *Exercitatio Anatomica de Motu Cordis et Sanguinis* (*Anatomical Treatise on the Movement of the Heart and Blood*).

Two reasons have been given for Harvey's delay. First, he was worried about how his findings would be received by the medical establishment. (Rightly, for the diarist John Aubrey records that, after Harvey published *De Motu Cordis*, "it was believed by the vulgar that he was crack-brained; and all the physicians were against his opinions, and envied him".) Second, he embarked on a long series of experiments to prove that he was correct.

Harvey's experience typifies the medical scene in the Enlightenment of the 17th and 18th centuries, with most physicians (mercilessly lampooned by the French dramatist Molière) perpetuating the antiquated theories of the Middle Ages, while anatomists, physiologists and physicists endeavoured to describe the universe (and the human body) according to scientific principles – a thirst for discovery summed up by the philosopher Emmanuel Kant's slogan for the era: 'Dare to know'.

ABOVE *The English artist, William Hogarth, satirizes the medical profession and its grisly obsession with the human body in* The Anatomy Lesson.

BELOW *A woodcut from William Harvey's treatise illustrates the one-way system of valves in the veins and its role in the circulation of blood.*

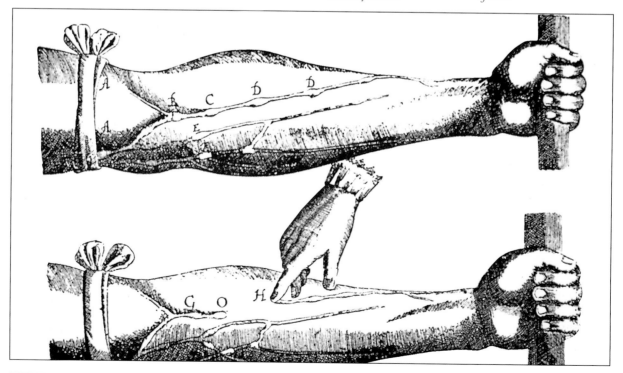

SCIENCE TO THE FORE

Many doctors and scientists who did discard the theories (and treatments) of the past grabbed wildly at any new theory that might explain all the new discoveries about the body. One group, the iatrochemists – among them Jan van Helmont, Sylvius, Georg Ernst Stahl, Friedrich Hoffman, Albrecht von Haller and John Brown – believed in a 'vital force' that could be balanced chemically or by increasing or decreasing stimuli. Another, the iatrophysicists inspired by Descartes, saw the body as a machine whose workings could be understood in terms of mechanics and chemistry.

In 1661, Robert Boyle, the 'skeptical chymist', rejected Aristotle's four elements and instead proposed an experimental theory of the elements, thus transforming alchemy into scientific chemistry. In addition, he revealed that air was necessary for life. Six years later, Boyle's former assistant Robert Hooke inserted a bellows into a dog's trachea to demonstrate that the key to respiration was the alteration of blood in the lungs.

ANATOMISTS ABOUNDED

By the end of the 17th century, at least half of all the structures of the body had been named after their discoverers – Graafian follicles, the circle of Willis, Tulp's valve, Cowper's glands. In addition, in 1761, Giovanni Battista Morgagni published a book describing over 500 post-mortems, comparing diseased organs with normal ones and linking symptoms to abnormalities within the body. He thus demolished for ever the theory of the four humours (although years passed before most physicians abandoned it).

Following Harvey's discovery, blood transfusion between animals was attempted with some success in 1654 by Francesco Folli in Italy. In 1667, Richard Lower in Britain twice transfused a divinity student, Arthur Coga, with the blood of a sheep (making the fortunate Coga a minor celebrity). In France, the mathematician Jean-Baptiste Denys also carried out human-animal transfusions, but although initially successful (through pure luck, as we now know), many deaths occurred later and the practice was outlawed.

At the end of the 16th century, the compound microscope was accidently discovered by the Dutch spectacle-makers Hans and Zacharias Jansen. Using one, Robert Hooke first described cells (and coined the word in the process), and in 1660, an Italian, Marcello Malphigi, discovered the missing link in Harvey's theory: the tiny capillaries that connect the arteries and veins. However, it was a Delft draper, Anton von Leewenhoek (1632–1723), who popularized the medical use of the microscope, describing spermatozoa, red corpuscles and striped voluntary muscles, as well as protozoa and bacteria.

In 1709, Gabriel David Fahrenheit, a German physicist, invented the alcohol thermometer and, five years later, the mercury thermometer and temperature scale that stood medicine in good stead for almost three centuries *(see p.53)*.

Gradually, scientific and medical research ceased to be an activity of isolated men of genius, but more organized in academies – such as the Accademia dei Lincei in Rome (1601); the Royal Society in London (1662), which grew out of informal tavern meetings of a group Boyle called the 'Invisible College'; and the Académie Royale des Sciences in Paris (1666).

TREATING PATIENTS

With this peering into, naming and measuring of the body and its functions, the scientific and medical community often seemed to lose sight of the prime purpose of medicine: treating patients.

One who did not was Thomas Sydenham (1624–89), an English Puritan who fought with Cromwell. He relied on observation and common sense – according to one writer, "he shut his books and opened his eyes to look at the patient". Sydenham was a proponent of the 'life force', and

THE RETURN OF THE PLAGUE

The plague did not disappear after the Black Death of the 14th century (see pp. 30-1); smaller outbreaks occurred over the centuries. In 1664, 24,128 died of it in Amsterdam. By July 1665, at least 1000 a week were dying of plague in London. Samuel Pepys rewrote his will, confiding in his diary "the town growing so unhealthy, that a man cannot depend upon living two days".

While the doctors argued theory, the common folk relied on amulets and tobacco (Eton schoolboys had to smoke or be flogged). The desolation of these times was vividly described by Daniel Defoe in his documentary novel A Journal of the Plague Year *(1722). By the end of 1665, between 75,000 and 100,000 had succumbed in London, approximately 20 per cent of the capital's population. Elsewhere in England, the epidemic continued unabated through 1666.*

The plague never recurred in England with such virulence. It is widely believed that its memory lives on in the nursery rhyme 'Ring-a-Ring o' Roses': the 'roses' refer to the red spots that appeared over the buboes, and 'A-tishoo! A-tishoo! We all fall down!' recalls the violent sneezing that accompanied pneumonic plague.

ABOVE *A town crier wanders the plague-ridden streets of London in 1665, calling to the* occupants of the houses: "Bring out your dead". Almost 20 per cent of Londoners died.

JENNER'S BREAKTHROUGH

Smallpox (Variola major) *replaced the plague as the foremost epidemic disease. The first reasonably effective method of control in the early 18th century was variolation – inserting pus from a smallpox pustule into a scratch on someone unaffected. In 1768, the 'inoculator' Thomas Dimsdale treated the Russian empress Catherine the Great, her son and her court, and was rewarded with a fee of £10,000, an annual pension of £500 and the rank of baron.*

Unfortunately, variolation could sometimes lead to a fatal attack or fail to give protection, and all who underwent it became infectious and had the potential to spread the disease.

It was common knowledge in the west of England that milkmaids who contracted cowpox (Variola vaccinae) *never caught smallpox. In 1774, farmer Benjamin Jesty, using a stocking needle, inoculated his wife and two sons with pus from a cowpox pustule. News of their subsequent immunity to smallpox spread, eventually reaching the ears of Edward Jenner (1749–1823), graduate of the Edinburgh Medical School and friend of John Hunter (see p.41).*

For almost 20 years, Jenner studied dairy workers and in 1796 he put his theory to scientific test by vaccinating eight-year-old James Phipps with cowpox and then, six weeks later, with smallpox: the boy proved to be immune. After inoculating 23 others, Jenner published his findings in 1798. His form of vaccination rapidly gained popularity, and by the end of 1801, about 100,000 people in Britain had been vaccinated.

The King of Spain then decided to vaccinate his colonies. In 1803, 22 children who had never suffered from smallpox were chosen and two were vaccinated. They all set sail for the Americas, and every ten days, two more were vaccinated from the arms of the previous pair. Thus when they arrived in Caracas in Venezuela, the living vaccine arrived with them, and over 50,000 people were treated in South America alone. Another ship with 26 children, sailed to the Philippines, Macao and Canton, where British and American missionaries carried the vaccine into the heartland of the Chinese interior.

With Jenner's vaccination, smallpox could be controlled, and by 1975, it had been eradicated (see pp.212-3).

ABOVE *French artist Constant Desbordes records a doctor vaccinating a child against smallpox early in the 19th century.*

---

all his treatment was designed to revitalize it, with prescriptions for fresh air, horse-riding, beer and simple remedies contained in such new standard works as Nicholas Culpeper's *Physicall Directory* (1649), now commonly known as *Culpeper's Herbal.* Sydenham was one of the first to describe individual diseases and to prescribe the first effective drug for a specific disorder – 'Peruvian bark', later to be known as 'quinine', as a treatment for malaria.

Hermann Boerhaave, a professor at the University of Leiden in Holland between 1718 and 1729, is said to have doffed his hat at every mention of Sydenham's name, and the Englishman's reliance on common sense certainly seems to have rubbed off on the Dutch doctor. He was an extremely popular lecturer (when he recovered from an attack of gout, the bells of Leiden rang out), and the thousands of students who flocked to hear him learned sound clinical practice – recording case histories, finding out about disease and treatment at patients' bedsides, and recognizing the need for science rather than abstract theories.

One of Boerhaave's best students was Gerhard van Swieten. He joined the court of Empress Maria Theresa in Vienna and transformed the university there into one of the most important centres for medical study in Europe. Among its students were the mavericks Franz Mesmer (*see p.43*) and Franz Gall (*see p.73*) as well as the more orthodox Leo Auenbrugger, who, while working in Spain in 1761, devised percussion – tapping the chest to establish the condition of the lungs and heart.

Another of Boerhaave's students, Alexander Monro (1697-1767), succeeded to the chair of anatomy at Edinburgh University in 1720, when he was only 22 – a post later held by his son and grandson (both called Alexander), a medical dynasty spanning 126 years.

Among the Edinburgh graduates were the two co-founders of the University of Pennsylvania Medical School, the first in North America: William Shipper and John Morgan. One Edinburgh graduate, William Withering, a notable botanist, listened with interest to the country folk of his native Shropshire as they described the benefits of foxglove tea for 'dropsy' (the oedema that often accompanies heart and kidney failure). Then in 1785, he wrote *An Account of the Foxglove*, an important study of digitalis, the primary drug in foxglove leaves, and its use in the treatment of cardiac disease.

THE SURGEONS

During the Enlightenment, surgeons at last achieved equal status with physicians. They tended to be more innovative, since many of the new anatomical discoveries and instruments gave them more scope.

By 1718, the French surgeon J. L. Petit – a surgeon's assistant at the age of seven – had invented an effective tourniquet for thigh amputations, which controlled blood flow while the surgeon carried out all of Paré's ligatures (*see p.35*). Claudius Amyand, surgeon to George II, performed the first appendectomy in 1736, while dealing with a boy's

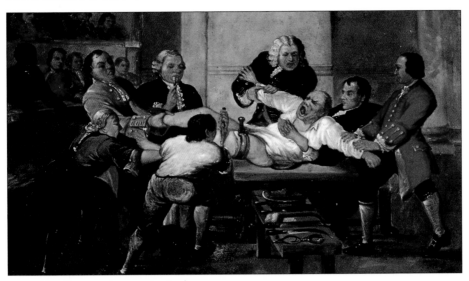

LEFT *Before anaesthesia and antisepsis, surgical operations were horrendously painful and exposed the body to a host of infections. Leg amputations were, perhaps, the most gruesome. First, a primitive, vice-like tourniquet was fixed around the thigh to reduce the flow of blood to the leg. Then, as the patient howled in agony, held down by half-a-dozen strong men, the surgeon severed the limb with a knife and saw — often within the span of a minute.*

hernia. However, such abdominal surgery was still rare in an era in which there were still no antiseptics.

William Cheselden (1688–1752), considered one of the greatest surgeons of his day, could perform a lithotomy (bladder stone removal) in 45 seconds. (Considering that the procedure was carried out without anaesthetic, his speed was a blessing for patients.) Percivall Pott, Cheselden's apprentice, achieved lasting renown for his description of the lower leg fracture he himself suffered, which now bears his name. Pott was also the first to link cancer with a particular substance and occupation — scrotal cancer with the soot to which chimneysweeps who worked naked were exposed.

Perhaps the most famous surgeons of the era were the Hunter brothers. William (1718–83) studied at Edinburgh under the first Alexander Monro, becoming a superb anatomist and a 'surgeon-man-midwife'. John (1728–93) eventually surpassed his brother in fame and achievement. Very different from his dignified, vain sibling, he "met temptation in a rollicking spirit — with a wine-bottle in his hand and a doxy on his knee". He was, however, dedicated to his work, particularly comparative anatomy: he collected at least 65,000 anatomical, embryological and pathological specimens, including the skeleton of Byrne, the 8-foot-tall 'Irish Giant', whose remains he pursued even while the unfortunate man was still alive.

Together, the Hunter brothers — sombre anatomist-obstetrician and boisterous pathologist-investigator — raised surgery to the rank of a scientific profession.

THE SECRET OF CHAMBERLEN'S FORCEPS

Sometime before his death in 1631, Peter Chamberlen (the Elder), surgeon to Queen Anne (consort of James I of England) and widely known as a 'man-midwife' (obstetrician), invented a pair of obstetrical forceps — two curved, hollow metal blades that could be inserted separately into a woman's pelvis and around her child's head, then brought together and locked in place with a pin and used to pull out the baby. The invention remained a family secret for about 130 years — with the help of a certain financially inspired deceit.

His nephew, Dr Peter Chamberlen — a qualified obstetrician — was rumoured to have special instruments to assist women in labour, but it was Dr Peter's son Hugh who made the most of the mystique and the commercial possibilities of the forceps. He used to arrive at a delivery with two men carrying a large gilt-covered box containing the forceps. The patient was blindfolded, the midwife ushered out, and as the forceps were readied, bells were rung and wooden sticks hit together to disguise the sounds made by the metal blades.

In 1670, Hugh Chamberlen approached Mauriceau, physician to the French king, offering to sell — for 10,000 crowns — an instrument guaranteed to deliver any woman in 15 minutes. Mauriceau instructed Hugh to deliver a woman dwarf with a deformed pelvis: after struggling for three hours, Hugh admitted defeat and the sale was off.

In 1693, he formed a corporation in partnership with Roger Roonhuysen in Amsterdam. This became so influential that no one could obtain a licence to practise medicine without first purchasing a pair of the Chamberlens' forceps, which were sold at a fabulous price.

When the Amsterdam obstetrician Rathlaw was refused a licence, he persuaded a former student of Roonhuysen's to give him a drawing of the instrument and published it in 1732. The forceps soon came into general use, often with disastrous results due to the lack of skill of those who used the instruments.

LEFT *Peter Chamberlen (1601–83), nephew of the man who invented the obstetrical forceps, was a qualified doctor — unlike his uncle, who was a barber-surgeon. The former went on to become a member of the Royal College of Physicians, graduating to physician to the King, Charles I.*

THE GOLDEN AGE OF QUACKS

A CENTURY OF NAIVETY

Talking black cats, bone-setters, and animal magnetism

'QUACK' IS AN ABBREVIATION of the 16th-century term 'quacksalver' – a person who sells salves by 'quacking', or noisy patter. During the Enlightenment, there were still plenty of these medical pedlars, many achieving notoriety and fame, and some acquiring immense fortunes.

PISS-PROPHETS AND WORM DOCTORS

Some practices harked back to medieval times and before. The 'piss-prophets' – including the German Theodor Myersbach, who had a medical degree from Erfurt – made great play of examining urine. John Moore, the 'worm doctor', made money by exploiting the fear that evil worms caused all disease.

The ex-footman Joshua 'Spot' Ward developed 'Ward's drops', cure-all pills consisting mainly of antimony, an emetic. When George II dislocated his thumb, Ward gave the digit a violent wrench and the King kicked his shins, but finding himself cured, rewarded the charlatan handsomely. And when the Apothecaries Act of 1748 was passed, to keep unqualified pill-makers out of medicine, Ward's pills were specifically excluded.

Joanna Stephens concocted a medicine – consisting of snail and egg shells, herbs and soap – that supposedly cured bladder and gallstones. In 1738, at the height of her fame, she announced that she would reveal the recipe for £5000, an enormous sum. When public subscription only raised £1365, a parliamentary commission (including the surgeon William Cheselden) recommended the amount outstanding be paid from public funds.

Gustavus Katterfelto, appeared in London in 1782 as an influenza quack, with two 'talking' black cats. He claimed that, with his 'solar microscope', the "insects which caused the late influenza outbreak will appear as large as birds".

Showmanship was all. Katterfelto's coach arrived in Durham preceded by two black servants blowing trumpets and distributing handbills. Dr Smith, the 'dancing quack', travelled with four outriders in a yellow coach that bore a coat of arms with the motto *Argento laborat faber* – 'Smith works for money'.

BONE-SETTERS AND STONE-CUTTERS

Other alternative practitioners may have been as showy as the charlatans, but some were actually very good at what they did. 'Crazy Sally' Mapp, physically repulsive and enormously strong, came from a long line of bone-setters (primitive orthopaedic surgeons). In 1736, she set up shop at Epsom, a fashionable watering-place, and was so successful that the townsfolk offered her a retainer of 300 guineas a year. When she moved to London, she was even consulted by the queen.

The self-styled 'Chevalier' John Taylor, a qualified physician, was skilled in treating eye problems, particularly cataracts. He claimed to have cured the kings of Poland, Denmark and Sweden, the pope, and the 88-year-old Johann Sebastian Bach (Bach died, blind, at 65). He did, however, treat the British king, George II, and afterwards styled himself – with remarkable pomposity and self-confidence – 'Ophthalminator Pontifical, Imperial and Royal'.

The Frenchman Jacques Beaulieu (1651–1714) was in a class by himself. At 46, he received a licence to practise as a 'stone-cutter' (lithotomist) from Louis XIV. For security on his travels and to take advantage of free hospitality, he donned the habit and black broad-brimmed hat of a Franciscan friar and called himself 'Frère Jacques' ('Brother John'), the name by which he is still remembered in the children's song.

LEFT *A visit to the dentist in the 17th century usually meant subjection to a largely unqualified tooth extractor, as in this painting by Theodor Rombouts.*

LEFT *Jacques Beaulieu, known more popularly as Frère Jacques, travelled Europe as a lithotomist and hernia specialist. In 1704, magistrates in Amsterdam made him a gift of his portrait and a set of gold pieces, which he sold, donating the proceeds to the poor.*

Frère Jacques travelled all over Europe practising his craft. In 1701, he returned to Paris and performed 38 lithotomies and 14 hernia operations without a single death – a record that stood for decades. In his 19-year career, he performed some 4500 lithotomies and 2000 hernia operations, before dying rich and leaving a fortune to charity.

Another practitioner who straddled the worlds of orthodox and dubious medicine was Franz Mesmer (*c.*1733–1815). Born in Germany, a graduate of the Vienna Medical School and a friend of Mozart, he moved to Paris, and set up a 'Magnetic Institute'. It became fashionable to attend Mesmer's sessions, where people stood, holding or touching hands, round a chemical bath and in contact with an iron ring, while Mesmer made elaborate ritual movements. The aim was to restore clients' health through 'animal magnetism' – according to Mesmer, a healing force transmitted from the cosmos. For whatever reason – the excitement of the occasion, Mesmer's hocus-pocus, the tension arising from the circle of people – many patients went into hypnotic trances and felt better on coming to.

Mesmer's popularity was such that the Académie des Sciences set up a commission to investigate his claims. In

ABOVE *Franz Mesmer claimed he could harness 'animal magnetism'* by the use of his hands, to restore his patients to health.*

1784, the members – including Benjamin Franklin (then US ambassador to France) and Dr Guillotin – reported: "The imagination without the magnetism produces convulsions, and ... the magnetism without the imagination produces nothing". However, while debunking 'mesmerism', the commission had stumbled upon a profound truth: the power of the imagination over health and well-being. It is for this, and for his practical methods of hypnotism, that Mesmer – who was certainly not a fraud – is remembered today, as a pioneer of psychiatry.

DR GRAHAM'S CELESTIAL BED

The twin appeal of science and sex was exploited by the Scottish 'masterquack' James Graham. In 1780, he opened the 'Temple of Health' in London, where for a fee of two guineas, visitors (ladies always veiled) could hear a lecture by 'Dr' Graham on the benefits of health, sex and beauty, assisted by his scantily dressed 'goddesses of health'.

However, the main draw was the 'Celestial or Magnetico-electrico bed'. Costing £10,000, it was 12ft (3.7m) long and 9ft (2.7m) wide, supported by 40 glass pillars and topped by a dome containing sweet-smelling spices and essences. At its head was inscribed 'BE FRUITFUL, MULTIPLY AND REPLENISH THE EARTH'. The mattress was stuffed with stallions' tails. Within the frame were 1680lb (762kg) weight of magnets, 'continually pouring forth in an everflowing circle', and the bed itself could be pivoted in any direction and tilted at almost any angle. Graham

promised that any couples that wished to conceive could, on payment of £50 (and some paid hundreds), spend the night in the bed, 'accompanied by soft music' and enjoying 'superior ecstasy'.

The bed was initially immensely popular, although no one knows whether it did the trick, but, by 1783, interest had waned, and Graham's Elixir of Life (at £1000 a bottle) also ceased to sell. After a few attempts at regaining fame – such as a venture into 'earth-bathing' – he returned to Scotland where, in 1794, he died insane.

LEFT *Mud baths were high on the list of Dr Graham's health treatments, whereby clients were encouraged to enjoy health and vigour, preserving – even exalting – their personal beauty.*

3 The Nineteenth Century

*I*n the second half of the 18th century, Britain's Industrial Revolution had laid the foundations for a following century of imperial affluence – enjoyed, too, by the other colonial powers of Europe and a United States that was opening up its country confidently and energetically.

This prosperity gave the men (and, later, the women) of medicine and science both the breathing space to indulge themselves in research, and the resources, financial and technological, to take advantage of it. Some of the basic instruments of medicine were invented: the stethoscope, for example, the hypodermic needle and a usable thermometer; and other machines were devised that could take physiological measurements, such as the sphygmomanometer. With data about patients now available, theories of biochemistry, physiology and the transmission and processes of disease could now be put forward, tested and modified, giving the art of the physician a solid scientific base. The skill of the surgeon, too, developed – primarily at the expense of women, for experiments in gynaecological surgery paved the way for the development of invasive surgery of all the body. And out of surgery came a new search for methods of pain relief: a century that opened with opium, alcohol or laughing gas as the only choices, closed with aspirin freely available.

But the century was not just a confident march towards scientific certainties and social order. It was interrupted by horrific conflicts: the Napoleonic and Crimean wars, for example, in Europe, and the Civil War in America. Nevertheless, some good came from these conflicts – not least, the new status of women in medicine, as nursing became a profession. Certainties were undermined, too, by Charles Darwin's work on evolution, and Sigmund Freud's ideas on the subconscious mind.

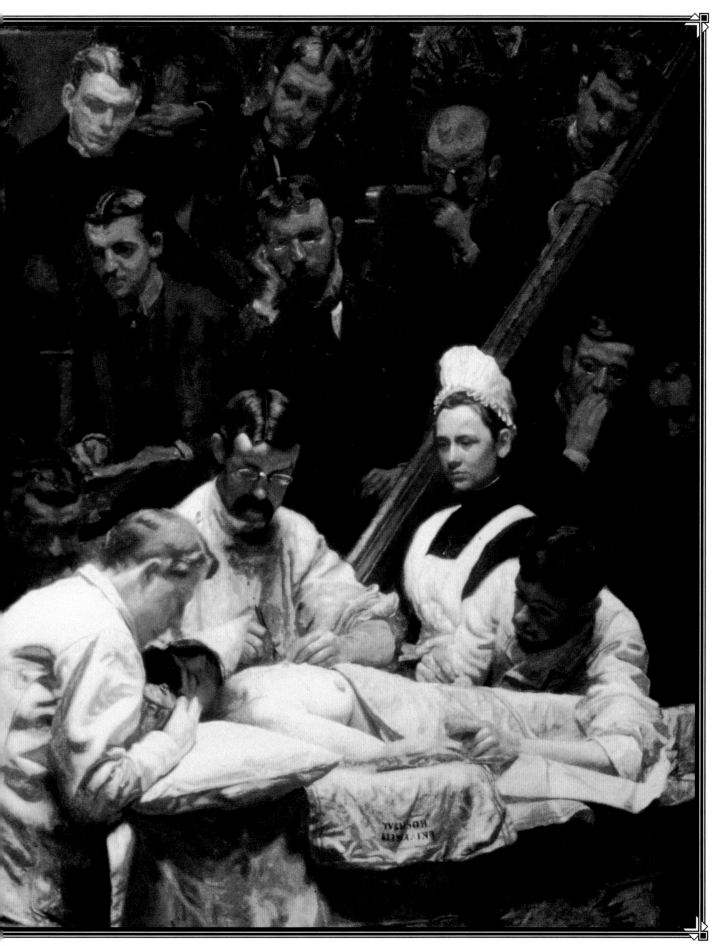

ABOVE The Agnew Clinic, by Thomas Eakins (1844–1916).

RELIEVING PAIN

FROM LAUGHING GAS TO COCAINE

"... a patient preparing for an operation was like a condemned criminal"

FROM VERY EARLY TIMES, attempts were made to find drugs to relieve pain – to make more types of surgery possible and to reduce or eliminate the aches and pains of illness and of everyday life. Two kinds of pain relief were sought: anaesthesia, both general (pain-free unconsciousness) and local (the numbing of particular parts of the body); and analgesia, the blunting of the conscious perception of pain.

The discovery of medical anaesthesia and analgesia is, ultimately, a story of triumph. For one thing, general anaesthesia removed one of the two major barriers to surgery – the other being the danger of infection – and both methods of pain relief have benefited countless numbers of people. However, it is also, in some cases, a tragic story, littered with episodes of bitter disappointment and suicide.

"A NEW ERA OF TOOTH-PULLING"

Over the centuries, opium, henbane and mandrake root were popular choices in attempts to induce general anaesthesia (as was making patients dead drunk), but it was soon recognized that the effective dose could also be lethal. Thus, from the 17th century, doctors gradually faced reality and

stopped trying, even though this meant that their patients would undoubtedly have to suffer agony. Consequently, as a veteran of anaesthetic-less surgery was to recall in 1848, "a patient preparing for an operation was like a condemned criminal preparing for execution".

However, the solution was drawing closer. In 1799, Humphrey Davy (who would later be better known as the British inventor of the miners' lamp) made up a quantity of nitrous oxide and, on inhaling it, felt so good that he burst into gales of laughter. 'Laughing gas' had been born, and Davy – who noted at one stage that the gas relieved his toothache – invited acquaintances to share this experience. Soon 'laughing gas parties' were being held on both sides of the Atlantic, but no one thought this jolly jape could have any medical application. The same was true of ether, which Michael Faraday (Davy's former assistant and another future scientific pioneer) showed to have a similar effect to nitrous oxide in 1815. Soon, 'ether parties', too, were all the rage among the fast set.

Just nine years later, Henry Hickman, a doctor in the small English town of Ludlow, published the results of his

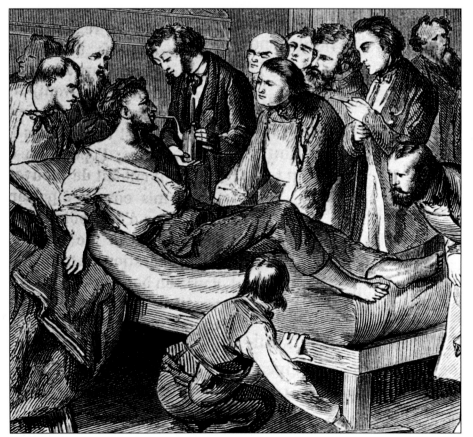

LEFT *This 1870 engraving has generally been thought to be of the first operation in which ether was used as an anaesthetic, by William Morton in October 1846 (see p.47). In fact, it is more likely that the scene depicts Horace Wells's unsuccessful attempt to use nitrous oxide as an anaesthetic prior to pulling a tooth, also at Massachusetts General Hospital, in early 1845.*

experiments anaesthetizing animals with both carbon dioxide and nitrous oxide, and suggested that this might prove useful in surgery. The British and French medical establishments branded him a crank, and Hickman died, broken-hearted, at the age of 29.

When Crawford Long, the dashing American country doctor of Jefferson, Georgia, took part in 'ether frolics', as well as enjoying the 'sweet kisses' he got from female participants, he noticed that, when his giggling companions fell over, they felt no pain. He decided to see if this effect could be used medicinally and, in 1842, successfully gave ether to a boy named James Venable before excising cysts from his neck. However, for some reason, Long did not publish his discovery until 1849.

In the meantime, the Hartford, Connecticut, dentist Horace Wells had become interested in the nitrous oxide demonstrations of the showman 'Professor' Gardner Colton. Wells wanted to find out if the gas could be used for painless tooth extraction, and decided on himself as the first victim. In 1844, Colton administered the gas while Dr John Riggs pulled out one of the molars of his friend Wells. When Wells regained consciousness, he exclaimed: "A new era of tooth-pulling!"

Wells started to give public demonstrations of his own. In early 1845, during one at Massachusetts General Hospital in Boston, the patient (who was having a tooth extracted) did not receive enough of the gas and groaned a great deal.

Although he later testified that he had felt far less pain than he had expected, many of the doctors in the audience derided Wells's attempts. Totally humiliated, Wells gave up experimentation and dentistry, and started selling chloroform, to which he soon became addicted. Arrested for hurling sulphuric acid at two prostitutes on New York's Broadway in 1848, he committed suicide in jail.

"NO HUMBUG"

An erstwhile partner of Wells', William Thomas Morton — who, already a dentist and owner of a false teeth factory, was studying medicine at Harvard University, — was told about ether's longer-lasting painkilling power (making it suitable for more operations) by one of his professors, Dr Charles Jackson. Morton experimented on his pet spaniel, himself and a dental patient. Then in October 1846, he persuaded the surgeon John Collins Warren to allow him, before another audience at Massachusetts General, to anaesthetize Gilbert Abbott before Warren removed a tumour from the young man's neck. Using his newly invented inhaler, Morton was successful, and Warren declared solemnly to the gathered medical men: "Gentlemen, this is no humbug".

Morton was also looking to make a profit. Adding ingredients to colour ether in its liquid form and change its smell, he announced that he had invented a new gas: Letheon. His commercial plans soon went awry, however, when doctors

PAINLESS CHILDBIRTH

James Young Simpson, Professor of Midwifery at Edinburgh, had become dissatisfied with ether in obstetric cases. He had found the heavy bottles difficult to carry up the many steps of the tenement blocks where his patients waited, and he worried that the newly invented gas light might cause the ether to explode.

Simpson decided to try chloroform, which had been discovered virtually simultaneously in the United States, France and Germany in 1831/2. In 1847, after experimenting on himself and friends, he used it on a woman just before she gave birth. Simpson thought the results so good that, within a week, he gave it to 30 or so of his patients. He later commented that, with chloroform, "the natural process [of childbirth] goes on with more regularity when not under the influence of the will of the patient".

However, when the news got out, Simpson faced an uproar. Straitlaced physicians claimed that pain in labour was a biological necessity. Scottish churchmen cried, "Heresy!" – for had not God told Eve: "In sorrow thou shalt bring forth children"?

Although Simpson continued to use chloroform, the outcry did not die down until 1853, when Queen Victoria consented to have chloroform for the birth of Prince Leopold. The volatile liquid was administered by John Snow, Britain's first specialist anaesthetist, who would go on to achieve world renown in the field of public health (see p.58). When Victoria had chloroform for her last confinement in 1857, the anaesthetic's position in obstetrics was secure for more than a century, until nitrous oxide and air machines, pethidine, and later 'natural' childbirth came into vogue (see pp.152-3).

ABOVE *Dr Simpson's chloroform inhaler of 1847. It must have been extremely uncomfortable to wear: the lead sides of the face mask were moulded to the patient's features.*

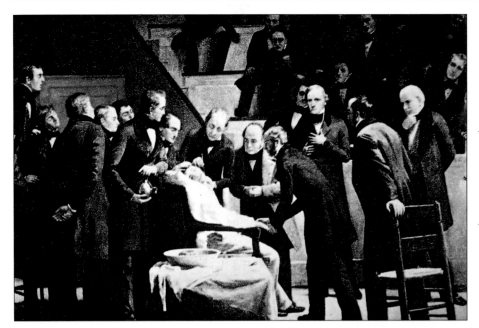

LEFT *This painting, by Robert Hinckley, shows John Collins Warren about to remove a tumour from the neck of house painter Gilbert Abbott, after he had been anaesthetized by William Thomas Morton. The operation, performed at the Massachusetts General Hospital on 16 October 1846, was a milestone in surgery: it was the first at which ether anaesthesia had been used successfully.*

discovered that what he was trying to sell them was simply ether, and Morton never regained their confidence. In addition, he was now being unfairly accused of responsibility for Wells's suicide, and when he read a magazine article crediting Dr Jackson with the discovery of surgical anaesthesia, he was furious. It proved too much: a few days later, at the age of 48, he died of a stroke.

As for Charles Jackson, although he gained much acclaim for his part in the discovery, he had by now become an alcoholic and, after Morton's death, was found screaming at his graveside. He was committed to an asylum for the insane for the rest of his life.

THE YANKEE DODGE

News of Morton's demonstration had soon reached Britain and the ears of Robert Liston. One of the most well-regarded surgeons of his day, Liston operated in a bottle green coat and rubber boots, and was famed for his speed: clasping the bloody scalpel between his teeth to free his hands, he once amputated a leg in 2½ minutes – and, in the rush, cut off the patient's testicles.

On 21 December 1846, having acquired an inhaler similar to Morton's, Liston waited while a colleague, Peter Squire, gave the ether to the patient, a butler called Frederick Churchill, who was to have his leg amputated. Then, watched by a number of students – including Joseph Lister (*see pp.62-3*) – Liston began, his knife flashing. The surgeon outdid himself: the leg was on the floor in 26 seconds. Liston turned to the students and said: "This Yankee dodge, gentlemen, beats mesmerism hollow".

The French writer Guy de Maupassant (1850–93) would have agreed. He believed that he wrote better if he had "a little something" beforehand – that is, ether, which he took to relieve his severe and frequent headaches.

'COCA KOLLER'

General anaesthesia could prove dangerous, and in any event, deep unconsciousness was not needed for a number of less invasive operations. The search was on for a substance that would simply numb a particular area.

Coca leaves had been used for centuries in South America for medicinal and pleasurable purposes. Its active chemical – cocaine – was isolated in 1859, and during the next 25 years, it was promoted as a treatment for morphine addiction and (for a time) as an ingredient in soft drinks. In 1883, Sigmund Freud, then a young physician in Vienna, was looking for a way to make enough money so that he could marry his sweetheart Martha Bernays, and he decided to find out if there was a specialized medical use for cocaine. Following "some dozen" experiments on himself, he recommended the drug for a variety of ailments, but it did not actually work.

Freud mentioned cocaine's tongue-numbing capacity to his friend, the ophthalmologist Dr Carl Koller. Koller was desperately looking for something that would keep the eye from moving during operations and which would dull pain. Cocaine proved to be the answer – and the eye doctor became known as 'Coca Koller'.

Cocaine's ability, when injected, to numb extensive areas was discovered by William Halsted, father of American surgery – with drastic results (*see pp.90-1*). (The drug later became subject to federal control in the United States when its abuse was perceived as a danger – primarily by white Southerners who misguidedly believed that many blacks indulged in it [in fact, most were too poor to afford it], and that the wildness it engendered would lead them to attack white communities.)

In 1883, doctors had found that needles could be inserted into the spinal canal to withdraw fluid. Two German researchers – August Bier and his assistant August Hildebrandt – decided to see if they could induce anaesthesia of the lower body by injecting cocaine into the spinal canal. With Hildebrandt as guinea pig, Bier withdrew a small amount of spinal fluid and, in its place, injected a cocaine solution. As Hildebrandt's legs grew numb, Bier drew one needle through his assistant's skin and drove another into his thigh bone; then he squeezed his skin with forceps, placed the end of a lighted cigar against his flesh, and hammered his shins. Poor Hildebrandt's injuries made possible all the techniques of spinal anaesthesia that we have today.

THE TREE AND THE FLOWER: THE STORY OF ASPIRIN

The majority of the pain suffered by humanity is not caused by surgery or acute injuries, for which anaesthesia can be used, but the pain caused by chronic disorders, such as arthritis, or short-term conditions, such as headaches and toothaches. For these miseries, another sort of drug was needed, one that would eliminate the pain while allowing people to carry on with their lives.

In the summer of 1758, the Rev. Edward Stone, of Chipping Norton, in Oxfordshire, England, was suffering another of his bouts of fever and rheumatic twinges. By accident, he chewed on a twig of the white willow tree (Salix alba), and despite its "extraordinary bitterness", he was astounded to find that it relieved his "ague". He devised a method of drying and pulverizing the bark, and then experimented to discover the best dosage. Over the next five years, he gave his remedy to 50 others, and it "never failed in the cure". Enthusiastic at his discovery, on 25 April 1763 he wrote to the Earl of Macclesfield, President of the Royal Society, but was ignored.

In the 1820s, the Swiss pharmacist Johann S. F. Pagenstecher began extracting a substance from the leaves of the plant Spirea ulmaria, commonly called meadowsweet and well known as a pain reliever in folk medicine. Pagenstecher's report in a scientific journal was read in 1835 by the German chemist Karl Jacob Löwig, who, using the extract, obtained an acid he called 'spirsäure' – later to be known as salicylic acid. Its molecular structure was discovered in 1853 by Karl Friedrich Gerhardt, a chemistry professor at France's Montpellier University. He also tried to modify it to eliminate its rather severe side-effect – the painful irritation of the stomach lining – but he found the procedure so time-consuming that he abandoned the drug as "of no further significance".

Salicylic acid was then used only by people whose pain was worse than that caused by the drug itself. One of these was a Herr Hoffman, who lived in the German town of Elberfeld and was crippled by arthritis. His son Felix worked as a chemist at the huge Bayer drug plant nearby, and in 1895, he decided to try to change salicylic acid to end his father's suffering. He simplified Gerhardt's methods and came up with acetylsalicylic acid. Hoffman then took home a small phial of the compound and gave it to his father, who had his first pain-free night for years. It was soon found to be not only a painkiller, but also to reduce fevers and inflammation.

Hoffman's colleague Heinrich Dreser reckoned that the new drug worked so well because it split in two in the blood. To test his theory, he swallowed some sodium acetyl-salicylate and then periodically examined his urine for the next 12 hours. He found traces of salicylic acid but none of the combined acetylsalicylate: the compound did indeed 'split'.

In 1899, Hoffman and Dreser invented a new name for their new drug: aspirin - a for 'acetyl', spir for the Spirea plant family and in to round it off. The following year, the Bayer drug company took out patents on aspirin, on the intermediate compounds in its manufacture and on the design of the manufacturing equipment, and began to make huge amounts of what was to become their bestselling product all over the world.

In 1914, in anticipation of the outbreak of war and a halt in supplies from Germany, the British government offered a prize of £20,000 to anyone in Britain or the British Commonwealth who could come up with a new formulation for aspirin that would circumvent Bayer's patents. When the Australian government added another £5000 as an incentive, the chemist George Nicholas took up the challenge. Using primitive equipment, and having been almost blinded by an ether explosion at his laboratory, he devised a process that yielded exceptionally pure aspirin – and won the prize.

Following Germany's defeat, the British Alien Properties Custodian confiscated the name 'aspirin', and the Bayer company lost its exclusive rights to both the name and the manufacture of the drug. Among the firms that began to make the compound was George Nicholas's; his product 'Aspro™' became the biggest selling aspirin outside the United States. In the US, the Sterling drug company – even though no longer connected with the original German enterprise – continued to market their aspirin as 'Bayer', with its well-known cross trademark.

But the Rev. Stone's discovery of willow bark all those years before did not remain completely unnoticed. In 1826, two Italians found the bark's active ingredient was salicin, and three years later a French chemist succeeded in obtaining its pure form. In 1839, another Italian chemist prepared salicylic acid from salicin, and from then on, the active ingredient in aspirin could be obtained from both the willow and the meadowsweet. It is now made syntheti-cally (from phenol), using a method not very different from one devised by Herman Kolbe of Strasbourg in 1874.

It was only in 1971 that researchers in Britain came up with at least one reason why aspirin works. Prostaglandins, a group of hormone-like substances found in virtually all the tissues of the body, seem to increase the sensitivity of nerve endings at sites of inflamma-tion – and aspirin appears to interfere with the effective action of these substances.

Aspirin eventually became part of a group known as non-steroidal anti-inflammatory drugs (NSAIDs), which now includes the more recent drug, ibuprofen. In the 1980s, aspirin was superceded by parac-etamol – first used in 1893, but first marketed in 1953 – as a popular painkiller for all ages.

OPIUM

The miracle cure that addicted millions

Opium is derived from dried juice from seed capsules of the white Indian poppy (*Papaver somniferum*). How it acts on the body and mind depends on the relative proportions of the more than 20 alkaloids it contains, including morphine, codeine, narcotine and papaverine. Some are depressants, others stimulants. But one thing is certain – opium is highly addictive.

FROM POTIONS TO LAUDANUM

Opium has been used for millenia as a medicinal and recreational drug. Sumerian writings 4000 years old refer to it, and relics of Stone Age lake dwellers in Switzerland give evidence of it. The pharmacies of ancient Egypt and Persia dispensed opium, and it was important in the medicine of Rome and classical Greece. (If the poet Homer is to be believed, Helen of Troy used it to relieve her sorrows.)

The extensive writings of the medieval physicians and scholars of the Arab world (*see pp.28-9*), which extolled the efficacy of the drug, ensured its spread. It was also a major component of theriac, a remedy of Galen's time that remained popular for centuries.

By the 16th century, opium was well established in western European medicine. Paracelsus (*see p.36*) called it the 'stone of immortality', and the Dutch physician Franz de la Boë, known as Sylvius (1614–72), swore that he could not practise without it. Even Shakespeare mentions it, in *Othello* (1602–4): "Not poppy nor mandragora/Nor all the drowsy syrups of the world/Shall ever medicine thee to that sweet sleep/Which thou ow'dst yesterday".

In the mid-17th century, the 'English Hippocrates', Thomas Sydenham (*see p.39*) first dissolved opium in alcohol to make the tincture known as 'laudanum'. This became wildly popular with the fashionable classes, and although addiction was recognized, it was rarely a cause for concern.

OPIUM WARS

By the 19th century, the opium trade was a significant part of British commercial life. In 1827, 17,000lb (7750kg) were imported, primarily from Turkey; by 1859, this amount had almost quadrupled. Opium preparations were sold not only by pharmacies but by, among others, shoemakers, factory workers, tailors and rent collectors. The many conditions for which opium was used included cholera, dysentery, toothache, flatulence, insanity and the menopause.

Export markets flourished. The East India Company, which grew opium poppies in Bengal, imported the drug illegally into China in exchange for silver to pay for tea and silk. The trade increased from no more than 400 chests of opium annually in the mid-18th century to 100 times that amount in 1839.

ABOVE *A seed capsule of the opium poppy – if used wisely, its products relieve untold misery; if unwisely, they cause it.*

China grew concerned about the moral dangers of the drug – and even more about the drain on silver reserves. The prospect of opening more of China to general trade spurred the British on to push the drug. China resisted, and there was a crackdown on the opium traders: the admirable Commissioner Lin alone saw to the destruction of more than 20,000 opium chests at Canton.

The result was two wars that are still remembered by the Chinese and others for the naked aggression shown by the British, made even more odious by the opium connection. After the First Opium War (1840–42), China lost Hong Kong and five treaty ports were opened. The Second Opium War (1857–60), an Anglo-French venture, led to further losses of Chinese sovereignty and the legalization of the opium trade.

"THE MILK OF PARADISE"

Back in Britain, opium had become fashionable among the Romantic writers and poets. Samuel Taylor Coleridge's *Kubla*

Khan (1797) – with its images of a sacred river, "stately pleasure dome", "sunless sea", and a frenzied poet who has drunk "the milk of Paradise" – was inspired by an opium-induced dream. Thomas de Quincey won his place in literature with his remarkable work *Confessions of an English Opium Eater* in 1822.

Pillars of society also indulged in opium. Clive of India, conqueror of Bengal, died in convulsions in 1774 after taking double his usual dose. King George IV was prescribed it for insomnia; the Duke of Wellington took laudanum to calm himself after a day's drinking, and in 1866, following treatment for back pain, Florence Nightingale (*see p.79*) commented: "Nothing did me any good, but a curious new-fangled operation of putting opium under the skin".

In the United States, the importation of crude opium grew from the time of the Civil War. Between the years 1898 and 1902, when the US population rose by only 10 per cent, the importation of opium increased by 500 per cent and morphine 600 per cent. Much of it was used in patent medicines (*see pp.82-3*); even baby-soothing remedies contained opiates. By 1900, it was reckoned that 250,000 Americans were addicts.

THE BEGINNING OF CONTROL

Throughout the 19th century, concern about opium increased. In 1803, the 20-year-old German pharmacy assistant Friedrich Serturner surmised that there was a specific component of opium that gave pain relief, but only when sufficiently concentrated. Using ammonia, he separated the various constituents of the drug, and called the narcotic substance he discovered 'morphine', after Morpheus, the god of sleep. Other researchers soon isolated codeine.

These discoveries, though of great medical benefit, brought increasing morphine and codeine abuse, exacerbated by the greater availability of the hypodermic syringe. In 1898, two new opium extracts were added to the list. The E. Merck drug company of Germany introduced Dionin, the first commercially available semi-synthetic morphine derivative (now used as a cough sedative); and Bayer enthusiastically welcomed Heroin (diacetylmorphine) – the 'heroic drug' – which, they said, had "the ability of morphine to relieve pain, yet is safer".

Restrictive legislation was first passed in Britain in 1860 in an attempt to control the new substances. In the United States, much of the fear that opium engendered had its roots in the prejudice against the opium-smoking Chinese of the West Coast. Calls for the control of opiates (and, by inference, of the Chinese) increased and the importation of smoking opium was prohibited in 1909.

Although patent medicine manufacturers lobbied feverishly, the US Pure Food and Drug Act of 1906 and its later amendments finally put paid to the legal availability of addictive drugs over the counter. It was not until 1914 that the Harrison Narcotic Act gave the US government control over the sale of opium and its derivatives. By 1938, 25,000 doctors had been tried for narcotics offences and 3000 of them sent to prison.

BELOW *Scientists at the drug company Bayer pose proudly in 1900, after producing heroin, the so-called 'heroic' drug.*

MEDICAL TECHNOLOGY

MICROSCOPES, SPHYGMOMANOMETERS AND SYRINGES

An American giant helped show the way to diagnosis of lung disease

THE 19TH CENTURY was the age of the machine, and while doctors and medical technicians did not come up with anything as spectacular as the steam engine and industrial weaving machines, advances were made in the instruments available for research, diagnosis and treatment.

BEYOND THE NAKED EYE
At the beginning of the century, microscopes had improved little from those of the Enlightenment. Then, in 1830, the British scientist J. J. Lister worked out a formula to determine the best distance between the two lenses of different materials that made up the achromatic lens, so that both chromatic and spherical distortions could be eliminated. This opened up microscopy to an abundance of modern applications. However, it was left to the Germans – including Robert Koch *(see p.57)* and Rudolf Virchow *(see p.65)* – to bring microscopes to a high level of development.

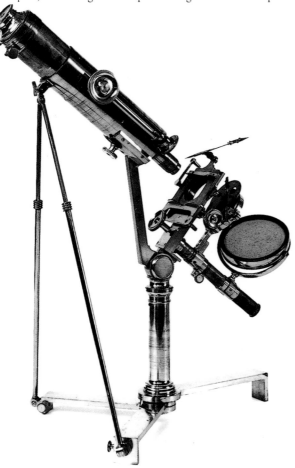

ABOVE *The achromatic microscope invented by Joseph Jackson Lister in 1830, and used by his son, Joseph (later Lord) Lister (see p.62).*

Another inventive German, Hermann Ludwig Ferdinand von Helmholtz, not only established that muscles are the main source of heat in animals, measured the speed of nerve impulses and studied the mechanism of hearing, but in 1851 also invented the ophthalmoscope. Previously, eye disorders could only be investigated with the naked eye or a magnifying glass. Now it was possible to see right to the back of the eye, to the end of the optic nerve – an extension of the brain itself.

BLOOD AND BREATH
In 1628, William Harvey *(see p.38)* wrote that blood spurted from cut arteries as if under some kind of pressure. The clergyman and amateur scientist Stephen Hales was fascinated by this phenomenon. According to a report he published in 1733, he inserted a glass tube at least 11ft (3.4m) long into the artery of a horse; the extent to which the blood in the tube rose indicated the force of pressure within the artery.

There the matter rested until 1828, when the French physiologist Jean Poiseuille discarded the long glass tube for a U-shaped one containing mercury. The mercury's weight counterbalanced the pressure of the blood, and the distance that the metallic element moved could be recorded in millimetres. Poiseuille also demonstrated that blood pressure was the same wherever it was measured on the body.

In 1881, Samuel Siegfried von Basch developed the first, rather inaccurate, sphygmomanometer (from the Greek *sphugmos*, 'pulse') to measure blood pressure from outside the body. Fifteen years later, Scipione Riva-Rocci, an Italian physician, produced a model with an inflatable arm band, which is virtually the same as that used today. His inventiveness is still remembered in some countries where the symbol 'R-R' represents blood pressure.

To measure another activity of the body, John Hutchinson devised the spirometer, which gauged the lungs' 'vital capacity' – the amount of air breathed out with as much force as possible following the deepest breath possible. He recorded the vital capacities of more than 2000 people, and in 1846 published his findings, claiming that his invention was better at detecting lung disease than either percussion or auscultation *(see box)*.

One unusual experiment seemed to bear him out. When Freeman, the American giant – who was more than 7ft (2.1m) tall – visited England, Hutchinson took spirometric readings of his lung capacity. Two years later, he repeated the tests and found a 20 per cent reduction in Freeman's vital capacity. A year later, the giant developed fatal

RIGHT *One of the first spirometers, dating from the late 1840s. Less than efficient, the device was modified a number of times over the following years, but soon went out of use.*

Fig. 3.

LEFT *A further attempt to design an efficient spirometer.*

tuberculosis. However, Hutchinson's spirometer could record deficient capacities in perfectly healthy people, and doctors were never sure if a low measurement indicated disease. As a result the spirometer soon went out of use.

BELOW THE SKIN

Syringes have a long history: Galen used one to inject blood vessels in the brain; Leonardo da Vinci filled the spaces within the brain with wax from a syringe; and William Harvey injected blood vessels with dye in his work on blood circulation. All were basically the same: a tube containing a piston plunger, ending with a pointed, open-ended extension.

Then, in 1713, the French surgeon Dominique Anel developed a small syringe with an extremely fine tube (*cannula*), which he used to treat diseases of the tear ducts. This was modified over the decades, but essentially remained restricted to openings already present in the body or to cuts made in the skin.

The last alteration produced the hypodermic syringe with its very fine, hollow needle through which drugs and other liquids could be injected directly into the tissues below the skin. In 1853, Alexander Wood of the Edinburgh medical school simply modified the cutting point of the needle of an existing syringe and introduced the hypodermic 'method'.

MEASURING TEMPERATURE

Today, a clinical thermometer is a basic diagnostic tool – one of the least complex items in a doctor's bag. But it took many centuries for the medical significance of temperature to be understood; and several more centuries before a practical thermometer was devised.

The first, crude thermometer was invented in the 16th century by the Italian scientist, Galileo. It was refined by Santorio Santorio (1561–1636), working in Padua, Italy, who spent his life assembling medical statistics, including body temperature, and published them in *Ars de Estatica Medicina* (*The Art of Statistical Medicine*) in 1614 – it contained a 30-year record of his bodily functions.

The British scientist Robert Boyle was unimpressed, however. In 1683, he spoke of the thermometer as "a work of needless curiosity, or superfluous diligence". And so the story rested for a while, with minor revivals. Gabriel David Fahrenheit (1686–1736) developed a mercury thermometer and fixed three temperature standards: for a mixture of ice, water and sea-salt (0°); the freezing point of water (32°); and the external body temperature (96°). Herman Boerhaave (*see p.40*) used this to investigate fever cases in Holland; and Anton de Haen (1704–76) introduced the thermometer at the Old Vienna School.

But the thermometer was still bulky, slow and impractical. Then, in the mid-19th century, the story gained momentum. In 1868, Carl Wunderlich (1815–77), Professor of Medicine at Leipzig, published *The Temperature in Diseases*, based on data from 25,000 patients; he also introduced temperature charts. Unfortunately, his thermometer was 1ft (30.5cm) long and took 20 minutes to register. But in the north of England, Sir Thomas Clifford Allbutt (1836–1925) had devised, in 1867, a 6-inch (15.25cm) thermometer, which registered quickly and accurately. The thermometer was ready to take its place in medical diagnosis.

HEARING THE HEART

The ancient Greeks had practised auscultation – listening to the sounds of the lungs and the heartbeat by pressing an ear against the chest wall. This technique was lost until the Renaissance, when it became an integral part of every doctor's practice.

In 1816, the French physician René Théophile Hyacinthe Laënnec was confronted with an extremely plump young woman with a heart condition. Overcome with embarrassment at the thought of pressing his ear against her truly ample flesh, he recalled having seen a child tapping a log while another listened at the far end. Laënnec rolled a sheaf of papers into a cylinder and, applying this to the woman's chest, heard her heartbeat "with much greater clearness and distinctness than I had ever done before".

He soon abandoned his paper cylinder, developing instead the first true stethoscope: a wooden tube about 9 inches (23cm) long and 1½ inches (4cm) in diameter. Before his death from tuberculosis in 1826, at the age of 45, he had invented most of the terms now used to describe chest sounds and matched many with chest diseases.

Wooden stethoscopes were used until about 1850, when pliable tubing was introduced. In 1852, the American doctor George P. Cammann added two earpieces for binaural sound, and in 1878, when the microphone was invented, it was connected to the other end to amplify the sound to better effect.

Training and experience are needed to interpret the information elicited from a stethoscope correctly. As a result, with the advent of easier diagnostic tools such as X-rays, the stethoscope is not as important today as it was in Laënnec's time – but it is still a useful, and portable, tool.

ABOVE *Laënnec's improved stethoscope, made of wood.*

SAVING MOTHERS

SEMMELWEIS AND CHILDBED FEVER

The story of "one of medicine's martyrs ... one of its far-shining names"

CHILDBIRTH TODAY IS USUALLY a time of great joy; once labour is finished and the mother at last holds her new baby, there is little worry about her health. However, in the past, many mothers died within a week or two of giving birth from a disease called 'childbed', or puerperal, fever: a high temperature, pain in the lower abdomen, swelling of the pelvic tissues, abscesses, peritonitis, septicaemia, delirium and heart failure.

Childbed fever was particularly common in women who delivered in hospital – and in the 19th century, these were almost always the poor, since the more well-to-do invariably gave birth at home.

PREFERENTIAL VICTIMS

One who refused to see the disease as the 'curse of Eve' was a Hungarian doctor, Ignaz Semmelweis. In 1847, as a 28-year-old assistant at the Vienna Lying-in Hospital, he noticed a striking difference between the incidence of deaths from childbed fever in the hospital's two obstetric wards: in ward no.1, 9.9 per cent of newly delivered mothers died (and

sometimes as many as 29.3 per cent); in ward no.2, it was 3.9 per cent. Ward no.1 became notorious, and patients would beg tearfully not to be placed in it.

The doctors in charge of the hospital, like others elsewhere in Europe, were certain that childbed fever was caused by a 'miasma' – an infectious vapour – present in the atmosphere. Semmelweis could not accept this, for surely the miasma would affect both wards equally? Other suggested causes were just as unsatisfactory.

Semmelweis found that ward no.2 was run almost exclusively by midwives, who were careful about cleanliness; ward no.1 was the province of medical students, who entered directly from the dissecting rooms without washing their hands, wearing the same blood- and tissue-splattered coats in which they had performed autopsies. When one of Semmelweis's friends died of blood poisoning from a cut received while dissecting, having developed many of the same symptoms as the victims of ward no.1, he was sure of the cause of both. Something – Semmelweis called it 'putrid particles' – was being transferred from the cadavers of the

ABOVE *Ignaz Semmelweis (1818 – 65), the Hungarian doctor and pioneer of antisepsis in maternity wards, to whom every mother of today owes a debt. Semmelweis's ideas of hygiene were ridiculed during his life, but vindicated after his death by Pasteur and Lister.*

LEFT *A colony of* Mycoplasma haminis *– a rare cause of childbed fever – cultured from the vagina of a woman suffering from sepsis after childbirth. Before Semmelweis's ideas were taken up, infections such as this made giving birth a highly dangerous business.*

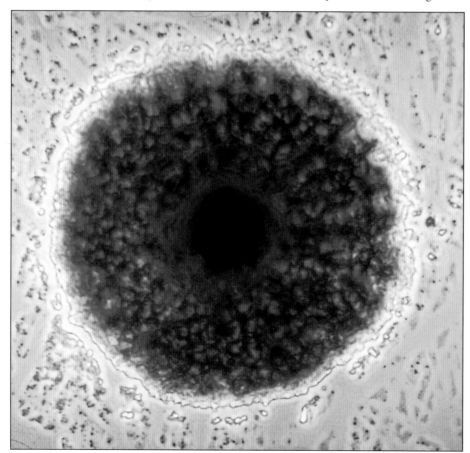

THE POET AND THE "TERRIBLE EVIL"

Semmelweis's crucial discovery was foreshadowed four years earlier by a theory proposed by a Boston gynaecologist/obstetrician who later became the dean of the Harvard medical faculty. Better known today as a poet and essayist – his Autocrat of the Breakfast-Table *first appeared in the* Atlantic Monthly *in 1857/8 – Oliver Wendell Holmes was the first to put together evidence that suggested that childbed fever was an infectious disease.*

In 1843, he read his paper On the Contagiousness of Puerperal Fever *at a meeting of the Boston Society of Medical Improvement. Using numerous examples, he showed how the infection had spread from physician, nurse or midwife as they moved from autopsy rooms or from attending infected patients to the bedsides of newly delivered mothers. Holmes offered no suggestions as to what might cause the fever; he simply presented the facts, adding his own common-sense recommendations.*

Like Semmelweis, Holmes' ideas met with forceful opposition. The eminent Professor Charles D. Meigs, of Philadelphia, who the year before had ruled that childbed fever was simply "a group of diverse inflammations within the belly", was particularly scathing, taking great exception to the idea that the hands of doctors – gentlemen all, according to

Meigs – could be unclean. Although a few doctors were convinced by Holmes' theory and took steps to implement it, most did not. (Semmelweis does not seem to have heard of it, and came up with his own quite independently.) Holmes' reply to his critics was couched in the same elegant language as his essays: "Medical logic does not appear to be taught or practised in our schools".

But Holmes could not let the matter drop. In 1855, he published an expanded version of his essay, retitled Puerperal Fever as a Private Pestilence. *(His new references included one for a paper by an 'M. Semmeliveis' [sic].) Holmes' passionate concern had not diminished: "I beg to be heard, on behalf of the women whose lives are at stake, until some stronger voice shall plead for them".*

Unlike Semmelweis, Holmes lived long enough (until 1894) to see his theory proved correct. The year before he died, he wrote with satisfaction: "Others had cried out with all their might against the terrible evil before I did ... But I think I shrieked my warning louder and longer than any of them ... before the little army of microbes had moved up to support my position".

LEFT *Oliver Wendell Holmes – poet, essayist and master obstetrician.*

dissecting rooms into a wound: the small cut on his friend's hand or the large 'wound' left behind after the placenta separates from the uterus following childbirth.

The young doctor must have been elated at his discovery, but he was also filled with guilt. He, too, had dissected many bodies, primarily to find out why so many of these poor women were dying: "Consequently must I here make my confession that God only knows the numbers of women whom I have consigned prematurely to the grave".

A VOICE IN THE WILDERNESS

Semmelweis acted quickly. Much to their surprise and anger, he insisted that the students wash their hands with a solution of lime chloride before entering ward no.1. The results were conclusive: within one year, the mortality rate in the ward fell to just over 3 per cent, and the following year, it further declined to 1.27 per cent.

If Semmelweis expected congratulations from his colleagues when he published his excellent results, he was to be disappointed: his suggestions were ignored. Despite the danger to his future prospects, the Hungarian refused to be silent, and in the ensuing row, he called his opponents "murderers". The director of the hospital, a Dr Klein, made sure that Semmelweis's contract was not extended.

Forced to leave Vienna, Semmelweis returned to Budapest to practise gynaecology and obstetrics. Here, too, his new theories met with resistance, but he spent all his

spare time writing the book that he thought would finally vindicate him. *The Cause, Concept and Prophylaxis of Childbed Fever* was finally published in 1861, but, having been born of a medical dispute, it proved to be terribly long, confusing and, above all, quarrelsome – and did not convince anyone of anything.

As time went on, Semmelweis became clinically depressed, and on 1 August 1865, he was admitted to a lunatic asylum. Twelve days later, he was dead. During one of his last operations, he had cut his hand and the wound had become infected. Ignaz Semmelweis died of streptococcal blood poisoning – the same infection from which he had tried so hard to shield the mothers under his care.

Semmelweis was finally vindicated in 1879. At a meeting of the Academy of Medicine in Paris, an eminent gynaecologist began to pour scorn on the Hungarian's theory of contagion. He was suddenly interrupted by the great French scientist Louis Pasteur (*see pp.56-9*) who, mounting the platform, began to draw on the blackboard a series of small circles joined together in a chain – the streptococcus bacterium. "There you are!" he said. "That's what it's like!" Semmelweis's methods were also later found to be well in advance of Joseph Lister's antiseptic surgery (*see pp.62-3*).

The Hungarian doctor is now regarded, according to the medical historian Fielding H. Garrison, as "one of medicine's martyrs ... one of its far-shining names, for every child-bearing woman owes something to him".

DISEASE TRANSMISSION

FROM MIASMA TO MICROBES

The removal of a parish pump handle stopped an epidemic returning

BEFORE THE 17TH CENTURY, how diseases spread was a mystery. A 2nd-century Roman, Marcus Terentius Varro, had made a stab at resolving the problem when he wrote about "minute creatures which cannot be seen by the eyes" and that might cause malaria (*see p.94*). There the matter rested – until 1546, when the Italian physician Fracastorius (*see p.100*) hypothesized on "seeds of contagion" that could be passed from person to person. However, his work had little impact, and it was only in 1683, when Leeuwenhoek, with the help of his microscopes (*see p.40*), revealed the existence of protozoa and bacteria, that the pieces of the puzzle began to fall into place.

Nevertheless, the vast majority of doctors and scientists continued to believe that diseases were caused and spread by certain combinations of climate, environment and poor hygiene, or, as in the case of childbed fever (*see pp.54-5*), by an ill-defined 'miasma' in the air – theories that were very little different from those of the physicians who had tried to come to terms with the Black Death in the 14th century (*see p.30*). Even many of those researchers who looked a little further became sidetracked by the enticing theory of 'spontaneous generation' – the supposed formation of new life in decaying matter. Evidence for this came from the apparently miraculous appearance of maggots in rotten meat, and the theory was clung to even in the face of Francesco Redi's experiments of 1668, which showed that, if you keep flies away from the meat, no maggots appear.

In the 19th century, scientists began to identify certain microbes that were at least intimately associated with certain diseases. However, were these germs the causes of particular illnesses or simply innocent bystanders? The work of Louis Pasteur and Robert Koch would answer the question.

WINE, BEER AND MILK

Louis Pasteur was born in 1822 in the Jura mountains on the French side of the border with Switzerland. With the encouragement of some eminent scientists, he took up chemistry, eventually becoming a professor at Strasbourg, Lille and then Paris. Pasteur remained a scientist all his life, and never had any medical training. Yet by lucky accident he ultimately gave more to medicine than perhaps any doctor before or since.

The first piece of luck was Pasteur's appointment at Lille, a wine-growing and beer-making centre. He was asked to look into the fermentation process, and he found that the fermentation of sugar into alcohol, and the souring of milk, were all due to the action of micro-organisms.

Now another question arose: how did these microbes come to be present – were they spontaneously generated or were they already in the air? By a series of experiments, Pasteur demolished the old theory, proving that life could only come from life, that the 'germs' involved – yeasts and bacteria – were, indeed, already in the atmosphere and that microbes were the cause, and not an effect, of fermentation, putrefaction and infection. These last two findings were eventually to lead Joseph Lister to develop antiseptic surgery (*see pp.62-3*).

Pasteur also devised a method of eliminating microbes from milk. With 'pasteurization' – the heating of milk to a certain temperature for a certain amount of time – this vital part of the diet could no longer spread such deadly diseases as tuberculosis and typhoid.

After spending three years in the south of France investigating silkworm diseases that were destroying the silk industry there, Pasteur became convinced that epidemics among animals and humans could be controlled using the appropriate scientific measures. With this thought (and much of his previous work), he transformed himself from a scientist researching alone in his laboratory into a public servant concerned with humanity – a trend that could be seen in the entire scientific/medical community during this century. He had also changed himself from a chemist into a brand new type of scientist: a bacteriologist.

Then, in 1868, tragedy struck: at the age of 46, Pasteur was felled by a stroke. At first, his life was in danger, but after a long and tedious convalescence, he regained his

LEFT *Louis Pasteur, in a tribute from French magazine* Le Petit Journal, *in 1895. Though* *handicapped by a succession of strokes, Pasteur's influence on the evolution of medicine was immense.*

health, although the cerebral haemorrhage had left his left arm and leg permanently weakened. However, he was able to forget about this as he became increasingly absorbed in his study of infectious diseases.

ON THE TRAIL OF ANTHRAX

While Pasteur showed that bacteria in general could cause disease, it was up to a German country doctor, Robert Koch, 21 years Pasteur's junior, to demonstrate which of these micro-organisms caused which diseases.

In his primitive home laboratory, with a microscope bought by his wife with her housekeeping money, Koch first developed a method of growing bacteria on a solid medium (first gelatin, then agar jelly with added nutrients), which could be sampled to produce a 'pure culture' of a particular microbe. Then, expanding on rules first expounded by his former teacher, the anatomist Jakob Henle, in 1840, Koch came up with the four 'Henle-Koch postulates'. These must still be fulfilled today before any bacterium can be stated to be the cause of a disease:

1. A specific organism must be identified in all cases of an infectious disease.
2. Pure cultures of the organism must be obtained.
3. Organisms derived from pure cultures must reproduce the disease in experimental animals.
4. The organisms must be recovered from the experimental animals.

In 1876, after using these methods and following his own rules, Koch was able to show that a large, rod-shaped bacillus (discovered in 1849) causes anthrax.

Koch would go on to reveal the bacillus that causes tuberculosis (1882), as well as (in Alexandria and Calcutta in 1883/4) the 'comma bacillus' (*Vibrio cholerae*) responsible for cholera, and its transmission through drinking water (*see p.58*). He also travelled to South Africa to study rinderpest,

India to investigate plague and Java to look into the cause of malaria. In his honour, the German government built the Institute for Infectious Diseases in Berlin in 1891, and he was awarded a Nobel prize in 1905.

Hearing of Koch's anthrax experiments, Pasteur decided to carry out some of his own. When he filtered solutions of anthrax bacilli through membranes fine enough to hold back the microbes, he found that rabbits injected with the resulting filtrate did not become infected with the disease.

Pasteur then began to wonder whether it were possible to immunize animals (and possibly people) against anthrax, as Jenner had done for smallpox (*see p.40*). The French scientist had first to create weakened (attenuated) bacilli. Initially, he tried adding weak antiseptics to his cultures; later, he settled on incubating the cultures at a relatively high temperature for eight days. On 28 April 1881, Pasteur injected 24 sheep, one goat and six cows with his new vaccine; he repeated this on 17 May. Two weeks later, both this group and another comprising 29 unvaccinated animals were injected with virulent anthrax bacilli. Pasteur and his assistants left; they would return two days later to examine the animals.

When they did, on 2 June, they were greeted with loud cheers: all the vaccinated animals were well, and the unvaccinated ones were either dead or dying.

Pasteur went on to develop vaccines against the animal diseases chicken cholera and swine erysipelas. Through his research, he found that medicine no longer had to be dependent on the lucky discovery of some naturally occurring immunizing agent such as cowpox. Instead, it was possible to create vaccines containing microbes with diminished virulence as a result of poisoning or heating them, or allowing them to remain in culture for long periods.

BELOW *In 1892, Death warns that a ship from cholera-ridden Hamburg has just decanted 2200 souls, possibly infected, into the US.*

JOHN SNOW AND THE BROAD STREET PUMP

In 1817, a new disease crept out of India and advanced on Europe. By 1832, it had reached London, where more than 7000 people died. The epidemic disappeared, only to return (this time via Afghanistan) in 1848; it would remain in Britain until the end of the following year. This time, 7000 Londoners died in one month alone.

Following an incubation of just one to six days, the disease began with faintness and sweating, and then a sudden and complete evacuation of the bowels – victims were often struck down in the street. Repeated bouts of diarrhoea followed, until nothing emerged but water and fragments of the membrane lining the intestines. Sufferers became desperately thirsty, but when they drank, they fell prey to violent vomiting and retching. Soon their bodies would appear to shrink; some people would lose a quarter of their body weight through loss of fluid. This dehydration, a change in the acid/alkali balance in the blood and a loss of potassium (resulting in a disturbance in the electrical impulses of the heart) would be rapidly lethal. More than half of the victims died.

The main sign of this disease is diarrhoea. The Greek word for this is kholera – hence 'cholera'.

Dr John Snow was one of the first specialist anaesthetists (see p.48), but this was not the limit of his interests. He was fascinated by cholera, and following the 1848/9 epidemic, he wrote a pamphlet about it. Since the main symptoms affected the intestines and not the lungs or the body in general, Snow said, the 'cholera poison' thought responsible could not be inhaled as a 'miasma', but must enter the body via the mouth and the digestive tract. The copious amounts of diarrhoea and vomit would dry, infect bed linen and clothes and spread as dust, to be touched and ingested by others, who would in turn succumb to the disease. Even more would fall victim by drinking water contaminated by sufferers' faeces. Snow's theories about the disease's transmission were, however, given little credence.

In 1853, cholera again struck Britain, but by June 1854, only a few cases had appeared in London. Then in July, there was a sudden upsurge and 133 died. This outbreak paled into insignificance when, between 29 August and 11 September, nearly 700 people died in a small area of Soho centring on Broad Street (now Broadwick Street) comprising incredibly overcrowded houses (54 people lived in one), workshops and taverns.

The local hospitals were soon overwhelmed and took on extra nursing staff. One of these was Florence Nightingale (see pp.78-9), who wrote to her friend, the novelist Elizabeth Gaskell: "One poor girl, loathsomely filthy, came in and was dead in hours. I held her in my arms ... I bent down to hear: 'Pray God you may never be in the despair I am in at this time.'"

Dr Snow, who lived nearby, immediately suspected the affected area's water supply. Although there was water from the mains, this was turned on for only two hours a day, Monday to Saturday. The rest of the time, residents depended on the pump at the corner of Broad and Cambridge streets, which was so renowned for the quality of its water that people from other neighbourhoods would come to sample it.

Dr Snow found that the pump water was indeed sparklingly clear, and for a moment he hesitated. But when he plotted all the cholera deaths between 27 August and 2 September, he found they were all clustered in an area no more than 500 yds (450m) across, at the centre of which was Broad Street. His pump water samples also began to show signs of contamination after two days.

Dr Snow decided to act, and, on 7 September, he addressed the Board of Guardians responsible for the

*ow John Snow,
sthetist and
ur of London's
d Street.*

Parish of St James in which Broad Street was situated. The officials were sceptical of the doctor's theories, but all around them, people were dying and none of their other efforts seemed to be making any difference. Besides, the action that Dr Snow wanted them to take was simplicity itself: the removal of the handle of the Broad Street pump. They agreed.

The epidemic ended three days later; no one (including John Snow) ever suggested that the removal of the pump handle had anything to do with its disappearance. However, in its aftermath, the Board of Health carried out an inquiry and came to the conclusion that the epidemic had been caused by "some atmospheric or other widely diffused agent still to be discovered"; the Broad Street pump and its well were completely exonerated.

Then in November, the committee of the St James's Church vestry decided to form its own committee of inquiry, on to which Dr John Snow was co-opted. It was decided to go from door to door, interviewing all the residents. One question the committee wanted answered was why some people had remained untouched while others, often those who lived next door or even in the same building, had fallen victim to the disease.

The filthy conditions did not seem to be a cause. Henry Whitehead, another of the members of the St James's inquiry, commented: "Want of cleanliness was by no means more characteristic of the diseased than of the survivors". However, the inquiry did find that, despite the sewage system, there were still many outdoor privies, which often overflowed their contents into the sewers and surrounding soil.

Following the interviews of the Broad Street residents, the statistics spoke for themselves: of the 137 people who had drunk water from the pump, 80 had caught cholera; of the 297 who had not used the pump, only 20 had become ill. Then Henry Whitehead discovered that the first cholera victim had been a five-month-old baby girl living next to the pump. Her mother had washed her dirty nappies in water that was then dumped into a privy in the front of the house, only a few feet from the pump. The drain from the privy to the sewer leaked badly – right into the well feeding the pump.

When other family members had become ill, they had been tended in upstairs rooms and their slops had simply been flung out the back window. However, when the baby's father had succumbed to the disease, he had been nursed in the front kitchen and his slops deposited in the privy. But by this time, Dr Snow had persuaded the Board of Guardians to remove the pump handle, and a resurgence of the epidemic had, unbeknownst to them, been avoided.

John Snow's theories were vindicated, but the world still ignored them. Recognition for his achievement would have to wait for Pasteur's work on germ theory and Koch's identification of the cholera microbe – long after Snow had died, in 1858, at the tragically early age of 44.

Pasteur then turned his attention towards rabies and, much against his will, the immunization of humans (see pp.60-1).

THE FOLLOWERS

Pasteur and Koch are important not only for their scientific work, but also for the influence they had on generations of scientists and doctors.

The Russian zoologist Ilya Metchnikoff (1845–1916) was studying sea anemones in Sicily when he noticed that they contained amoeba-like cells that were able to engulf small particles and even bacteria. In 1888, after quarrels erupted between Metchnikoff – by then the non-medical director of a scientific institute in the Ukranian city of Odessa – and his medical subordinates, he left the institute and went to Paris, where he became Pasteur's most devoted pupil. Remembering his observations in Sicily, the Russian (who, whatever the weather, always wore overshoes and carried an umbrella) eventually developed his theory of phagocytosis – the destruction of bacteria by the white corpuscles in the blood – for which he was awarded a Nobel prize (sharing with Paul Ehrlich; see pp.100-1) in 1908.

Emil von Behring spent some time at Koch's institute in Berlin before becoming a professor. His greatest achievements were the discovery of immunizations against both diphtheria (1890) – for which he received the Nobel prize in 1901, the first awarded for medicine and physiology – and tetanus (1892) by injections of serum containing antibodies against the relevant microbe. This he called 'antitoxin', a term he introduced into medicine. His work has saved the lives of countless millions of children.

The Japanese bacteriologist Shibasaburo Kitasato worked under Koch for six years before returning to his home to found an institute for the study of infectious diseases. He collaborated with von Behring on tetanus, and in 1894, he identified the bacillus responsible for plague (a discovery that was also made, independently, by the Swiss scientist Alexandre Yersin). Four years later, he isolated the bacterium that causes dysentery.

By the end of the 19th century, the majority of the bacteria causing common diseases had been identified by Pasteur, Koch or one of their followers.

BELOW *Robert Koch (1843–1910), the German country doctor who,* *together with Louis Pasteur, influenced generations of scientists.*

RABIES

"... the sick person is tormented ... with thirst and the fear of water"

RABIES MAY BE a relatively rare disease, but when it strikes it is also one of the world's most appalling.

People infected by the virus usually first develop a headache and vomiting, followed by a high fever and powerful spasms of the jaw, throat and breathing muscles. It is at this stage that hydrophobia – terror at the sight and sound of water – may appear; however, not all victims develop this, and some have the same violent reaction to a slight breeze across the face. Delusions and hallucinations then set in, often with biting and spitting. Swallowing becomes impossible, the spasms increase in frequency and intensity, until finally paralysis, coma or exhaustion sets in. Death usually comes as a result of heart failure or suffocation in about four days.

A minority of rabies victims develop different symptoms. Following a high fever, paralysis sets in, first attacking the area where the virus first entered the body and then progressing inexorably upwards.

The virus responsible is present in the saliva of infected animals – foxes, squirrels and many others, but especially dogs – and is most often transmitted to other animals and humans by bites (although a lick on an open wound will also transmit the disease). Humans develop rabies within 20-90 days, depending on how far away the bite is from the brain. Without modern treatment, the condition is invariably fatal.

DIANA'S HOUNDS

Rabies has been with us since the very earliest times. In Greek mythology, the hounds that pursue and savage Actaeon after he has seen the goddess Diana bathing are supposed to represent rabid dogs. The Roman writer Celsus (*see p.21*) described it: "a most wretched disease in which the sick person is tormented at the same time with thirst and the fear of water, and in which there is but little hope".

Celsus recommended throwing patients without warning into a pond and holding them under until they are forced to swallow water. As well as amputation of the limb that had been bitten, another early treatment was to swallow a hair of the rabid dog or lay one on the bite – the grisly origin of the hangover cure: the 'hair of the dog that bit you'.

The first known epizootic (an epidemic affecting animals) occurred in the Franconia region of Germany in 1271. By the 18th century, rabies was widespread in Europe and the North American colonies, and when the disease appeared in London in 1752, the Government issued orders for all dogs to be shot on sight.

In 1794, Samuel Bardsley, a doctor working in the northern English city of Manchester, wrote a paper in which he was perhaps the first to describe rabies as a specific and identifiable disease. He stated that rabies was not generated

ABOVE *An anti-rabies vaccination at the Pasteur Institute, in Paris.*   *Pasteur was criticised, baselessly, for 'infecting' patients with the disease.*

spontaneously but communicated from animal to animal. Reckoning that the incubation period averaged less than two months, he recommended that all dogs coming into the British Isles should be confined in quarantine for that length of time, and that those showing signs of the disease should be killed. Unfortunately, Bardsley's sensible suggestion was ignored for more than a century, and rabies raged on.

ENTER PASTEUR

A severe outbreak of rabies in the Jura mountains of France lasted from 1803 to 1835. Louis Pasteur (*see p.56*) was born there in 1822, and he may later have been attracted to the idea of a rabies vaccine because he had witnessed the havoc and misery caused when a rabid wolf rampaged through his home village.

He began his research in 1880, first looking for the organism responsible. Despite ascertaining that the disease affected the central nervous system, and theorizing that whatever caused it should be found there as well as in the saliva, he failed completely to identify the correct microbe. (This is hardly surprising, since the rabies virus is so small that it can be seen only under an electron microscope.) Because of this, Pasteur could not fulfil the Henle–Koch postulates (*see p.57*), and he had to tackle the disease from another direction.

He began by injecting rabies-riddled material (usually nerve tissue) into rabbits' brains. When rabbit after rabbit had been injected with the same virus, a consistent incubation period of about six days was produced, much shorter than would happen normally. The virus that acted in this way was called 'fixed virus', and it seemed to have been weakened: dogs inoculated with it sometimes did not produce rabies.

By 1884, Pasteur had developed a method whereby he injected 'fixed virus' into rabbits and removed their spinal cords after they died of the disease. He would then suspend the cords over a vapour of potassium hydroxide to dry them out. The more the cords dried out, the fewer viruses survived, until, after two weeks, most were ineffective.

He decided to make a series of 14 graduated vaccines, the strongest comprising emulsified infected spinal cord that had dried for one day, the weakest from cord that had dried for 14 days. He then set up an experiment with 42 dogs: 23 each received 14 injections, starting with the weakest vaccine and ending with the strongest, one injection a day; the remaining 19 dogs were the control group. At the end of the two weeks, all the dogs were exposed to the rabies virus, either by having it injected in their brain or blood-stream, or by being bitten by a rabid animal. None of the 23 immunized dogs got rabies; 13 of the control group did. Pasteur later showed that, because the rabies incubation period is so long, vaccination worked even if dogs had been infected for some time.

RABIES TODAY

In 1897, 103 years after Dr Bardsley first suggested it, the British government established quarantine for all imported animals that could be infected with rabies. Within five years, the disease had disappeared from Britain, and the country is still clear, despite a brief relapse following World War I when returning soldiers smuggled in their pets. Australia and certain other islands also remain free of rabies.

However, in the rest of Europe, North America and elsewhere, rabies is endemic, and because it exists in animals in the wild, will continue to be so. Laws compelling American dog owners to have their pets inoculated with rabies vaccine have greatly reduced the incidence of human rabies in the US, although rabid skunks and squirrels still pose a risk,

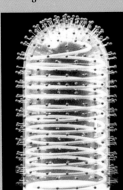

as do foxes in continental Europe. With the building of the Channel Tunnel, Britain, too, is now threatened with a return of the disease.

LEFT *A structural model of a rhabdovirous particle — the bullet-shaped rabies virus, invariably fatal without treatment.*

THE BOY JOSEPH

Pasteur hesitated over inoculating humans – rabies was so terrible and always fatal – although he certainly did consider vaccinating himself. Fate made up his mind for him.

On 6 July 1885, a nine-year-old Alsatian boy, Joseph Meister, and his mother appeared at the door of Pasteur's laboratory. Two days before, Joseph had been bitten 14 times by a dog thought to be rabid, and his doctor, knowing that there was nothing he could do, had suggested that the boy and his mother come to Pasteur.

The scientist was torn – he desperately wanted to save the boy, but his reputation was also at stake. He consulted two of his assistants, both physicians, to help him make up his mind. They both urged him to vaccinate Joseph.

His mind made up, Pasteur ordered the 14-day series of increasingly virulent injections (containing a total of up to 0.09oz [2.5g] of animal spinal tissue). Because he was not medically qualified (and therefore could not legally carry out procedures on humans), and because he was partially paralyzed from his stroke, Pasteur called in Professor Grancher of the Hôpital des Enfants Malades in Paris to inoculate Joseph. Halfway through the series of injections, the boy developed a headache, and Pasteur had the nightmare thought that this presaged the remainder of the symptoms. But it passed, and Joseph Meister stayed well.

Shortly after, Pasteur was approached by his second patient. A 14-year-old shepherd lad, Jean-Baptiste Jupille, from Pasteur's home district of the Jura, had been severely bitten by a rabid dog as he tried to protect some other children. Again the injections; again the nerve-wracking wait – but Jean-Baptiste, too, survived.

Over the next 15 months, the vaccines were received by at least 2490 people. The first failure was Louise Pelletier, who only sought Pasteur's help 37 days after she had been bitten on the face; by then, the disease had taken hold and, despite the treatment, she died. Then other deaths occurred that could not be explained away so easily (it is probable that they resulted from intense allergic reactions to the animal spinal tissue), and while Pasteur received much praise, criticism, too, began to mount.

One argument the scientist could not ignore was that, while rabies was still a rare disease, he was actually infecting patients with the virus. Accusations of 'homicide by careless-ness' followed, and the controversy spread from the Academy of Medicine into the political arena. While the public dug into their pockets to fund 'Pasteur Institutes' in Paris and elsewhere in Europe as well as in South America and Mexico to honour the great scientist, Pasteur himself was deeply upset by the criticism, and in 1887, he suffered two serious strokes. When he died eight years later, he was still working to improve his vaccines.

Pasteur's work was vindicated in 1915, when a ten-year study revealed that, of 6000 people who had been bitten by a confirmed rabid animal, only 0.6 per cent of those who had received his vaccines had died, compared to 16 per cent of those who had not.

A statue of Jean-Baptiste Jupille now stands in front of the Pasteur Institute. When Joseph Meister grew up, he never forgot what Pasteur had done and returned to Paris where he became gate-keeper at the Institute.

JOSEPH LISTER

THE FIRST ANTISEPTIC OPERATION

Carbolic and tin foil helped cut post-operative mortality rates to 5%

ANYONE ENTERING HOSPITAL for surgery in the 1860s was, according to Sir James Simpson, the doctor who popularized chloroform anaesthesia in childbirth (*see p.47*), "exposed to more chances of death than was the English soldier on the field of Waterloo".

The reason seems simple today: "When almost every wound was foul with sappuration," wrote another contemporary doctor, "it seemed natural ... to postpone the cleansing of hands and instruments until the process of dressings and probings had been finished." As a result, open wounds often became infected and, all too frequently, limbs had to be amputated. The mortality rate of patients in hospital from all causes was about 12 per cent, but the rate for those following amputations could climb as high as 50 per cent.

LAUDABLE PUS
Despite the work of such men as Ignaz Semmelweis who had cut maternal deaths from puerperal fever in the late 1840s (*see pp.54-5*), doctors still believed that disease in general – and rampant hospital infection in particular – was due simply to 'bad air'. And since suppuration was held to be an inevitable part of wound healing, the presence of "laudable pus" – that oft-repeated phrase attributed to the 2nd-century Greek physician Galen (see *pp.22-3*) – was still cheerfully recorded in patients' case notes.

But Joseph Lister did not view putrefaction with such equanimity. After many years research into the causes of inflammation he understood that wound sepsis was not due to "something in the air", and became a convert to the "germ theory" of disease and "the beautiful researches of Monsieur Pasteur" (*see pp.56-9*). Lister chose carbolic acid as his antiseptic agent – "having heard of its remarkable efficacy in disinfecting sewage" – and performed his first antiseptic operation in March 1865. This, a wrist operation, and another a couple of weeks later to reset the bones in a compound leg fracture, failed because of what Lister later termed "improper management".

BREAKTHROUGH
Then came the breakthrough. On 12 August 1865, an 11-year-old boy, James Greenlees, suffered a compound fracture of the left leg when he was run over by a cart. He was taken to Glasgow Royal Infirmary, where Lister first washed the wound with a solution of carbolic acid and linseed oil, then dressed it with a sheet of tin foil to prevent evaporation. Except where the acid had burned the skin, the leg – both the bone and the wound – healed perfectly, and young James walked out of the Infirmary six weeks later. In other hands, he would certainly have lost his leg and, quite possibly, his life.

THE UNPUNCTUAL CHIEF

Joseph Lister was born in London on 5 April 1827, the son of Joseph Jackson Lister (see p.52). Following a brilliant student career at University College, London, he moved to Edinburgh to work for Professor Syme, whose daughter, Agnes, he married in 1856. A religious, shy woman, Agnes was devoted to Joseph, and, like him, very unpunctual. She was both his assistant and secretary, for these were lean years for the young doctor: "Poor Joseph and his one patient," murmured long-suffering Agnes.

But, in 1859, Lister became Regius Professor of Surgery at Glasgow University and, two years later, surgeon at Glasgow Royal Infirmary, where he was to perfect his antiseptic techniques. He also found time to improve the range of surgical ligatures, choosing absorbable catgut in preference to silk – silk could not be absorbed, was an irritant and increased the risk of sepsis.

In 1869, following the death of his father-in-law, Lister ascended to the chair of surgery at Edinburgh University, where his fame grew. Although a bad communicator, Lister was a brilliant demonstrator, and much loved by his students, who called him 'Chief': they were horrified when he was invited to take the chair at King's College, London, in 1877, and 700 signed a petition asking him to stay. Nevertheless, Lister went to London, where he was given a cold welcome by the suspicious medical establishment.

Despite this, Lister became President of the Royal Society in 1895, and of the British Association in 1896. The following year he was created Baron Lister of Lyme Regis, and, in 1902, he received the Order of Merit. He died in 1912, having lived to see the universal acceptance of his techniques and knowing he had saved the lives of thousands.

These pioneer antiseptic procedures, which Lister published in *The Lancet* in 1867, provoked a mixture of bewilderment and abuse. "This carbolic acid fuss," wrote one of Lister's critics, "is frivolous and unscientific"; others pointed out that they had tried carbolic acid without success. Lister countered by saying that it was the method, not the carbolic acid, that was vital – any chemical capable of destroying micro-organisms was as good. Nurses also opposed Lister's technique, resenting the extra work involved in keeping operating theatres germ-free. But Lister persevered. A year after his first successful operation, he extended the principle of antisepsis to the drainage of life-threatening abscesses.

ROYAL APPROVAL

It was Lister's famous carbolic spray, introduced in 1870 to "destroy microbes in the air", that attracted the most invective. However, the spray gained acceptance a year later when Lister used it on Queen Victoria during the lancing of an abscess in her left armpit. The monarch was very pleased with the outcome, and fashion followed her lead. Unfortunately, though, Lister did not enjoy the fruits of royal patronage for long: Victoria was very annoyed with Lister when he refused to condemn the practice of vivisection.

Another reason why Lister had difficulty in gaining acceptance among his peers was that he was a far from brilliant communicator. His written accounts of the antiseptic principle were – and still are – extremely heavy going. Nor was this reserved man, who fought a life-long stammer, a good public speaker. Invariably arriving late at the podium, he came across as earnest, humourless and dull, and frequently overran his allotted time. But he was a compelling demonstrator: as one visitor to his wards put it, those who saw him in action came away "driven to belief". In later years, Lister came to accept that he could only spread his doctrines effectively and persuasively by means of his fascinating personal demonstrations.

In any event, it was becoming clear that Lister was correct – only 2 per cent of the operations that he performed resulted in death; after his ideas gained general acceptance, the general mortality rate following surgery fell

ABOVE *Lister's first antiseptic spray, introduced in 1870, relied on hand-power to atomize the carbolic acid. Later, Lister connected the device to a steam pump for greater efficiency. But only Queen Victoria's endorsement gave it credibility.*

BELOW *Lister with his surgical team in Victoria Ward, King's College Hospital, London, in the 1890s. By now, Lister was at the height of his considerable fame and reputation: President of the Royal Society and Baron Lister of Lyme Regis.*

to about 5 per cent. In fact, although aseptic methods were later developed – by William Halsted at Johns Hopkins (*see pp.90-1*), and Johann von Micuhcz at Breslau, among others – from 1865 on, medicine was to be divided into the pre-Lister and post-Lister ages.

George Bernard Shaw, the Irish man of letters and playwright, carped, "The *fin de siècle* stank of carbolic acid". Nevertheless, Lister had opened the way for really innovative surgery – a whole range of operations that could now be ventured with greatly reduced risk. Lister's work even compelled the German pioneer in orthopaedics, George H. Stromeyer, to burst into poetry:

Mankind looks grateful now on thee
For what thou didst in surgery
And Death must often go amiss
By smelling antiseptic bliss.

COMMUNITIES OF CELLS

THE WORK OF BERNARD AND VIRCHOW

A Frenchman and a German take a new look at the basis of disease

ALMOST ALL 'DISCOVERIES' are the sum of the work of many individuals. However, sometimes a man or woman can take an imaginative leap and transform our thinking on a subject that, for years, has been considered settled. So it was with two men – one French, the other German – who, together, altered for ever the way we look at life at its most basic level: the cell.

CLAUDE BERNARD

Bernard's greatest ambition as a young pharmacy student was to be a dramatist. At least one of his plays – *Rose du Rhône* – was performed in Lyon in 1833 when he was just 20, but after he had finished his five-act historical drama *Artur de Bretaigne*, a critic persuaded him that his true *métier* was medicine and medical research.

Moving to Paris, he became a student of the physiologist François Magendie at the Collège de France. Magendie was a fanatic when it came to rejecting all previous theories and only believed what his eyes could see from his experiments. These generally involved vivisection; hundreds of animals perished at his hands. Bernard followed in his master's footsteps; his wife, on the other hand, was a supporter of the French equivalent of the Royal Society for the Prevention of Cruelty to Animals (they separated in 1870).

In 1865, in his *Introduction to the Study of Experimental Medicine,* Bernard set out a system whereby conclusions could only be drawn from experiments, which would then lead to further questions and further experiments. There was no room for purely speculative hypotheses in his world.

Over the years, as evinced by the more than 300 papers and books he published between 1834 and 1878, he made major contributions in a number of areas. In his study of digestion and carbohydrate metabolism, he proved that, like plants, animals could synthesize complex substances (previously it had been thought that animals could only break down fats, sugars and proteins). He found that, as well as producing bile, the liver could manufacture glucose with the assistance of a substance he named glycogen. (It was later discovered that the liver did this directly, by converting glycogen into glucose.) He also worked out the digestive function of the secretions of the pancreas: they split fat in the duodenum into a fatty acid and glycerol, which could then be absorbed.

Bernard also studied blood vessels and how their diameters (and thus the flow of blood in them) were regulated by nerves. In addition, through his work on carbon monoxide, he found that it was the red corpuscles that carry oxygen from the lungs to the rest of the body; and his investigation of the effects on muscles of curare, the South American arrow poison, would later lead to this being used as an adjunct to anaesthetics during operations.

However, Bernard's main achievement was his concept of the unchanging 'internal environment' (*milieu intérieur*) in which live communities of cells – the basic units of all living things, discovered by Theodor Schwann in 1839. The entire human body, said Bernard, did not have to adapt to a continually changing environment in order to survive. Rather, the fluids that bathed the cells – blood and lymph – had to be altered. This was done by changes in the amount of water they contained, temperature regulation (through skin flushing and sweating), alterations in oxygen supply (such as through panting) and blood pressure, and changes in the amounts of certain chemicals (called collectively electrolytes) in the blood. This concept – now expanded and called 'homoeostasis' – is today the crux of much emergency treatment and is vital in surgery.

LEFT *An 1899 painting by L'Hermitté of Claude Bernard vivisecting a rabbit. To modern-day sensibilities, this is an appalling image; 19th-century morality, however, was more pragmatic – and Bernard's work undoubtedly led to the saving of many lives.*

Bernard's later years were disturbed by ill health, which he blamed on the upset of his own *milieu intérieur* – he even claimed that French setbacks during the Franco-Prussian war of 1870–71 were responsible for his bad digestion. When he died in 1878, the French nation made up for having worried him: he was the first scientist ever to be given the honour of a state funeral.

RUDOLF VIRCHOW

The son of a Pomeranian farmer, Virchow could be considered the 'Renaissance man' of the 19th century, so wide-ranging were his interests and accomplishments. After taking his degree in 1843, he worked as a pathologist in Berlin and founded the medical journal that is now called, in his honour, *Virchow's Archiv*. In 1848, that year of revolutions, he was sent to Silesia to investigate a typhus epidemic. His report condemned the government for the conditions there and for refusing to provide the Polish population with even basic sanitary facilities. The government promptly banned him from Berlin. Virchow moved to Würzburg, where he was Professor of Pathology until his return to Berlin in 1855, and began in earnest his study of cells.

When Schwann had discovered these in 1839, he had thought that they arose spontaneously from a formless ground substance he called 'blastema'. The pathologist Carl von Rokitansky of Vienna, who carried out and described more than 30,000 autopsies, surmised that conditions that affected the blood caused the blastema to produce abnormal cells resulting in disease – a theory that was simply the four humours in disguise, and which succeeded in sullying Rokitansky's reputation.

Now Virchow discovered that *omnis cellula e cellula* – 'every cell comes from a cell': all cells are multiples of one cell, the fertilized ovum (egg), which itself is derived from cells from two parents and on back through the ancestral line. All these cells live in what he called – using a political analogy – a 'cellular democracy' or 'republic of the cells', in which cells are social classes and the organs and tissues are their territory. In addition, he said, all diseases come from abnormal changes within cells, and these abnormal cells in turn multiply through division.

Virchow published his findings in his book *Cellularpathologie* in 1858, and from then on, each disease had to be looked at differently. No longer were organs seen as statically diseased; instead, it was understood that processes continued within the cells of which the organs were made.

Virchow's theory of the origins of cells was vital for medicine, but his ideas on how disease starts, while they were brilliantly effective in describing what happens in cancers, were not adequate to explain many other conditions. For one thing, he concentrated wholly on internal events in cells, and did not take into consideration what effect external factors could have. The problem was that Virchow was sceptical of Pasteur's germ theory, primarily because he feared it would reawaken the concept of disease as a living entity, which had enthused – and misled – doctors during the Enlightenment and before.

While many medical researchers applauded his findings and others criticized them, Virchow continued his work, describing leukaemia for the first time, collecting and mounting 23,000 specimens, devising the fifth sign of inflammation (disturbed function; *see p.21*) and other important tasks. But he had other interests, too.

Having retained liberal political views from his days in Silesia, he co-founded the Progressive Party and was for many years its leader. In 1860, he was elected to a seat in the Prussian Parliament, where his debates with Bismarck almost led to a duel, and from 1880 to 1893, he was a member of the Reichstag, where he championed social reform and public hygiene. In his spare time, he carried out a huge investigation into the physical anthropology of German children, as well as looking into tattooing, lake dwellings and other subjects. In 1879, he accompanied Heinrich Schliemann to the excavations of what they thought was Troy (it turned out to be too old) and wrote a book about their discoveries.

Virchow's 80th birthday in 1901 was celebrated as a national holiday, and when he died of heart disease a year later, he, like Bernard, received a state funeral.

THE CENTURY OF EPONYMOUS DISEASES

Whereas, during the Renaissance and Enlightenment, many body parts were named after those who first described them, the 19th century saw medical men describing scores of different diseases and conditions and naming them after themselves. The following is just a selection.

Addison's disease: Thomas Addison (1855)

Banti's disease: Guido Banti (1882)

Basedow's disease: Karl von Basedow (1840)

Bell's palsy: Sir Charles Bell (1828)

Bright's disease: Richard Bright (1827)

Cheyne–Stokes respiration: John Cheyne and William Stokes (1818)

Colles' fracture: Abraham Colles (1814)

Corrigan's pulse: Sir Dominic John Corrigan (1832)

Dupuytren's contraction: Guillaume Dupuytren (1831)

Graves' disease: Robert Graves (1835)

Hodgkin's disease: Thomas Hodgkin (1832)

Jacksonian epilepsy: John Hughlings Jackson (1875)

Korsakoff's syndrome: Sergei Korsakoff (1887)

Menière's syndrome: Prosper Menière (1861)

Paget's disease: Sir James Paget (1876)

Parkinson's disease: James Parkinson (1817)

Reynaud's disease: Maurice Reynaud (1862)

Stokes–Adams attack: William Stokes and Robert Adams (1826)

von Recklinghausen's disease: Friedrich von Recklinghausen (1882)

Weil's disease: Adolf Weil (1886)

Wilms' tumour: Max Wilms (1899)

LEFT *Richard Bright (1789–1858) was the archetypal 19th-century polymath: he was a zoologist, biologist, geologist and doctor. Wearing the latter hat, he described, in 1827, Bright's disease – a collection of kidney disorders in which albumin is present in the urine and there is often dropsy.*

BACK TO BASICS

THE BEGINNINGS OF GENETICS

"How extremely stupid not to have thought of that"

FOR SOME TIME, scientists had been puzzling over the question of inheritance. Animal and plant breeders had for centuries been developing stronger, more fertile or more productive specimens simply by concentrating their efforts on individuals with these characteristics, but no one knew why this worked. Many suggestions had been put forward, but there was not yet a coherent theory that explained everything that was happening.

VOYAGES OF DISCOVERY

As a young man, Charles Darwin (1809–82) preferred collecting expeditions to studying medicine or theology. He was a great disappointment to his father, Robert, a doctor: "You care for nothing but shooting, dogs and rat-catching, and you will be a disgrace to yourself and all your family!" he once exclaimed. Robert was persuaded against his better judgment to allow his wayward son to serve as the official naturalist on the research vessel HMS *Beagle*, which set sail in December 1831. For the next five years, the younger Darwin would travel to South America, the Pacific islands and beyond, and what he saw and learned on that voyage would provide him with enough food for thought to last a lifetime of study and analysis.

Following his return to England, Darwin read Thomas Malthus' *Essay on Population*, in which the dour economist commented that all species tend to produce far more offspring than can be expected to reach reproductive maturity. Darwin began to speculate that those offspring that did survive might have some favourable characteristic that their more unfortunate brothers and sisters did not, and that this favourable characteristic might be passed down through generations, eventually – over many generations – changing an entire species and enabling it to survive. He wrote down his new theory in a short essay, which he expanded to book length in 1844.

LEFT *Darwin's theory that humans shared a common ancestry with apes led to a storm of controversy, as this cartoon from* The London Sketch Book *shows. Benjamin Disraeli, British Prime Minister and novelist, commented: "The question is, whether man is descended from the apes or the angels. I am on the side of the angels".*

However, before he could publish, another, very superficial work on evolutionary theory came out and touched off a furore. The subject was now in the spotlight, and Darwin knew that he would have to treat it thoroughly if the critics were not to ride roughshod over his work. He retreated to his home and his family in Kent, to spend the next 15 years reading, thinking and classifying barnacles. His health began to fail: from having been a robust youth, he could now work no more than four hours a day, and he constantly visited doctors and dubious hydrotherapy establishments (*see pp.84-5*).

Finally, in 1858, Darwin began to write down all his conclusions. The result was *On the Origin of Species*, published in 1859, which was, and remains, an extraordinary book. Darwin examined all the available evidence to come up with a theory on how species change, or evolve, over time through natural selection, which the philosopher Herbert Spencer would later encapsulate in the phrase 'survival of the

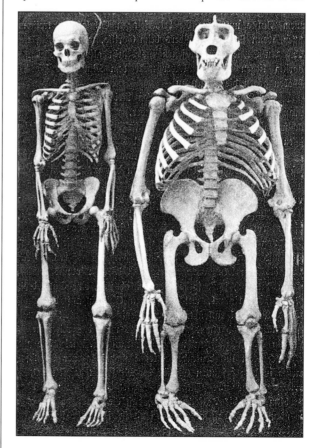

ABOVE *This photograph of a human skeleton, side-by-side with one from a gorilla, at once shows the evident similarities between the two, and looking with the eye of prejudice, shows why many scientists and churchmen refused to believe the connection.*

fittest'. After reading the book, the eminent biologist Thomas Huxley could only sigh: "How extremely stupid not to have thought of that!".

For all his pains, Darwin's theory (or 'Darwinism' as it came to be known) created an uproar throughout the Western world, for two reasons. First, by stating that species change, he was contradicting the literal teaching of the Bible, that the world and all the species on it were created by God at the same time. Second, when he said that higher species evolve from lower ones, he included humans; this meant that humans were in some way 'related' to other primates – the monkeys and apes – and this was completely unacceptable to many people.

"A LITTLE TRICK"

However, Darwin could not explain how various characteristics were inherited from generation to generation, to enable species to change and survive. That piece of the puzzle came from a monk in the town of Brno, now in Czechoslovakia but at that time a part of the Austro-Hungarian empire.

Johann Mendel was born in 1822, taking the name of Gregor when he entered a monastery in 1843. A lack of family money decided his vocation, for the Church would pay for his education. At Vienna in the early 1850s, he studied under Franz Unger, who, some years before Virchow (see p.65), taught that all plant cells arise from other previously existing ones. He also said that variants develop within natural populations, which are then passed on to succeeding generations. This view contradicted that held by other scientists, and Mendel decided to carry out experiments to decide the issue.

Between 1856 and 1863, he planted 34 varieties of edible peas and crossed 12 of them to see how often various characteristics reappeared in succeeding generations of hybrids; he then repeated the experiment using French and bush bean plants. His results were expressed in simple mathematical ratios, one of the first biological studies to employ statistics. He found that certain characteristics reappeared in fairly precise ratios; the ones that occurred most often he called 'dominant' and the others he called 'recessive'. He believed that these characteristics were passed on from plant to plant as 'particles', of which each plant had two, one from each parent.

Mendel published an account of his work in a local naturalist journal in 1866, but although a few scientists noted his findings, they made no impact and were forgotten. In 1878, Mendel, then abbot of his monastery, was asked how he had achieved the beneficial changes in the pea plants in his garden. "It is just a little trick", he replied, "but there is a long story connected with it that would take too long to tell", and he changed the subject.

It was only in 1900, 16 years after his death, that his work was rediscovered and fully appreciated. From the 1920s, population geneticists such as J. B. S. Haldane (see p.116) melded together Mendel's and Darwin's work to come up with a coherent explanation of evolutionary change. However, the final piece of the puzzle would not be slotted into place until 1953, when Francis Crick and James Watson discovered the structure of DNA (see pp.160–3).

ABOVE
Gregor Mendel, the monk who devised the theory of heredity.

GALTON AND EUGENICS

Fascinated by statistics and a keen observer, Francis Galton (1822–1911) had initially studied meteorology, and was a pioneer in the cataloguing of fingerprints. However, when his cousin Charles Darwin's **On the Origin of Species** *was published in 1859, he began to concentrate on heredity and, in particular, the inheritance of 'natural ability'.*

He thumbed through biographical dictionaries, noting that a large proportion of distinguished scientists, military men, statesmen, jurists, painters, poets and composers were related by blood. Therefore, he said, not only are physical features inherited, but also talent and character. He denied that eminence in a particular field was dependent on either social advantage or disadvantage. Inheritance was all, and thus it was "quite practicable to produce a highly gifted race of men by judicious marriages during several consecutive generations" – a system he would call 'eugenics' (literally, 'well born').

These ideas, which he discussed in his book **Hereditary Genius** *(1869), were taken up enthusiastically by many people both in Britain and in the US, where fears that the country was being swamped by immigrants of 'inferior' quality gave added impetus. The Eugenics Society was founded in London in 1907, and although its membership never numbered more than about 800 at its peak, its influence was considerable in such fields as birth control, artificial insemination, sex education, marriage guidance, abortion reform, family allowances and taxation.*

From the beginning, eugenists were divided between those advocating 'positive' eugenics – encouraging those perceived as 'fit' to have more children – and those plumping for 'negative' eugenics who were in favour of discouraging and even preventing the 'unfit' from breeding. The 'negative' eugenists were particularly concerned about the fecundity of the lower orders of society and the mentally handicapped and ill. Mutilating sterilization operations were carried out by gynaecologists on supposedly 'hysterical' or insane women, and a large number of state legislatures in the US passed laws allowing the forcible sterilization of women in mental asylums. Through the 1930s, negative eugenic ideas took an even more sinister turn, culminating in the extermination by the Nazis of thousands of mentally handicapped people and the genocide of Jews, gypsies and others.

After World War II, overt interest in eugenics receded. However, in 1986, Singapore became the first democratic country to adopt an openly eugenic policy: female graduates were offered pay rises after giving birth, while non-graduates were promised housing grants if they agreed to be sterilized. In addition, it is said by some that eugenic theory can be seen in the practice of genetic counselling, when prospective parents of handicapped children are offered the option of abortion.

WOMEN UNDER THE KNIFE

EXAMINATION AND SURGERY

"One of the most important discoveries of the age for the relief of suffering"

BY THE LATE 18TH CENTURY, surgeons were eager to tackle abdominal operations, but the problems involved in any procedure in this area were enormous. With no anaesthesia, patients were subjected to excruciating pain, and speed, not skill, made surgical success more likely. Antisepsis was also unknown, and if the person under the knife did not die of shock, he or she usually succumbed to infection.

Still, the surgeons were keen to try, primarily in the prevailing spirit of research and experimentation, although there were some eager to spare humanity pain and suffering through surgical cures. Gradually, they focused on women's diseases, and from the ovaries, they eventually extended their expertise to the rest of the body. Along the way, however, many of them were harshly criticised for their methods and their attitudes towards their patients.

WOMEN AND DOCTORS

Women's diseases were not a medical specialty at the beginning of the 19th century. They were either treated by general surgeons or by physicians, depending on the precise nature of the complaint.

Women, especially those of the middle class, were considered nervous, frail, swooning creatures, and men had an exaggerated sense of delicacy when dealing with them.

This made examination of their genital organs extremely difficult: touch alone was usually employed, and as late as the 1870s, William Goodell of the University of Pennsylvania Hospital Dispensary went so far as to urge his students to keep their eyes fixed firmly on the ceiling while making their first vaginal examination.

Use of the speculum, which had been invented at least as early as classical Rome (*see p.21*), caused grave concern. It was felt to erode a woman's decency, and some doctors even believed that it gave sexual gratification. Philadelphia's Charles D. Meigs (*see p.55*) congratulated women who refused to be examined in this way.

"I confess I am proud to say that in this country generally", declared Meigs, "there are women who prefer to suffer the extremity of danger and pain rather than waive those scruples of delicacy which prevent their maladies from being explored."

Despite these 'scruples', the speculum came into general use, but the treatments that followed the diagnoses differed little from those of previous centuries. As well as the usual blood-letting, purging and starvation, the uterus might be prodded into what was considered (usually erroneously) a better position, and the cervix might be cauterized with powerful caustics or a red-hot iron. Even leeches were placed on the cervix to reduce swelling, inflammation and vaginal discharges. Disturbingly, one medical book of 1864 advised doctors to count the leeches inserted into the vagina and those that, after feeding, dropped off, so that they would not lose any.

LOSING OVARIES

None of these treatments was particularly effective, and many women continued to suffer, particularly from ovarian cysts – tissue masses often filled with fluid, which grew out from one of a woman's ovaries and which could become so enormous that the victims looked as if they were in late pregnancy (one is known to have weighed 149lb [68kg]). Many sufferers were confined to their beds; some cysts were cancerous. Faced with such terrible disability, it was not surprising that some women were prepared to do almost anything to be well once more, but until 1809, there was no effective treatment.

In December of that year, the Edinburgh-trained American surgeon Ephraim McDowell received a message asking him to ride 60mi (96km) cross country from his office in the frontier town of Danville, Kentucky, to

LEFT *A bashful compromise to overcome the reluctance of female genital examination was portrayed in 1822 by Jacques-Pierre*

Maygnier — the woman stands as the physician kneels, both apparently completely unconcerned by what is happening.

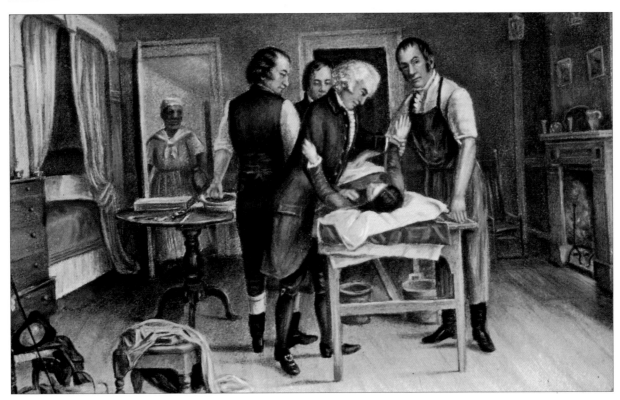

examine 47-year-old Jane Todd Crawford. Because her abdomen had swelled, Mrs Crawford thought she was pregnant, but although she began to have pains, labour had not begun. The local doctors had conferred and agreed that the delivery would be too complicated for them.

When McDowell arrived, he soon realized that, rather than pregnancy, Mrs Crawford's swollen belly was caused by an enormous ovarian cyst. Consequently, as McDowell later wrote: "I gave to the unhappy woman information of her dangerous situation. She appeared willing to undergo an experiment". McDowell returned to Danville, to be followed a few days later by Mrs Crawford, who had ridden on horseback through the forests and had forded several rivers to reach him.

The 25-minute operation took place at McDowell's home on Christmas Day. While his patient sang hymns to turn her mind from the agony, the surgeon removed 15lb (7kg) of a "dirty gelatinous substance" from Mrs Crawford's cyst and then the Fallopian tube and the ovary that had contained the cyst, the latter weighing in at $7^1/_2$lb (3.4kg). His patient was up and about five days later, and lived in good health for another 31 years.

Today, we would say that McDowell had performed a salpingo-oöphorectomy (removal of the ovary and Fallopian tube on one side), but in the 19th century, the procedure was called an 'ovariotomy'. The fact that McDowell was working in the United States had much to do with his agreeing to tackle such a risky operation: American medicine was far less regulated than in Britain and the rest of Europe; there were fewer constraints on trying something new; and, especially in the South, some doctors (although not McDowell) took advantage of the opportunities provided by slavery to provide subjects for their research (see p.70).

When, eight years later, McDowell sent a description of his operation for publication in Britain, the news was

ABOVE *In 1809 and in his own home, American surgeon Ephraim McDowell operated on Mrs Crawford to remove her ovarian cyst by abdominal section. News of the operation — and its success —* reached John Lizars at Edinburgh University some eight years later. *In 1824, Lizars performed the first British ovariotomy on a woman whose abdomen was so large she looked nine months pregnant.*

received with hostility and incredulity. Despite this, the first successful ovariotomy was performed there in 1824, and between 1838 and 1855, it was carried out at least 200 times. However, the death rate was 44.5 per cent, and controversy raged within the medical establishment between those who claimed that ovariotomy was the only solution to a grave and dangerous condition, and those who believed that the operation itself was too dangerous. One of the latter was the surgeon Robert Liston (see p.48) who labelled the ovariotomists 'belly rippers'. Some doctors were also said to perform ovariotomies either to make a name for themselves or to make money, or both.

French doctors considered the operation a wholly Anglo-American invention and said that no prudent practitioner would ever resort to it. They also likened it to vivisection — the operation was only being done, they said, so that surgeons could practise pelvic surgery and carry out research on the internal organs in a live woman. This worry was also found in Britain: in 1888, during Jack the Ripper's gruesome serial killings, a rumour circulated that 'Jack' was really a vivisecting surgeon from the University of London.

The desire for knowledge at almost any cost was certainly a factor in the ovariotomy's increasing popularity with British and American surgeons (from 1843 to 1883, John and William Attlee of Pennsylvania performed 465 between them) — and even the French scientist Claude Bernard (see p.64) was in favour of it for this reason. However, it cannot be denied that, especially in the early decades of its use, it also helped a great many of the surviving women.

DR SIMS AND THE SLAVE WOMEN

Prior to 1852, one of the most appalling conditions that women had to suffer was vesico-vaginal or recto-vaginal fistula, in which a hole develops in the vagina and extends into, respectively, the bladder or the rectum (and sometimes both). It commonly occurred following mismanaged labour, when the head of the baby pressed too long against the tissues of the vagina, depriving them of blood and allowing gangrene to set in. The result was incurable incontinence. The skin between the sufferer's legs became inflamed, covered in sores and intolerably itchy, and because of the smell, she was forced to retreat from society.

The eminent Berlin surgeon Johann Friedrich Dieffenbach wrote that "the cure for such an evil is the prize for which we all labour". The man who won the prize was James Marion Sims, who, upon graduation from medical school in 1835, settled in Montgomery, Alabama.

Sims has become a figure of immense controversy in recent years. Following his death in 1883, he was hailed as the 'father of gynaecology', yet feminist historians have condemned him for not only experimenting on women, but on black slave women, and becoming rich in the process. The truth seems to lie somewhere in between.

In 1845, Sims was called to visit a black slave girl called Anarcha, who following a three-day labour developed a vaginal fistula leading to both her bladder and rectum. Although Sims was touched by her suffering, and that of two other slaves, Lucy and Betsey, who had vesico-vaginal fistulae, it was probably the challenge of finding a cure that inspired him. Soon he had found four more slaves with the same condition, and with their owners' consent, he began to operate – without anaesthesia, trying a variety of techniques and always failing. Along the way, he invented a new speculum, a new catheter and a new suture using silver wire and silk thread. Finally, as Anarcha underwent her 30th operation in four years, he was successful.

In 1852, Sims published a description of his work, later describing it (with typical immodesty) in his autobiography as "one of the most important discoveries of the age for the relief of suffering humanity".

He then moved to New York and established the Women's Hospital, the first of its kind in the United States. His statue now stands opposite the New York Academy of Medicine; sadly there is no memorial to the pain and suffering of Anarcha, Betsey, Lucy and the rest of Sims' 'experiments'.

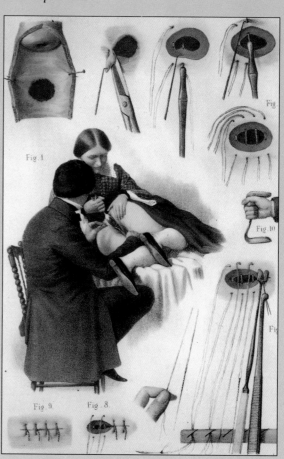

ABOVE *A step-by-step illustration of Dr. James Marion Sims's famous operation to close a vesico-vaginal fistula adorns the pages of* Henry Savage's The Surgery, Surgical Pathology and Surgical Anatomy of the Female Pelvic Organs *(1882).*

BATTEY AND BAKER BROWN

But it was the attitude towards women in general of 19th-century doctors – almost all of them men – that seems to have coloured their acceptance of operations on female reproductive organs. The physician Thomas Radford defended caesarean sections (with a mortality rate very similar to that of ovariotomies) by arguing that, since a woman's main reason for living was her ability to bear children, if the organs involved in this did not function because of disease, then it did not matter so much if she lost her life during an operation to fix them. The brilliant scientist Rudolf Virchow (*see p.65*) took the argument even further. "Woman is a pair of ovaries with a human being attached", he wrote, "whereas man is a human being furnished with a pair of testes".

Not all doctors were as blunt as Virchow, but many shared his belief. To them, a woman's uterus and ovaries were not only involved in the reproduction of the species but they were also the source of much illness – both physical and psychological. The result was that, on both sides of the Atlantic, and especially with the advent of anaesthesia, there was an increasing number of ovariotomies for the treatment of such relatively minor conditions as period pain and such spurious diseases as 'menstrual epilepsy', regardless of the very real symptoms that were produced by the ensuing premature menopause.

From 1872, the American surgeon Robert Battey popularized an operation he called 'normal ovariotomy', in which completely normal ovaries were removed to relieve 'symptoms' in women who were considered insane, hysterical, unfaithful to their husbands or just plain unhappy. Dr Elizabeth Blackwell (*see p.81*) claimed that this extension of the operation to the treatment of mental conditions was the result of doctors' *prurigo secandi* ('itch to cut'), but this is not the whole story. Some doctors, such as William Goodell, advocated 'Battey's operation' to prevent a woman transmitting the 'taint' of her supposed insanity to her descendants – a direct reference to the eugenics craze (*see p.67*) then sweeping across Britain and the US, where the operation was particularly popular.

The use of surgery to control women reached its dubious apotheosis with the work of Isaac Baker Brown, a London surgeon who specialized in removing the clitoris and, thus, a woman's sexual feeling. Baker Brown and his disciples performed clitoridectomies on women whom they (or their husbands) felt were suffering from uncontrolled sexuality, as evinced by masturbation or 'nymphomania'. In a number of cases, one of the primary 'symptoms' for which the operation was recommended was that the woman wanted a divorce, which had only become possible in Britain in 1857.

In 1867, at the height of his success, Baker Brown was suddenly faced with ruin, being expelled from the Obstetrical Society and forced to resign from the Medical

Society of London. However, the reason for this was not the fact that Baker Brown had been responsible for the mutilation of hundreds of women, but that he had carried out the operation without informing many of his patients of its consequences and, more importantly to the doctors, because he was guilty of self-promotion. Baker Brown went to the United States, where his operation became standard treatment for many years.

FROM OVARIES TO THE BRAIN

The controversies over ovariotomies and clitoridectomies also revealed profound tensions between surgeons and the physicians who were gradually becoming known as 'obstetricians' concerning the question: Who is qualified to perform gynaecological operations? This was to lead to the formation, in Britain, of the Royal College of Obstetricians and Gynaecologists in 1929, and the unity of practitioners in this specialty throughout the world.

The gynaecological surgery of the 19th century had, however, a far greater influence, for it truly opened the way for invasive surgery. In 1873, the eminent British surgeon Sir John Erichsen declared: "The abdomen, the chest and the brain [will] be for ever shut from the intrusion of the wise and humane surgeon", but by the end of the century, none of these parts of the body was any longer off-limits to the surgeon's scalpel.

For instance, the German surgeon Theodor Billroth (1829–94), a friend of Brahms and one of the first to follow Lister's antiseptic procedures, devised most of the operations still performed on the stomach, intestines and thyroid gland. A tumour was first removed from the brain in 1884, and two years later, an oesophagus was reconstructed. And blood loss during all sorts of operations was limited by the British surgeon and keen ovariotomist Thomas Spencer Wells, whose 'Spencer Wells forceps' are still in common use.

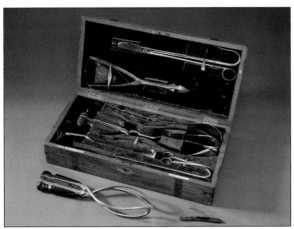

ABOVE *A set of 19th-century obstetrical instruments that may look fearsome but, in fact, represented a major advance for women by easing the rigours of difficult childbirth.*

RIGHT *Recognized as one of the most able of British surgeons, Sir Thomas Spencer Wells, skilfully performed abdominal operations for many years. The forceps he invented were designed to clamp the bleeding ends of open blood vessels – when the two blades are closed over the vessel, a catch locks them firmly in position.*

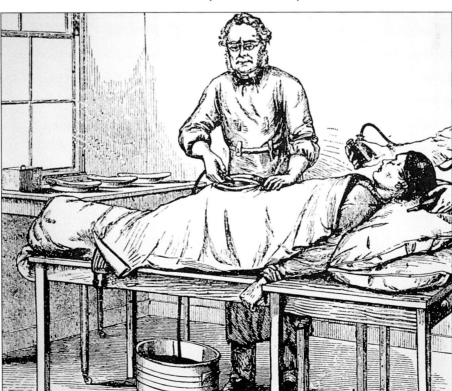

THE DAWNING OF PSYCHIATRY

FROM CRUEL SPECTACLE TO LEGAL PROTECTION

Patients in special chairs whirled at 100 revolutions per minute

FROM EARLIEST TIMES, people thought that the mentally ill were possessed by demons, and 'treatments' as extreme as trepannation (*see p.11*) and as fatal as being burned at the stake were carried out. Then, in the great surge of learning of the Renaissance, new voices began to be heard.

Paracelsus (*see p.36*) rejected the supernatural, theorizing instead that the cause of unreasonable behaviour could be serious emotional disturbance. After his son was beheaded for poisoning his wife, the medical humanist Geronimo Cardano (1501–76) wrote a treatise in which he described immorality as a disease of the spirit, saying that there was a difference between those who did wrong through wickedness and those who fell foul of the law through 'passion'. And in his book of 1563, *De Praestigiis Daemonum*, Johann Weyer, court physician to the Duke of Cleves, maintained that witches were simply unhappy people whose minds had become unhinged.

Unfortunately, the study of the mind and mental illness did not, after these promising beginnings, keep pace with the extensive investigations of the body and physical disease that followed. Until well into the 19th century, there was little or no distinction drawn between mental illness and mental handicap, and problems of the personality were ignored for almost as long. For instance, the American doctor, Benjamin Rush, a signatory of the Declaration of Independence, believed that the brains of the insane were overcharged with blood; therefore, the cure was 'heroic' bloodletting and purging, which sometimes killed patients in the process.

The mentally ill were rejected by society and gradually came under the care, first, of the Church, and then of government asylums. The most famous of these – London's Bethlem Royal Hospital, commonly known as 'Bedlam' – was a popular sightseeing spot, with tours costing a penny undertaken by the fashionable rich of the capital city. Here, as elsewhere, the insane, dressed in rags, were herded together with no heat, little lighting and poor ventilation,

chained and gagged if they were violent or difficult and ducked in cold water to bring them to their senses.

THE FIRST REFORMS

Interest in a different, kinder way of treating the insane – what came to be called 'moral care' – increased in Britain as people became familiar with the insanity of the king, George III. Possibly suffering from the rare hereditary disease porphyria, he had five distinct periods of insanity before his final breakdown and death in 1820.

From the end of the 18th century, the Quaker Tuke family ensured that at least some of Britain's insane would receive proper treatment. In 1792, the wholesale tea and coffee merchant William Tuke and his son Henry formed a society of like-minded people in York to improve the care of the mentally disordered, and, four years later, they founded the York Retreat, a hospital for 30 patients that, in contrast to Bedlam and its like, was clean, quiet and orderly. Inmates were treated like guests, often being invited for tea with the superintendent and matron, and for an extra fee, they could be looked after by their own servants. (William's great-grandson Daniel Hack Tuke carried on the family tradition: he became president of the Medico-Psychological Association, the forerunner of the Royal College of Psychiatrists; and his scathing report of 1885 on asylums in the United States and Canada resulted in major reforms there.)

In 1792, in the midst of the French Revolution, Philippe Pinel was placed in charge of the 17th-century asylum of Bicêtre in Paris. The horrors of the revolution were never far away: in September of that year, 162 Bicêtre prisoners (including 43 under the age of 18) were butchered by the mob, led by the chief warden.

The following year, Pinel bravely (some said foolishly) decided to test a theory – that madness was the product of the deprivation of liberty and movement – and unchained a group of 49 inmates. One man escaped but was soon caught,

LEFT *In the courtyard of La Salpêtrière, Paris, (part of the same hospital that contained the Bicêtre asylum) Dr. Philippe Pinel presides over the 49 mental patients liberated from their chains. An advocate of a more humane treatment of the insane, Pinel believed that patients who were manacled grew agitated and dangerous. Kindness, on the other hand, prompted sociability and encouraged confidence.*

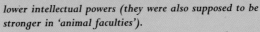

READING THE BUMPS

Like Mesmer, Franz Josef Gall (1758–1828) was one of the mavericks of the Vienna medical school. A talented anatomist and physiologist, he claimed to have discovered 26 organs in the brain (later increased to 42), each responsible for a particular mental function. The larger these organs were, he said, the better they worked and the more they affected the overall shape of the skull, which could be studied to discover a person's personality and character traits. Gall's 'science of protrusions' eventually grew into the pseudo-science of phrenology.

The practise of phrenology grew rapidly during the early decades of the 19th century. People flocked to phrenological surgeries to have their 'bumps' felt and their heads measured and weighed: those of superior intellect averaged 24 to 25in (61 to 64cm) in circumference, and, because women's brains weigh less than men's, this was said to account for their lower intellectual powers (they were also supposed to be stronger in 'animal faculties').

Phrenology became fashionable even among the upper classes. Queen Victoria had her children's heads 'read', and the novelist George Eliot twice had her hair shaved off to make it easier for the phrenologist to get at her cranium.

The comic writer Mark Twain, author of such American classics as **Tom Sawyer**, was a confirmed critic: when, in disguise and giving a false name, he had his bumps read, he was told that he lacked a sense of humour.

Phrenology reached its peak in the mid-1800s. Thereafter, it declined, but it still maintains a foothold in the West.

LEFT A phrenologist reads the bumps on a boy's head in an attempt to predict the child's potential and capabilities.

and the experiment was deemed a success. Although, before and after this, Pinel made great headway in his classification of various forms of mental illness, his aim at Bicêtre was more a matter of hospital administration: chaining made inmates worse, and that was inefficient.

INCARCERATION

Unfortunately, Pinel's system depended on individuals with forceful personalities to manage these 'open' asylums. There being few people like this, the trend was towards the incarceration of the insane in new, ever bigger hospitals. These at least were healthier places than the Bedlams of old, and provided more care than the almshouses and local jails into which many mentally ill people were thrown and then put out of mind.

Some lay people began, like the Tukes before them, to take an interest in the welfare of the mentally ill. For example, from the 1840s the formidable American campaigner Dorothea Dix investigated the abuse and neglect of these unfortunate people outside state care. By striking out at public indifference and lobbying state legislatures, she was eventually credited with the establishment of more than 30 state asylums.

Doctors began to see mental disease as far less curable than they had in the glory days following the work of the Tukes and Pinel, and in the large factory-like asylums, patients received less individual attention. However, this was the age of the machine, and some of the new psychiatric specialists – called 'alienists', because their charges were 'alienated' from society – came up with mechanical methods of treatment. Patients were strapped into the newfangled strait jackets and fastened into 'tranquillizer chairs'. Some, whirled at speeds of up to 100 revolutions per minute in special beds, chairs, cages and padded hollow wheels, became incontinent, vomited and fainted. Placed under a 'douche', inmates would be hit on the head with water thrown down from varying heights. There is no evidence that any of these methods had the slightest beneficial effect.

However, the cause of the mentally ill was advanced in at least one sphere – that of the law. By the mid-19th century, most Western nations had passed legislation that prevented to some extent the abuse of incarceration, and ensured that asylums were licensed and inspected. In addition, mental illness as a legal defence finally came into force in 1843. In that year, Daniel McNaughten was tried in London for the murder of Edward Drummond, private secretary to the Prime Minister, Sir Robert Peel (the intended victim), and was found not guilty on the grounds of insanity.

THE DISCOVERY OF THE UNCONSCIOUS

Meanwhile work was progressing slowly towards at least an inkling of how the mind works. One of the first neurologists was Jean-Martin Charcot (1825–93) of La Salpêtrière in Paris. Concentrating on the physical origins of mental disorders, he examined each of his patients in complete silence, so that his scrutiny would be unbiased. In the late 1870s, he became fascinated by hysteria, a form of emotional instability that he was sure had a physical basis.

Charcot experimented with the application of metals and magnets, to see if these had any effect on his patients. Then he turned to hypnosis – which he considered a form of 'experimental hysteria' – which was still suffering from the Mesmer scandal of 1784 (see p.43). From 1878, Charcot demonstrated the effects of hypnotism on a variety of patients during lectures at La Salpêtrière. However, his subjects tended to be sensitive 'somnambulists', and other practitioners were unable to achieve the same results. In addition, a number of doctors were taken to court, accused of having seduced their patients while under hypnosis; and criminals claimed to have been forced to rob while in a trance. As a result, the use of hypnotism fell into disrepute.

Despite this, Charcot's efforts were not in vain. Among his students was a young Viennese doctor, Sigmund Freud, who only abandoned hypnotism when he discovered other methods that could more effectively reach into the 'mental darkness' that was the unconscious (see pp.118-21).

THE GREATEST HAPPINESS

ACTION ON PUBLIC HEALTH

"Suffering and evil are nature's admonitions, they cannot be got rid of"

SINCE THE TIME OF WILLIAM HARVEY, the body had been viewed as a machine that only had to be understood mechanically or chemically in order to be cured. However, as hardly any effective cures were discovered (only the scientific bases of some diseases), a few people attempted to eliminate the external causes of ill health.

FIGHTER AGAINST FILTH

At the forefront of the fight was British civil servant Edwin Chadwick (1800–90), a follower of the economist and philosopher Jeremy Bentham whose utilitarianism professed the motto: "The greatest happiness of the greatest number". Through his work on the Factory Act of 1833 and the Poor Law Amendment Act of 1834, Chadwick came to the conclusion that ill health was the direct result of poverty. In 1842, he wrote *A Survey into the Sanitary Condition of the Labouring Classes in Great Britain*, which has become a monument in the history of public health.

Much of Chadwick's evidence was already apparent to many. The great cholera epidemics (*see pp.56-9*) had shown the conditions under which the poor were living, especially in rapidly growing cities. Charles Dickens wrote about the almost indescribable squalor within which a large proportion of British citizens tried to survive. Among the many facts that Chadwick and his team uncovered was that deaths from infectious diseases were almost exclusively confined to the

RIGHT *The public works inspired by the zeal of Sir Edwin Chadwick laid some of the foundations for the establishment of the British welfare state.*

poor parts of towns, and that only 12 per cent of Britain's urban areas had pure water supplies.

Chadwick recognized the need for radical reform, including a comprehensive medical service and a centralized Board of Health with full-time medical officers to implement the changes he advocated, among them "the removal of all refuse from habitations, streets and roads, and the improvement of the supplies of water".

However, the laws that he pushed through Parliament in 1848 were weak. Except for areas with unusually high death rates, their implementation was not compulsory, and the Public Health Act was limited to five years and to London alone. Despite all the evidence of suffering and wastage of human resources, there was opposition in high places. *The*

LEFT *Clearing up the slums where barefoot Victorian children played became a top priority for Edwin Chadwick and the civil servants who followed him — though opposition in high places meant that this was often an uphill struggle.*

ABOVE *St Thomas' Hospital, standing proudly beside the river*   *Thames, was opened by Queen Victoria in 1871.*

Economist thundered: "Suffering and evil are nature's admonitions, they cannot be got rid of".

When, in 1854, the Public Health Act came up for renewal, it was defeated. The Board of Health was disbanded and Chadwick was pensioned off, "so that", he remarked, "dirt and disease would be left alone". Although a magnificently competent administrator, Chadwick was unable to adapt to the prevailing political wind: "Unable to bend", wrote his biographer, "he was made to be broken". His opponents crowed. "We prefer to take our chance with cholera and the rest rather than be bullied into health," said *The Times*.

DOCTORS AND CONSULTANTS

In the 19th century, differing patterns of medical practice were established throughout the world. In Australia, general practitioners (GPs) had open access to hospitals, and could also undertake major surgery. In Britain, the medical profession had become fairly evenly divided between GPs and consultants, although a consultant was often, as the **British Medical Journal** *put it in 1876, simply "a practitioner among the rich" and not the specialist he or she has now become. American practice did not at first conform to any set pattern, but then large numbers of doctors started to specialize. Today, there are very few GPs in the US.*

In Britain and elsewhere, the distinctions within the profession depended on whether doctors (both surgeons and physicians) held an appointment at a voluntary hospital. This was particularly important for surgeons, whose status increased through their hospital work.

The licensing of doctors had begun in England in Tudor times. By 1830, some 13 American states had passed laws to license doctors, but in the following decade, they were repealed. This was due to three factors: pressure from irregular practitioners, such as homoeopaths and Thomsonians (see pp.82-83); dissatisfaction of patients who were worried about the extreme treatments they were receiving; and a general distrust of state regulation. Licensing was not reinstituted in the US until the 1870s.

Nevertheless, Chadwick's ideals lived on. A royal commission revealed that, in places, infant mortality was as high as 250 per 1000. In the 1860s and 1870s, various Acts of Parliament paved the way for an overhaul of public sanitation, slum clearance and rehousing, together with improved safety standards for food and drugs. In addition, with agricultural advances and better food distribution, a higher nutritional standard was achieved. All this resulted in far better health for the general public. For example, in 1869, there were 716 deaths from typhus in London; by 1885, this had been reduced to 28; and, at the beginning of the 20th century, to none.

Industrialization and its problems hit Britain first, and this was where sanitary measures were first adopted. Other Western countries gradually followed suit. In the US, the New York Metropolitan Board of Health, founded in 1866, was responsible for cutting infant mortality by two thirds within 50 years. In France, the cholera epidemics influenced Napoleon III to rebuild Paris in the 1850s.

A PUBLIC HOSPITAL SYSTEM

Most of the great hospitals of Britain were built by 1760. They were charitable institutions dedicated to the care of poor people who had fallen sick. However, they soon began to exclude children, pregnant women and people suffering from infectious diseases, and gradually became voluntary, depending on subscriptions from potential patients. Later, they excluded those with chronic illnesses, mental disorders and other maladies that were expensive to treat. The result was a chronic shortage of hospital care.

In 1861, when the population of England and Wales had climbed to 20 million, there were only 117 hospitals containing fewer than 12,000 beds in total.

The very poor could be treated at one of the pauper hospitals, established by Poor Law boards as the ill person's alternative to the workhouse. In 1867, Parliament authorized the construction of infirmaries separate from workhouses, and to a standard similar to that of the voluntary hospitals. Thus, the beginnings of a public hospital system could be seen, which would reach fruition in the National Health Service (*see pp.140-1*).

Other European countries developed hospitals on more or less the same lines but primarily under government auspices. In the US, however, such institutions as the Pennsylvania Hospital of Philadelphia (1751) and the New York Hospital (1791) set the pattern of private medicine that, with few exceptions, still exists today.

THE RESURRECTION MEN

They went on strike when the surgeons refused to pay another two guineas per corpse

SINCE THE TIME OF HENRY VIII, only executed criminals were legally available for dissection in the British Isles – a form of after-death punishment. With the increase in medical schools and research, cadavers were soon in extremely short supply – even the great William Harvey was reduced to dissecting the bodies of his father and sister.

A criminal subculture soon arose. Medical students moonlighted as graverobbers to supplement their income and provide bodies for their own studies. However, professional gangs soon muscled in on what was a fairly lucrative business, and these 'resurrection men' were actively supported by respectable surgeons and anatomists.

SIR ASTLEY COOPER AND THE BOROUGH GANG

The surgeon Sir Astley Cooper (1768–1841) was an inspiration to a whole generation of doctors at the medical school of Guy's Hospital, London. He was also the first to streamline the delivery of bodies, working hand in glove with resurrection men known as the Borough Gang.

ABOVE *Surgeon Sir Astley Cooper, benefactor of the resurrectionists, located and named the ligaments that support the breasts – today, these are snipped and shortened in cosmetic operations.*

The Borough boys were highly professional. On Sundays, when most funerals took place, they would reconnoitre various burial grounds, and take orders from their surgeon clients. During the rest of the week, they would dig up the corpses, deliver them to the medical schools, and send any surplus to the Edinburgh school.

They followed exacting rules. The position of any pebbles, shells or other markers – placed on graves by suspicious relatives – were noted before removal. The graverobbers would then dig down to uncover only the head of the coffin, carefully placing the soil on a cloth. They would prise up the exposed part of the coffin lid and remove the corpse by placing a rope round its neck or hooking the shroud. Once the corpse was free, it would be stripped of its shroud, which would be put back into the coffin. (Taking a shroud was theft; taking a body was not.) After stuffing the body into a sack, the soil would be carefully tipped back into the grave and any markers carefully replaced. Even though graverobbing was illegal, the fines were minimal – and were almost always paid by the surgeons.

In October 1811, the Borough Gang demanded an increase in the price of an adult corpse from three guineas to five. The Anatomical Club, to which all teachers of surgery belonged (including Sir Astley), decided to resist – and were

GRAVEROBBING IN THE USA

Two groups who had little influence and could offer only slight resistance – blacks and white paupers – were the focus of bodysnatchers in the United States.

In 1788, both free and slave blacks petitioned the New York City Common Council to halt the removal by medical students of their dead loved ones, protesting that the students "mangle their flesh out of a wanton curiosity, and then expose it to Beasts and Birds". The Council ignored the petition. When the bodies of some well-respected whites were also snatched, a two-day riot ensued during which the Columbia Medical School was ransacked and a number of city physicians harangued.

Although 17 states had passed anatomy laws by the early 1880s, the supply of legal, unclaimed bodies was still too small: in Maryland, in 1893, there were only 49 cadavers for the 1200 students at Baltimore's medical schools. Legislation did little to stem the trade, and as late as the 1920s graverobbers in Tennessee were supplying the four medical schools in Nashville, and sending any bodies surplus to requirements to Iowa City.

into a tea chest and had it taken straight to Knox's house, where it was found the next day.

Burke and his lover Helen McDougal went on trial on Christmas Eve, 1828; Hare and his common-law wife turned King's evidence. The jury acquitted McDougal – "Nelly, you are out of the scrape!" exclaimed Burke – but found her lover guilty. Burke was hanged on 18 January 1829 before a crowd of 25,000 people; his body was sent for dissection. No charges were ever brought against the fortunate and privileged Robert Knox.

A CHANGE IN THE LAW

In 1828, a committee of Parliament had been appointed to look into the study of anatomy and the obtaining of bodies for dissection. Its first witness was Sir Astley Cooper.

In August 1832, the Anatomy Act was passed. Now, anyone without a licence who was in possession of a body for anatomical purposes could be imprisoned or fined. The Act also made it legal for all unclaimed bodies – that is, those of paupers – to be used for medical research. As the British psychiatrist Ann Dally has written: "What had long been a feared and hated punishment for murder became a punishment for poverty".

immediately faced with a strike by the resurrection men. The surgeons refused to budge. The gang held out for a month, but finally agreed to compromise at four guineas.

THE TALE OF BURKE AND HARE

Some bodysnatchers decided to skip the hard work and supply medical schools with freshly murdered corpses. The most famous were two Irish emigrants living in Edinburgh: William Burke and William Hare. They, too, worked closely with a surgeon – Robert Knox, the most popular anatomist at Edinburgh's medical school.

In November 1827, an old pensioner named Desmond died at the doss-house run by Hare's common-law wife, owing £4 in back rent. Hoping to recoup his loss, Hare, with Burke, removed Desmond's body from its pauper's coffin and took it to Knox, who gave them nearly twice that amount. Thrilled by this easy money, the two no longer waited for their victims to die: they hurried the process along by suffocating them after getting them drunk. In this way, at least 16 Edinburgh residents lost their lives.

One was old Abigail Simpson; Knox himself commented favourably on the freshness of the body. Another was Peggy Haldane, a beggar in the Grassmarket. After her disappearance, her daughter Mary began to haunt the streets of the area, crying and asking if anyone had seen her mother. Burke got rid of this nuisance on his own.

Burke and Hare finally ran out of luck after they killed old Madge Docherty. A couple lodging with Burke discovered her body under a bed and reported it to the police. Before the law arrived, Burke and Hare bundled the corpse

ABOVE *Two unsavoury characters, Messrs Cruncher and Son, hail from the pen of Charles Dickens in his story* The Tale of Two Cities, *published in 1859. Inspired by the sensational stories of body-snatching in the first quarter of the 19th century, Cruncher and Son were bank messengers by day and resurrectionists by night.*

RETURN OF THE WOMEN

NURSING AND FEMALE DOCTORS

A 'wild swan' founded a profession — through sheer force of will

FROM THE 14TH CENTURY, women found it increasingly difficult and ultimately impossible to become physicians and surgeons. Entry into medical schools was forbidden to them, as was membership of the organizations that licensed and regulated doctors.

In the new hospitals built in the 19th century, women formed the basis of the nursing staff. Yet they were – if not as slatternly and intemperate as the nurse-midwife Sairey Gamp in Charles Dickens's *Martin Chuzzlewit* (1843–4) – at least illiterate, ill-trained and ill-paid. However, even before Mrs Gamp began entertaining Dickens's readers, steps were being taken to transform nursing.

NURSING SISTERS

The first sign of reform was the Protestant deaconess movement in northern Europe in the early 19th century. Sober young women were gathered together in 'mother-houses' to undertake good works, particularly visiting and

BELOW *Philanthropist Elizabeth Fry reads the Bible to women prisoners at Newgate prison, London. She* *founded soup kitchens throughout the capital and campaigned ceaselessly for prison reform.*

assisting the sick at home. These women were similar to the Roman Catholic Sisters of Mercy, begun in Ireland in 1831, but unlike them, they took no vows.

The Reverend Theodor Fliedner (1800–64), the Lutheran pastor of the German village of Kaiserwerth, saw the work of Mennonite deaconesses in Holland, and in England, he met Elizabeth Fry, the Quaker prison reformer. Both experiences led him and his wife Friederike to set up, in 1836, their own three-year course for nurse-deaconesses, who as graduates, could dispense medicines and nurse acutely ill and convalescent patients. By 1864, the school had trained some 1600 deaconesses, and motherhouses had been set up as far afield as Milwaukee, in Wisconsin, and Constantinople.

In 1840, Elizabeth Fry visited Kaiserwerth and, on her return to London, founded the Institute of Nursing. The women who joined were well-to-do and religious. They called themselves Protestant Sisters of Charity, but when there were protests that this smacked too much of Catholicism, they changed their title to 'nursing sisters' (a term still in use in British hospitals). However, unlike the Kaiserwerth nurses, they received no classroom instruction and were trained only for practical home nursing.

ABOVE *The daughter of a prosperous family, Florence Nightingale decided, at an early age, to devote her whole life to the care of the sick. Her achievements in this field owe much to her determined and fearless personality – regardless of whom she upset.*

Nursing as an act of Christian charity was taken up by the Church of England, and especially by adherents of the 'High Church' (Anglo-Catholic) movement. A number of nursing sisterhoods were established, the most important being St John's House (1848), which undertook the systematic training of middle-class Anglican 'ladies'. In 1856, St John's House took over full responsibility for nursing at King's College Hospital in London, and the following year, Sister Mary Jones established a five-year training school.

NURSING IN THE CRIMEA
Another visitor to Kaiserwerth was Florence Nightingale (1820–1910). Born into a wealthy middle-class family, her early and continuing obsession with the care of the sick was a mystery to her parents: "We are ducks", wept her mother, "who have hatched a wild swan". Forbidden to become a nurse, Florence read every hospital and public health report she could, and made alliances with powerful friends within the British establishment.

Finally, when she was 31, she was allowed to go to Kaiserwerth for three months. Two years later, she was appointed superintendent of the small Establishment for Gentlewomen during Illness, in London, and turned it into what she knew a hospital should be.

In 1853, Britain, France and Turkey went to war against Russia in the Crimea. There was an outcry when it was realized that, while French soldiers were being cared for by Catholic Sisters of Charity, British soldiers had to make do with untrained male orderlies – and the soldiers were dying like flies. Florence Nightingale and her friend Sir Sidney Herbert, then in the War Office, simultaneously wrote to

ABOVE *Toiling in the heart of the conflict, Sisters of Charity assist a doctor as he tends wounded French soldiers at the Battle of Inkerman, fought in 1854 during the Crimean War.*

each other, she asking and he requesting that she take a party of nurses to the front.

On 4 November 1854, Nightingale and 38 nurses arrived at the Barrack Hospital in Scutari, where 1800 wounded and sick men lay in poorly ventilated, rat-infested wards with virtually no sanitation. Within six months, and in the face of almost intractable opposition from the staff, Nightingale had transformed the place – through sheer force of will. The death rate fell from about 40 to 2 per cent.

Florence Nightingale was not, however, the only nurse to make an impact in the Crimea. Mary Seacole (1805–81), having served in Panama and Cuba during cholera and yellow fever epidemics, wrote to the British government from her native Jamaica asking to join Nightingale, but being black she was refused. Undaunted, she financed her own journey to the Crimea, where she set up 'The British Hotel' between Balaclava and Sebastopol, with a hospital on the upper floor where she saved the lives of many hundreds of soldiers. In 1867, she was honoured with the 'Seacole Fund', raised to care for her in her old age and supported by, among many others, Queen Victoria.

ABOVE *By 1915, when this image appeared on the front cover of the French magazine* Le Flambeau, *nurses and the International Red Cross had come to play a vital role in the support-services for the troops.*

LADIES BOUNTIFUL

By 1856, when Nightingale returned to England, the 'Nightingale Fund', raised from the British people to express their gratitude, had reached a staggering £50,000. She decided to use part of it to found a school of nursing in conjunction with St Thomas' Hospital in London. The school opened in June 1860.

Nightingale's aim was "to train training matrons" – that is, to produce graduates who would take untrained staff in a hospital and train them to their high standards. The St John's House school, on the other hand, simply trained nurses. Florence Nightingale and Sister Mary Jones worked closely together and they came up with the concept of the district nurse, to provide health care in the homes of the poor.

The Nightingale matrons often proved to be imperious "ladies bountiful" who frequently had less practical nursing experience than those they had come to train. St John's House nurses were criticized for their adherence to the High Church, and some were more

LEFT *Formal, starched, prim and proper, an* *English nurse of the 1900s wears her award proudly.*

concerned for their patients' spiritual welfare than for their physical well-being. Gradually, though, hospitals opened non-sectarian nursing schools that enrolled women of all classes and trained all nurses (including potential matrons) in the same careful way.

Florence Nightingale's influence on nursing was immense: she set the standards for a new style of caring. Her book, *Notes on Nursing* (1859), became required reading for all those within the profession that she had helped to found:

"[Nursing] has been limited to signify little more than the administration of medicines and the application of poultices. It ought to signify the proper use of fresh air, light, warmth, cleanliness, quiet, and the proper selection and administration of diet."

Nightingale School graduates emigrated to many countries around the world where they set up nursing schools: in Sweden (1867), Australia (1867), the United States (1873), Canada (1874) and Denmark (1897). Nightingale's work also inspired Jean Henri Dunant's work on the Geneva Convention and, in 1864, the International Red Cross.

Florence Nightingale was not satisfied with simply transforming nursing. Her amazing energy enabled her to study and make recommendations on military and civilian hospitals, sanitation in India, and infirmaries and workhouses for the poor. In 1907, she received the Order of Merit, one of Britain's highest awards.

MEN, WOMEN AND MIDWIFERY

As early as the 18th century, a few men such as the surgeon William Hunter (see p.41) had become "man-midwives". But for the most part, midwifery was restricted to women. However, as the body began to be viewed as a machine and medical instruments were increasingly developed, childbirth came to be seen as a mechanical procedure, more suited to men's talents. According to Augustus Granville, founder of the Obstetrical Society of London in the 1830s, women were "unfitted by nature for all scientific mechanical employment", and within two decades, this opinion was reinforced by the advent of anaesthesia during childbirth (see p.47).

By the 1840s, several medical schools in Britain had added midwifery to the curriculum, and in the next decade, the Royal Colleges of Physicians and Surgeons began to award diplomas in midwifery. However, many of the new specialist "obstetricians" believed that they would never achieve their rightful status while there were still midwives, many of whom were untrained.

The Nightingale Ward, dedicated to training nurses in midwifery, opened at King's College Hospital in 1862. However, the Midwives Institute (later the Royal College of Midwives), founded in 1881, pressed for more and better training, and finally saw the Midwives Act reach the statute book in 1902. This provided for supervised training and registration of all midwives in England and Wales, and marked the moment when midwifery became an established profession for British women.

In America, the opposite occurred. By 1910, the proportion of births in the United States supervised by midwives had declined to about 50 per cent. Male obstetricians railed against the practice, promoting science and reform in opposition to the midwives who were, they said, "hopelessly *dirty, ignorant and incompetent". Under intense pressure, state after state passed legislation outlawing midwives and restricting midwifery to registered obstetricians.*

In Canada, the Medical Act of 1869 made it illegal for anyone to practise medicine without first obtaining a university degree and being licensed by the College of Physicians and Surgeons. This disqualified virtually all midwives, and by 1899, they attended only about 3 per cent of births in Ontario.

BELOW *A cartoon from 1793 satirizing the somewhat pompous way the man-midwife, with his* *scientific instruments, overcame the more down-to-earth domestic woman midwife.*

NURSING IN THE UNITED STATES

Two months after the outbreak of the Civil War in April 1861, the redoubtable Dorothea Dix was appointed 'Superintendent of the United States Army Nurses'. At first, she demanded very high standards: "No woman under 30 years need apply ... very plain-looking women... no bows, no curls, no jewelry, and no hoop skirts". But as the war progressed and hundreds of thousands of soldiers required nursing, she reconciled herself to taking virtually anyone.

Among those who excelled was the tiny black woman Harriet Tubman (1820–1913). Before the war, she had been dubbed the 'Conductor of the Underground Railroad', having led more than 300 slaves to freedom on 19 clandestine trips to the South. During the Civil War, she nursed on the Sea Islands off South Carolina. In recognition of her outstanding work, a Union general urged Congress to grant her a pension, which she finally received in 1892.

Perhaps the most famous nurse of the Civil War was Clara Barton (1821–1912). In 1862, she became the first to work directly at the front, earning her the nickname 'Angel of the Battlefield'. After the war, she travelled to Europe to study the work of the International Red Cross, and established close contact with Florence Nightingale. In 1882, she founded the American Red Cross and, two years later, was responsible for the 'American amendment' to the Geneva Convention, which enabled the Red Cross to be active in peacetime emergencies as well as wartime.

WOMEN DOCTORS

The real name of the first modern woman doctor in Britain is unknown. In 1865, an autopsy revealed that 'Dr James Barry', who had graduated from Edinburgh's medical school and served with distinction at the Battle of Waterloo and in South Africa, had, in fact, been a woman.

The first woman to become a doctor in her own right was Elizabeth Blackwell (1821–1910). She graduated from the Geneva (New York) Medical School in the United States, to which her family had emigrated from Britain in 1832. Unable to receive hospital training in the US, she moved to Paris and then London to continue her studies. In 1859, she became the first woman to be registered as a doctor by the British Medical Association (BMA). The following year, the BMA forbade registration to anyone who had not studied at a British university, which were open only to men.

Elizabeth Garrett Anderson decided to follow in Dr Blackwell's footsteps, but was turned down by every medical school in Britain. Finally, the Society of Apothecaries was forced to license her when she produced the necessary certificates of medical proficiency, having studied privately with medical professors. She was able to take her final medical examination in Paris, and this, with the licence from the Society of Apothecaries, enabled her to begin practising as a doctor in 1870.

In that year, Sophia Jex Blake and Edith Pechy passed their examinations at the Edinburgh Medical School, against the fierce opposition of the male student body, only to be awarded certificates of proficiency and not medical degrees. The certificates were not recognized by the BMA.

RIGHT *The first woman to qualify as a doctor in Britain, and Britain's first woman mayor, Elizabeth Garrett Anderson (1836–1917) was responsible for opening up the way for women to study medicine.*

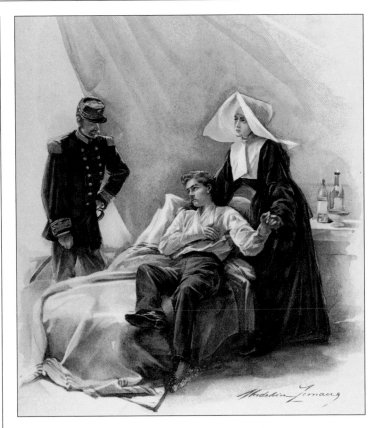

ABOVE *The successful nursing of the Sisters of Charity often turned the hearts of the war-wounded as they recovered, giving rise to the notion that the nurses were guardian angels protecting them from death.*

In August 1876, Parliament, swayed by popular opinion, finally passed a bill allowing women to attend university and become doctors. Across the Atlantic, American medical schools reluctantly began to open their doors; by 1894, 10 per cent of the students at 18 medical schools were female.

AN ALTERNATIVE PATH

PATENT CURES AND COMPLEMENTARY MEDICINE

Laxatives, vegetable compounds and herbel remedies made fortunes for some

IN THE 19TH CENTURY, many people still viewed doctors with suspicion, condemning them for spending their time propounding theories rather than finding solutions to the needs of common people. But this was not the only problem. Working-class people simply could not pay for doctors' services, and they were easy prey for anyone with a persuasive manner who had a cheap nostrum to sell.

The 19th century was the age of patent medicines – those bearing proprietary names protected by trademarks and intended for self-medication. "Since professional practice chiefly consisted in giving a great many drugs", wrote George Eliot in *Middlemarch* (1871–2), "the public inferred that it might be better off with more drugs still if only they could be got more cheaply".

THOMSONISM AND BOOTS THE CHEMIST

The drugs concocted by doctors – usually containing such poisons as antimony and mercury – were often as mistrusted as their manufacturers: from about 1770, the verb 'to doctor' had come to have an alternative meaning: "to adulterate, to tamper with, to falsify".

One reaction to this was a renewed interest in herbalism. The barely literate Samuel Thomson (1769–1843), of New Hampshire, developed a simple theory of disease: all ills are produced by cold and any treatment that generates heat will aid recovery. His favourite herbal remedy was *Lobelia inflata*, the ground seeds of which caused vomiting and heavy sweating. (The use of the herb in remedies is now banned in the United States.) Having patented his 'Thomsonian' system in 1813, he appointed agents across America.

One of these agents was 'Dr.' Albert Isaiah Coffin, who claimed to have learned many medical secrets from the native Americans. In 1838, Coffin arrived in England where he soon had a large following, his own team of agents and a chain of 'Friendly Botanico-Medical' societies.

A farm labourer by the name of Boot came under the spell of one of the agents. Boot's son Jesse (1850–1931) found that he had a gift for making herbal remedies and, at the age of 13, left school to help his mother in her tiny herbal shop in Goose Gate, Nottingham. In 1877, Mrs Boot handed over the shop to Jesse. Within six years, he had opened ten branches in Nottingham and surrounding towns and, in 1892, began to manufacture drugs. When he died in 1931, Jesse Boot – by then the first Baron Trent – had more than 1000 'Boots the Chemist' shops, and today the firm is one of the world's largest retail pharmacists.

OINTMENTS AND PILLS

One of the most successful British purveyors of patent medicines was Thomas Holloway (1800–83). When he set himself up as an import–export agent in London in 1828,

ABOVE *A late-19th-century, mahogany medical chest contains bottles of drugs and patent remedies, and syringes.*

RIGHT *Forerunner of the modern dispensing pharmacist, an apothecary mixes up medicines in his shop, using pestle and mortar.*

THE SPREAD OF HOMOEOPATHY

'Homoeopathy' means 'like disease', and is a system of medicine based on choosing remedies that mimic the symptoms of the ailments that they are meant to cure. This criterion was used by both Hippocrates (see p.118) and Paracelsus (see p.136), but was expanded on by the German doctor Samuel Hahnemann (1755–1843).

In the late 1780s, Hahnemann gave up his medical career, disgusted at the extreme treatments he had been forced to carry out. He developed an interest in the use of quinine to treat malaria and, after some self-experimentation, came to the conclusion that quinine works because it produces some malarial symptoms. The symptoms, he reasoned, were simply signs of the body's fight against disease.

When Hahnemann began experimenting on his family and friends, he found that his patients often got worse before they got better. To overcome this, he began to dilute his remedies more and more, shaking each successive dilution to make the most of the infinitesimal amount of the drug left. He found that, paradoxically, the smaller the dose, the greater the effect. In 1811, he published his findings in the **Homoeopathic Materia Medica.**

Hahnemann moved to France, where his homoeopathic treatments were more effective than orthodox methods in the typhus epidemic that followed Napoleon's retreat from Moscow in 1812. Homoeopathy spread rapidly after that. In 1825, it arrived in the United States, and in 1833, the Academy of Homoeopathy had been established in Allentown, Pennsylvania, and three years later, the Hahnemann Medical College was thriving in Philadelphia. It reached England in 1832, and by 1849, a large homoeopathic hospital had been founded in London.

---

one of his best lines was an ointment from an Italian client, Felix Albinolo, which began to sell briskly after Holloway obtained a testimonial from a surgeon at St. Thomas'

THE **JEOPARDY** OF LIFE IS IMMENSELY INCREASED without such a simple precaution as

ENO'S "FRUIT SALT"

ABOVE *Eno, health's winged messenger, offers a fruit salt for ailing livers, courtesy of the Beecham family.*

Hospital. Disregarding Albinolo's protests, Holloway decided to make his own ointment, and spent huge amounts of money on advertising – £5,000 in 1842, growing to £50,000 per annum by his death. He accumulated a fortune, and gave well over £1 million to various charities, including a college for ladies in Egham Hill, Surrey, now part of the University of London and called Royal Holloway College.

The Beecham family became another successful purveyor of patent medicines. In 1847, Thomas Beecham (1820–1907) began selling 'Beecham's pills' – a mixture of laxative drugs – in the north of England. Ten years later, he found that local press advertisements boasting that his pills were "worth a guinea a box" paid off. However, it was his son Joseph who spent the most on advertising – £120,000 in 1891 alone. The Beechams' firm was soon worth millions, and the family thrived: the grandson of the former shepherd boy became the world-famous conductor Sir Thomas Beecham.

"SAVIOUR OF THE HUMAN RACE"

In 1873, 54-year-old Lydia Estes Pinkham of Lynn, Massachusetts, began selling the remedy that would transform her into perhaps the first millionairess in America. 'Lydia E. Pinkham's Vegetable Compound', originally marketed as a cure for "all female weaknesses", was soon proclaimed as "the greatest remedy in the world", a panacea for virtually any complaint.

Mrs. Pinkham's sympathetic face, the image of everyone's old mother, appeared on every bottle and in virtually every newspaper in the United States. "Write to me about your female troubles", Mrs Pinkham commanded the nation's women, and the women did, receiving in return personal letters from Mrs Pinkham – even after she died in 1883.

By 1881, the Pinkham family were grossing $30,000 a month. However, the popularity of the Compound probably had more to do with the fact that two bottles of the mixture were the equivalent of one bottle of whisky. Perhaps this is why British medical students sang in praise of Mrs Pinkham:
"And so we drink, we drink, we drink to Lydia Pink,
The saviour of the human race,
She invented the Vegetable Compound,
Most efficacious in every case".

HYDROTHERAPY

TAKING THE WATERS

Treatment with 'dripping sheets', 'lamp baths' and wet stomach packs

THE MEDICINAL QUALITIES of water have been known for thousands of years: the ancient Greeks and, particularly, the Romans (*see pp.20-1*) were great fans. In the Middle Ages, water was viewed with distrust and bathing discouraged but, by the mid-18th century, immersion in water was again seen as a good thing.

FATAL CURE

In the early 1750s, Dr Richard Russell went bathing at the small English seaside village of Brighthelmstone. With the publication of his *Dissertation on the Uses of Sea Water in the Diseases of the Glands* in 1754, visitors flocked there, transforming the village into the fashionable health spa that would later be known as Brighton. Here, said Dr Russell, they could avail themselves of "that vast collection of waters … which the omniscient Creator of All Things seems to have designed to be a common defence against the corruption and putrefaction of Bodies".

Saltwater bathing may well have helped many people, but for some, it proved fatal. In 1796, the Scottish poet Robert Burns was told to stand up to his armpits in the freezing waters of the Solway Firth for two hours a day. Shortly after, the 37-year-old Burns died of rheumatic fever.

Such rugged treatment was not to the taste of the dandies of English society, who turned to inland towns where sulphurous springs could be found. They went to Tunbridge

RIGHT *A health spa poster features Hygeia, Greek goddess of health and daughter of Asklepios, Greek god of physicians.*

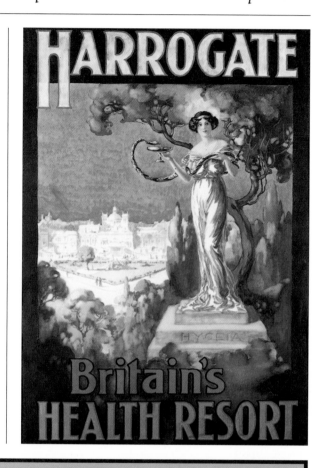

MALVERN WELCOMES DARWIN

In 1842, many of Priessnitz's treatments were transposed in modified form to the English spa of Malvern by two doctors: James Wilson (1807–67) and James Manby Gully (1808–83). Soon, about 6000 visitors were descending on the spa every year, among them Charles Dickens with his wife Kate, and Alfred, Lord Tennyson. In March 1849, Charles Darwin arrived with his family for a three-month visit, during which the scientist hoped that Gully could treat the giddiness, nausea, boils and headaches that plagued him.

He was prescribed the 'dripping sheet' – a wet sheet draped over him through which his skin was rubbed vigorously – and the 'lamp bath', during which Darwin was heated by a spirit lamp until he streamed with

sweat and then was rubbed violently with cold, wet towels. The scientist was also told to wear a wet stomach pack at all times except during meals, and to climb up the steep hills nearby four times a day.

Darwin complained that, by the end of his time at Malvern, he had turned into a walking and eating machine, but he did feel much improved. He visited Gully's establishment four more times and, in the interim, carried out the doctor's instructions at home. He built himself an outdoor douche and bath in his garden, and had his butler, Parslow, rub and sluice him.

LEFT *Portrait of Charles Darwin as an old man, ravaged by his treatments, painted by the English artist John Collier.*

LEFT *In 1901, some 51,000 visitors bathed in the 17 warm springs that escape from the hard* *rock below Carlsbad, a spa town formerly in Austria but now Carlovy Vary in Czechoslovakia.*

Wells for a cure for colic, to Epsom to partake of Epsom salts, and to Bath – once revered by the Romans – to be rid of their boredom. Here, in the lavish Pump Room, the overindulgent drank water containing some 30 minerals and elements, which gushed out of the earth at a constant temperature of 120°F (49°C). Bath retained its popularity even in the slightly more restrained early 19th century: "Oh! who can ever be tired of Bath?" wrote the novelist Jane Austen, in *Northanger Abbey (1798)*.

MEDICINE WATERS

Taking the waters also became fashionable in the New World. Saratoga – "the place of the medicine waters of the great spring" – was the Mohawk name for a collection of hot springs in the mountains of New York State. In 1774, Saratoga Springs became North America's first pleasure resort, visited by, among others, George Washington and Alexander Hamilton. By the mid-19th century, various medical establishments had been set up there. For instance, the Remedial Institute offered a selection of baths (Turkish, Russian, Roman and electro-thermal), as well as compressed and rarified air and vacuum treatments.

In western Virginia, another group of springs also became established as a resort. Warm Springs was a favourite of Thomas Jefferson, but after he stayed in the water for two hours (instead of the recommended 15 minutes), he wrote to a friend that this had so damaged his health that he had

never fully recovered. In the mid-1830s, a Dr Goode set up a spout bath in the neighbouring town of Hot Springs, and soon it became a firm fixture on the society circuit, visited by Henry Ford, John D. Rockefeller, Andrew Mellon and the Vanderbilts.

DISCOMFORT IS GOOD

In Europe, Victorian worthiness was getting a grip on society, and the point of watering holes was no longer pleasure but discomfort – for the good of body and soul. At Wiesbaden, visitors were compelled to drink water resembling hot chicken soup and submerge themselves in baths covered in dirty scum. At Franzenbad, they submitted themselves to mudpacks of black ooze. At Aix-la-Chapelle, the vapour baths were the dubious attraction: "You breathe, swallow, live in brimstone", wrote one commentator.

However, it was the water university of Gräfenberg, high in the mountains of Austrian Silesia (now Jesenik, Czechoslovakia), that exploited the Victorians' masochism. Run by Vincenz Priessnitz (1799–1851) on Spartan lines, it offered a full range of treatments: head baths (patients would lie on the floor with the backs of their heads in basins of cold water); wet stomach packs, or Neptune's girdles; and the wet sheet treatment, for which patients would be wrapped, mummy-fashion, from shoulders to ankles in wet bandages, covered in a blanket and left for four hours.

It was, though, the cold douche, or fire engine treatment, that was the most alarming. As patients held on grimly to grab rails, icy water would be poured over them from a height of up to 20ft (6m), the force likened by one victim to standing under a falling load of gravel. Priessnitz also invented the ascending douche, which sent chill spouts of water up from the floor to treat the genitals.

Priessnitz's establishment became immensely popular. In 1839 alone, it played host to one royal highness, one duke, one duchess, 22 princes and princesses, and 149 counts and countesses. In the 1840s, it was flooded by members of the British upper classes willing – and brave enough – to make the 10-day carriage journey.

RIGHT *English caricaturist Thomas Rowlandson satirizes the interest in drinking mineral water in his 1815 cartoon entitled* Sailors Drinking the Tunbridge Waters. *The woman (LEFT) offers a glass of the water, saying: "Be assured it is an excellent beverage for gentlemen who have been a long time at sea".*

4

Medicine Before World War II

By the end of the 19th century, the emphasis of medicine in Europe and America was beginning to shift. No longer did research concentrate on the infectious diseases that had once spread through continents. Instead, scientists were more concerned with chronic degenerative disorders.

There were several reasons for this. First, many of the epidemic diseases, such as cholera and smallpox, were understood, if not yet completely controlled – the influenza pandemic of 1918-19 was to claim 20 million lives – by vaccination, new treatments and public health measures. Second, the increased availability of medical care, together with the growing perception that illness belonged in the hospital rather than the home, meant that more symptoms that were not immediately life-threatening were investigated. Third, increasing longevity brought with it an increase in death rates from chronic disease.

Advances in general scientific understanding, and in the technology available, also helped the investigation of disease: the workings of the endocrine system were unravelled, for example, and insulin discovered; radiation was harnessed, and X-rays used for diagnosis; electron microscopes, ECGs and EEGs, allowed the body to be probed in detail as never before.

But the advances in medicine and science were paralleled by great strides in the technology of warfare, as the super-powers of the world girded themselves for conflict. In a terrible irony that seems to sum up the age, Alfred Nobel left the fortune he had made by inventing a manageable form of dynamite to establish an annual series of prizes that would encourage medical and scientific research. The carnage caused by explosives during the horrors of World War I made this more necessary than ever.

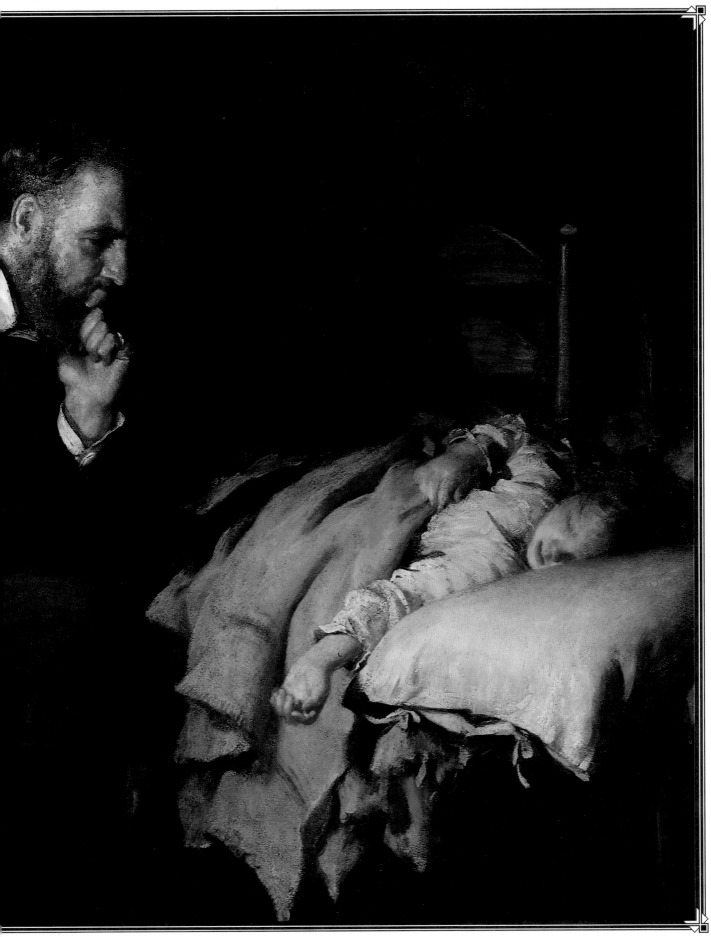

ABOVE The Doctor, *painted by Sir Luke Fildes in 1891.*

PRACTICE AND EDUCATION

AT THE TURN OF THE CENTURY

Britain's Harley Street was "the valley of the shadow of death"

I N 1900, PATIENTS UNDER a doctor's care had only a 50 per cent chance of being better off than if they and their diseases had been left alone.

Infectious diseases were the great killers: in the United States, pneumonia, tuberculosis, gastrointestinal infections and diphtheria were responsible for more than a third of all deaths. However, in the doctor's little black bag were only a handful of remedies that acted specifically against infection: quinine for malaria, mercury for syphilis (*see p.100*), ipecac for amoebic dysentery and the diphtheria and tetanus antitoxins that were still not universally accepted.

There had been progress, however, particularly in such areas as the state of Massachusetts. Here, vaccination had almost eliminated smallpox, some public health measures had been adopted, cholera had been virtually wiped out and typhoid fever was in decline. But in other parts of the US, and in other countries, public health was hampered by a lack of knowledge of how infections spread and by a dearth of vital statistics.

THE BEGINNING OF SPECIALIZATION

By the turn of the century, it was impossible for individual doctors to know everything about the body. As a result, many began to specialize in certain parts or systems of the body or in certain diseases. It became quite acceptable for doctors to admit openly that particular ailments were outside their range, and for them to refer patients to other doctors with specific expertise.

By 1910, sweeping and widespread measures to eradicate infectious diseases had gone so far as to include visits by public vaccinators to places of work, such as this printing works ABOVE.

In Britain, the new 'consultants' banded together in centrally located group practices. The most famous grouping was in and around Harley Street, a fashionable housing development in central London. From the 36 doctors who had taken premises there by 1873, the medical population exploded until, by the end of the century, there were 157 and the area had acquired the nickname 'The valley of the shadow of death'. One of the first to put up his shingle was Dr Arthur Conan Doyle, author of the Sherlock Holmes stories.

This pattern of medical specialization proved so popular in the United States that, by 1890, there were few doctors in general practice. American patients could choose their own doctors for specific problems (instead of being referred

JOHNS HOPKINS MEDICAL SCHOOL

The shining example of medical education against which Abraham Flexner compared all others was the Johns Hopkins Medical School and hospital in Baltimore, Maryland — the result of a bequest of $7 million from the Quaker merchant and banker, Johns Hopkins.

The medical school, unfettered by tradition could be innovative The heads of various hospital departments also headed the corresponding departments of the school. The medical school staff – who, for the first time, were hired full-time and relieved of earning money from private practice – were the finest in the US. Members included William Osler, a Canadian regarded as the greatest medical teacher of his generation, and the brilliant but flawed William S. Halsted (see p.90). These men were not only fine teachers but also researchers in their own right, and Johns Hopkins had well-equipped laboratories in which they could carry out their work.

The hospital opened in 1889 but the medical school was unable to open until 1893 because of a shortfall of $500,000. In 1890, a women's committee offered to donate $200,000, but only if women were admitted to the medical school on equal terms with men. (The first class to graduate, in 1897, would consist of 15 men and 3 women.) Mary Elizabeth Garrett then agreed to make up the balance, but on one condition: students had to have a bachelor's degree from a good college and a reading knowledge of French and German. William Osler later confessed that he was lucky to get into Johns Hopkins as a professor, since he would never have been admitted as a student.

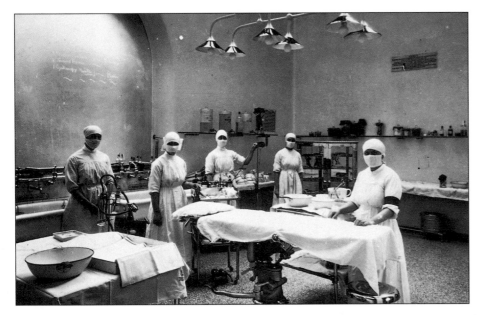

LEFT *The clean and sterile enviroment of Theatre A at St Bartholomew's Hospital, London, epitomizes the advances made in attitudes to surgical procedure, around 1920. Operating personnel wear masks, hats and gowns; the operating table is adjustable in height and inclination; a battery of ceiling lights provides bright illumination; and the latest equipment for anaesthesia stands at the ready.*

to a consultant by their family doctors as in Britain and elsewhere), but sometimes it was difficult to know which specialist to choose.

The referral system was also prone to corruption. There were rumours (and some proof) that referrals were occasionally unnecessary and only made so that the two doctors could split the fees.

MEDICAL EDUCATION IN NORTH AMERICA

One of the greatest obstacles to an improvement in health in the US and Canada was bad medical education. Many doctors still learned their craft through apprenticeships, and

numerous students who attended the 155 medical schools in operation in 1910 had not even finished high school.

The American Medical Association (AMA) was acutely aware of these educational shortcomings but felt that it would be unethical for doctors to criticize other doctors. It asked the Carnegie Foundation for the Advancement of Teaching to launch an independent investigation, and in 1908, Abraham Flexner was commissioned to carry it out.

Flexner visited every medical college in North America. He did not enlighten those college administrators who assumed that he was advising the Carnegie Foundation on grants: hoping to qualify, they enthusiastically pointed out all their schools' faults. Flexner was appalled by what he discovered. When asked if there was a physiology laboratory, the dean of one school went to get it, returning with a small pulse-measuring instrument. Others simply granted medical degrees on receipt of fees for non-existent tuition.

In 1910, Flexner published his report, *Medical Education in the United States and Canada*. In it, he recommended:

- a reduction in colleges to 31.
- at least two years of college education prior to entry.
- teachers to be full time, not practising physicians.
- learning from observation of patients, not just from books and lectures.
- medical schools to become integral parts of universities.
- fees from students not to be the sole source of funding.

Within ten years, 46 American colleges had closed. This had a number of unforeseen consequences. Many of them had been the only places in which women could study medicine, and only two black medical schools remained open. The greater educational requirements meant that many newly arrived immigrants and their children, as well as black people, women and poor whites, were shut out of medicine. Flexner also did not take into consideration the need for doctors in an expanding population: in 1910, 4400 doctors had graduated; by 1920, this number had declined to 3047.

LEFT American artist Thomas Eakins captures a poignant moment in his painting The Gross Clinic *(1875). Samuel Gross, Professor of* *Surgery at Jefferson College, Philadelphia, pauses mid-operation and offers words of comfort to the patient's companion.*

WILLIAM STEWART HALSTED

THE FATHER OF AMERICAN SURGERY

The drug addict who invented rubber gloves and revolutionized surgery

WILLIAM STEWART HALSTED's entry into medicine came as a surprise to many of his fellow graduates at Yale: prior to becoming a student at the College of Physicians and Surgeons in New York in 1874, he had devoted most of his time to football, baseball, gymnastics and rowing. However, the young man excelled and was awarded his medical degree with honours.

In November 1878, Halsted travelled to Vienna. For the next two years, he studied there and at the other German-speaking medical centres that had overtaken London and Paris as leaders in research, learning from such luminaries as the surgeon Theodor Billroth.

Soon after his return to New York in 1880, Halsted became one of the most successful young surgeons in the city, appointed to a variety of hospital posts and entertaining incessantly. Then in 1884, the year in which the work of Carl Koller (*see p.48*) was published, Halsted and a few colleagues began to investigate cocaine.

COCAINE ADDICTION

The young medical men soon became aware of cocaine's intoxicating and sinister side-effects. Some became addicted, including Halsted, and all but him were eventually destroyed by their addiction.

Halsted's work deteriorated sharply. When his friend William Welch realized what was happening, he arranged for Halsted to go on a cocaine-free cruise (Halsted broke into the ship's medical stores). Then, after the addict had spent some months in a psychiatric hospital, Welch offered him a research post in Baltimore, where, as Professor of Pathology, he was involved in the planning for the new Johns Hopkins Medical School. Within six months, Halsted was back in the psychiatric hospital; it was probably at this time that he

BELOW *The amphitheatre at Johns Hopkins Medical School, Baltimore, provides a modern, clean setting for* *William Halsted to conduct an operation while simultaneously teaching a rapt audience.*

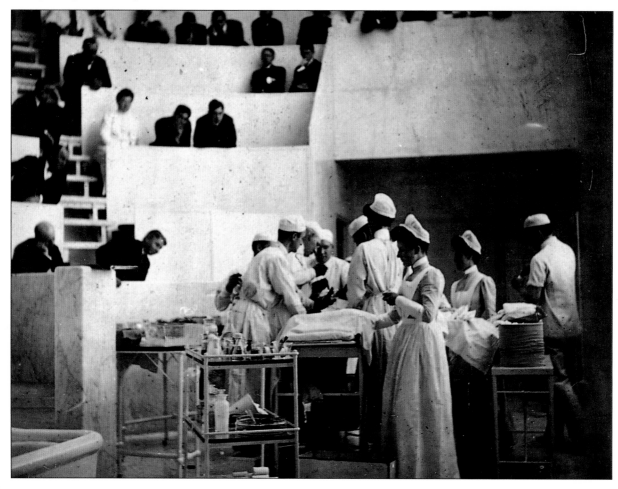

switched from cocaine to morphine in an attempt to gain control of his addiction.

On his release in 1889, the 36-year-old Halsted was appointed Associate Professor of Surgery at the medical school (on the recommendation of Welch, who believed, wrongly, that Halsted was off morphine), and then was made full Professor as well as Surgeon-in-Chief of the hospital. It was the beginning of a stunning career that spanned 33 years.

However, this Halsted was very different from the exuberant doctor who had captivated New York. He was remote and uncommunicative, sharply sarcastic if pressed, prone to disappearing from the medical school at odd moments and to making mysterious trips to Europe, from which he would return in bespoke suits from London and handmade shoes from Paris.

TRAINING THE NATION'S SURGEONS

As a surgeon, Halsted was now highly cautious. Yet this very cautiousness ushered in the new 'surgery of safety', where care was taken not to injure patients' tissues more than was absolutely necessary, with the result that they recovered far quicker and in better shape.

Halsted also adopted an equally cautious approach to training. After receiving their medical degrees, former students would become interns for one year. Above them were assistant residents, the survivors of the previous year's internship. At the top, a single house surgeon (chief resident) chosen from the previous batch of assistant residents, was in charge of all surgical patients at Johns Hopkins. The young surgeons at each level were responsible for the training of the ones below, and the house surgeon was trained personally by Halsted. The whole procedure, from intern to house surgeon, took about eight years.

Halsted trained 17 house surgeons during his years at Johns Hopkins. Eleven established similar residency programmes at other medical schools throughout the U.S., from which a further 166 chief residents graduated; in this way, Halsted's methods gradually became the standard throughout the country. The finest Halsted house surgeon was Harvey Cushing (1869–1939), who developed the basic principles of neurosurgery.

Halsted's plodding research methods resulted in a series of exceptional operations. His experiments with intestinal sutures and his knowledge of anatomy led him to invent the Halsted II procedure for repairing inguinal hernias. The recurrence rate for his patients – 7 per cent – has been improved only slightly since. Halsted also made great advances in the surgery of the bile duct, intestines and thyroid gland, as well as for arterial aneurysms and breast cancer (see box).

RUBBER GLOVES

Today, Halsted is perhaps most famous for inventing equipment that made an enormous difference to aseptic surgery. Halsted used mercuric chloride as a sterilizing solution, and in the winter of 1889/90, one of his nurses complained that the chemical was causing dermatitis on her hands and arms. Halsted asked the Goodyear Rubber Company to run up some thin rubber gloves. These proved so successful they first became standard wear in Halsted's operating room, and then in operating rooms worldwide.

HALSTED AND BREAST CANCER

Halsted believed that when cancer of the breast spread to other parts of the body, it did so through the lymph system. In the late 1890s, he devised an operation called a 'radical mastectomy', in which the breast, all the lymph glands in the nearest armpit and the muscles of the chest wall were removed. This became the treatment of choice for breast cancer (see pp.198-9) for the next 75 years.

It has been suggested that this mutilating operation was easier for Halsted and his followers to justify, because they felt that most women who underwent it, being past the menopause, no longer had to breastfeed or be sexually attractive. In any event, in 1937, the British Medical Journal reported that the same percentage of women survived after less severe surgery, and today serious questions have been raised regarding Halsted's operation.

The nurse whose complaint had been the germ of this invention was Caroline Hampton, who, in June 1890, became Halsted's wife. In her own way, Caroline was as strange and unusual as her husband, but despite this, their marriage was a great success.

In 1922, Halsted was operated on for gallstones by two of his former house surgeons, using a technique invented by Halsted himself. The operation was a success, but Halsted died – on 7 September – of post-operative pneumonia. It was later revealed that his consuming drug addiction had never left him and he had continued to take large doses of morphine to the end of his life.

BELOW *Prior to operating on a patient, Halsted holds an X-ray up to the light. The professor developed a technique that* simplified the repair of inguinal hernias – the Halsted II procedure; the survival rate has only improved slightly since his day.

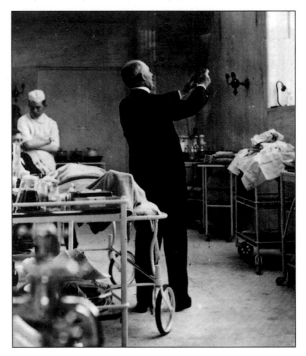

LANDSTEINER AND BLOOD

THE A-B-O AND RHESUS SYSTEMS

A small monkey from India helped solve the mystery of stillbirths

ATTEMPTS AT BLOOD TRANSFUSIONS had been more or less abandoned after the unsuccessful experiments of the Enlightenment (*see pp.38-41*). In the 19th century, new research revealed that transfusions were more likely to work if blood was exchanged between members of the same species. Moreover, advances in the antiseptic control of bacteria reduced the danger of infection during transfusions. Yet there was still the inescapable fact that a good proportion of those transfused had extremely bad reactions to donors' blood.

BLOOD GROUPS

In 1900, Karl Landsteiner (1868–1943), an Austrian physician working at the University of Vienna, set himself the task of investigating what factors might be responsible for the unsuccessful tranfusions.

He made a series of 30 mixtures using samples of blood from himself and five colleagues. He found that mixing the blood of some individuals with that of others caused the red cells to clump together, or agglutinate. But this agglutination did not happen with all the different sets of mixtures.

Landsteiner concluded that whether or not clumping occurred depended on the presence or absence of two antigens (substances that cause the body to produce antibodies) on the surfaces of the red cells. He labelled these antigen A and antigen B.

The red cells from two of his colleagues carried antigen A (group A) and two carried antigen B (group B): when blood from each group was mixed together, clumping would occur. When the blood of another colleague and Landsteiner's own produced no clumping when mixed with samples from either group, he decided that these blood cells carried no antigens and named their blood group 'O' (for 'nil').

Landsteiner was very lucky. Since his experiments involved so few people, it was statistically possible for all of them to have had blood of the same group, especially since it was later discovered that blood groups are not equally distributed. For instance, in Britain, 46 per cent of people are group O and only 9 per cent are group B.

Discs packed with haemoglobin to capture oxygen, red blood cells BELOW *carry antigens — proteins that distinguish their blood group.*

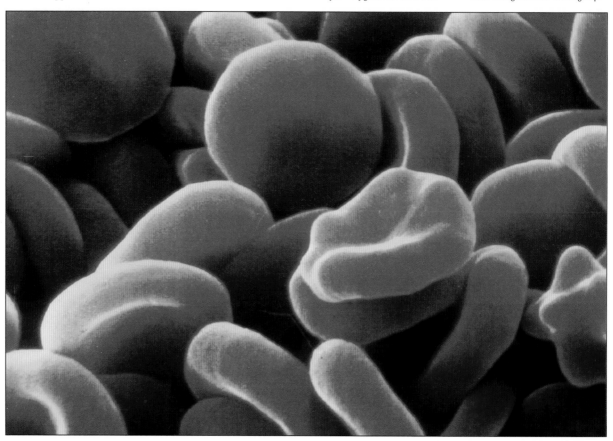

In fact, it was not until 1902 that he realized, after further experiments, that he had missed another blood group – AB, in which the red cells carry both antigens. To date, at least 14 different blood systems have been discovered.

Despite the enormous significance of Landsteiner's discovery of the A-B-O system, the laurels were slow in coming. His work received so little initial recognition that researchers elsewhere – J. Jansky in Prague in 1907, and W. L. Moss of Johns Hopkins, Baltimore, in 1910 – independently came to the same conclusions. It was only in 1930 that Landsteiner received a Nobel prize for his work.

red cells, causing them to clump together and producing the severe reaction that she barely survived.

At the time, Landsteiner was experimenting with blood tranfusions from the little Indian Rhesus monkey (*Macacus rhesus*) into rabbits and guinea pigs. He found that the anti-Rhesus antibodies produced by the rabbits and guinea pigs not only caused the monkey's red blood cells to clump

BELOW *The legacy of Landsteiner's work on blood groups, blood transfusions – even on the front line – saved the lives of hundreds of thousands of soldiers wounded during World War II.*

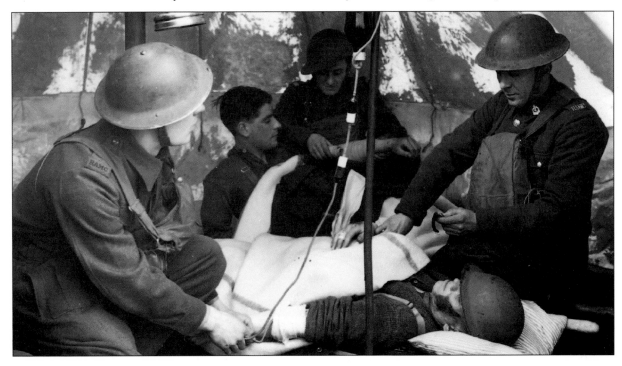

In the meantime, he had emigrated to the United States and was working at the Rockefeller Institute for Medical Research in New York, where in 1927 he uncovered a further blood system – the MN blood groups. And, in 1936, his book *The Specificity of Serological Reactions* helped to establish the science of immunology. He continued to work towards discovering more about the nature of blood – a matter that became of even greater importance with World War II and the necessity for battlefield transfusions.

THE RHESUS FACTOR

In 1939, two American scientists, Philip Levine and Rufus Stetson, reported an unusual case. A woman had had a stillbirth after eight months of pregnancy. She had lost a great deal of blood during the delivery and was given a transfusion of her husband's blood which, like hers, was group O. Despite this apparent compatibility, she suffered a severe reaction. Levine and Stetson showed that the woman's blood serum caused red cells from her husband to agglutinate. When they mixed her serum with red cells from 104 donors, all group O, clumping occurred in 80 of the samples.

Levine and Stetson concluded that the woman's red cells lacked a hitherto unknown antigen. She had developed antibodies after exposure to it from her unborn baby, who had inherited the antigen from its father. When the woman had received her husband's blood, her antibodies attacked his

together but also those of six out of seven white New Yorkers. Both the monkey and the majority of New Yorkers must, surmised Landsteiner, have an antigen in common, which he called the 'Rhesus factor'. Thus the blood of the monkey and of the affected New Yorkers was 'Rhesus positive' (Rh+) and the unaffected blood was 'Rhesus negative' (Rh–). Other researchers discovered that anti-Rhesus antibodies could be found in the serum of those who had experienced bad reactions after transfusions with supposedly compatible blood.

However, as important as this discovery was – making blood transfusion virtually safe – it also had immense implications for the health of unborn babies. In 1941, using Landsteiner's findings, Levine and Stetson discovered that the woman who had had the stillbirth was Rh– and her husband was Rh+. Other women who had had stillbirths were investigated, and many also proved to be Rh–. In addition, many of their stillborn babies had died from a blood disease called erythroblastosis foetalis, which was already recognized as recurring in some families without anybody knowing why. Now they did. The researchers realized that this was just one of a range of diseases with one cause – Rhesus incompatibility between mother and baby. The diseases were now renamed 'haemolytic disease of the newborn'. With Landsteiner's work, it became possible for women to be tested for the antigen, and treatment developed.

TROPICAL MEDICINE

MALARIA AND SLEEPING SICKNESS

"O Death, where is thy sting? Thy Victory, O Grave?".

FOR MANY YEARS, scientists had suspected that insects were involved in the transmission of diseases, especially tropical ones. But it was only at the turn of the 20th century that they were established as actual carriers of some diseases. However, finding out exactly how the insects communicated these illnesses to humans was a far more difficult task.

MOSQUITOES AND MALARIA

Of all the infectious diseases, malaria (*mal aria*, 'bad air') has affected the most people. As a result, it has been partly responsible for the decline of great civilizations, among them classical Greece, the Roman empire and ancient Ceylon. As early as the 2nd century BC, the Roman scholar Marcus Terentius Varro (*see p.21*) said that swamps, the breeding grounds of mosquitoes, were areas to avoid. But no one began to pinpoint the true cause of malaria until the 19th century, when several doctors theorized that the mosquito could be a carrier, or vector, for yellow fever (*see pp.96-7*).

The breakthrough came during the investigation of another disease – elephantiasis, a gross enlargement of the legs and testicles. Patrick Manson became intrigued with this disease following his appointment (from 1866) as a medical officer to the Chinese Imperial Maritime Customs on the islands of Formosa (now Taiwan) and Amoy (now Hsaimen). In the 1870s, he heard that Timothy Lewis in Calcutta and Joseph Bancroft in Brisbane had discovered the parasitic filarial worm in elephantiasis sufferers. Manson then devoted seven years to finding out at what point in its life cycle the filarial worm could penetrate a human blood vessel, thereafter to lodge in a lymph node and cause such an obstruction that enormous swelling occurred.

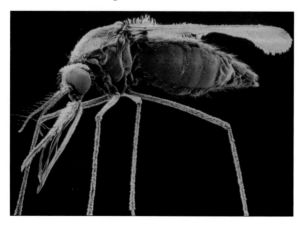

The deadly scourge of malaria is transmitted by female mosquitoes – the species ABOVE *is Anopheles gambiae. The female has distinctly fewer bristles than the male on her antennae. The female's belly is swollen after a meal of human blood – a rich environment in which the malaria parasite, Plasmodium, can develop.*

Improved sanitation and preventive medicine are deemed the best preventive against the Anopheles *mosquitoes. In 1949,* UNESCO *health experts* ABOVE *studied the water in the pools and swamps near Marbial, Haiti. Measures were then taken to drain the water, or keep it moving, depriving the mosquitoes of their breeding habitat.*

Manson wondered if the *Culex* mosquito might be an intermediate host in the worm's life cycle. He dissected hundreds of mosquitoes, and found that, inside their stomachs, the membranes containing the worm embryos had broken down. Thus released, the worms could bore through the insects' stomachs into their thoracic muscles. The worms then metamorphosed, developing mouths and alimentary canals, in preparation for their entry into humans.

Manson came to the conclusion, albeit erroneously, that the mosquitoes died as they laid their eggs in water, and their corpses, containing cargoes of filarial worms, were then drunk by humans. However, his discovery that mosquitoes acted as intermediate hosts to a disease was to have profound consequences for the future.

"I KNOW THIS LITTLE THING"

Ronald Ross never wanted to be a doctor, preferring to play music and compose poetry. However, in 1881, succumbing to parental pressure, he entered the Indian medical service. To his surprise, he found himself interested in the role mosquitoes might play in the spread of disease, and in 1892 he began to concentrate on malaria.

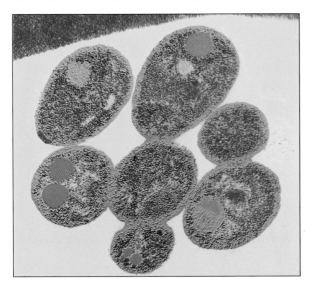

The malaria parasite – the *Plasmodium*, a protozoan slightly smaller than a bacterium – had been discovered in victims of the disease by the French scientist Charles Laveran in 1880. In 1894, on leave in London, Ross visited Manson, who had returned permanently to Britain in 1889. Manson showed him the parasite and discussed with him the ways in which it might enter a human host, not forgetting to mention the part the mosquito played in the filarial worm's development.

Ross returned to India and continued his research, with Manson encouraging him by letter: "Look on it as a Holy Grail and yourself as Sir Galahad, for be assured you are on the right track".

LEFT *Marauding clusters of* Plasmodium *merozoites are the culprits responsible for the shivering, fever and sweating suffered by malaria victims. Every now and then, these merozoite cells enter a red blood cell and divide in two — not sporadically, but as a synchronized offensive that the body is unable to handle.*

On 20 August 1897 – thereafter known as 'Mosquito Day' by Ross and his disciples – he located in the stomach wall of an *Anopheles* mosquito the oöcysts that are the intermediate stage of the *Plasmodium* life cycle. Once he was sure of the parasite's presence, he was then able to follow its history within the mosquito: first, as a zygote in the stomach; then as an oöcyst in the stomach wall; and finally as a mature sporozoite that reaches the mosquito's proboscis and, ultimately, a human host when the insect bites and injects its saliva preparatory to sucking blood.

Ross never abandoned his poetry, and on 'Mosquito Day' he wrote a poem of thanksgiving: "I know this little thing/A myriad men will save./O Death, where is thy sting?/Thy Victory, O Grave?". But it was for his work on malaria that Ross received his Nobel prize in 1902.

Once it was certain that mosquitoes carried malaria, eradication programmes could be devised. Following the pioneering work of Colonel Gorgas (*see p.97*) and Sir Malcolm Watson in Malaya, the US Public Health Service started a war on the mosquito in the southern states. The incidence of malaria dropped by 50 per cent and, by 1927, it had been largely eliminated from American cities and towns. When, in the 1940s, DDT was used against the insects, it seemed a miracle weapon. However, DDT later proved to be very harmful to the environment.

SLEEPING SICKNESS

As white European empire builders penetrated Africa in the late 19th century, one of the most puzzling diseases they came across was what, in those illiberal times, was called 'Negro lethargy', or 'sleeping sickness'. Victims eventually became so drowsy that they would starve for want of energy to eat, and could die of any opportunistic infection. Epidemics were known to wipe out whole communities, and it seemed that the opening up of territories by the Europeans was spreading it.

After a particularly bad epidemic in Uganda, the British government sent out a commission to study the disease. One member was the Italian doctor, Aldo Castellani, who in November 1902, while carrying out post-mortems, discovered the presence of unknown protozoa in the spinal fluid of victims of sleeping sickness.

The following year, the commission was joined by Colonel David Bruce, who had been working on nagana, a related disease in livestock. He had

established that nagana was spread by the tsetse fly (Glossina palpalis) *from wild animals to domesticated cattle and horses, and was caused by a protozoan called a trypanosome. He and Castellani now found trypanosomes in the spinal fluid of 70 per cent of sleeping sickness victims. Bruce went on to discover that the tsetse fly was also involved in the spread of what came to be known as human trypanosomiasis.*

RIGHT *Resting in front of his quarters, one of the main collaborators of the Bayer expedition to Africa in 1921/22 considers how best to tackle the endemic disease of sleeping sickness in his area.*

YELLOW FEVER

"I shall never forget the expression of alarm in his eyes when I last saw him alive"

I N JUNE 1900, four American medical researchers met for the first time in Havana, Cuba, then under American rule following the Spanish-American war two years earlier. Their brief was to form a Yellow Fever Commission to investigate yellow fever, the disease responsible for at least 35,000 deaths in the city during the previous half century and which was now decimating American troops.

Yellow fever (yellow jack) starts with a high temperature, which drops to below normal after two or three days. The skin takes on a characteristic yellowish tint – a sign that the liver has become involved. Victims are nauseous and, in severe cases, blood from haemorrhages produces *vomito negro* (black vomit). Sufferers may now begin to recover, but for many a deceptive remission period is followed by more intense jaundice, a recurrence of *vomito negro* and blood in the urine. A feverish coma can then lead inexorably to convulsions and death.

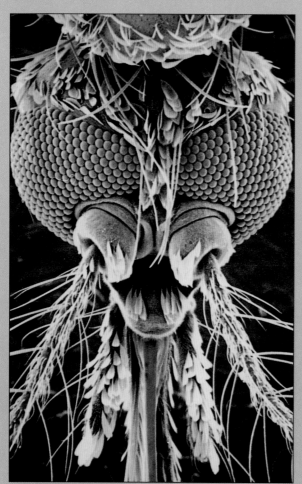

In 1900, yellow fever was endemic in the New World, having probably arrived there from Africa with the first slaves. It had cut a swathe through the Americas in the 17th and 18th centuries, killed 8101 people in New Orleans in 1853 and produced a mortality rate of 94.5 per cent in Rio de Janeiro in 1898. Many thought that, because it tended to occur in hot, damp, filthy places, it was the result of a 'miasma'. However, as early as 1807, Dr John Crawford of Baltimore, Maryland, made the first connection between mosquitoes and yellow fever, and the work of Manson and Ross (*see pp.94-5*) seemed to corroborate this.

In Havana, a doctor called Carlos Finlay had been trying to prove for 19 years that mosquitoes were responsible for yellow fever, but all of his 104 experiments had proved unsuccessful. To his great excitement, and possibly his relief, the American researchers – James Carroll, Jesse W. Lazear, Aristides Agramonte and their leader Walter Reed – agreed to test his theory.

SELF-EXPERIMENTATION

Because no animals were known to suffer yellow fever, the researchers agreed that they would be their own first experimental subjects. Before they could start, Walter Reed was called back to the US, where he remained throughout the Yellow Fever Commission's initial work.

Using *Aëdes aegypti* mosquitoes raised by Dr Finlay, the remaining three researchers began. Lazear allowed some to bite yellow fever patients and then his arm. After a tense wait, nothing happened. Carroll repeated the exercise and, within four days, developed a severe case of the illness, complicated by an apparent heart attack. However, because he could have picked up the disease elsewhere in Havana, his illness proved nothing. Then a soldier, who had not had any contact with yellow fever, volunteered to be bitten by the same mosquito that had bitten Carroll. He came down with a mild attack of the fever – the first proof that mosquitoes spread the disease.

By chance, Lazear was bitten while working in a yellow-fever ward, and this time he became ill with yellow fever. However, unlike Carroll, who recovered, Lazear's condition worsened, and on 25 September 1900, he died. Carroll later wrote, "I shall never forget the expression of alarm in his eyes when I last saw him alive". Walter Reed, who had

Like the Anopheles *mosquito that transmits malaria, it is only the female* Aëdes aegypti *mosquito that transmits yellow fever. In addition, the female can be distinguished in the same way – the relatively sparse number of hairs on her antennae.* LEFT *The head of a female* Aëdes aegypti *has been magnified 45 times in the scanning electron micrograph. The beginning of the proboscis can be seen at the bottom of the picture, below the large compound eyes.*

CLEANING UP CUBA AND THE CANAL

The American Chief Sanitary Officer in Havana, Cuba, Surgeon-Major William Gorgas, probably supplied the most convincing evidence against the Aëdes mosquito. In February 1901, following the Yellow Fever Commission's successful experiments, he ordered the quarantine of all suspected victims of the disease (to prevent mosquitoes biting them and thus picking up the illness) and the destruction of all mosquito breeding places. By September, yellow fever had been eradicated in Havana.

In 1888, the French had abandoned construction of a canal through Panama linking the Atlantic to the Pacific, primarily because of yellow fever: in one month alone – October 1884 – 654 workers had died of it. The Americans took over and, in 1904, began building, with Gorgas in charge of the medical department. With thousands of non-immune workers about to arrive, the potential for disaster was immense. Curiously, Gorgas met with complete opposition from the governor of the Canal Zone, General G. W. Davis, who exclaimed: "Spending a dollar on sanitation is as good as throwing it into the Bay!".

However, in November 1905, when a yellow fever epidemic began and all the workers tried to leave, Gorgas was given the go-ahead. A pumped water supply was installed and all domestic water receptacles removed; traps were set for mosquitoes to lay their eggs (which were then disposed of); undergrowth was burned; all remaining mosquitoes were hunted down. By September 1906, the last yellow fever victim had died in the Canal Zone.

BELOW *A lethal cluster of yellow fever virus particles: these kill cells in the liver and kidneys, and also* give rise to internal haemorrhaging throughout the body, with fatal effect.

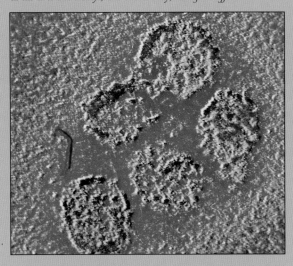

returned to Cuba in October, would confess: "I have been so ashamed of myself for being in a safe country, while my associates have been coming down with yellow fever". Later that month, he announced the Yellow Fever Commission's findings at a meeting of the American Public Health Association.

INVIOLABLE DATA

Carroll's severe case and the soldier volunteer's mild one were not accepted as sufficient proof that yellow fever and mosquitoes were linked. (Lazear's illness and death were considered inadmissible as evidence). In order to obtain data that would be beyond suspicion, the researchers set up an experiment in isolated hospital tents in the Cuban countryside, which they named Camp Lazear in honour of their dead colleague.

Soldier volunteers were split into two groups. One lived among the clothing and bedding of yellow fever victims to see if it contained anything contagious. The other group was isolated from yellow fever victims and from mosquitoes and other insects. Its members were allowed to be bitten only by mosquitoes deliberately infected by the researchers from yellow fever patients. None in the first group contracted yellow fever; 80 per cent of those bitten by the infected mosquitoes did. All 23 volunteers survived.

The researchers realized that the mosquitoes have to incubate the disease before transmitting it: Dr Finlay's experiments had not worked because he had not waited long enough. And, in 1901, Carroll discovered that the microbe responsible for yellow fever was one of a group that had just been recognized: the viruses (*see pp.108-9*).

BELOW *A group of three nurses, working for the US Marine Hospital Services, looking less than* relaxed off-duty, outside a yellow fever hospital in a photograph dated 1898.

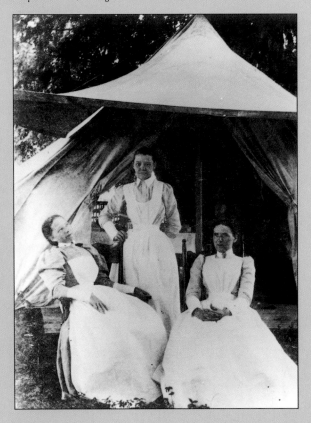

ARCS AND IMPULSES

DISCOVERIES IN NEUROLOGY

Frogs' hearts and leech muscles help in the discovery of neurotransmitters

By the late 19th century, scientists had revealed many of the functions of the brain and spinal cord – the central nervous system. These revelations had begun in 1766 when the Swiss biologist Albrecht von Haller showed that some nerves carry impulses from the central nervous system to the muscles to stimulate them into action, while others carry sensory impulses from the body to the brain. Thus, it is the brain not the body part that 'feels' sensation. Seventy years later, the British doctor Marshall Hall demonstrated that reflex actions still occur even when the spinal cord has been severed from the brain. However, these men and others were unable to explain how the nervous system works as an integrated whole.

"THE PHILOSOPHER OF THE NERVOUS SYSTEM"

In 1891, the British scientist, Charles Scott Sherrington (1857–1952), became interested in spinal reflexes – controlling such activities as sneezing, coughing and recoiling from pain. Working at the University of London, he undertook a massive series of animal experiments during which he untangled and identified the nerves leading to and from the spinal cord and the brainstem.

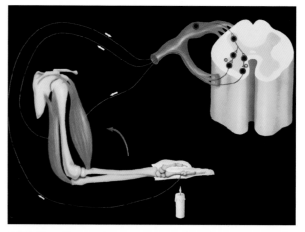

ABOVE *The reflex arc: when a candle heats the hand sensory nerves transmit a pain impulse to a direct connection with motor nerves in the spinal cord; these trigger arm muscles to remove the hand from the flame.*

Then he decerebrated a number of animals, removing the upper parts of their brains so that only the primitive brainstems and spinal cords were left. He experimented on these "brainless beasts" to discover the action of the central nervous system without the interference of thought. Sherrington was able to establish the existence of the reflex arc: the path by which sensory signals are gathered together and passed through the decision-making central nervous system, which reacts by turning related muscles on and off.

Sherrington then realized that reflex arcs do not work independently; rather, thousands operate together in a coordinated 'system of systems'. Sensory signals might have one specific mission, but once they have passed through the central nervous system, they might be joined by others. The nerve leading to the muscle might be shared by many reflex arcs – what Sherrington called the "common path". This nerve's activity would then be a summation of signals from a number of sources.

Sherrington's early discoveries – which led one scientist to describe him as the "philosopher of the nervous system" – were published in 1906 in his book *The Integrative Action of the Nervous System,* a classic of neurophysiology.

TRANSMISSION OF NERVE IMPULSES

Sherrington could not have reached his conclusions without his acceptance (before many others) of the neurone theory put forward by the Spanish histologist, Santiago Ramón y Cajal. This theory stated that each nerve cell branches, and each branch meets another at a junction. To describe the junction, Sherrington coined the term 'synapse'. According to the British scientist, Cajal "solved at a stroke the great question of the direction of nerve currents". It was for this and other research that Cajal shared the 1906 Nobel prize.

The question of how these nerve currents are transmitted from nerve to nerve, across synapses, to their targets, remained unanswered. In 1914, Henry Hallett Dale, working in Britain, isolated a compound called acetylcholine from the ergot fungus. He later found that, when applied to certain nerve endings in a muscle, the acetylcholine produced a response in that muscle. Then the German scientist Otto Loewi discovered that a similar substance secreted by the vagus nerve had an effect on a frog's heart. In 1929, Dale and H. W. Dudley established that acetylcholine occurred naturally in animals: after mincing 24 horse spleens obtained from a slaughterhouse, they were left with an extract containing 334 mg of acetylcholine.

In a further series of experiments, Dale forced a special solution through the tissues of a muscle in which a motor nerve was being stimulated electrically. The same solution was then applied to a muscle from a leech, making it react in exactly the same way as if acetylcholine had been applied. So acetylcholine must be secreted by motor nerves in response to electrical stimulation. Later experiments showed that acetylcholine was the chemical agent by which nerves worked on muscles – the first neurotransmitter identified.

However, if nervous impulses were transmitted chemically, wouldn't their action be continuous rather than brief and transitory as their name implied? Loewi was puzzled, but then he read Dale's paper in which he stated that acetylcholine might be broken down by an enzyme. Loewi looked

for just such an enzyme, and in 1926, he and a colleague discovered cholinesterase in a frog's heart. It was the alternating production of acetylcholine and cholinesterase that produced nerve impulses. Loewi and Dale shared the 1936 Nobel prize for their complementary discoveries.

ALL-OR-NOTHING

Researchers had theorized that the electrical activity of a nerve fibre did not change: it gave all or nothing. However, this 'all-or-nothing' theory could not be proved until someone measured the electrical activity of a single fibre – an impossibility until the invention of amplifiers capable of detecting the few millivolts involved.

The British scientist Edgar Adrian (1889–1977) devised such an amplifier and a way of showing the tiny electrical differences involved: a special oscillograph recorded on a moving strip of photographic film. He and Detlev W. Bronk spent many tedious hours slicing through the nerves of small animals to obtain single nerve fibres. They connected an intact part of a nerve to the amplifier and recorded the impulses of the single fibre.

Throughout these experiments, Adrian found that the all-or-nothing theory held true. However, an increased stimulation would bring into play increasing numbers of nerve fibres and so stimulate more muscle cells until contraction occurred.

In addition, Adrian discovered in the 1920s that a nerve adapts to a stimulus by first responding and then ceasing to respond even though the stimulus continues. In this way, we are able to sense our environment without being inundated by millions of signals every second of our lives.

Adrian shared the 1932 Nobel prize with Sherrington, for their work on describing the nervous system. In 1949, the 92-year-old Sherrington set the stage for later research: "Aristotle, 2000 years ago, was asking, 'How is the mind attached to the body?' We are asking that question still".

BELOW *A false-colour electron micrograph scan of the grey matter in the cerebral cortex of the brain.* *The nerve cells are yellow-green; also shown are nerve fibres and sensory receptors.*

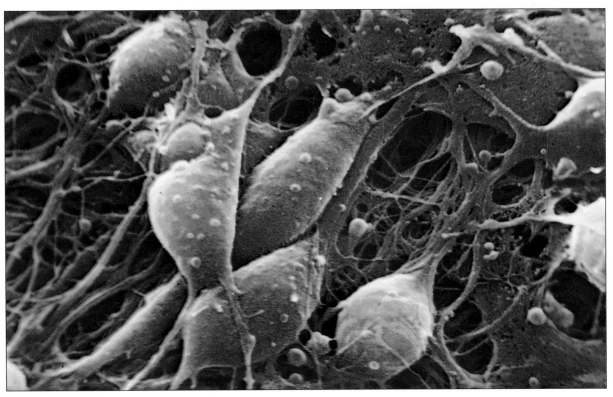

SYPHILIS

*Until 1910, "A night with Venus meant
a lifetime with Mercury"*

IN 1494, THE POX-RIDDLED cosmopolitan army of Charles VIII of France was forced to break the siege of Naples and disband. As the troops returned home, they generated the first syphilis epidemic to hit Europe. The disease acquired its name in 1530, when the humanist Fracastorius published *Syphilis, or the French Disease,* a poem in which Syphilis, a shepherd, offends Apollo and is punished by a pestilence.

A number of theories have tried to explain how syphilis could have appeared in Europe. One is that Columbus's sailors (and perhaps the captain himself) brought it back from the New World; another that it was already present, masquerading as another disease (such as leprosy) and, in 1493/4, took on a particularly virulent form. More recently, however, it has been proposed that, because the microscopic spirochetes (*Treponema pallidum*) responsible for syphilis are identical to those that cause yaws, bejel and pinta in the tropics, syphilis must be the same disease, adapted for a more temperate climate.

The original epidemic moved swiftly, producing hideous disfigurement and causing many victims to die in the early stages. Gradually, however, the infection changed to a chronic form. After the initial sores on the genitals and the somewhat later rash, the micro-organisms can remain dormant for up to 25 years. Then, serious heart damage may occur, or damage to the spinal cord leading to paralysis, or a form of insanity known as 'general paralysis of the insane' (GPI) marked by character changes and delusions of grandeur. At one time, as many as 10 per cent of patients in insane asylums were suffering from GPI.

The Renaissance was marked by the reigns of such syphilitics as Charles VIII, François I, Henry VIII and Ivan the Terrible, believed to have been in the final throes of the disease when he slaughtered more than 3000 of his opponents. Artists such as Dürer and Cellini were afflicted, and the great humanist Desiderius Erasmus commented cynically that a nobleman without syphilis was either not very noble or not much of a gentleman. The list of eminent syphilitics grew relentlessly: Cardinal Richelieu, Peter the Great, Catherine the Great, Goya, Keats, Schubert, Nietzche, Lord Randolph Churchill, Gauguin, De Maupassant, Oscar Wilde and Emil von Behring.

DEFINING THE DISEASE

Syphilis was often confused with gonorrhoea, and in 1767, the British surgeon John Hunter (*see p.41*) decided to self-experiment to settle the question. He infected himself with pus from a patient known to have gonorrhoea, and waited for the symptoms to appear. Unfortunately, the patient also had latent syphilis, and when Hunter developed symptoms of both diseases, he decided that they were the same.

The spread of syphilis was mirrored by an increase in quack remedies. However, early in the initial epidemic, the mercury-containing ointment, *unguentum Saracenicum,* proved effective and, for 400 years, mercury remained the only reliable therapy. It was said that "A night with Venus meant a lifetime with Mercury". However, mercury is a poison, and those prescribed it suffered hair and teeth loss, stomach pains and mouth ulcers; in fact, many preferred the horrors of syphilis to the treatment.

It was not until 1879, when the German bacteriologist Albert Neisser identified the gonococcus, that scientists finally agreed that gonorrhoea and syphilis were actually two diseases. Then, in 1905, Fritz Schaudinn and Eric Hoffmann identified the corkscrew *T. pallidum,* and the following year, August von Wassermann developed a test that could diagnose symptomless syphilis.

SEEKING THE MAGIC BULLET

In 1908, Paul Ehrlich (1854–1915) shared the Nobel prize with Elie Metchnikoff for their work on immunity. For years, Ehrlich had been seeking a specific chemical that could kill microbes causing a specific disease, just as an individual's own antibodies, which Ehrlich called "magic bullets", zero in on invading bacteria.

Since the mid-19th century, the Germans had been making great headway in inventing synthetic dyes, and Ehrlich thought some might selectively destroy micro-organisms. He tested compounds containing arsenic, and

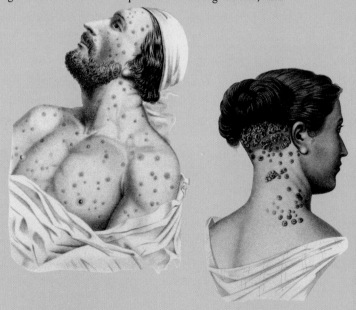

ABOVE *Two patients with syphilitic pustules, from an 1885 engraving.*

ABOVE *Paul Ehrlich, discoverer of*   *Salvarsan, in his laboratory in the*
the synthetic "magic bullet",   *early 1900s.*

found that one – which he called 606 because it was his 606th experiment – killed the *T. pallidum* responsible for syphilis. On 19 April 1910, he announced his findings at the Congress of Internal Medicine at Wiesbaden.

Initially, there were severe shortages of the drug, soon renamed 'Salvarsan', and doctors from all over the world arrived at Ehrlich's laboratory in Frankfurt to beg for supplies. At first, Ehrlich said Salvarsan should be injected intramuscularly, but reports came back of disasters caused by careless technique, and, in October 1910, he said that all injections should be made intravenously. However, doctors were still unused to injecting into veins and some even believed that they had to cut the vein before injecting and then tie it off, making it useless for further injections.

By 1914, only 109 deaths were attributed to Salvarsan therapy – many fewer than for mercury treatment – and Ehrlich soon developed a more soluble version, which he called 'Neo-Salvarsan'. In the meantime, moralists had begun a campaign against the drug, saying that, by curing syphilis, Ehrlich was removing the fear that had kept people from fornication. Quacks, too, came out against Salvarsan, resentful of losing many of their best clients. Ehrlich died in 1915, exhausted by work and the criticism he was receiving.

As World War I approached, American doctors became concerned that, as with aspirin (*see p.49*), supplies of the German-manufactured Salvarsan would be disrupted. They were also dismayed at the great increase in price – from $3.50 for a dose to $35.00 – which threatened programmes devised to treat working-class patients. In October 1917, the US Congress abrogated the German patents, under the Trading with the Enemy Act, and American manufacturers began to make a Salvarsan-like product called Arsphenamine.

For all its great advance in the treatment of syphilis, Salvarsan was still not a very good drug, requiring many painful injections before a cure could be pronounced. It was not until the advent of penicillin (*see pp.136-7*) that the spread of syphilis was slowed.

BELOW *Reminiscent of today's*   *poster commands attention to the*
AIDS campaign, this 1930 French   *threat of syphilis.*

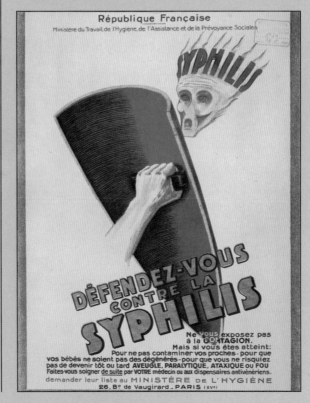

THE ENDOCRINE SYSTEM

THE DISCOVERY OF HORMONES

Injections of pulverized testicles helped reveal the endocrine orchestra

IN 1893, THE SCIENTIST George Oliver went to University College, London, to see the physiologist Edward A. Schäfer (known as Sharpey-Schaefer after World War I). Schäfer was measuring a dog's blood pressure, and was irritated by the interruption. When Schäfer had finished, Oliver asked him if he would repeat the measurement after injecting the dog with an extract of adrenal gland he had brought. This time the blood pressure reading went almost off the scale.

The two scientists investigated the properties of the extract, but were unable to isolate the active ingredient: adrenaline (epinephrine in the US). Jôkichi Takamine and Thomas Bell Aldrich achieved this independently in 1901, however, and three years later, Friedrich Stolz synthesized it. Adrenaline was the first hormone to be synthesized – even though the term 'hormone' had not yet been invented.

On 16 January 1902, William Maddock Bayliss and his brother-in-law Ernest Henry Starling introduced hydrochloric acid into a dog's duodenum that was connected to the rest of the body only by its blood vessels. They found that, in response, the dog's pancreas began to secrete pancreatic juice. The two scientists realized that the duodenum must be secreting a substance that travels through the bloodstream to stimulate the pancreas. They called this substance 'secretin'. "It was", reported their colleague Charles Martin, "a great afternoon".

A brand new field now opened up: the study of chemical messengers that travel from one organ (primarily a ductless, or 'endocrine', gland) to other parts of the body via the bloodstream. These messengers regulated various body systems – a concept that Claude Bernard had presaged with his 'internal environment' (*see p.64*). A term for these new substances had to be found, and two Cambridge dons suggested 'hormones', from the Greek *hormao*, meaning 'to excite or arouse'. Starling first used the term in 1905.

THE PITUITARY AND THE THYROID

In 1909, Henry Hallett Dale (*see p.99*) produced an extract from the posterior lobe of the pituitary gland, whose active hormone – oxytocin – stimulates contractions of the uterus during childbirth (*see pp.150-1*). But the scientist who was to unravel more of the pituitary's secrets was the eminent neurosurgeon Harvey Cushing of Johns Hopkins, Baltimore.

ABOVE *A false-colour electron micrograph of the part of the pituitary gland that secretes the hormones (dark pink 'packets') that control the release of sex hormones in the reproductive organs; the orange mass is the cell nucleus.*

RIGHT *Dr Harvey Cushing, an American neurosurgeon, unravelled the secrets of the pituitary gland; he also named Cushing's syndrome, in which a pituitary tumour causes obesity, hairiness and red lines over the skin.*

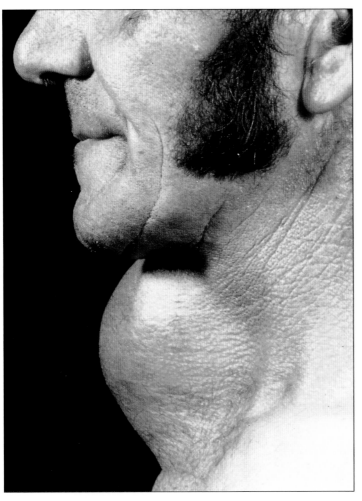

ABOVE *The enlarged thyroid gland (goitre) in Graves's disease leads to over-production of thyroid hormone,* *and pop-out eyes, sweating, a fast pulse, tremor, anxiety and weight loss are often the result.*

Cushing knew that the pituitary secreted growth hormone and was keenly aware of the effects of over- and under-secretion of this tiny gland. But it was some years before the other six hormones produced by the pituitary were identified. However, Cushing was the first to perceive that all the elements of the endocrine system are interrelated, and that the pituitary is "the conductor of the endocrine orchestra".

People with thyroid gland deficiency (myxoedema) had been prescribed sheep thyroid extracts since the 1890s, with some success. However, a young biochemist at the Mayo Clinic in Rochester, Minnesota, was sure that a purer, more powerful extract could be developed. Edward Kendall set to work in 1910, but it was not until Christmas Day, 1914, that he finally succeeded in refining the hormone that came to be called 'thyroxine'.

Producing thyroxine crystals was difficult: about 3 tons (2,720kg) of pigs' thyroids were needed to obtain 1oz (33g) of the hormone. Only minute amounts were available for biological tests before thyroxine was synthesized in 1927.

SEX HORMONES

That the body was affected by the absence of sex organs had been known for many years. But how the changes occurred was still a mystery at the beginning of the 20th century,

despite attempts at treatment with organ extracts by Brown-Séquard (*see box*) and others.

Biochemist Edward Doisy and zoologist Edgar Allen had become friends playing together on a faculty baseball team at Washington University in St Louis, Missouri. In March 1923, Allen told Doisy about experiments he was carrying out: when he injected fluid from follicles on pigs' ovaries into spayed mice, the mice came into heat. So, he reasoned, the fluid must contain a female hormone.

Allen and Doisy worked together to create concentrated extracts of the fluid, but had trouble obtaining enough. Then they heard of the discovery of two Berlin gynaecologists, Selmar Aschheim and Bernhard Zondek, who, trying to find a simple way of diagnosing pregnancy, had hit on injecting a patient's urine into an immature laboratory mouse or rat. If the woman was not pregnant, there would be no change in the animal, but if she were, it would go into heat. Thus, the urine of pregnant humans and other animals must contain a female hormone.

In the autumn of 1929, Allen and Doisy announced the isolation of the female sex hormone oestrin (oestrone). By 1933, two more had been discovered: oestriol and oestradiol. (These three and others form the family of oestrogens.) A year later, a completely different hormone, progesterone, was isolated from the *corpus luteum*, the 'yellow body' that remains when the egg leaves the ovarian follicle.

In 1931, the German scientist Adolf Butenandt isolated a few grains of crystalline hormone from about 5500 gallons (6600 US gallons; 25,000l) of male urine, and called it 'andosterone'. Four years later, a team in Amsterdam led by Ernst Laqueur succeeded in extracting the pure hormone from ground-up bulls' testicles, calling it 'testosterone'.

THE REJUVENATION OF DR BROWN-SÉQUARD

In 1889, the 72-year-old Dr Charles Edouard Brown-Séquard reported to the French Academy of Sciences and set the august audience buzzing.

The previous year, he had begun injecting himself with an extract of blood, semen and pulverized testicles from both dogs and guinea pigs. He described how, in the preceding 12 years, he had suffered a decline. However:

"By the ... third day after starting these injections ... I had recovered at least all my former vigour ... I can now, without effort or even thinking about it, run up and down stairs ... My digestion and the working of my bowels have also improved considerably ... I also find mental work easier than it has been for years".

Within weeks of Brown-Séquard's report, doctors began to prescribe testicular extracts for aging men, and a plethora of patent medicines hit the market.

Even though Brown-Séquard's theory was eventually disproved, his experiments were of immense importance to medicine. They led to an increased interest in the substances that would eventually be known as hormones, and could be said to have been the first attempt at hormone-replacement therapy.

THE DISCOVERY OF INSULIN

Two men made the breakthrough — but only one received the prize

ALTHOUGH THE SYMPTOMS of diabetes had been known for thousands of years, the first diagnostic description of the disease – then invariably fatal – was made in the mid-17th century. Thomas Willis, personal physician to Charles II, advised colleagues: "Taste thy patient's urine. If it be sweet like honey, he will waste away, grow weak, fall into sleep and die".

In about 1775, Matthew Dobson found sugar not only in the urine but also in the blood, thus suggesting that diabetes was not a disease of the kidneys but one of the metabolism. A century later, Richard Bright, Queen Victoria's physician, noticed that the pancreases of patients who had died of diabetes often contained small crystals (calculi), indicating that this organ was somehow involved.

In 1889, two Strasburg doctors – Oskar Minkowski and Joseph von Mering – confirmed this. The day after Minkowski removed a dog's pancreas, flies clustered around the sweet-smelling urine in its cage, and within weeks, it died of diabetes. The two researchers then showed that it was only the complete removal of the pancreas that had this effect. Finally, they tied off the ducts carrying the pancreatic juice to a dog's small intestine, and found that, although this affected digestion, it did not result in diabetes. Therefore, the dog's pancreas must have produced some other secretion that passed directly into the bloodstream.

Earlier in the 19th century, the physiologist Paul Langerhans had described distinct clusters of tissue scattered throughout the pancreas. In 1901, Eugene Opie of Johns

LEFT Thomas Willis, physician to King Charles II of England, and the first man to describe diabetes.

Hopkins, Baltimore, showed that in diabetics these islets of Langerhans partly or completely degenerated. Following the work of Bayliss and Starling (*see p.102*), scientists realized that diabetes must be a hormone-deficiency disease. The race was on to extract and isolate the active substance produced by the islets of Langerhans, a substance which Edward A. Schäfer (*see p.102*) dubbed 'insuline' from the Latin *insula* ('island').

BANTING AND BEST

In the spring of 1921, a 29-year-old Canadian orthopaedic surgeon abandoned his unsuccessful practice in London, Ontario, determined to develop an effective and safe extract of insulin (as it came to be spelled). Frederick Banting went to the University of Toronto, where, although he had neither salary nor research budget, Professor John J. R. Macleod, gave him permission to use his physiology laboratory while he was on a three-month holiday in Scotland. Before he left, Macleod offhandedly instructed his assistant Charles Herbert Best, then 22, to help Banting if he could.

Banting believed that other researchers had failed because pancreatic juice had inactivated the insulin secreted by the

BELOW An islet of Langerhans, from a human pancreas — the part of the organ, named by physiologist Paul Langerhans, that secretes the vital hormone insulin into the surrounding blood capillaries.

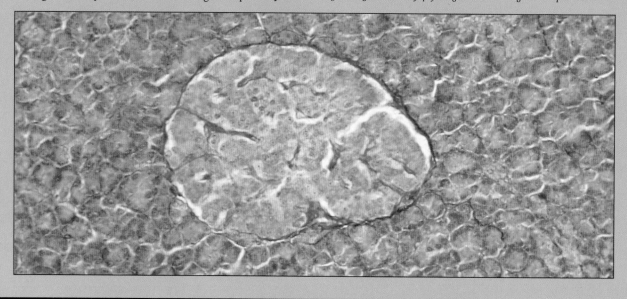

ABOVE *Charles Best* (LEFT) *and Frederick Banting, with the first dog to survive as a result of* *insulin, in the summer of 1921. Banting won the Nobel prize, but Best was ignored.*

islets of Langerhans. He and Best finally obtained a dog's degenerated pancreas by tying off its pancreatic ducts; when they opened it, they found the islets of Langerhans still intact. After making an extract from this, Banting injected some into a diabetic dog that was close to death. Then the two young men waited. Within a few hours, the dog sat up, wagged its tail and barked.

The euphoria of the two researchers was soon dampened when they realized that the extract from one pancreas would keep a diabetic dog alive for less than two days. For their discovery to be a success, they had to find a source from which large quantities of insulin could be produced.

Then Banting remembered reading that the pancreases of unborn animals are composed almost entirely of islet cells; he was also aware that farmers often breed cattle just before slaughter to increase their weight. A local slaughterhouse supplied them with a large number of immature pancreases, and enough insulin was extracted from these to keep their diabetic dogs alive and healthy indefinitely.

When Professor Macleod returned from Scotland, he was impressed with the progress of his protégés. On 14 November 1921, Banting and Best summarized their conclusions in a paper for a local physiology society, and submitted a revised version to the *Journal of Laboratory and Clinical Medicine*. This appeared in February 1922, three months after an abstract of their findings had been published in the *American Journal of Physiology*.

RIGHT *A scanning electron micrograph of just one of the* *millions of islets of Langerhans in the pancreas.*

The next step was to try out insulin on humans, but Banting and Best were still concerned about its safety. Bravely they injected each other, and except for a pair of sore arms, the experiment was a complete success. (They were extremely lucky: if the dosage had been higher, they might have gone into a coma.)

Now sure of their extract, they went to nearby Toronto General Hospital and, on 11 January 1922, gave injections to 14-year-old Leonard Thompson, who was dying of diabetes. Almost immediately, his blood sugar level fell; within days, he was out of bed; and within weeks, he was home and well, although dependent on insulin injections.

When Banting and Best's insulin began to produce toxic reactions, Macleod turned to a talented biochemist, James B. Collip, for help. In 1923, Collip devised a method of further purifying the extract and it was this purified insulin that made the control of diabetes possible.

PRIZES AND DISAPPOINTMENT

The world soon heard of Banting and Best's accomplishments, and so did the Nobel prize committee, who, in 1923, decided to honour the men responsible. Unfortunately, two terrible mistakes were made.

Best, who had worked so closely with Banting throughout the discovery, received no prize, and neither did Collip, without whose work insulin therapy would have been impossible. Instead, Banting shared the prize with Macleod, who had been thousands of miles away when the discovery was made. As the committee defended its decision, saying that no one had remembered to nominate Best and Collip, the two winners attempted to make up for the disappointment by sharing their prizes, Banting with Best and Macleod with Collip.

Having made his mark on medical history, Banting later abandoned endocrinology and researched the new field of aviation medicine; he died in 1941 in an air accident. Best, despite having been shunned by the Nobel committee, went on to further achievement, heading the University of Toronto's physiology department from 1929 to 1965. After Banting's death, he became chief of the university's Banting–Best Department of Medical Research until he retired in 1967.

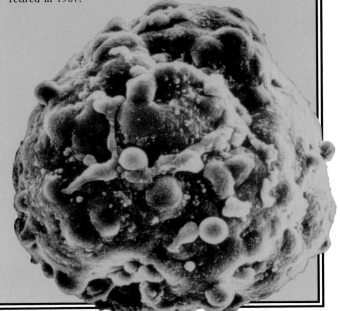

FIGHTING INFECTION

THE SEARCH FOR MAGIC BULLETS

The first attempt was a dye that turned patients bright red

FOLLOWING EHRLICH'S spectacular success with Salvarsan, researchers began to test virtually every substance that might be effective against infectious diseases. Although there were some successes – antimalarial drugs and those that fought protozoal infections such as amoebic dysentery – everything else proved either as destructive to the patient as to the bacteria, or unable to kill the germs once they had started to multiply. Scientists began to despair of finding any more 'magic bullets'.

There was one sign of hope. In 1931, René Dubos and Oswald Avery, of the Rockefeller Institute, announced that they had discovered an enzyme derived from a soil bacillus that could break down the capsule that protected one particular type of pneumococcus, the bacterium most often the cause of pneumonia. Although this proved too toxic for human use, the discovery gave new life to the search for anti-bacterial drugs.

THE CURIOUS CASE OF PRONTOSIL

In 1927, Gerhard Domagk was appointed research director of the German chemical company, I. G. Farbenindustrie. Its main products were azo dyes used to colour textiles, and Domagk decided to find out whether they had any adverse effect on streptococci, the bacteria responsible for many serious infections. In 1932, he found that one azo compound – Prontosil red – cured mice injected with a lethal dose of haemolytic streptococci.

Oddly enough, he did not publish his findings until February 1935. His employers later explained the delay by saying that Domagk had spent the intervening years confirming his results. However, when his report was finally issued, it consisted of only one animal experiment and a few sketchy case histories of human subjects.

Intrigued by Domagk's report, scientists at the Pasteur Institute in Paris asked for samples of Prontosil for investigation; again there was a delay. In the meantime, the French team synthesized the drug themselves and verified Domagk's results. However, they found that Prontosil would work only when the compound split into two parts within the body, and that one of the two parts – later called sulphanilamide – was largely responsible for Prontosil's bacteriostatic action (it did not kill bacteria like an antibiotic, but prevented them from multiplying).

Scientists were surprised that Domagk had made no mention of sulphanilamide, which was superior to Prontosil if only because it did not turn patients bright red. A British bacteriologist, Ronald Hare, came to the conclusion that Domagk had been aware of sulphanilamide but, for commercial reasons, had kept its existence secret.

Hare believed that Domagk and his associates knew that sulphanilamide was unpatentable because it had already been synthesized – by a Viennese student, Paul Gelmo, who had published his findings (concerning the chemical's efficacy as a dye) in his doctoral dissertation in 1908. Therefore, surmised Hare, Domagk had spent the years between 1932 and 1935 in a vain attempt to find a drug similar to but better than sulphanilamide and one that could be patented. In the meantime, thousands of patients had suffered, and some had died — all for the sake of profits.

In 1939, despite the rumours about possible suppression of research results, Domagk was awarded the Nobel prize for his discovery of the bacteriostatic effects of Prontosil. However, the Nazis prevented the scientist from accepting.

FIGHTING THE COCCI

Test samples of Prontosil eventually reached the rest of the scientific world. At Queen Charlotte's Maternity Hospital in London, Leonard Colebrook used it to treat puerperal (childbed) fever, and was able to reduce the mortality rate from 26 to 4.7 per cent. Ignaz Semmelweis's dream had at last come true (*see pp.54-5*).

However, neither Prontosil nor sulphanilamide proved very effective against pneumococcal infections, and scientists began to look for other drugs. In 1938, a British team, led

LEFT *German biochemist Gerhard Domagk (1895–1964), who won the Nobel prize for his work on* *the azo dye, Prontosil. His integrity, though, was later called into question.*

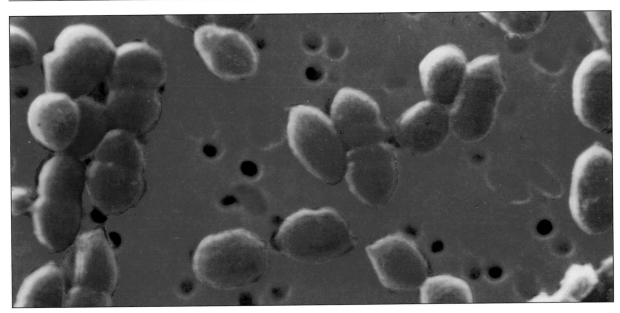

ABOVE *A false-colour electron micrograph of pneumococcus bacteria, responsible for pneumonia;* *sulphonamides were the first effective treatment, and saved millions of lives.*

by A. J. Ewins of the firm May & Baker, developed 'M&B 693' (later called sulphapyridine). This chemical not only worked well against pneumococcal infections but even better than sulphanilamide against streptococci. It soon displaced its older relative, and as it took its place in the world's pharmacopoeia, the family of sulphonamide drugs was born.

Sulphapyridine, however, could cause serious nausea and sometimes kidney and bladder stones, so chemists at the American Cyanamid Company began to search for a less toxic analogue. They came up with sulphadiazine in 1940, but this still produced kidney stones in a few patients taking large doses. The firm Hoffman-La Roche developed the much more soluble sulphasoxazole, which was then used almost exclusively for treatment, while sulphadiazine continued to be employed (in small doses) as a preventive.

Doctors began to prescribe these new 'sulpha drugs' almost immediately: in 1941, 1700 tonnes were given to at least 10 million Americans. As well as puerperal fever, they were found to be extremely effective against pneumonia, erysipelas (a serious skin infection), mastoiditis and meningitis. In 1939, doctors at Columbia University and Johns Hopkins reported that the percentage of patients experiencing recurrences of rheumatic fever had been reduced from 13 to 2 per cent by taking small daily doses of sulphanilamide. And the sulpha drugs also proved to be the first successful treatment for gonorrhoea.

However, in 1941, it was reported from New York that 28 people had died from adverse reactions to sulpha drugs, and it was suggested that 1 in every 1600 pneumonia cases treated with them died as a direct result. Since these tragedies were more likely with high doses, more care was taken with prescribing the drugs.

Even in low doses, sulpha drugs could in some circumstances produce unexpected – and unwanted – effects. During World War II, because streptococcal infections were common among recruits, small daily doses of sulpha drugs were prescribed as a preventive to large numbers of soldiers living and working together in close proximity. At first, the therapy was a success, but eventually strains of sulpharesistant streptococci appeared and spread widely because the drugs had also eradicated competing bacteria.

Luckily, sulpha-resistant strains only developed where the transmission of the bacteria could happen easily and rapidly. In normal civilian life, sulpha drugs continued to be responsible for saving millions of lives, and it was only with the advent of penicillin (*see pp.136-7*) that they lost their place at the vanguard of the anti-bacterial army.

BELOW *Streptococcus viridans, causing throat, mouth and gut* *infections, was a scourge of the troops in World War II.*

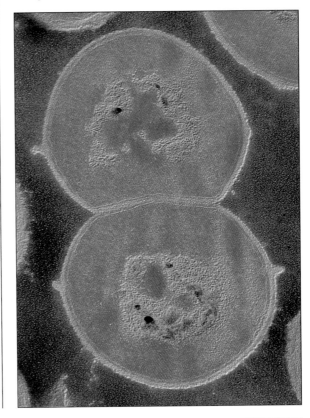

VIRUSES

THE SEARCH FOR SAFE VACCINES

World War I killed 8.5 million, but flu took 20 million in a year

Tracking down invisible viruses became much easier when, in 1884, one of Pasteur's pupils, Charles Chamberland, invented a filter with pores small enough to hold back bacteria but large enough to allow viruses to pass through. In 1892, the filter was used to identify the tobacco mosaic virus and, six years later, the one responsible for foot-and-mouth disease in animals. Finally, in 1901, James Carroll reported that an agent that could pass through a filter caused yellow fever in humans (*see p.96*).

In 1911, an American pathologist, Francis Peyton Rous, found that, by injecting healthy chickens with an extract made from cancerous tumours, he could induce cancer. Passing the extract through a filter, he repeated the experiments. The chickens again developed tumours – so the cancer must be caused by a virus. Rous was finally rewarded for his discovery 55 years later when, in 1966, he shared the Nobel prize.

In 1912, Rous and a colleague, J. B. Murphy, reported that they had been able to reproduce tumours by injecting a cell-free filtrate into a chick embryo. This should have suggested the possibility of reproducing other viruses in this way, as researchers had by now realized that viruses required living cells to survive. But it was not until 1931 that Ernest Goodpasture and A. M. Woodruff of Nashville, Tennessee, were able to grow fowl-pox virus in embryos. The technique then began to be used widely, until smallpox, *herpes simplex* and influenza viruses had all been reproduced.

POLIOMYELITIS

Polio epidemics were greatly feared for attacking healthy children, but research was hampered by the fact that polio affected only humans. Then, in 1909 in Vienna, Karl Landsteiner (*see p.92*) and Erwin Popper infected Rhesus monkeys by inoculating them with a filtered extract of spinal cord taken from two human cases that had proved fatal. Not only did this demonstrate that the disease was caused by a virus that was infectious, but it also meant that research could progress at a faster pace.

In 1916, an American scientist, Simon Flexner, discovered that monkeys became immune to polio after inoculation, when neutralizing antibodies appeared in their blood serum. Other researchers found similar antibodies in human victims, and the search for a vaccine began.

The first vaccines tested on humans came from the spinal cords of infected monkeys. In 1935, two independent trials were carried out. Dr John A. Kolmer of Philadelphia's Temple University used a live but very dilute polio virus

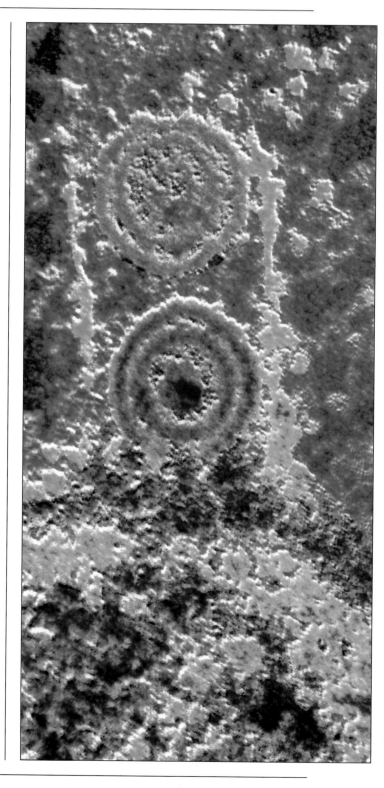

RIGHT Herpes simplex *virus particles (orange) migrate from the nucleus (green) of a host cell,* *potentially to cause cold sores. A closely related virus,* Herpes zoster, *causes shingles.*

THE INFLUENZA PANDEMIC OF 1918–19

In March 1918, during World War I, a relatively mild form of influenza spread across the United States, affecting people between the ages of 20 and 40 more than the very young and very old. By April, American troops had carried it to France, and thousands of soldiers and civilians were laid low: General von Lüdendorff blamed it for halting Germany's victory drive in July. It circled the globe in about four months, and affected so many in Spain that it had acquired the name "Spanish flu".

Then, in August, the disease changed to a far more vicious form. Again, it spread around the world, and this time, vast numbers of people died, primarily from subsequent pneumonia for which there was no drug treatment. The American Expeditionary Force's Meuse-Argonne offensive floundered as 69,000 troops fell ill. At San Francisco Hospital in California, 3509 pneumonia cases were admitted, of which 26 per cent died, and 78 per cent of the nursing staff fell ill. All over the US and elsewhere, public gatherings were banned, schools, churches, cinemas and businesses were closed, face masks were worn – but nothing did any good. Influenza travelled too fast and spread too widely to be stopped.

When the war was over and the flu pandemic had subsided, church bells were rung in celebration. Yet, almost as soon as they had faded, another wave of flu spread

ABOVE *A London bus is disinfected in March 1920 in an* attempt to prevent the return of the flu pandemic.

throughout the world. From December 1918 to April 1919, many of those who had so far escaped fell ill, but the death rate was only half that of the previous wave.

In just over a year, influenza had killed between 15 and 25 million people; by contrast, about 8.5 million military personnel had died as a direct result of World War I. No place was safe: the US lost over 500,000, England and Wales, 200,000; on the Pacific island of Samoa, a quarter of the population perished; 176 out of the 300 Eskimos living in Nome, Alaska died; about 5 million succumbed in India. And at least half of these fatalities had been in the prime of their lives.

Little was understood about the disease, which only seemed to affect humans. In 1932–33, at the National Institute for Medical Research in England, many unsuccessful attempts were made to transmit it to a variety of animals. Then Wilson Smith inoculated ferrets with filtered throat-washings from a colleague who had flu; the ferrets developed the illness. The researchers were initially unable to reverse the process (from ferret to human), but in 1934, an inoculated ferret sneezed violently while being examined by Dr Charles Stuart-Harris, who contracted the disease 45 hours later. They now knew that humans were affected by this influenza virus, and work could begin on developing a vaccine.

---

treated with a chemical derived from castor oil; and Dr Maurice Brodie of the New York City Health Department used viruses that he had attempted to inactivate by treating them with formalin. Some 17,000 children had been vaccinated by the two teams, when J. P. Leake of the US Public Health Service reported that polio had occurred among unvaccinated children living in an area previously unaffected by the disease but where the vaccines were being evaluated. In all, 12 children developed polio and six of them died. Both vaccines were deemed to be unsafe and inoculation was immediately stopped.

In 1938, President Franklin D. Roosevelt, himself crippled by the disease in 1921, established the National Foundation for Infantile Paralysis. Hundreds of research projects were funded through the Foundation's 'March of Dimes' campaign.

One project was led by Dr Charles Armstrong of the US Public Health Service. In 1939, he succeeded in infecting cotton rats and then white mice with polio. The sacrifice of many thousands of these prolific creatures, which were much cheaper and easier to maintain than monkeys, would eventually lead to prevention of the disease (see pp.202-3).

RIGHT *President Franklin Roosevelt, himself a polio victim, threw his personal support behind the* campaign to find a safe, reliable vaccine to fight the disease by establishing a National Foundation.

THE STRUGGLE AGAINST TB

THE GREAT WHITE PLAGUE

For centuries, the only cure was rest, a good diet, hygiene and fresh air

TUBERCULOSIS HAS STALKED humankind for centuries. The characteristic lesions caused by the rod-like tubercle bacillus *Mycobacterium tuberculosis* have been discovered in Neolithic skeletons in Europe, and in Egypt in mummies dating back to 3700 BC. Pulmonary tuberculosis, or 'leprosy of the lung', was described and known as phthisis by Hippocrates *(see pp.18-9)*.

BELOW *The rod-like bacteria* Mycobacterium tuberculosis, *inhaled into the lungs to cause 'consumption', or tuberculosis.*

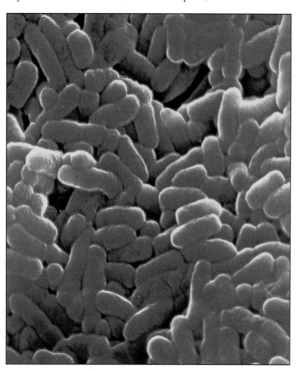

THE KING'S EVIL

A disfiguring form of tuberculosis, called scrofula, was prevalent in the 17th century. Swollen lymph glands in the necks of scrofula sufferers gave them a pig-like expression that easily identified the disease. An extraordinary custom in France and England decreed that the touch of a king could cure scrofula, or the 'king's evil' as it became commonly known. From the reign of Robert the Pious (966–1031) until the French Revolution in 1789, monarchs underscored their divine right to rule with the God-given gift of healing. King Charles II of England was said to have touched more than 92,000 victims between 1660 and 1664.

The virulent microbes of tuberculosis thrived as civilizations and cities developed throughout the 19th century. Poverty helped to spread the disease. Immigrant populations from Europe poured into the United States and died in the squalor of the slums in their thousands. Being overcrowded, overworked and undernourished in unsanitary conditions put further strain on immune systems already debilitated by famine and hardship in the immigrants homelands. The infectious and resilient nature of the tubercle bacillus ensured a smooth passage across every frontier – including those of social standing, age and race. At one time, the 'Great White Plague' of tuberculosis was responsible for one in five deaths in the industrialized world.

THE TB BACILLUS

At the height of the tubercular epidemic of 1882, the self-trained Prussian bacteriologist, Robert Koch *(see p.57)*, isolated and identified the tubercle bacillus, thereby proving the contagious nature of the disease. He then developed the tuberculin test, a skin test able to detect the infection. This marked the beginning of the decline of tuberculosis. From a peak death-rate of 400 lives lost per 100,000 of the populations of Europe and America, the number was halved by 1900. Improved living standards and another breakthrough in diagnosis, Röntgen's discovery of X-rays in 1895 *(see p.126)*, helped bring the epidemic under a degree of control.

At the time, the only treatment for tuberculosis was a long stay of months, or sometimes years, in a sanatorium. The strict regimes enforced by sanatoria consisted of complete rest, a nutritious diet, scrupulous hygiene and fresh air. Such treatment did not so much cure tuberculosis as help the body's immune system – its natural defences – confront the problem, and help damaged tissue to scar and seal, and so contain the bacilli. The climate and beautiful scenery of Switzerland made the country a favourite sanatorium resort for those who could afford it.

ABOVE *This solarium, at Aix-les-Bains, France, revolved slowly during the day, to give TB patients the maximum amount of sunshine.*

THE PERILS OF CONSUMPTION

The course of tuberculosis, before the advent of effective treatment, was characterized by fever, night sweats, a delicate, pale complexion (often, tragically, thought by young Victorian bucks to be entrancing when it affected young ladies) the coughing up of blood and wasting: the disease was known as 'consumption', because victims were almost literally consumed before their relatives' eyes.

For centuries, there had been a general perception that emotional deprivation and stress were causative factors in the onset of tuberculosis. This idea has been given some credence by research carried out by David Kissen, a Scottish scientist, who published a report called *Emotional Factors in Pulmonary Tuberculosis,* in 1958. Certainly, it would go some way to explain the classic image of the poet, artist or novelist as a tragic consumptive, coughing his or her life away in a turmoil of passion, sensitivity and unrequited love. For this image is not just a caricature: Keats, the Brontë sisters, Elizabeth Barrett Browning, D. H. Lawrence and Franz Kafka all succumbed to the wasting disease.

THE BCG VACCINE

Bovine tuberculosis is carried by cattle and can be ingested by humans through infected milk, though tuberculin tests and pasteurization have largely eradicated the risk from this source of infection. In the US, 280 million cattle were tuberculin tested between 1917 and 1940. This resulted in the slaughter of 4 million carriers, to the health and benefit of the nation. But the bovine link formed the basis of a significant medical advance – an effective vaccine. Two French scientists, Albert Calmette and Camille Gurin, had been working on a bovine strain of tuberculosis since 1906.

Despite the efficacy of their 'BCG' (Bacilli-Calmette-Gurin) vaccine, there was still no cure for tuberculosis until the introduction of streptomycin (*see p.164*) in the late 1940s. From 1920, sanatorium treatment included the surgical induction of a pneumothorax and thoracoplasty (respectively, the deliberate introduction of air between the lung and the chest wall, so that the lung collapses; and the removal of ribs to collapse the chest wall and close an abscess) to aid the long, slow process of healing. Unfortunately, remissions were often followed by relapses and further tissue damage. In 1930, Dr. R.C. Wingfield, the Medical Superintendent of Brompton Hospital Sanatorium in Frimley, England, expressed a healthy respect for the tenacity of the illness: "No patient should be regarded as cured of tuberculosis until he is safely dead of some other disease".

BELOW *A multiple-puncture tuberculin test, more commonly known as a 'Heaf test' in action: this six-needled device punctures the skin and places a highly concentrated solution of tuberculin* beneath it. *Three to ten days later, a lack of reaction shows there has been no previous exposure to the disease, and, therefore, no immunity: vaccination is needed and the BCG vaccine is given.*

TB TODAY

Tuberculosis is still an active adversary. The bacilli lie dormant in millions of people, most of whom have enough immunity to stop the disease developing – unless living conditions deteriorate. Poverty is the greatest ally of the disease, which is happy to colonize many areas of the developing world, particularly Asia, Africa and South America. Wealthier societies are also still vulnerable. In 1979, more than 30 years after the discovery of an effective cure, there were two outbreaks of tuberculosis in the UK; in one, 56 children were infected. And, in the period between 1985 and 1992, the number of new cases reported annually in the US has risen by 16 per cent – a worrying statistic in a country where streptomycin is almost unobtainable.

The weapons of vaccination, drug treatment and X-ray screening continue the fight against tuberculosis. But the 'Great White Plague' may only finally be eradicated when the war against poverty is won.

LEFT *Rather unwillingly, a senior citizen submits to an X-ray in the drive to eradicate TB in Glasgow,* *Scotland, in the 1950s. A six-year screening campaign lowered death rates significantly.*

ALLERGY

HISTAMINE AND ANAPHYLAXIS

"A fine big dog by the name of Neptunus" demonstrated sensitization

REFERENCES TO ALLERGIC REACTIONS stretch back as far as ancient Greece. The *Hippocratic Corpus (see p.19)* mentions that some foods make a few people ill but not the majority. Six centuries later, Galen reported adverse reactions to certain plants. In 1565, Leonardo Botallo gave the name 'rose cold' to the catarrh and asthma that a few suffered near blooming roses, and in 1819, the London doctor John Bostock described a seasonal nose infection that eventually bore his name: 'Bostock's summer catarrh'.

No one knew what caused these symptoms. Then two scientists, Charles Blackley in England and Morrill Wyman at Harvard University, independently came to the conclusion in the early 1870s that pollen from grass and weed caused hay fever. In 1903, a German researcher, Wilhelm P. Dunbar, induced hay fever by giving sensitive subjects pollen extracts in a saline or alcohol solution. He showed that hay fever did not occur simply because the pollen mechanically irritated the nose lining. Some other factor was involved.

Charles Blackley, in England, and Morrill Wyman, at Harvard University, realized independently in the 1870s that pollen – such as that from ragweed, BELOW – *caused hay fever.*

RICHET AND THE JELLYFISH

In 1898, Charles Richet (1850–1935), Professor of Physiology at the University of Paris, had found that dogs reacted strangely when injected with blood serum from eels: not only did the dogs react to the serum as if it were a poison, but they suffered even worse symptoms if they received a series of injections.

Richet remembered this when, in 1902/3, he accompanied the Prince of Monaco on a tropical cruise. To give himself something to do, he decided to make a study of the poisonous giant jellyfish, the Portuguese man-o'-war, whose painful sting can be fatal.

Then, remembering the ancient king, Mithridates, who took minute doses of poison to make himself immune to assassination, Richet carried out experiments with dogs, injecting them with tiny amounts of jellyfish poison. One subject – "a fine big dog by the name of Neptunus" – remained perfectly healthy after the first injection. However, when he was injected a second time, he became extremely ill and died suddenly.

Neptunus's shocking death impelled Richet to carry out more experiments, and in 1903, he published his results. A substance that might be only moderately toxic when first taken, he said, could produce far worse symptoms and even death when injected again. Rather than providing protection, or prophylaxis, the repeated injection removed whatever protection there had been. He coined the term 'anaphylaxis' to describe this. Richet, who was also a poet, novelist, dramatist and, later, an aviation pioneer, won the 1913 Nobel prize for his discovery. .

Soon after Richet's experiments with Neptunus, Maurice Arthus demonstrated that anaphylaxis can occur not only with poisons but also with supposedly non-toxic substances such as horse serum and cows' milk. When he injected rabbits with horse serum, a strong reaction occurred at the site of the injection, with inflammation and, occasionally, tissue destruction. This local reaction became known as the 'Arthus phenomenon'.

At about the same time in Vienna, two paediatricians – an Austrian, Clemens von Pirquet, and a Hungarian, Béla Schick – were researching diphtheria antitoxin. They discovered that some patients given the antitoxin developed symptoms – fever, swollen glands, an extensive rash – and a few even died. They eventually found that it was not the antitoxin that caused the adverse reaction but the horse serum in which it was carried.

Von Pirquet devised the term 'allergy' by combining two Greek words – *allos* ('different' or 'changed') and *ergos* ('work' or 'action'). An allergy denoted that, in these adverse reactions, the action of a substance in the body was somehow changed.

RIGHT *In an allergy skin test for asthma, small quantities of potential allergens — household dust, pollen and aspirin, for*

RIGHT *In an allergy skin test for asthma, small quantities of potential allergens — household dust, pollen and aspirin, for example — were injected beneath the skin. Reddening around the site showed a positive reaction to the allergen responsible.*

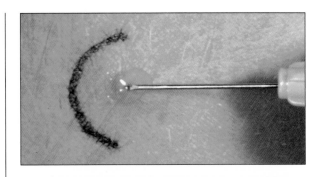

HISTAMINE AND MAST CELLS

In 1877, 23-year-old Paul Ehrlich, the future discoverer of Salvarsan (*see p.100*), described a special cell in connective tissue, which contained granules of some kind. However, Ehrlich never found out the cells' purpose.

In 1910, while carrying out the ergot fungus studies that would lead to his startling findings on nerve impulse transmission (*see p.99*), Henry Hallett Dale identified a substance in the fungus that caused smooth muscle to contract and blood pressure to drop. He also found that, when this substance was injected, it produced anaphylaxis.

It was almost 16 years before other scientists agreed that something like Dale's substance — now called histamine — was released during the destruction of invading proteins or when cells were slightly damaged by the reaction between antibodies linked to them and allergens (substances to which an individual is sensitized). In Britain, Thomas Lewis showed that injured cells do, indeed, manufacture histamine, and an American scientist, Charles F. Cole, then invented a test to detect it. Finally, in 1932, Carl Draystedt of Northwestern University in Illinois and Wilhelm S. Feldberg in Berlin showed independently that histamine is released by damaged cells and causes anaphylaxis.

However, it was only in 1953 that J. F. Riley and G. B. West revealed the presence of histamine in the granules of Ehrlich's mysterious cells, which are now known as mast cells. About a decade later, scientists realized how widely these mast cells are distributed within the body. By the mid-1970s, they were able to describe how allergens trigger the release of the histamine contained in the approximately 1000 granules in each cell.

BELOW *A human mast cell, part of the immune system. The red granules contain histamine, released during allergic reactions.*

RELIEF FOR ASTHMATICS FROM ANCIENT CHINA

Ephedrine, originally derived from the **Ephedra** *plant, is one of the major drugs used to treat asthma. It also has one of the longest histories of any drug.*

In China, from about 2000 BC, doctors prescribed the herb, which they called **ma huang**. *Completely independently, doctors of classical Rome gave their asthmatic patients* **ephedron**.

With the fall of Rome, ephedrine disappeared from the Western pharmacopoeia until it was rediscovered by chance by the young American doctor Carl Frederic Schmidt, in 1924. Working in Peking, he was sifting through 2000 of the most popular traditional Chinese herbal medicines in the hope of finding a new active compound when he came across **ma huang**. *Schmidt then learned that a substance called ephedrine had already been extracted from* **ma huang** *in 1885 and subsequently synthesized. However, because large doses killed experimental animals, it had been discarded. Schmidt was able, with his knowledge of Chinese medicine, to persuade drug companies to reintroduce ephedrine.*

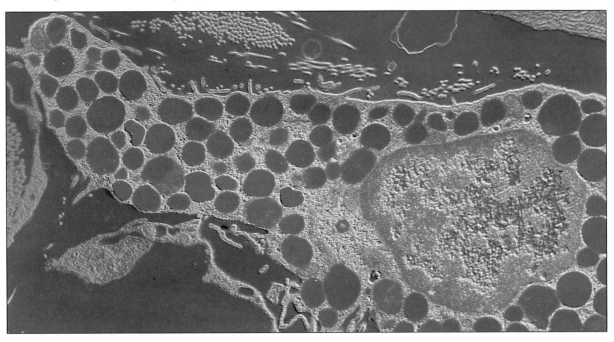

OBSTETRIC ADVANCES

TOWARDS SAFE CHILDBIRTH

In the 1930s, almost half of mothers' deaths were avoidable

IN THE EARLY 20TH CENTURY, childbirth was still highly dangerous, claiming at least 17 per cent of all mothers' lives. In 1932, it was reported that, in Britain, just under half of these deaths could have been prevented, and in the United States, two thirds had been avoidable.

In 1924, the Ministry of Health in Britain listed five reasons why maternal mortality was so high: poor sanitation and housing; rickets causing deformed pelvises; women's work (primarily heavy household chores); abortion or miscarriage leading to infection; and the lack of quality professional care before, during and after childbirth.

CARE OF UNBORN BABIES

Action had already been taken towards improving the care of unborn babies, the fates of whom had previously been considered secondary to the survival of their mothers. In 1901, the Scottish obstetrician J. W. Ballantyne proposed a 'pre-maternity hospital' where pregnant women could be cared for and doctors could study the pregnant state closely. He was one of the first to recommend the chemical and microscopic examination of pregnant women's urine and blood to discover the condition of their babies.

Within a year, the first 'pre-maternity', or antenatal, bed was endowed in the Edinburgh Royal Maternity Hospital, soon to be copied elsewhere in Britain. Curiously, Dr Ballantyne did not ask for outpatient facilities, but clinics were set up in Australia in 1910 and 1912, and 1911 saw one started at the Boston Lying-in Hospital, in the US.

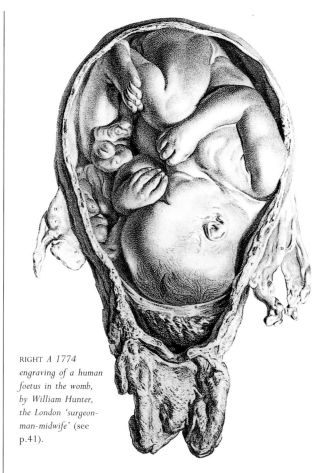

RIGHT *A 1774 engraving of a human foetus in the womb, by William Hunter, the London 'surgeon-man-midwife' (see p.41).*

FIGHTING CANCER

Before World War II, some progress was made in the battle against two major killers – uterine and cervical cancer.

In 1898, the Austrian surgeon Ernst Wertheim devised an operation for advanced cancer – still known as 'Wertheim's hysterectomy' – in which, as well as removing the uterus, far more tissue was taken from a woman's pelvis than previously.

Of even more benefit was the early detection of cancer. At Cornell University in the late 1930s, while working with the gynaecologist Herbert Traut, the Greek-born pathologist George N. Papanicolaou discovered abnormal cells in the vaginal smears of women with uterine cancer. In 1943, the two researchers published a monograph entitled **Diagnosis of Uterine Cancer by the Vaginal Smear** *– and the 'Pap smear' was launched, allowing the detection of precancerous changes to the cervix.*

During the next two decades, antenatal care became widespread. In Britain, the percentage of women receiving it increased from almost nil in 1915 to 80 per cent by 1935. However, while other adverse factors remained, antenatal care could not reduce mortality in childbirth on its own.

From the 1920s, doctors routinely ordered X-rays (*see pp.126-7*) to help them in antenatal diagnosis, assuring their patients that there was absolutely no danger. It was not until 1956 that a study revealed the association between antenatal X-rays and childhood cancer.

GIVING BIRTH

Meanwhile, medical understanding of the process of childbirth improved only gradually, and new beneficial techniques were slow to be developed.

Late in the 19th century, the French obstetrician Adolphe Pinard was responsible for several important advances. He invented a stethoscope to listen to the foetal heart, and his method of external version – massaging the pregnant woman's abdomen in late pregnancy to turn the baby from a breech (buttocks first) to a normal, head-down presentation – greatly reduced risks for mother and child. In addition, he developed a way of estimating whether a baby's head was too big to pass through its mother's pelvis, thus allowing caesarean section (much safer with the new antiseptic surgery and anaesthesia) to be anticipated.

In 1910, a Norwegian obstetrician, Christian Kielland, demonstrated a new set of forceps in Copenhagen. He was adamant that the exact position of the baby's head should be determined before any forceps delivery was made, and that the blades of the forceps should be so designed that the obstetrician could get an accurate grip on the head. With this in mind, he designed what came to be called 'Kielland's forceps', which were used primarily to correct head position during the last stage of labour by rotation.

The increasing availability of blood transfusion also saved lives, as did the introduction in the 1930s of such new antibacterial drugs as the sulphonamides (*see pp.106-7*). In addition, there were new techniques to prevent eclampsia (convulsions in pregnancy).

PAIN RELIEF IN HOSPITAL

After World War I, there was a significant increase in hospital deliveries. This trend was due partly to the attraction of 'specialist' care provided by consultants, and partly to the new 'germ–free' image of hospitals. However, what drew most women was the promise of pain relief.

Early in the century, researchers in Germany had developed a new type of anaesthesia: 'Twilight Sleep'. Women were injected with morphine and scopolamine (hyoscine) at the beginning of labour, and then given chloroform or ether as the baby's head was born. Pain was dulled, the memory of it removed, and women regained consciousness with the feeling that their babies' births had been a pleasant and fulfilling experience.

Twilight Sleep was popular in Britain and even more so in the United States, where feminist and suffrage groups campaigned for it. However, it had drawbacks: the drug dosages had to be finely tailored to each woman; it could prolong labour; and it could cause foetal distress.

Having a baby in hospital was not, however, always pleasant and safe. It became routine for women to have

enemas and their pubic hair shaved as precautions against infection. Yet, infection was far more likely in hospital, because of slips in personal hygiene and antiseptic routines by staff, as well as interventionist techniques such as caesarean sections and forceps deliveries.

In the US, obstetrical standards were low. A 1932 report revealed that, between 1915 and 1930, the number of maternal deaths had not fallen, and the deaths of babies from birth injuries had actually increased.

In Britain, family doctors were allowed to carry out home deliveries. Many, to save time, induced labour by giving castor oil, with or without quinine. Occasionally, the force of induced contractions ruptured the uterus and caused the death of the mother. Some doctors used forceps incompetently and had to rush their patients into hospital; in one study of such cases, one in ten women and two thirds of the babies died. It was found that about a third of these doctors had been too impatient or anxious to allow the cervix to dilate fully.

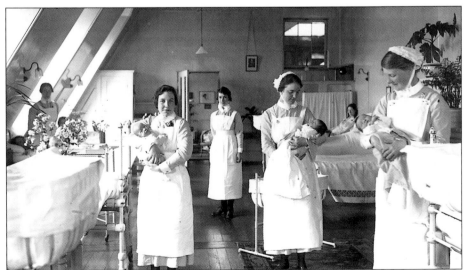

LEFT *The Elisabeth Maternity Ward, at London's St Bartholomew's Hospital, around 1925. The nurses look happy and reassuring; the babies appear cherubic. Nevertheless, in both Britain and America, 17 per cent of mothers died during childbirth; many were given dangerous drugs, such as morphine, scoplamine and chloroform; and routine antenatal care was years away.*

HALDANE & SON

They recited Shakespeare while breathing firedamp

JOHN SCOTT HALDANE and John Burdon Sanderson Haldane, respectively father and son, combined all that was best in 19th-century science with the changes and promise of the 20th century. Although they specialized in very different fields, both demonstrated the finest scientific method, great intellectual curiosity and enormous courage in self-experimentation: 'Suffer' was, after all, the Haldane family motto.

LIKE FATHER …

J.S. Haldane (1860–1936) was born in Edinburgh into a well-off and well-connected Scottish family, and graduated from the city's university medical school. Early in his career, he became fascinated by the subject of respiration – how the body breathes and what happens to the gases taken into it. In 1893, he carried out a series of experiments with himself and a colleague as human guinea pigs. In one, they remained in an airtight box (which they called 'the coffin') for up to eight hours, breathing twice as fast as normal, rebreathing the air and noting their reactions. Through this and other trials, JS learned that breathing is primarily regulated by nerves in the respiratory centre of the brain, and that these nerves are sensitive to any alteration in the amount of carbon dioxide in the blood.

JS then focused his attention on breathing difficulties in the world of work. In 1895, he investigated a serious accident in which five London sewer workers had died, overcome almost immediately by poisonous gases while down a deep shaft. After descending the shaft to take samples of the air and the sewage, JS found that, in certain conditions, sewage produces highly poisonous hydrogen sulphide – 'sewer gas' – and recommended aerating sewers and attaching safety ropes to all sewage workers.

He next turned to coal mines, where he found that the carbon monoxide in 'firedamp' (a combination of carbon monoxide, carbon dioxide and nitrogen) was far more lethal to the underground workers than the effects of explosions. Again he experimented on himself:

"At 7 per cent [oxygen concentration in air] there is usually distinct panting, accompanied by palpitations, and the face becomes a leaden blue colour. At the same time the mind becomes confused."

The mental confusion led him to send one telegram after another to his family, each one saying 'All safe'.

Among the many recommendations he made, one had an immediate practical effect:

"In view of the difficulty of recognizing by ordinary means the presence in poisonous amounts of this gas [carbon monoxide], [I] proposed the plan of making use of a small warm-blooded animal (a mouse or very small bird) as an indicator of CO."

As a result of his experiments, JS discovered that carbon monoxide is attracted to the haemoglobin in blood 300 times

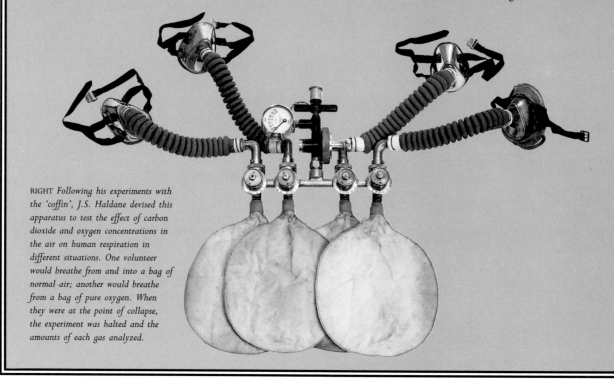

RIGHT *Following his experiments with the 'coffin', J.S. Haldane devised this apparatus to test the effect of carbon dioxide and oxygen concentrations in the air on human respiration in different situations. One volunteer would breathe from and into a bag of normal air; another would breathe from a bag of pure oxygen. When they were at the point of collapse, the experiment was halted and the amounts of each gas analyzed.*

BELOW At the Coal Face *by William Dring. J.S. Haldane realized the lethal potential of* carbon monoxide in mines and advised the use of a bird to warn of a build-up of the caged gas.

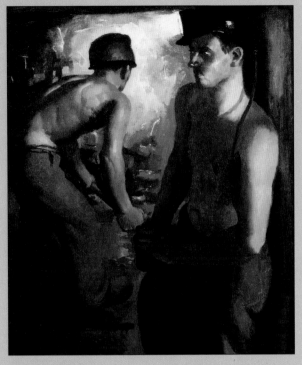

more strongly than oxygen. He also devised ingenious methods of measuring blood gases, and invented the precursors of the haemoglobinometer and blood gas analyser still routinely employed by doctors.

JS went on to investigate decompression sickness ('the bends') suffered by deep-sea divers. The compression and decompression schedules used today are based on his work. In addition, he studied the effects of high temperatures on the body – becoming, in the process, the 'father of the salt tablet' by recommending the replacement of salt lost during excessive sweating.

... LIKE SON

J.B.S. Haldane (1892–1964) became his father's assistant at the age of three, when he provided blood samples for an experiment, and by the time he was eight, he was taking down the numbers his father called out while reading his gas analysis apparatus. But it was while he was at Eton (where he was mercilessly bullied) that he worked most closely with JS, carrying out deep dives during his father's work on decompression and investigating working conditions in mines.

On one occasion, in a north Staffordshire mine, they entered part of a tunnel containing firedamp. "To demonstrate the effects of breathing firedamp", wrote JBS later, "my father told me to stand up and recite Mark Antony's speech from Shakespeare's *Julius Caesar*, beginning 'Friends, Romans, countrymen'. I soon began to pant, and somewhere about 'the noble Brutus' my legs gave way and I collapsed on to the floor, where, of course, the air was all right. In this way, I learnt that firedamp is lighter than air."

In 1911, JBS entered Oxford to study mathematics, but since, as he later claimed, no one could study that subject for more than five hours a day and remain sane, he spent a great deal of time attending a zoology course. But this was not JBS's first exposure to the study of the living world.

In 1901, when he was eight, his father had taken him to a lecture on the recently rediscovered work of Gregor Mendel (*see p.67*). Despite his youth, he remembered what he had heard, and when he was 15, he attempted to put Mendel's principles into practice by breeding his sister Naomi's guinea pigs (there were soon 300 of them). He read all the literature on the subject, and by the time he attended the Oxford zoology course he had discovered the concept of genetic 'linkage', in which the inheritance of certain characteristics appeared to be linked, possibly because the genes responsible for them are located near each other on the same chromosome. JBS published a paper on this in 1912, and linkage has played a major role in genetics ever since.

That same year, he co-authored (with his father and an associate) a paper, published in the *Journal of Physiology*, on how haemoglobin combines with oxygen, to which he contributed the complex mathematical analyses. He also switched from reading mathematics to classics and philosophy: thus one of the 20th century's greatest scientific minds did not earn a science degree.

During a long, fulfilling career, JBS successfully married Darwinism to Mendelian genetics, and his book *The Causes of Evolution* (1932) was a landmark in population genetics. Among many scientific 'firsts', he investigated the biochemistry of gene action and the genetic control of enzyme actions; calculated mutation rates of genes; created linkage maps for human chromosomes; and analysed human pedigrees to understand different modes of inheritance.

In addition – and very unlike his father – he was a great popularizer of science and a life-long Marxist. "This was a very exciting atmosphere to grow up in," wrote JBS's sister, the writer Naomi Mitchison, "and [because of it] I think my brother set his mind on science and on the kind of science which is likely to help people". In 1957, in protest at Britain's involvement in the Suez crisis and desiring to live in a warm climate – "Sixty years in socks is quite enough", he said – JBS emigrated to India. He died there seven years later, leaving his body to medical research.

LEFT *A genius, by any standard, J.B.S. Haldane was also a notorious eccentric and prone to be truculent and quarrelsome. A life-long Marxist, he resigned from the Communist Party in 1956 – because of "Stalinist interference in science" – then emigrated to India, taking up Indian citizenship.*

PSYCHIATRY & PSYCHOLOGY

FROM SIGMUND FREUD TO B. F. SKINNER

"Never hug and kiss them, never let them sit on your lap"

THE STUDY OF THE MIND evolved from the medical science of the 19th century. However, researchers soon discovered that, unlike Pasteur's germ theory, when it came to the mind there were very few clear-cut guidelines: it resisted classification and testing was extremely difficult.

The result was a fragmentation of approach: some investigators concentrated on mental illness, others on the basic functions of the mind in animals and humans, and still others on how medical drugs and operations could treat certain mental conditions.

FREUD AND PSYCHOANALYSIS

Shortly before receiving his medical degree from the University of Vienna in 1881, Sigmund Freud (1856–1939) became fascinated by a patient of his friend, Dr Josef Breuer: the 21-year-old Bertha Pappenheim, whom Breuer and Freud later wrote about as 'Anna O'. What they learned from her became the basis of psychoanalysis.

Anna O suffered intermittently from a variety of hysterical symptoms: leg and arm paralysis, sight and speech disturbances, memory loss, general disorientation, nausea. Breuer found that, after hypnotizing her, asking her to remember when she first experienced a particular symptom

and tracing the first occurrence to a long-suppressed traumatic event, the symptom would disappear. Anna O called Breuer's treatment the 'talking cure'.

After more than a year of daily visits, Anna O began to act as if Breuer were her father, expressing all the emotions that she had felt towards her real father. Breuer, too, began to feel quite strongly about Anna. (Freud would later call these phenomena 'transference' and 'countertransference'.) When his wife became jealous of this doctor–patient relationship, Breuer decided to end the therapy. Anna promptly developed an hysterical pregnancy, which Breuer reluctantly agreed to treat with hypnosis. This was the last time he treated Anna – or any other hysterical patient – and, sensibly, he placated his wife by taking her to Venice on a second honeymoon.

The year 1895, when Breuer and Freud published Anna O's case in *Studies on Hysteria*, marked the official founding of the school of psychoanalysis. Ten years earlier, Freud had visited Charcot in Paris (*see p.73*), studying his hypnosis

BELOW *Sigmund Freud at his desk. Though later criticized by one-time colleagues, such as Jung and Adler,* and less than fashionable today, Freud was undeniably the true father of psychoanalysis.

SHOCK TREATMENT AND LOBOTOMIES

While Sigmund Freud delved into the unconscious and Watson and Skinner tested white rats, medical researchers experimented in more traditional ways, sometimes with regrettable results.

Although insulin had been unsuccessful in treating morphine addiction, Manfred Sakel discovered that the physical shock caused by an overdose of insulin, although dangerous, sometimes had positive benefits in the treatment of schizophrenia. Ladislaus Joseph von Meduna devised another shock treatment, with camphor as the agent, but this often produced convulsions so violent that patients suffered broken bones. Eventually, in 1938, Italian psychiatrist Ugo Cerletti used electric shocks to produce seizures. Today, his electro-convulsant therapy (ECT), despite a chequered career, is still used in parts of the world to treat severe depression.

Psychosurgery was also popular during the late 1930s and 1940s. The Portuguese neuro-psychiatrist Egas Moniz, impressed by the disappearance of aggression in animals after removal of the frontal lobes of their brains, performed the first lobotomy on a human in 1935. The procedure became standard in patients resistant to shock therapy. Although Moniz was awarded the Nobel prize in 1949 for this surgical development, the irreversible operation was eventually seen as almost as bad as the mental disorders it treated, and it fell out of favour.

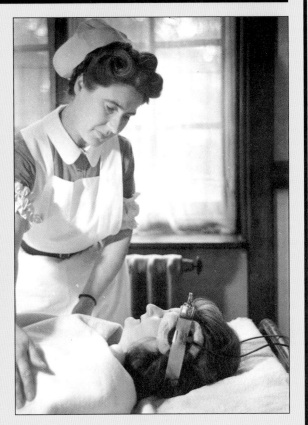

RIGHT *The original, sensational caption to this 1946 photograph of ECT in action was: "she is jolted out of hell".*

techniques and picking up the idea that there was a relationship between hysteria and sex. However, on returning to Vienna to practise, Freud found that hypnotism did not work as well as he had hoped.

As a result, he gradually developed a technique – free association – in which patients would lie on a couch with their eyes closed, speaking freely about whatever came into their minds. Many displayed what Freud called resistance – the avoidance of recalling traumatic experiences – but when they did talk about them they were, unlike hypnotized patients, able to deal with them rationally. Such experiences, Freud saw, did not go away but continued to motivate troubled minds unconsciously.

Freud realized that, to be an effective analyst he, too, would have to be psychoanalysed. Since he could not use free association on himself, he examined his dreams, which he saw as symbolic manifestations of repressed thoughts. For him, dreams became the "royal road to the unconscious" and the subject of his most popular work, *The Interpretation of Dreams* (1900).

One of the major outcomes of Freud's self-analysis was his discovery of the Oedipus complex, which led to his outline of the psychosexual development of children. He also constructed a triad of frequently warring factions within the unconscious – the id, the ego and the superego – with the libido (primarily sexual energy) as the motivational force.

Freud's achievements were enormous. All his hypotheses added up to the first comprehensive theory of personality, and psychoanalysis was a new and, in the opinion of many,

very effective way of dealing with mental disorders. Yet Freud dealt not only with abnormal behaviour, but also made the normal comprehensible, and his theories were applied by him and others to almost every area of human activity.

However, psychoanalysis attracted as many critics as fans. A major criticism was that it was too unscientific: there were no controlled experiments, the data collected (chiefly observations of patients) were influenced by Freud himself, and the terms he used were impossible to quantify or define completely; recently, too, his records of Anna O have been questioned. In addition, many people felt he overemphasized sex as a motive for human behaviour.

BREAKING WITH FREUD

Despite these criticisms, Freud's methods and theories were taken up by many psychiatrists and psychologists, and, in 1908, 42 practitioners attended the first international congress on psychoanalysis. However, serious rifts within Freud's own ranks soon appeared.

Within a year of becoming president of the Vienna Psychoanalytic Society in 1910, Alfred Adler (1870–1937) resigned and never saw Freud again. In Adler's 'individual psychology', powerlessness – not sex – is the driving energy in people's lives, beginning with the helplessness felt in infancy: feelings of inferiority either lead people to strive to attain power, to take control of their lives, or overwhelm them so that they accomplish nothing. According to Adler, humans are not victims of biology or environment, but are free to choose their own destinies.

At about the same time, the Swiss psychoanalyst Carl Jung (1875–1961) began to have serious doubts about Freud's emphasis on sex in his theories, and in 1914, Freud terminated their relationship. In Jung's 'analytical psychology', the libido comprises not only sexual energy but a pool of generalized creative energy that can be used for positive growth throughout life. Jung also believed that people adopt one of two attitudes in relating to the world: introversion or extraversion.

In addition, he developed theories on the mystical and spiritual side of life (which Freud derided) – in particular, the concept of the 'collective unconscious'. Jung described this as the "deposit of ancestral experience from untold millions of years, the echo of prehistoric world events". According to this theory, humans inherit predispositions to react emotionally to certain basic experiences, such as "birth, death, the sun, darkness, power, women, men, sex, water, magic, mother, heroes and pain". As a result, people are pushed by the past and pulled by the future.

PAVLOV AND THE CONDITIONED REFLEX.

While Freud was grappling with the darker aspects of the unconscious, a Russian scientist was developing a different view of human motivation. For his work on the functions of the digestive system, Ivan Petrovitch Pavlov (1849–1936) won the 1904 Nobel prize. It also led him to make sweeping generalizations about why people behave as they do.

Pavlov created artificial channels (fistulae) leading from dogs' digestive organs to the outside, so that he could view the secretion of gastric juices. (The dramatist George Bernard Shaw later labelled him "a scoundrel and a vivisectionist,

BELOW *Ivan Petrovitch Pavlov, in 1935, who according to George* *Bernard Shaw would "boil babies alive just to see what happens".*

whose habit was to boil babies alive just to see what happens".) He found to his surprise that the sight of food or even just the sound of his footsteps would cause the dogs' stomachs to secrete. This he called a 'psychic reflex', later amending the term to 'conditioned reflex' when he realized it resulted from the animals' experience.

Pavlov decided to test this phenomenon more rigorously. He had noticed that, when he appeared with food, his dogs would begin to salivate. He decided to ring a bell when the food was presented, and eventually he found that the dogs would begin to salivate simply when the bell was rung.

Pavlov had no time for untestable theories about the human unconscious. Instead, he believed that all human behaviour was the result of innate and conditioned physical reflexes, all sorted by the brain into usable patterns, and all of which could be investigated scientifically.

SKINNER'S UTOPIA

By 1913, John B. Watson (*see box*) had taken Pavlov's thesis and applied it to a theory of human behaviour, which he called 'behaviourism'.

Watson's most famous disciple was B. F. Skinner, who at the age of 22 began to research Watson's approach, following the publication of the latter's book *Behaviorism,* in 1925. Skinner's first success was an invention – the 'Skinner box'. He mounted a lever bar on the wall of a cage large enough to hold a rat comfortably, and when the animal pressed the bar, a food pellet would drop into a tray. Every press of the bar was recorded on a cumulative record.

Skinner found that the rate at which his rats would press the bar increased dramatically once they realized that they would be rewarded by food; the young psychologist called these rewards 'reinforcement'. He began to vary the situation. Sometimes he would withhold food when the bar was pressed; the rats at first continued to press but, with growing frustration, eventually gave up. Sometimes he would give food only after a certain time interval or number of presses; the rats would learn to press more as the end of the interval approached, and would continue to operate the lever bar even when they received food at only every 192nd press. When he varied randomly the intervals or number of presses, Skinner found that the rats, like slot machine players, became 'hooked' and continued to respond.

Skinner published his results in his book *The Behavior of Organisms* in 1938. His theory, which he called 'operant conditioning', stated that an organism's behaviour can be strengthened or weakened by altering the reinforcement it receives. He later expanded this, saying that complex behaviours consist of chains of simpler ones that can be reinforced – and proved it by teaching pigeons to play ping-pong. When he visited his nine-year-old daughter's school class, he realized that the techniques he had been using with pigeons could be used with children; the result was programmed instruction and teaching machines.

Skinner eventually applied his theories to society as a whole. His novel *Walden Two* (1948) describes a utopia in which children are rigorously conditioned by positive reinforcement, allowing them to grow up into happy, intelligent, cooperative adults. Skinner had no time for the idea of free will; to him, all behaviour was the result of either negative or positive reinforcement. Many people vociferously criticized his 'utopia' as a totalitarian state.

THE RISE AND FALL OF JOHN B. WATSON

For most of his life, John Broadus Watson (1878–1956) got what he wanted. From inauspicious beginnings in Greenville, South Carolina, he had by the age of 30 become Professor of Psychology at Johns Hopkins University in Baltimore.

Until then, he had devoted himself to studying animals, particularly the learning processes of white rats. When he turned his attention to human behaviour, he found little difference. Like Pavlov, by whom he was influenced, he believed that consciousness could not cause behaviour; it was something that occurred when certain stimuli produced certain physical reactions — i.e. conditioning. To Watson, humans and animals were the same, and humans should be studied as objectively.

"Psychology as the behaviourist views it", he said in 1913, "is a purely objective experimental branch of natural science. Its theoretical goal is the prediction and control of behaviour". This credo proved to be immensely popular, appealing as it did to the American belief that all people are created equal and anyone can achieve success. And the 36-year-old Watson was successful: in 1914, he was elected President of the American Psychological Association.

Watson and a research student, Rosalie Rayner, carried out a cruel experiment to demonstrate conditioning. When they first placed a white rat near 11-month-old 'Little Albert', the baby showed no fear. However, after Watson and Rayner struck a steel bar with a hammer behind Little Albert's back every time he reached out for the rat, he first jumped, then cried and eventually became frightened of the rat. This fear extended to anything furry, including rabbits, dogs and a Santa Claus mask.

Just when Watson must have felt that nothing could stop him, something did. In 1920, his wife discovered that he was having an affair with Rosalie Rayner and sued him for divorce; the scandal proved too much for Johns Hopkins and he was forced to resign. A year later, broke, out of work and married to Rosalie, he became a temporary employee of the J. Walter Thompson advertising agency. By 1924, he was vice-president of the company and considered one of the leading lights of advertising. By 1930, in the middle of the Depression, he was earning well over $70,000 a year.

He continued to air his views on child behaviour, becoming the Dr Spock of the 1920s and 1930s with his book Psychological Care of the Infant and Child *(1928): "Never hug and kiss them, never let them sit on your lap. If you must, kiss them once on the forehead when they say good night". However, he was generally forgotten by psychologists until the 1950s. By then, Watson was old and bitter, and when the American Psychological Association awarded him their gold medal, in 1956, he refused to go to the presentation. He died a few months later. History does not record what became of 'Little Albert'.*

NUTRITION

THE DISCOVERY OF VITAMINS

When chickens were fed whole, rather than polished, rice, they recovered

IN THE EARLY DECADES of the 20th century, Pasteur's germ theory was in the ascendant, and many believed that all diseases were caused either by specific infectious agents or by toxins. It was generally held that the ingredients for satisfactory growth and health were adequate amounts of carbohydrates, fats, proteins and mineral salts – and nothing else.

LEMONS AND RICE HUSKS

Nutrition deficiency diseases were, however, suspected as long ago as the 18th century. In 1753, the Scottish ship's surgeon James Lind recommended that sailors on long voyages should drink lemon juice to prevent scurvy, in which bleeding occurs in the gums, skin and joints.

At the end of the 19th century, Dr Christiaan Eijkman was posted to Batavia (Jakarta), in the Dutch East Indies, to study beriberi, a disease that causes numbness, loss of muscle power and, eventually, heart failure. He found that chickens at the local military hospital, fed mainly on kitchen scraps of polished rice, developed a similar condition. When he fed them with whole rice, he was astonished to find that they recovered.

ABOVE *James Lind, the first doctor to realize, in 1753, that more than* protein, carbohydrate and fat *is necessary for health – he prescribed lemon juice.*

ABOVE *British biochemist Frederick Hopkins, 'Hoppy' to his colleagues,* whose work eventually led to the *discovery of vitamins.*

Eijkman thought that there must be a toxin in the polished rice, the antidote being in the husk of whole rice. His colleague, Gerrit Grijns, disagreed, demonstrating that the chickens thrived if fed lightly cooked meat as well as polished rice, but did not if the meat was well-cooked. So some essential substance in the food must be destroyed by heat.

In 1906, British biochemist Frederick Gowland Hopkins fed young rats on casein, lard, starch, sugar and salts – supposedly everything essential to growth and health – and also gave some a little milk. The rats that did not receive milk failed to grow; the others thrived. 'Hoppy', as his Cambridge colleagues called him, concluded that "astonishingly small amounts" of certain substances in food – which he called "accessory food factors" – were necessary for the body to utilize protein and energy for growth. In 1929, Hopkins and Eijkman were awarded the Nobel prize for their work leading to the discovery of vitamins.

THE FAMILY OF VITAMINS

The term 'vitamin' was coined in 1912, after the Polish-Jewish chemist Casimir Funk, working at the Lister Institute in London, had isolated the active substance in rice husks that prevented beriberi in pigeons. He called this and other similar substances 'vitamines' – from 'vital amines' – believing they were amines, compounds derived from ammonia. (The final 'e' was dropped in 1920 when it became known that not all vitamins are amines.) Funk was also one of the first to link vitamin deficiency with specific diseases, such as beriberi, scurvy, pellagra and rickets.

Funk's discoveries ushered in a new age of scientific endeavour in nutrition. A former Kansas farmboy, E. V. McCollum, showed that certain fats contained an essential ingredient for normal growth, which he called 'fat-soluble A'. Later, he found that a substance in watery extracts of wheat, egg yolk and yeast was also essential: this became 'water-soluble B'.

In Britain, in 1918, Edward Mellanby cured puppies with rickets by giving them fat-soluble A in the form of cod liver oil. He established the difference between the substance that prevented rickets and the substance that ensured normal growth: he called the former 'vitamin D', and the latter 'vitamin A'.

The name 'vitamin C' was given to the still unidentified scurvy preventive found in fruit and vegetables. In 1928, a Hungarian biochemist, Albert von Szent-Györgyi, isolated the substance from the adrenal glands (receiving a Nobel prize in 1937). Nevertheless, it took another four years before the substance was generally recognized to be a vitamin.

The B vitamins proved more complicated. Water-soluble B in yeast was found to have two actions, so the two substances involved were called vitamins B_1 and B_2. Then, vitamin B_2 was found to have various other actions, and gradually the list expanded as far as vitamin B_{12}. Eventually, some of the B vitamins proved to be already known, and there are now only vitamins B_1 (thiamin), B_2 (riboflavin), B_6 (pyridoxine) and B_{12} (cobalamin).

BELOW *During World War II, the British public enjoyed free vitamins, courtesy of the government – nutrition standards had never been higher.*

THE SEARCH FOR THE INTRINSIC FACTOR

Pernicious anaemia is a disease in which too few red blood cells are produced and the ones that exist are fragile and misshapen. It was once invariably fatal.

In 1917, an American doctor, George H. Whipple, reversed induced anaemia in dogs artificially by feeding them beef liver. In 1925, after reading about Whipple's work, George R. Minot and William P. Murphy fed pernicious anaemia patients at a Boston hospital 8oz (225g) of raw liver daily. The results were spectacular, some patients being brought back virtually from the dead. Whipple, Minot and Murphy shared the 1934 Nobel prize.

After hearing Minot lecture in 1926, William B. Castle performed a dramatic experiment. He knew that 'cured' pernicious anaemia patients still produced abnormal stomach juices. So he decided to find out whether some substance (the 'intrinsic factor') present in normal stomach juices aids the absorption of another substance (the 'extrinsic factor') in food in order for normal blood to be produced. In his experiment, he cured pernicious anaemia patients by feeding them on the partially digested contents of his own stomach (having vomited one hour after eating 10½ oz [300g] of finely ground beef). And he demonstrated that his stomach juices did indeed contain the intrinsic factor (later shown to be a protein). In 1948, the 'extrinsic factor' in liver and beef was found to be vitamin B_{12}.

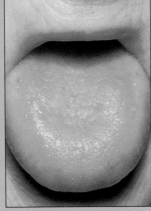

LEFT *The smooth appearance of the tongue of a sufferer from pernicious anaemia betrays a lack of papillae (taste buds) characteristic of the disorder, which also causes inflammation of the tongue.*

MEDICAL TECHNOLOGY

MICROSCOPES AND ELECTRICAL MONITORING

Dressed in black, hooded and full-gowned, they grew 'immortal' cells

AT THE END OF THE 19TH CENTURY, access to the body's interior was limited to surgery or post-mortems. However, it was just possible to peer into an opening – the vagina, say, with a speculum or the throat with a tongue depressor.

In 1911, the London doctor William Hill developed a gastroscope – a rigid tube slipped down the oesophagus and into the stomach. A periscope at the end increased the field of vision, so that the entrance of the small intestine could be seen. In 1913, Chevalier Jackson, in America, invented a direct-vision laryngoscope to view the larynx, followed by a bronchoscope to see into the lungs and pass through anaesthetic gases.

LEFT *'Boyle's Machine', to give nitrous-oxide, oxygen and ether – one of several anaesthetic devices designed by Edmund Boyle between 1917 and 1933.*

MICROSCOPIC MAN

Microscopes were first used directly on the body in 1899, when the cornea of the eye was investigated with a large-field stereomicroscope (with two eyepieces to show three dimensions) designed by Siegfried Czapski. An improved and widely used version brought a revolution in diagnosis and treatments.

The next step was microsurgery. In 1921, the Scandinavian ear specialist C. O. Nylen performed an operation using a monocular microscope. A year later, L. Holmgren, with a stereomicroscope, carried out the delicate procedure of fenestration – making an opening into the inner ear from the middle ear when superfluous bone blocks transmission of sound waves.

What could be seen was, however, limited. The wavelength of light is about one-thousandth of a millimetre, so things smaller than this, such as viruses, would not show up under a light microscope. In 1925, the London businessman and amateur microscopist Joseph Bernard developed the ultraviolet microscope, which achieved magnifications of up to 2500 and allowed some of the larger viruses to be seen.

Meanwhile, research had shown that electrons travel with a wave motion similar to light, but that these waves are 100,000 times shorter – thus, in theory, objects so much smaller should be visible through an electron microscope. The first was developed by L. L. Marton, at the Université

Libre in Belgium in December 1932. However, the first micrograph of a biological specimen using this technology was only made technically possible with Marton's second microscope, built 15 months later.

By 1934, researchers had achieved the same magnification as the best light microscopes; within three years, objects could be magnified 7000 times; and, by the end of World War II, electron microscopes were capable of magnifying over 200,000 times. Many aspects of cell structure were then revealed – for example, synapses between nerve fibres; histamine-releasing granules in mast cells (*see p.113*); and macrophages impaled by asbestos fibres (*see p.132*).

THE BODY ELECTRIC

Scientists were eager to observe and measure the minutest activities of the body, including impulses generated by the electrical activity of the heart. In 1903, Willem Einthoven, of Holland, published details of the first electrocardiograph. This was the 'string galvanometer': a 600lb (275kg) unit comprising a silver-coated quartz fibre suspended between the poles of an electromagnet.

Electrical current from the heart was conducted through the fibre, which bent at right angles to the field of the electromagnet. The fibre's shadow, cast by a strong light beam directed through holes drilled through the poles, showed up on a moving glass photographic plate – in effect, the first electrocardiogram (ECG, or EKG in America).

Einthoven, who was awarded the 1924 Nobel prize for his invention, eventually went into partnership with Horace Darwin, youngest son of Charles Darwin, to manufacture the string galvanometer. By 1928, portable devices weighing

ABOVE *One of the first effective scanning electron microscopes (SEMs), at Cambridge University.*

Such machines revolutionized understanding of cell structure and function.

ALEXIS CARREL AND THE MUMBO-JUMBO OF TISSUE CULTURE

In 1907, Ross G. Harrison of Yale University published a short paper on his work on the development of nerve fibres. However, what most excited the scientific community was his technique for growing tissues in culture. It gave researchers enormous potential for experimentation, because, completely dissociated from the human body, cell growth and the effects of certain substances on tissues could now be observed.

The name most linked with tissue culture is that of surgeon Alexis Carrel, who, in 1912, won the Nobel prize for his surgical work on blood vessels and organs. Born in France in 1873, he left the University of Lyon in 1904 following political and medical disagreements and emigrated to the United States, where two years later he joined the Rockefeller Institute.

ABOVE *A* Time *magazine cover from 1938, showing Alexis*   *Carrel (*RIGHT*) with US aviator Charles Lindbergh.*

In 1910, shortly after Harrison published his full paper, Carrel's colleague M. T. Burrows visited him to learn his technique. It was not ideally suited to their purpose, which was primarily to grow cells from warm-blooded animals (something already achieved in 1908 by Margaret Reed in Berlin), but Carrel and Burrows devised a method that consisted, according to Burrows, of "a simple surgical technique, freshly sterilized glassware and instruments".

However, by 1912, and in Carrel's hands, this 'simple' technique had become increasingly elaborate. He and Burrows worked in two separate suites of rooms, each comprising animal preparation rooms, scrub-up room and culture/operating room, the latter having built-in sprays so that dust could be settled by spraying with water before work began. The technicians (one was the future aviator Charles Lindbergh) were dressed somewhat sinisterly in black, hooded, full-length gowns.

The influential Carrel warned that "the technique is delicate, and in untrained hands, the experimental errors are of such magnitude as to render the results worthless". However, F. P. Rous (see p.108) had carried out procedures in embryology demanding more skill than those for tissue culture, but with much simpler apparatus and non-specialist technicians.

The result was that others were discouraged from attempting tissue culture because of its supposed complexity – what one of Carrel's critics termed his "mumbo-jumbo" – and because of the cost of the equipment and laboratory space. Progress was held back for years.

However, Carrel did make some advances. For instance, the 'Carrel flask' reduced the risk of bacterial contamination, the major cause of failure in tissue culture until the advent of antibiotics in the 1940s. He achieved popular fame for his 'immortal' cell strain, cultures of chick embryo heart first established in January 1912, and maintained by him and his disciple A. H. Ebeling until at least 1942. However, how this was done, when it is now known that cells have a finite lifespan, is still a mystery.

Carrel retired from the Rockefeller Institute in 1938 and went to Paris to set up his Institute for the Study of Human Problems. During World War II, he accepted help from the Vichy government and negotiated with the Germans. After the liberation, in August 1944, he was charged with collaboration, and avoided arrest only by dying.

only 30lb (14kg) had been developed. Later, the fibre was replaced by amplifying valves.

Using the string galvanometer, Johannes Berger discovered brain waves in 1924. His findings were ignored at first, but ten years later, the British physiologists Edgar Adrian (*see* p.99) and B. H. C. Matthews admitted their importance. Brain wave measurements – electroencephalograms (EEGs) – were initially used to diagnose epilepsy and, during World War II, proved invaluable in detecting brain injuries.

RIGHT *A scientist at the controls of a scanning electron microscope at the University of Utah, looking at the scanned images on a TV screen.*   *The diagonal line across the left-hand screen is a human hair, included for comparison with a micromechanical device.*

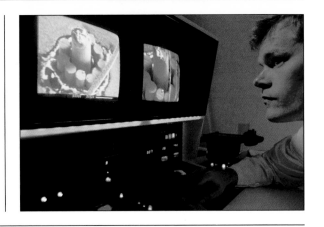

RÖNTGEN AND X-RAYS

REVEALING THE BODY BENEATH

A life-saving invention that also led to 'X-ray proof underwear'

IN 1895, A GERMAN-BORN Dutch citizen working at a German university transformed medicine when he discovered a way to look through the skin and soft tissues of the body to reveal the hard structures beneath.

Wilhelm Konrad Röntgen was born in Germany in 1845, but when he was three, his family moved to Holland and took Dutch citizenship. He was not a particularly successful student. In 1862, caught laughing at a caricature of an unpopular teacher, he was expelled from a technical school in Utrecht when he refused to name the offending artist. So he never obtained the correct credentials to enter university, and only gained entrance to – and a degree from – the Zurich Polytechnic by persuading the authorities to admit him without first passing the required examination.

Nevertheless, in 1888, after working at a number of colleges and universities, Röntgen finally landed the position of Professor of Physics at the University of Würzburg as well as the directorship of the new physics institute.

A FAINT GREEN CLOUD

Röntgen grew interested in cathode rays – the glow that radiates from one of two wires sealed in a vacuum in a glass Crookes tube when a high voltage is applied between them. Late on the afternoon of 8 November 1895, he was working alone in his laboratory. Having darkened the room and wrapped a Crookes tube in black cardboard to screen out the light it emitted, he was surprised to find that, on turning on the current, a small object on his workbench glowed – an effect like a faint green cloud. He discovered that the object was a small, fluorescent, cardboard screen that he had coated with barium platinocyanide. The tube was obviously producing something else besides cathode rays; invisible rays emitted by it were passing through the cardboard covering the tube and hitting the screen.

With increasing excitement, he moved the tube further away; the screen continued to glow. Completely absorbed, he had to be called to dinner several times before the message sank in. He ate little, and that in silence, and his wife thought he was in a bad mood.

Things did not improve for Frau Röntgen: during the following weeks, her husband virtually vanished from home as he carried out experiment after experiment. If the rays could pass through cardboard and air, thought Röntgen, they must pass through other things as well. He tested a double deck of playing cards, a 1000-page book, wood, hard rubber and sheets of various metals. It appeared that only lead blocked the rays completely, and to make doubly sure

BELOW *One of the first X-ray photographs, by S. Rowland in 1896, the year that Röntgen's discovery swept the world.*

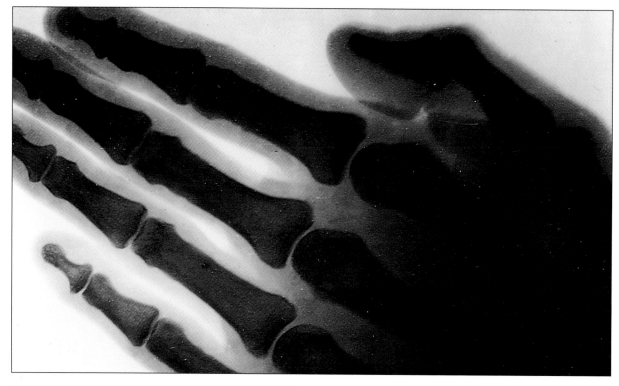

Röntgen held a small piece of lead between tube and screen. Not only was the shadow of the lead clearly visible on the screen, but also the outline of his thumb and finger and, within this, the dense bones of his hand.

Knowing that cathode rays could darken a photographic plate, he asked Frau Röntgen to hold her hand on a plate, while he directed rays on to it for 15 minutes. When the plate was developed, her hand was clearly outlined, and its bones and the two rings she wore were distinct light areas within the dark shadows of the surrounding flesh. She shuddered at the sight of her own skeleton.

Röntgen announced his discovery in a paper – *Eine neue Art von Strahlen* (*A New Kind of Ray*) – which he sent to the Würzburg Physical-Medical Society a few days before Christmas. News of the rays – which Röntgen called X-rays because their nature was unknown – reached the newspapers, and, in January 1896, the story swept the world.

Röntgen was suddenly famous, and he received, in 1901, the first Nobel Prize for Physics. However, he retained his humility, refusing to use the aristocratic 'von' conferred on him by the Bavarian government, donating his Nobel prize

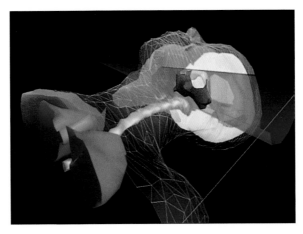

ABOVE *A computer 3-D image of a patient undergoing radiation therapy - another by-product of Röntgen's discovery. The tumour is coloured brown, and the green cone shows the radiation path.*

BELOW *A double-tube X-ray machine of the type invented by US physicist William David Coolidge in 1913. Electrons stream toward the central plate: a few turn into X-rays; the rest diffuse as heat.*

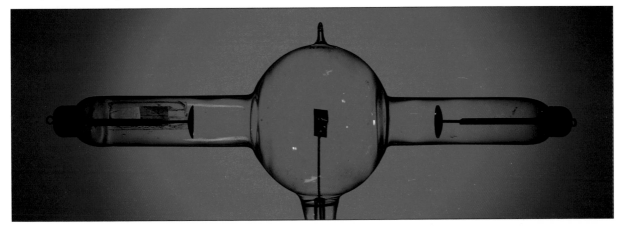

money to the University of Würzburg to be used in the interest of science, and deprecating the practice of calling his X-rays 'Röntgen rays'.

UNDERWEAR, OPERA GLASSES AND GOLD

Röntgen's discovery had an immediate impact on medicine. Initially, only bones were examined with this new diagnostic tool, but soon other things were seen: a broken needle in a seamstress's wrist; a coin swallowed by a child; gallstones; bullets. In 1898, a mobile X-ray unit accompanied the British army to the Sudan, where Kitchener was attempting to defeat the Dervishes. Past and future touched as some of those whose wounds were examined in this, the first military use of X-rays, had participated in the last British cavalry charge, at the Battle of Omdurman.

Researchers began experiments to discover a medium opaque to X-rays that would allow hollow internal organs to show up. One unsuccessful attempt to visualize the oesophagus involved patients swallowing small rubber bags containing lead. Then, in December 1896, an American medical student, later the distinguished physiologist Walter B. Cannon, found that when laboratory animals ingested bismuth salts it was possible to observe the workings of their intestines on a fluorescent screen. Eight years later, in 1904, the procedure was tried successfully on humans with the

substitution of the less dangerous barium sulphate. Barium meal and barium enema X-rays became routine for decades, until largely superseded by endoscopy.

X-rays prompted a variety of outlandish claims. When concern was expressed that X-rays would enable peeping Toms to look through women's clothing, an enterprising London firm advertised its underwear as X-ray proof, and the state of New Jersey outlawed non-existent X-ray opera glasses. An Ohio farmer claimed to have turned base metal into gold with X-rays, and a New York paper reported that the state college of physicians was using X-rays to imprint anatomical drawings on to the brains of medical students.

The dangers of X-rays were recognized as early as 1902, when the researcher A. Frieban reported a relationship between exposure to them and skin cancer. Despite this, until well into the 1950s they were extensively used for antenatal diagnosis and even in shoe shops to measure children's feet. Then, in 1956, a study demonstrated the link between childhood cancer and exposure to X-rays.

Yet there was a place for X-rays in medical treatment. Shortly after Röntgen's announcement of his discovery, the German surgeon Georg Perthes used them to treat a malignant tumour, and with the Curies' discoveries (*see pp 128-9*), radiation therapy became increasingly common in the fight against cancer.

RADIATION

The Curies discovered radiation in a "cross between a stable and a potato-cellar"

A FEW WEEKS AFTER Röntgen's discovery, the French scientist Henri Becquerel set aside a Saturday to discover the X-ray potential of uranium salts placed over a photographic plate shielded by aluminium and exposed to sunlight. However, the day was dull and he wrapped up the uranium and shielded plate and put them in a drawer.

For some reason, he later developed the plate without carrying out the intended experiment, and found it had darkened at the spot where the uranium salts had been placed; so, he reasoned, the mineral must emit rays that, like X-rays, penetrate matter. Becquerel published a number of papers on the subject but then lost interest.

POLONIUM AND RADIUM

Two years later, in 1897, 30-year-old Marie Curie chose the study of uranium rays for her doctoral thesis. Born in Warsaw as Marie Sklodowska, she had left Poland in 1891 to study at the Sorbonne in Paris, and by 1894 had earned herself master's degrees in both physics and mathematics.

In that year, Marie met fellow scientist Pierre Curie, and despite her homesickness, they married in July 1895. Two years later, their daughter Irène was born; within months, Marie was investigating uranium rays at the Sorbonne's School of Physics and Chemistry, where Pierre taught.

ABOVE *Marie and Pierre Curie in their laboratory, from the cover of* Le Parisien, a *French magazine, of January 1904.*

During her study of uranium compounds, she had noticed that pitchblende – uranium oxide ore that occurs in tar-like masses – was four times as active as uranium itself. In April 1898, she wrote a short paper for the Acadèmie des Sciences announcing the probable existence of a new element far more active than uranium.

Pierre abandoned his own work on crystals and joined Marie in the race to discover the mysterious new element. Laboriously, they refined the $3^{1}/_{2}$ oz (100g) of pitchblende available to them and, by the end of June, had isolated a substance that was 330 times as active – or, as the Curies described it, 'radioactive' – as uranium. In July, they announced the discovery of the new element 'polonium', named after Marie's beloved Poland.

By November, it was apparent that the refined pitchblende liquid left over after the polonium had been removed was still very radioactive: there had to be another undiscovered element in pitchblende. Further refining eventually produced a substance that was 900 times more radioactive than uranium. On 26 December 1898, the Curies announced the discovery of radium.

TOILING IN THE POTATO-CELLAR

Radium turned out to be only a one-millionth part of pitchblende. The Curies despaired when they realized that they needed a vast quantity of the expensive ore to recover any significant amount of the element.

However, they were able to buy cheaply several tonnes of pitchblende residue (with the costly uranium already conveniently removed), which was deposited outside the abandoned shed, once a dissecting room, loaned to them as a workplace by the Sorbonne. The glass roof leaked and they roasted in summer and froze in winter; a visiting German chemist described their 'laboratory' as "a cross between a stable and a potato-cellar".

For almost four years, they worked in these primitive conditions: grinding, dissolving, filtering, precipitating, redissolving, crystallizing and recrystallizing the pitchblende to produce radium. Yet Marie later wrote that these were "the best and happiest years of our life". Their progress could be measured by sight: the refined liquid and crystals glowed in the dark. By 1902, they had isolated one tenth of a gram of pure radium.

Pierre's teaching job could not support a family and research. Although he had offers of professorships abroad, the Sorbonne refused to recognize his genius, and, finally, Marie was forced to teach science at a girls' school at Sèvres. In 1903, she became pregnant again, but the baby was premature and died – perhaps a result of Marie's overwork, or the materials with which she was working.

Then, in late 1903, the Curies shared the Nobel prize for physics with Henri Becquerel for their work on radioactivity. Their prize money – 70,000 francs – solved their financial worries and the Sorbonne created a professorship for Pierre and provided him with a laboratory, with Marie as his chief assistant. She became pregnant again and this time her daughter, Eve, was born safe and well.

THE BIRTH OF NUCLEAR MEDICINE

Both Marie and Becquerel had burned themselves accidently when carrying phials of radium in their pockets, and in 1901, Pierre burned himself deliberately by strapping some to his arm. The phenomenon excited him – X-rays were being used to treat cancer, so perhaps needles of radium would work as well. When, in 1904, it was proved that radium rays killed diseased cells preferentially, there was great commercial interest in the element. However, dedicated to science, the Curies refused to patent their refining process, thus failing to gain any financial benefit from their discoveries.

In 1906, tragedy struck when Pierre was killed by a heavy horse-drawn cart. Refusing a state pension, Marie was offered Pierre's professorship, so becoming the first woman professor at the Sorbonne. In 1911, she was rewarded twice: she was the first to receive a second Nobel prize, this time for chemistry, for the discovery of radium; and the Sorbonne and the Pasteur Institute provided funds for a Radium Institute. With the outbreak of World War I, she flung herself into supporting her adopted country, spending her Nobel money on French war bonds, organizing a fleet of X-ray field ambulances and establishing more than 200 X-ray departments in hospitals.

Although Marie never equalled her early discoveries, the Curie connection with the new science of nuclear medicine continued. Her daughter Irène, also a scientist, married Frédéric Joliot, a colleague at the Radium Institute, and in January 1934, the Curie-Joliots succeeded in inducing radioactivity in non-radioactive elements, the results being

known as 'radioisotopes'. Later, when their manufacture was made easier with the 1931 invention of the cyclotron by the American physicist Ernest O. Lawrence, these isotopes would be used extensively in medical diagnosis. In 1935, Irène and Frédéric were awarded the Nobel Prize for Chemistry, but Marie was not there to share their triumph. In July 1934, she had died of radiation sickness, the toll that her long years of work had taken.

PUBLIC HEALTH

IMPROVING THE WELL-BEING OF ALL CITIZENS

'A new concept of dirt' led to organized gymnastics and physical culture

IN THE EARLY 20TH CENTURY, infectious diseases still killed millions, but there had been improvement in health, as war statistics show. In the Crimean War of the 1850s, disease killed ten times more soldiers than did battle wounds. In the Boer War of 1899–1902, five times as many died of disease – 11,000 from typhoid alone, even though

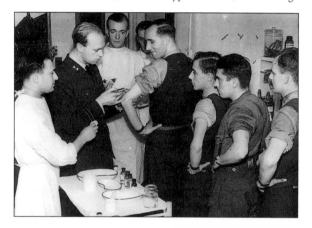

the British scientist Almroth Wright had developed a vaccine in 1898. Because of improved living conditions and food, an unpolluted water supply and a mass vaccination programme, the Russo-Japanese War of 1904–5 became the first in which more soldiers died directly from warfare than from disease.

THE PUBLIC VERSUS THE INDIVIDUAL

World War I and the influenza pandemic that followed (*see p.109*) reinforced the belief that the state must be concerned with the health of all citizens. Schemes for systematically surveying, monitoring and keeping track of people and their health were set up and public health laboratories were founded.

However, many also believed that individuals should take more responsibility for their own health. In part, this was due to 'a new concept of dirt'. No longer were massive environmental problems a great cause for concern, but rather

LEFT *Vaccination was vital if the fighting men and women were to stay healthy and fit for combat during World War II – here RAF recruits line up to get their 'jabs' in January 1942.*

ASBESTOS AND DISEASE

In 1906, the British doctor Montague Murray officially named asbestosis (scarring of the lung tissue, leading to chronic debilitating illness) as the cause of death of a former asbestos worker.

When a third victim was diagnosed in the late 1920s, the British Home Office authorized two researchers, Merewether and Price, to carry out the first study of the mineral's effect on occupational health. Their report, published in 1930, found that, of a sample of 374 asbestos workers, 105 had lung scarring, and a quarter of these had definitely contracted the disease through their work. They concluded that reducing dust levels would reduce the incidence of asbestosis, and advised that efficient exhaust ventilation be provided, and that some workers should be replaced by machines. Within 18 months of their report, the British government recommended their conclusions to all asbestos manufacturers.

The link between asbestos and cancer took longer to confirm. Reports of high rates of lung cancer in asbestos workers appeared in 1935, 1947, 1949 and 1951. Then, Dr Irving Selikoff of Paterson, New Jersey, began working with local branches of the asbestos insulator workers' union. In 1964, with Jacob Churg and E. Cuyler Hammond, he published an influential article describing how, out of 632 asbestos workers with 20 or more years in the industry, 255 had died of either mesothelioma, lung cancer or digestive cancer.

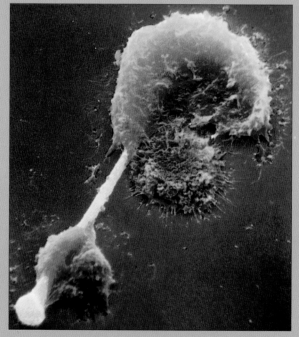

ABOVE *Normally, macrophages – a type of white blood cell (green, on this scan) – destroy foreign bodies, but the virtually indestructible asbestos fibres (white) can break them up.*

THE HUNT FOR TYPHOID MARY

During the first 15 years of the 20th century, one woman was an American public health nightmare. Mary Mallon, born in Ireland in 1867, was a good cook and never out of work – which was unfortunate as she was also a symptomless typhoid carrier.

For seven years, she cut a swathe through the northeastern United States: 19 people were certainly infected by her, of which one, a household laundress, died. She may also have been responsible for starting an epidemic of at least 1300 cases in Ithaca, New York, in 1903.

Mary was identified as a carrier at Oyster Bay, Long Island, by Dr George A. Soper. By then she had left for Tuxedo, New York (one person infected), and travelled on to New York City: two servants where she worked became ill and the daughter of the family died. When, in 1907, Dr

Soper finally tracked her down and presented his evidence, she attacked him with a cleaver. She had to be physically restrained when the City Health Department transported her to Riverside Hospital.

There she remained until 1910, becoming notorious through the press as 'Typhoid Mary'. Finally gaining her release with a promise to give up cooking, she immediately disappeared, but a cook known as 'Mrs Brown' popped up all over New York City.

In 1915, she fled from the Sloane Hospital for Women after an epidemic had broken out, with 25 infected and two dying. Police arrested her at her new job on Long Island and she was sentenced to quarantine for life at Riverside Hospital. Mary, who had become known as the 'human culture tube', died there in 1938.

BELOW *The public health drive for 'physical culture' gave rise to events such as this display at the* 'English-Scandinavian Summer School of Physical Education', in the summer of 1936.

the presence of invisible 'germs' passed from person to person. The middle and upper classes responded to this by an increasing interest in 'physical culture': gymnasia, athletics festivals, new types of organized sport and outdoor activities.

Another response was the emphasis placed on health education, which had its beginnings in the fight against sexually transmitted diseases (STDs). In 1910, Sir William Osler, then Regius Professor of Medicine at Oxford, estimated that, in England and Wales, 60,000 adults died of syphilis each year. This figure did not decline, despite Ehrlich's discovery of Salvarsan (*see pp.100-1*). Indeed, 25 per cent of all troops in Europe during World War I were incapacitated by syphilis and gonorrhoea.

The French dealt with STDs by establishing *maisons tolerées*, or regulated brothels. British soldiers simply received a warning from Lord Kitchener:

"... You may find temptations both in wine and women. You must entirely resist both temptations, and, while treating all women with perfect courtesy, you should avoid any intimacy. Do your duty bravely, Fear God, Honour the King".

The British did, however, realize that returning soldiers would soon make this a civilian problem, and in 1916 and 1917, laws were passed to enable local authorities to provide diagnosis, treatment and public education. This educative role – concerned almost exclusively with sexual continence – was primarily carried out through meetings, school biology lessons, pamphlets and films by the National Council for Combating Venereal Disease, formed "to fight the terrible peril of our imperial race".

OPPOSITION TO CHANGE

After World War I, American medicine, led by such institutions as Johns Hopkins, overtook the European. The United States model was research-based, but, in Britain and in Europe, there was great hostility towards the basic sciences, despite the legacies of such medical innovators as Claude Bernard and Louis Pasteur.

There were other differences, too. In Europe, and especially in Germany and Britain (*see pp.140-1*), the trend was towards national health insurance schemes. Some Americans were enthusiastic about the 'Zemstvo system' of free medical care for the rural population of pre-revolutionary Russia, and attempted to enact similar programmes in New York, California and elsewhere. However, with the Bolshevik takeover in Russia, the 'Red scare' had already begun in the US.

Accusations that these programmes were steps towards communism were blamed by public health reformer C. E. A. Winslow on the "overactive hormonal secretions" of the accusers, but they effectively stopped the schemes. Only one large public health programme saw the light of day: in 1921, the Sheppard–Towner Act provided federal grants to set up state infant health clinics.

During the Depression of the 1930s, the federal government financed a survey of 800,000 families, which revealed unemployment, starvation wages, appalling housing, inadequate nutrition and a stark connection between poverty and illness. The National Health Conference in Washington in 1938 recommended a programme including maternal and child welfare, care of the indigent, and health and disability insurance. It was defeated by the American Medical Association, which remained adamantly opposed to change.

5 The World at War

*T*he two world wars of the first half of the 20th century claimed lives at a rate unimaginable in former ages. And, for the first time, civilian populations were closely involved: in World War I, starvation was employed as a weapon against a whole country; while gas and high explosives caused havoc at the front. In World War II, area bombing wiped out whole towns; and the use of the atomic bomb led to long, slow deaths from radiation sickness, as well as causing indescribable destruction.

Yet some good – in medical terms, at least – did come from the horrors of war. For example, the major problem of wound infection in World War I was eased considerably during the next war by sulpha drugs and, on the Allied side, by penicillin; while treatment of the grotesque burns suffered by aircrew in World War II led to extraordinary advances in plastic surgery.

However, some of the most wide-ranging progress brought about by war came in the area of social medicine. Food rationing in Britain, the content of the ration being based on the latest research on diet and nutrition, made the population healthier between 1939 and 1945 than it had ever been before, or has been since. And the sacrifices of the fighting men and women, as well as those of civilians, led to a demand for the state provision of medical care, free and by right – in 1948, despite objections by the medical profession Britain's National Health Service came into being.

At the end of World War II, though, it became clear that something had taken place that was more terrible than war itself. It seemed almost inconceivable, but the truth was that both German and Japanese doctors and scientists had broken all codes of medical and humanitarian ethics, by experimenting methodically, cruelly and cynically on prisoners of war and civilians.

ABOVE St Mary's First Aid Post by Candlelight *by Anna Katrina Zinkeisen.*

NEW WOUNDS AND DISEASES

WAR BRINGS DIFFERENT CHALLENGES

Gas attacks killed 91,000 and left 1.3 million troops with inflamed lungs

THE MEDICAL AND HYGIENE lessons learned in the Crimean, Boer and Russo-Japanese wars were put to good use in the two world wars of the 20th century. Few major discoveries were made during the conflicts, but existing knowledge was refined and expanded.

THE HOME FRONT

Rejection rates of potential soldiers are a good indication of the general health of a population. In Britain, during World War I, medical examinations showed that a great many working-class men were unfit for military service: in September 1916, 28.9 per cent were rejected. However, by 1939, only 2.3 per cent of army applicants were declared unfit – a remarkable turnaround.

This improvement in health applied to the population in general. In England and Wales in 1910, life expectancy was 48.5 years for men and 52.4 years for women. By 1939, the figures had risen to 60.2 and 64.6 respectively.

Paradoxically, despite the casualties and dead, civilians on both sides thrived during World War II. Food rationing gave the British, and to a lesser extent the Germans, a far better diet, and children and pregnant women had free or cheap milk and vitamin supplements. The trend towards national health care (*see pp.140-1*) and social service provision accelerated. In Britain, a progressive tax structure redistributed wealth away from the middle classes and towards the working classes: the proportion of those poor enough to receive free milk fell from 30 per cent in 1940 to 2 per cent in 1945. As a result, in Britain the rates for infant, neonatal and maternal mortality and stillbirth were the lowest on record, and the birthrate was the highest for 15 years.

GAS, HIGH-EXPLOSIVE AND SHRAPNEL

The two world wars brought new wounds and illnesses. In World War I, high-explosive and shrapnel shells tore bodies apart and riddled them with metal splinters and parts of uniform already covered with the bacteria-filled mud of Flanders' fields. The trenches gave soldiers two louse-borne disease – a kidney disease (trench nephritis) and a million cases of trench fever – and trench foot, the result of prolonged standing in water.

Artillery shells bursting close by made some men shell-shocked, while others suffered heavily from head wounds. Attacks of poison gas – chlorine, phosgene and mustard – killed 91,000 and left 1.3 million troops with inflamed lungs, almost drowning in their own fluids, or with bodies covered in first- and second-degree burns.

World War II saw a 50 per cent reduction in troops laid low by disease. This was due not only to mass immunization programmes and the new drugs that had been discovered (*see*

LEFT "Travoys Arriving with Wounded at a Dressing-Station at Smol, Macedonia in September 1916", *by British artist Sir Stanley Spencer, a medical orderly in World War I. "I was standing a little way from the old Greek church", he remembered, "... and coming there were rows of travoys and limbers crammed full of wounded men .... I felt there was a terrible grandeur... all those wounded men were calm and at peace .... I felt there was a spiritual ascendancy over everything."*

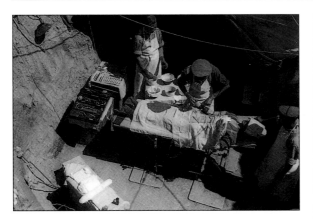

ABOVE *A British Army surgeon* *arm in the operation dug-out of a*
removes a bullet from a soldier's *World War II Field Ambulance.*

below), but also to the fact that trench warfare had been
abandoned and part of the fighting was carried out on the far
more sterile soil of the North African desert. However,
terrible new injuries were visited on the young aircrews who
fought the Battle of Britain (*see pp.138-9*), and after 6 and 9
August 1945, at Hiroshima and Nagasaki, Japan, the world
had to deal for the first time with the deadly and long-
lasting effects of radiation.

NEW TREATMENTS

If the servicemen of the two world wars were exposed to
new horrors in the art of warfare, they were also able to
take advantage of treatments that had been unavailable to
their predecessors.

Soldiers of World War I benefited, first, from Almroth
Wright's typhoid vaccine, and then, in 1916, from the new
typhoid-paratyphoid A & B (TAB) vaccine. Deaths from
typhoid were only 1 per cent of those of the Boer War.

Many had died in previous wars when oxygen-hating
tetanus spores penetrated deep wounds. Although a vaccine
was produced during World War I, the disease was still
commonplace. But it was rare by 1939: during the 1940
British retreat to Dunkirk, only seven of the 16,000
wounded developed tetanus. Typhus, too, was largely eradicated during World War II (*see box*).

However, infectious disease remained a problem as long
as there were few drugs to fight bacteria. In the 1914–18
conflict, the astonishingly inventive physiologist Henry
Hallett Dale (*see p.102*) introduced bismuth iodide, taken by
mouth to treat amoebic dysentery. The soldiers of World
War II reaped the benefit of the discovery of sulpha drugs
(*see pp.106-7*). Quinine was in short supply, but with the
synthesis of mepacrine, soldiers in the Far East were
protected from malaria. However, the biggest breakthrough
was the development of penicillin (*see pp.136-7*).

Other treatments also had a major impact. On the eve of
World War II, the British army established its own blood
transfusion service, where plasma – the liquid part of the
blood which can be given to anyone, regardless of blood
type – was dried and powdered. It could be kept almost
indefinitely and then turned back into a liquid with the
addition of sterile, distilled water.

The low death rate among those wounded during the
Normandy landings of June 1944 was largely due to the
blood carried by landing craft, ships, transport planes and

gliders. Plasma was dropped in wicker baskets to isolated
troops, and blood transfusions were the first and most vital
treatment for horribly burned aircrews.

The speed at which medical services were available was
also important. Doctors frequently parachuted into remote
areas. In one instance, when a hospital was destroyed, 80
American aircraft flew in a new 200-bed unit with all its
equipment in one day. Casualties were also transported
quickly to sophisticated medical treatment centres. In 1943,
the US army evacuated 173,527 sick and wounded by air to
base hospitals, losing only 11 men during the flights.

BELOW *Plasma transfusion techniques* *care of casualties in World War II,*
and sulpha drugs revolutionized the *and greatly increased survival rates.*

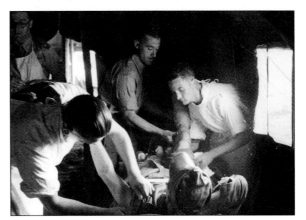

PENICILLIN

THE DISCOVERY OF THE FIRST ANTIBIOTIC

It took 12 years for anyone to realize a strange growth was a life-saver

A BRILLIANT MEDICAL STUDENT, Alexander Fleming (1881–1955) intended becoming a surgeon. However, in 1906, simply to stay in the hospital's rifle shooting team, he took a temporary job at London's St Mary's Hospital, Paddington. The post was in the Inoculation Department headed by the famous scientist Almroth Wright. Fleming remained there for 49 years.

Fleming's discovery of the strange mould *Penicillium notatum* has achieved the status of folklore. In 1928, a culture dish on which he was growing bacteria became contaminated by mould spores – not blown in through an open window as once supposed, but probably having floated up the stairs from a laboratory below where an allergy researcher was investigating rare moulds. The culture dish was probably left on a workbench in the unheated room while Fleming went on a three-week holiday. The weather – first cold enough to allow the mould to grow, then warm enough to make the bacteria flourish – did the trick. On his return, he noticed that the bacteria near the mould had been killed. Obviously a powerful antibiotic substance – which he called 'penicillin' – had seeped out from the mould.

Fleming investigated his new specimen for a couple of months. He found that penicillin was effective against microbes responsible for a variety of serious infections, but it did not interfere with the action of white cells. He even showed that it was non-toxic to healthy animals. However, he did not take the next obvious step: to give it to animals deliberately inoculated with deadly bacteria.

The reason behind this important omission was that, after mixing pencillin and blood in his laboratory, he found that the drug lost most of its power. Fleming, the supreme technician, did not realize that what might happen in a test tube could be very different from what happens in the human body. In 1929, he published a rather vague description of his discovery, and then turned to other things. He never made another breakthrough.

"IT LOOKS LIKE A MIRACLE!"

Penicillin would never have reached the world as an antibiotic medicine if it had not been for the brilliant, if irascible, Australian pathologist, Howard Florey. In 1935, at the age of 37, Florey became head of the Dunn School of Pathology at Oxford, where he hired the ebullient biochemist Ernst Chain, a German Jew who had just fled from the Nazis. Together they searched the scientific literature systematically, looking for anti-bacterial substances.

After examining more than 200 papers, Chain came across Fleming's report. Luckily, he and Florey already had a sample of *P. notatum*, and they began to grow it. They soon discovered the difficulties involved in isolating the active ingredient from the liquid the mould produces – only one

BELOW *This stained-glass window in St James Church, Paddington, London, shows Sir Alexander Fleming at work in his laboratory* at nearby St Mary's Hospital, *where penicillin was discovered in 1928 – but not recognized for another 12 years.*

part in two million is pure penicillin. They might have given up if Norman Heatley, another biochemist on the team, had not devised a way of transferring the penicillin back into water by changing its acidity.

By then, Britain was at war. Despite lack of funds and equipment and the risk of air raids, the scientists continued purifying the drug and began to test it. On Saturday, 25 May 1940, they inoculated eight mice with fatal doses of streptococci; four were then given penicillin. By 3.45 a.m. the following morning, the mice that had not had the drug

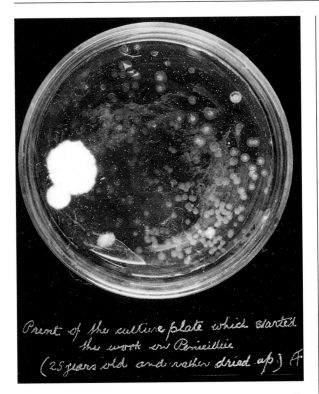

Print of the culture plate which started
the work on Penicillin
(25 years old and rather dried up) F

LEFT *A photograph of the original culture plate on which Sir Alexander Fleming grew* Penicillium *notatum, taken some 25 years after the event and, as one would expect, "rather dried up".*

were dead, but the four treated mice were alive and well. Florey, normally noted for understatement, exulted: "It looks like a miracle!"

Florey realized the potential of the drug, especially for treating war wounds, and his university department soon became a factory. Heatley found that the best container for growing penicillin mould was a hospital bedpan. Finally, they thought they had just enough of the drug to try it on a human patient: a policeman, Albert Alexander, who was near death, his body covered with abscesses. There was, in fact, so little of it available that, during the first day of treatment, all of Alexander's urine was collected to recover as much penicillin as possible. This was given to the policeman on the third day; by the fourth, he had improved remarkably, but then the drug ran out and he died.

The team later treated four other patients successfully, but Florey soon concluded that his laboratory could not produce enough penicillin for a proper clinical trial. He approached British pharmaceutical companies, but they were too busy trying to supply the country's wartime needs. So, in July 1941, with Norman Heatley in tow to explain the details of the team's production methods, Florey went to the United States.

BRITISH VERSUS AMERICAN

Florey generated enough interest from the US Department of Agriculture for its staff to refer him to the Northern Regional Research Laboratory in Peoria, Illinois. Here, researchers were experts on fermentation processes.

Heatley remained there for several weeks, working with Andrew J. Moyer, who extracted as much information from the British scientist as possible, but refused to share his own findings. By now, the Americans had entered the war. Moyer had managed to increase the yield of penicillin 34 times, and three US pharmaceutical companies were showing interest. So was the US government, and soon the penicillin

project was sharing top priority for federal funds with the development of the atomic bomb.

Florey returned to Britain with the promise of sufficient penicillin to conduct proper trials. However, he received only three tiny samples, and was thrown back on the extremely limited resources of his Oxford laboratory. All the US penicillin was reserved for American troops.

Even fame eluded Florey. In 1942, Fleming asked for some penicillin to treat a dying friend; when news of the man's dramatic recovery appeared in *The Times*, Almroth Wright followed with a letter ascribing the discovery of the drug to his protégé Fleming – and the myth began.

By 1943, British drug companies had begun to mass-produce penicillin, and, in May, Florey travelled to North Africa, where tests of the drug on war wounds were extraordinarily successful. Penicillin also cured gonorrhoea, and the generals were keen to treat the thousands of troops affected, so that they could join the invasion of Sicily. Florey was opposed to diverting treatment from the seriously wounded to the self-infected, but was overruled.

By D-Day, in June 1944, enough penicillin was available to allow unlimited treatment of all Allied servicemen. The Germans, Japanese and Italians never discovered the secret, hence the significant number of amputees to be seen in these countries after the war was over.

In 1945, Alexander Fleming, Howard Florey and Ernst Chain shared the Nobel prize for the discovery of penicillin. The hard-working Norman Heatley received nothing – except the proverbial slap in the face. Andrew Moyer had written up his carefully guarded research and published it in his name alone, even though Heatley's work had been its basis. Then, in 1945, Moyer took out a British patent on the production process, from which he earned millions of dollars. It was not until October 1990 that Norman Heatley was rewarded for his contribution, receiving an honorary doctorate of medicine from Oxford University.

ABOVE *Sir Alexander Fleming in his laboratory. He discovered* penicillin, but never realized its extraordinary significance.

McINDOE'S 'GUINEA PIGS'

ADVANCES IN PLASTIC SURGERY

A tartar in the theatre, he was much loved outside it

PLASTIC SURGERY WAS PRACTISED in ancient India (*see p.17*), and, during the Renaissance, Gasparo di Tagliacozzi grafted skin, still attached to the upper arm, on to faces to form new noses. In 1869, the French surgeons F.J.C. Guyon and Jacques Reverdin independently reported that they had grown grafts on large wounds using very thin, millimetre-sized, free skin transplants.

However, this method was time-consuming, and while the wound remained uncovered, the risk of infection increased. A great breakthrough was made by the German surgeon Carl Thiersch, who proved that, by initially cleaning the granulation tissue off the wound, it was possible to graft on pieces of skin the size of postage stamps, cut with a thin double-edged knife or razor blade.

SOLDIERS' FACES

The new weapons of World War I caused horrific facial injuries, and to deal with these, Harold Delf Gillies set up a jaw and plastic surgery unit at Aldershot in southern England. Gillies was one of the first plastic surgeons to take the patient's appearance into consideration, unlike his counterparts in Germany and in France, where, it was said, "a plastic patient looked horrible when he went in and ridiculous when he came out".

After the Battle of the Somme in 1916, Gillies dealt personally with some 2000 cases of facial damage, but his war work brought him little recognition. However, he made the headlines in January 1924 when he was rushed to Copenhagen to treat about two dozen Danish seamen who had been burned in an accident.

In 1932, Gillies hired as his assistant Archibald Hector McIndoe (1900–60), a distant cousin from New Zealand, who had been working at the Mayo Clinic in Rochester, Minnesota. Under Gillies' tutelage and with the amount of available work, McIndoe's technique soon became remarkably sophisticated, and in 1938, he replaced his cousin as consultant in plastic surgery to the Royal Air Force.

Shortly after World War II began, McIndoe founded a unit at the Queen Victoria Hospital in East Grinstead, Sussex. He remained a civilian, and so was able to fight for what he wanted unhindered by military red tape. The Battle of Britain in 1940, and the air war that followed, brought McIndoe some 4000 young men with new injuries: terrible burns to the face and hands from ignited high-octane fuel.

McIndoe felt that 'plastic surgery' did not truly describe what was required for these injuries, which frequently took years and dozens of operations to rectify, so he coined the term 'reconstructive surgery'. For whole-face injuries, he first used Gillies' tubed pedicle graft – a large piece of skin from the donor site, which remained attached by a stalk to give a blood supply until a new one established itself. But this was laborious, and when an epidemic of haemolytic streptococci swept the hospital and the pedicle grafts proved to be very susceptible to infection, he changed to free grafts, which 'took' more quickly.

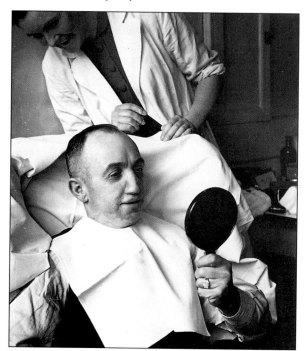

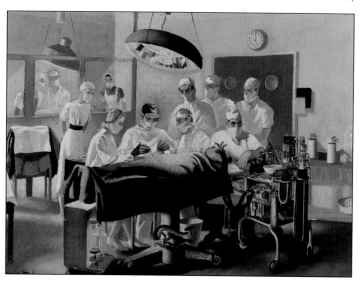

LEFT *'Archie' McIndoe in the operating theatre at East Grinstead in 1944, painted by Anna Katrina Zinkeisen, a nurse at the hospital.*

ABOVE *McIndoe's techniques were used on minor injuries, too: here a soldier admires his reconstructed nose and skin graft in 1944.*

ABOVE *In July 1955, McIndoe opened a children's wing at East Grinstead, where this child is recovering from plastic surgery.*

McIndoe was a surgical artist, cutting complicated shapes from skin freehand, but it was probably his attitude towards his patients that made him a great surgeon. He ensured that, in his ward, the radio and loudspeaker system emitted a barrage of sound to take the men's minds off their injuries and drown out the groans of those in the salt baths having their dressings changed. Knowing that those under his care did not want sympathy but straight talk, he discussed his intended surgical procedures thoroughly with each man, and even invited patients to watch him operate. A tartar in the operating theatre, outside it he was completely informal, and known as 'Archie'.

In the summer of 1942, McIndoe's patients decided to form a society for those who had passed through the East Grinstead ward. At first, they called themselves the 'Maxillonians', since the hospital was officially a maxillo-facial unit. However, a few months later, a burned RAF man, waiting for what must have seemed like his hundredth operation, was heard to grumble: "We're not fliers any more. We're nothing but a plastic surgeon's guinea pigs!".

The name stuck, and 'McIndoe's Guinea Pigs' soon numbered more than 600 members of 16 nationalities – British, Canadian, Polish, Czech, and Australian among others. With McIndoe's support – he was voted life-time president – the club raised morale enormously, and even long after the war, inspired intense loyalty.

MICROSURGERY AND LEECHES

Re-attaching severed fingers, hands, arms and feet became theoretically possible when, in 1908, Alexis Carrel (see p.125) invented the method of suturing blood vessels for which he was awarded the 1912 Nobel prize. However, sewing up the smaller vessels – some only a third of a millimetre in diameter – was impossible until about 1960, with the invention of efficient operating microscopes and appropriate suturing material – thread finer than a human hair permanently attached to the end of a needle about three millimetres long.

When the technique of nerve reconstruction was introduced in 1967, the way was clear for full re-attachment of severed extremities. A year later, the surgeons Komatsu and Tamai successfully replanted a severed thumb.

One astonishing result of microsurgery was the reintroduction of leeches to medicine in the 1980s. Sometimes, when the tiny arteries and veins of, say, a severed finger are sewn back together, the reattached veins do not immediately recover and must be allowed to rest. To keep the finger well supplied with oxygen, fresh blood is continuously pumped through the arteries; but with no outlet through the veins, the finger can become engorged, threatening its survival.

A leech attached to the finger for about 20 minutes drains off the surplus blood; and even when it is removed, the blood continues to flow out for up to 12 hours, relieving the congestion until the veins recover and take over. This bleeding occurs because a leech's saliva contains hirudin, a substance that prevents blood coagulating. The only alternative to a leech would be to give the patient anticoagulant drugs, which would affect the whole body, not just the affected part.

BELOW *Today, twin binocular operating microscopes allow two doctors to work on a patient simultaneously during microsurgery.*

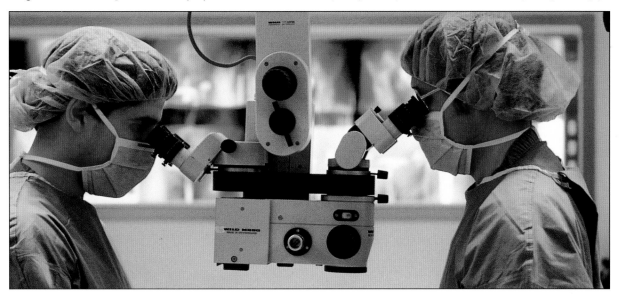

HEALTH CARE FOR ALL

BRITAIN'S NATIONAL HEALTH SERVICE

Doctors were bitterly opposed, but a radical firebrand won the day

ON THE EVE OF WORLD WAR II, British experts predicted that 300,000 people would die and 600,000 would be wounded each month as a result of German bombing raids on Britain. The figures, as it turned out, were a gross overestimate. But their impact on political leaders of the day played a large part in the creation of Britain's National Health Service. In scope, scale and accessibility, this NHS provides a yardstick against which other countries still measure their own public health programmes decades later.

A NATIONAL JIGSAW

The prewar British hospital system (*see p.130*) could not have coped with casualties on the levels predicted. It was impossibly fragmented, with each hospital functioning more or less as an independent unit under the auspices of a local authority or voluntary board, and restricting admissions according to a host of varying geographic, medical, financial and other criteria. To meet the anticipated needs of war, it had to be reorganized on national lines. In 1938–9, the government created the Emergency Medical Service (EMS) to do the job.

Through the EMS, more than 1000 of the biggest hospitals (between one quarter and one third of the total number) were brought under the administrative and financial control of the state. Their resources were assessed and their roles allocated to fit them as pieces into a national jigsaw. Hospitals in towns, for example, became casualty clearing centres, while those in rural areas, away from the worst dangers of bombing, were used for long-term care. The medical and ancillary staff, now EMS employees, could be directed to serve anywhere in the network where their particular skills were needed. The government pumped in funds to build new operating theatres and wards, to create ambulance and blood transfusion services, and generally to ensure that EMS patients received the best treatment available – promptly and at no charge.

At first, the EMS facilities were open only to military personnel and civilians wounded as a direct result of the war. Gradually, however, the service was extended to others whose occupations were vital to the war effort, such as munitions workers and firefighters, or those who had injuries, such as fractures or serious burns, in which the EMS was developing particular expertise. The system generally worked well, demonstrating to all who had dealings with it the advantages of centralized planning over the old, diffuse and inefficient arrangements.

CONVERGING TRENDS

When the EMS was established, a fierce debate had already been raging over the way in which medical treatment and benefits were administered and financed in Britain. The rich, as always, could buy all the care they required, paying as

ABOVE *A miner at a dispensary in industrial South Wales – Bevan knew how hard life was in such areas, and insisted that help was given.*

they went. The very poor could obtain it for nothing from municipal or charitable institutions, if they were judged to be needy enough. But most Britons fell somewhere between the extremes of wealth and poverty, and it was on this gap that the debate focused.

Under the National Insurance Act, which came into operation in 1911–3, working people were obliged to contribute from their wages to health insurance funds. The funds' committees, dominated by representatives of private insurance companies, then allocated the money to secure medical facilities for their members, pay doctors and provide cash benefits for those too sick to work. The scheme, worthily conceived, was rife with shortcomings.

Both the unemployed and the non-employed dependants of workers were excluded; they still had either to pay in full for treatment or go through a humiliating scrutiny of their means to determine whether they could get it free from municipal medical services. The vested interests of the insurers on the committees often took precedence over medical necessity, antagonizing doctors. On occasion, too, the insurers shamelessly flouted their obligations to pay

LEFT *A Scot born in India, Sir William Beveridge had a distinguished academic career before entering government service and producing the brilliant 'Beveridge Report' in 1942. Its wide-ranging recommendations (which were even studied by Hitler's propagandist, Goebbels) have underpinned a considerable amount of social legislation since. To mark his success, Beveridge was created the 1st Baron Beveridge in 1946.*

compensation – for example, to victims of industrial accidents – thus antagonizing the trade unions.

By 1936, the British Medical Association (BMA), speaking for most family doctors, and the Trades Union Congress (TUC), speaking for National Insurance members and their families, had linked forces to press for a comprehensive health service covering most of the population, organized under the control of the state. In 1941, with the example of the EMS apparent to all, the government established a commission, headed by the economist Sir William Beveridge (1879–1963). His brief was to survey the whole of British social policy and his *Report on Social Insurance and Allied Services* was published in 1942. It was to attain a status almost akin to that of King John's Magna Carta in British popular history.

BEVERIDGE AND BEVAN

In one sense, the Beveridge Report was a morale booster, holding out to ordinary Britons fighting Hitler the pledge of a new, fairer society when victory had been achieved. Its starting-point was the premise that, with a single National Insurance payment each week, all working people could secure for themselves and their families protection against the hardships arising from unemployment, ill health and old age, by ensuring that no individual's income fell below subsistence level. The protection would be granted as of right, not as charity – the basis of the welfare state.

Beveridge's broad recommendations on medical welfare proposed that everybody, irrespective of financial means, age, sex and occupation, should be entitled to the best and most up-to-date medical, dental and related care available, without direct charge except, in some cases, for appliances. In an equally radical vein, the document called for a "new attitude to health", with emphasis on the promotion of well-being as well as on the treatment of disorders – prevention as well as cure. All was to be paid for out of a combination of central taxes, including National Insurance, and local authority charges on property owners (rates).

ABOVE *The British Medical Association debates the proposed National Health Act – at first, opposition was bitter.*

The BMA opposed many of the recommendations regarding doctors' employment, particularly the idea of a salaried service run by a local authority. Their opposition redoubled in 1945, when the war ended and a Labour government was swept to power, with the left-wing firebrand Aneurin Bevan given the job of introducing the NHS. For three years, the BMA, in particular would conducte a campaign against the reforms, and against Bevan himself. But through a series of political manoeuvres and concessions to certain sectors of the medical world, Bevan managed to outflank the BMA.

Bevan's reforms were adopted into law in November 1946, and the appointed day for a universal, free National Health Service to come into being was fixed for 5 July 1948. The diehards of the BMA continued to huff and puff, but under pressure from public opinion, deserted by their hospital colleagues and wooed by Bevan's Welsh charm, family doctors were coming round to the NHS idea. By October 1948, 86 per cent of them had signed up to participate – a proportion that eventually rose to 98 per cent.

BUILDER OF THE NHS

When Aneurin ('Nye') Bevan (1897–1960) was appointed Minister of Health in Britain's Labour government at the end of the World War II, the leaders of the medical establishment had every reason to be suspicious of him. His background was impeccably left wing – the miner son of a Welsh mining family and a leading participant in the General Strike of 1926, who had entered Parliament as Member for Ebbw Vale in 1929. He was, in the Welsh tradition, a fiery orator, and he was no respecter of persons. During the war, when party rivalry was largely abandoned in the name of national unity, he was one of the few persistent parliamentary critics of Prime Minister Winston Churchill.

Nye Bevan's upbringing and political beliefs made him a natural supporter of a free universal health service, as well as the other principles of the welfare state. His guile, even cynicism, acquired over years as a trade union leader enabled him to create it. He was quick to court hospital doctors, in particular the professionally influential senior staff of the teaching hospitals,

and effectively bought them off. Only someone with Bevan's undisputed socialist credentials could have persuaded his fellow-socialists that this was not a cynical betrayal of their egalitarian goals.

Other aspects of socialist dogma were discarded, too, if they hampered Bevan's overall aims. By 1948, many doctors who would never share his politics were forced to concede he appeared a model of conciliation and reason. That year, he produced another master-stroke only he could have got away with. As surgeries and dentists' waiting-rooms filled to the doors with people eligible for free attention for the first time in their lives, he appealed to them publicly not to overload "their" NHS – and they accepted the rebuke.

From 1951, when he was made Minister of Labour, Bevan kept a fatherly eye on his baby. When the government proposed to introduce fixed charges for some NHS facilities, he resigned his office in protest, to become, until his death, a thorn in the flesh of his colleagues as the leader of a left-wing 'Bevanite' faction within the Labour Party.

THE OTHER SIDE OF WAR

Internationally recognized doctors experimented on death-camp inmates

WORLD WAR II BROUGHT a number of medical advances. Unfortunately, it also saw the worst abuses of medicine, when millions were deliberately killed in the name of 'racial hygiene' and others underwent horrific experiments in the cause of what has been called 'murderous science'.

MEDICINE UNDER THE NAZIS

The idea of eugenics (*see p.67*) appealed to many in the German medical establishment from the 1920s, but it did not become institutionalized until after the Nazi takeover in 1933.

The first eugenic crimes were compulsory sterilizations of, among others, people who were mentally handicapped, mentally ill, epileptic, alcoholics – at least 350,000 individuals between 1934 and 1939. Soon murders (which Hitler called 'mercy deaths') were being carried out, including 'euthanasia by starvation' at mental hospitals, and then the deliberate gassing of 70,723 mental patients between January 1940 and September 1941, all chosen from lists prepared by nine professors of psychiatry and 39 medical doctors. Only one psychiatrist objected.

In March 1943, the Nazi leaders decreed that only doctors and pharmacists could 'select' prisoners on arrival at Auschwitz and other extermination camps and supervise the killing process. Many Jews, gypsies and others were specifically chosen for death so that Nazi anatomists could take 'anthropological' measurements and their skeletons could be added to the doctors' collections. Camp doctors – many internationally recognized in their fields – also used inmates to study mustard gas, gas gangrene, freezing, high altitude, ingestion of seawater, typhus and other fatal diseases.

The most infamous of the Nazi doctors was Josef Mengele, a promising scientist and SS captain, who arrived at Auschwitz in 1943. He found the camp an endless source of human guinea pigs, particularly for his studies of twins. Mengele 'selected' over 100 pairs of twins (almost all children), injected them with typhoid and tuberculosis bacteria, took blood samples and, after their deaths, sent any

BELOW *An emaciated survivor of Bergen Belsen Concentration Camp,* *in summer 1945, some three months after liberation by British troops.*

THE CODE OF PEACE

Medical ethics are still based on the Hippocratic Oath (see p.18), although doctors no longer swear it. Following revelations of Nazi medical war crimes at Nuremberg in 1946–7, the 'Nuremberg Code' on human experimentation was issued by the American military tribunal.

Among other things, the Code requires the voluntary consent of human subjects. Experiments must be necessary for the good of society and not simply a matter of scientific curiosity, and must be justified by the results of previous study (e.g. animal experiments). They should be designed to prevent all unnecessary physical and mental suffering and injury, and should not be conducted if there is good reason to believe that death or disabling injury will occur. Subjects must be free to terminate an experiment at any point, and researchers must do so if it looks likely that continuing will result in a subject's injury, disability or death.

RIGHT *Dame Laura Knight's impressionistic painting of the Nuremberg War Crimes Trials, in 1946, with the accused seated in* the rear two rows — guards behind them, and lawyers in front — contemplating Europe devastated by war and 'murderous science'.

organs of scientific interest to Berlin. The children were also injected with phenol and petrol, suspended upside down in cold water or simply killed with an injection of chloroform in the heart so that they could be dissected. Many were killed just because a genetic oddity had made their eyes different colours.

After the war, Mengele escaped to South America, although 20 doctors were tried at Nuremberg for crimes against humanity (four were hanged). However, most were allowed by the Allies to return to medical practice and to their teaching posts.

JAPAN'S UNIT 731

In 1936, on the command of Emperor Hirohito, a new Japanese army unit was formed and given the innocuous name of 'Epidemic Prevention and Water Supply Unit', or Unit 731. Within two years, hundreds of doctors, scientists and technicians led by Shiro Ishii were based in the small town of Pingfan, near Harbin in northern Manchuria, then occupied by the Japanese. Officially, the unit was concerned with hygiene and disease prevention; unofficially, it was engaged in intensive research into bacterial warfare.

Eventually the personnel of this highly secret unit produced enough lethal microbes — those causing anthrax, dysentery, typhoid, cholera and especially plague — to kill the world's population several times over. They also raised hundreds of thousands of rats and millions of fleas to act as vectors for disease, and, to spread them through enemy troops and civilians, invented ceramic and paper bombs, which were dropped on several occasions in China, causing local epidemics and many deaths.

Ishii's bacterial empire had a 'secret of secrets': facilities for testing human guinea pigs. Initially, the victims — known by the Japanese as *marutas*, 'logs of wood', and eventually

totalling 3000 — were White Russian and Soviet 'spies', as well as 'disloyal' Chinese and innocent job-seekers.

Unit 731 needed the *marutas* to determine the best routes of infection, how many lethal bacteria were needed to ensure epidemics and how to immunize efficiently. The Unit's doctors observed their victims suffer the worst diseases in the world. Others were deliberately shot in ballistics tests, had their limbs frozen to investigate frostbite, were electrocuted, boiled alive, or died from prolonged exposure to X-rays. An unknown number were dissected while still alive.

A few of the medical staff were horrified to discover the true purpose of their work, but were threatened with secret execution. Most, however, simply treated the *marutas* as experimental animals, or as enemies who could only achieve an honourable death by contributing to medical science.

In 1943, Shiro Ishii, like Dr Mengele, turned his attention to racial differences in infectious disease. Until then, almost all Unit 731's 'research' had been on those of Mongol race, but now he used the American, British and Commonwealth prisoners-of-war incarcerated at Mukden, 350 miles (560km) from Pingfan. The prisoners there were frequently visited by Japanese doctors, to be given 'beneficial' injections and have blood samples taken; those who died were dissected. Information is sketchy, but it seems fairly clear that, at the least, some soldiers were infected with dysentery and cholera bacteria. Most were Americans, the British and Commonwealth troops acting as a control group.

At the end of the war, all the surviving *marutas* at Pingfan were gassed or poisoned, 600 labourers machine-gunned and the facilities destroyed; thousands of plague-infected rats were released, causing a local epidemic. Astonishingly, neither Ishii nor any of his associates were prosecuted by the Allies as war criminals. All had made a deal with the Americans, exchanging their bacterial research for freedom.

Medicine Since World War II – Perinatal Advances

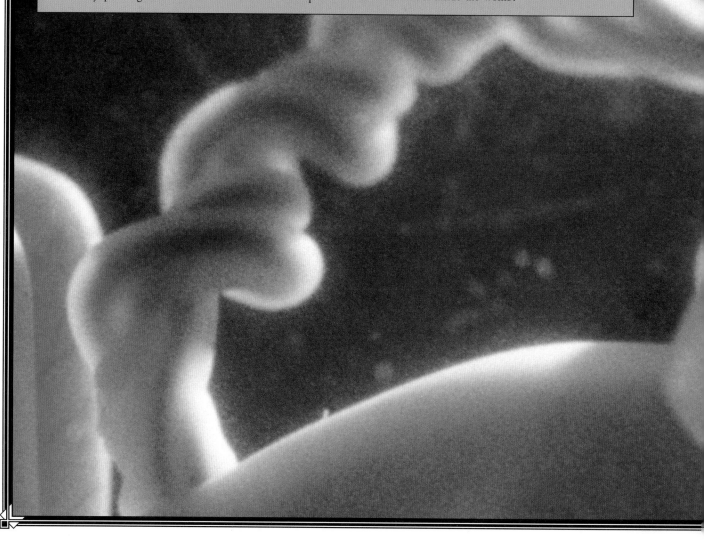

The end of World War II brought with it a new sense of purpose – a feeling among ex-combatants that now was the time for rebuilding and working for the future. It was a time when people believed that everything was possible, driven by the advances in science and technology that the war had brought.

Scientific and medical workers shared this feeling, and paid particular attention to those who were the planet's future: children and the women who bore them. The first step was to ensure that women could take control of their bodies by planning their families: the result was the pill.

Next came a focus on better management of childbirth, on new ways of relieving pain during it and on methods of ensuring that babies survived. Pain relief was improved, but, unfortunately, only at a price, and medical intervention during labour became almost routine – criticism grew, leading to the movement towards natural childbirth.

Improvements in the care of babies, though – including such milestones as Helen Taussig's work on the treatment of blue babies – were an unqualified success. So, too, were the attempts to find vaccines to control childhood diseases and, eventually, to eradicate them, and to detect foetal abnormalities inside the womb.

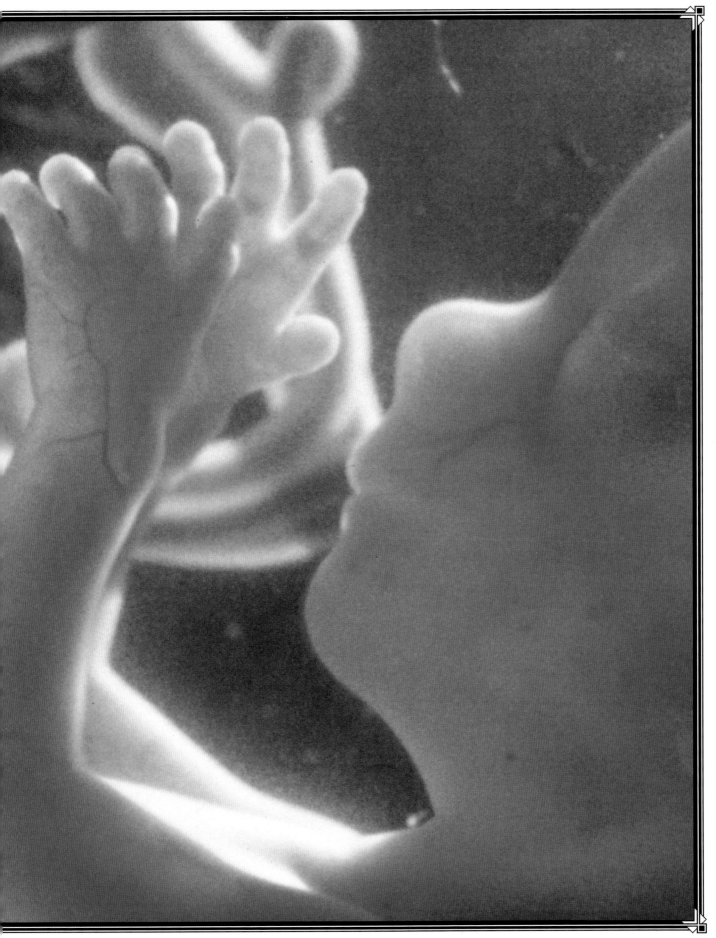

ABOVE *A human foetus in the womb, at about four months.*

BIRTH CONTROL

FROM CROCODILE DUNG TO PLANNED PARENTHOOD

Frankincense, olive oil, tortoiseshell and sheep gut ... all were tried

SINCE ANCIENT TIMES, breastfeeding has been nature's contraceptive – the hormone prolactin, which is responsible for the production of breastmilk, also acts to suppress ovulation. *Coitus interruptus*, the biblical 'spilling of seed', is probably the oldest active form of birth control. However, as time passed and society changed, so did breastfeeding patterns, and birth rates increased. As a result, various chemical concoctions and mechanical devices were tried in the attempt to prevent pregnancy.

TORTOISESHELL AND RUBBER GOODS

From at least the 3rd millennium BC, Egyptian women inserted pessaries of honey and crocodile dung into their vaginas, and Arab women mashed together pomegranates, rock salt and alum to use in the same way. According to Aristotle, a mixture of frankincense, cedar and olive oil did the trick – and, in fact, all these methods would have had some effect since their ingredients increase acidity within the vagina and make it less welcoming to sperm.

By the late Middle Ages, contraception had taken a step backwards, with the drinking of herbal decoctions as the primary yet ineffective method. Progress had to wait for the

16th-century anatomist, Gabriel Fallopio, to invent the moistened linen condom. However, he was more concerned with protecting his fellow man from the ravages of syphilis (*see pp.100–1*), and for the next four centuries, the condom would be associated with prostitution and disease.

Japanese men are reputed to have worn sheaths made of leather, horn or tortoiseshell, but, in Europe, the new style utilized the gut of a sheep, chemically treated, softened and dried. Oddly enough, wherever the condom became popular, its common name indicated a foreign origin. For instance, in France it was known as an 'English cap', and the 18th-century Italian sexual adventurer Casanova called it an 'English overcoat'. Although in England it was dubbed a 'French letter', packets of rubber (and, later, latex) condoms in the late 19th century were decorated with a portrait of Queen Victoria (herself the mother of nine).

The first 'rubber goods' for women were the cervical caps made by a German, Frederick Adolphe Wilde, in 1838. A mould of the cervix would be made from wax, and the

BELOW *A Marie Stopes mobile Birth Control Clinic brings* *contraceptive advice direct to the public, in London in the 1920s.*

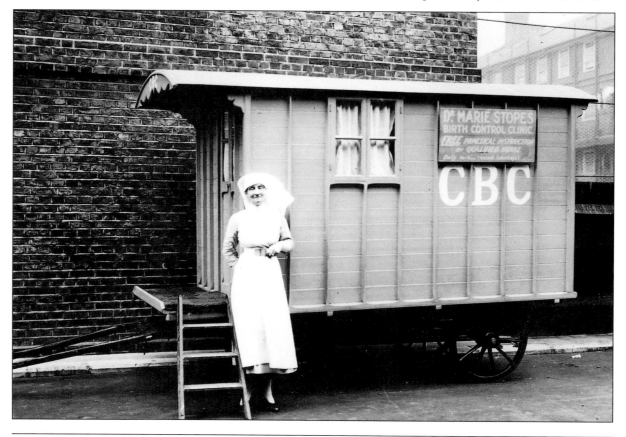

TWIN CRUSADERS

Birth control became a crusade for two women. Both were particularly keen to reduce working-class fertility, to improve the 'quality of the race', and both regarded sexual pleasure not only as the right of every wife but also a duty, to preserve marriages.

Margaret Sanger (1879–1966), a New York housewife and nurse who briefly became a radical socialist, ascribed her conversion to the cause to a visit to France in 1913, where she was astounded at how much ordinary women knew about sex and contraception. On her return to the US, she coined the term 'birth control' and wrote Family Limitation *(1914), which recommended the use of condoms, pessaries and douches for working-class couples. Sanger achieved notoriety when the Federal government prosecuted her for obscenity (the charges were later dropped). However, in October 1916, when she opened her first clinic in Brownsville, New York, she was charged with creating a public nuisance and sent to the workhouse for 30 days. On her release, she founded the American Birth Control League, the forerunner of the Planned Parenthood Federation of America. Later, she founded the International Planned Parenthood Federation, whose first home was in the offices of the Eugenics Society in London.*

BELOW *Margaret Sanger, spent 30 days in a workhouse because of her pioneering activities in America.*

RIGHT *Marie Stopes campaigned tirelessly for British women to take responsibility for their own bodies.*

Marie Stopes (1880–1958) was the first English woman to receive a doctorate in palaeobotany, but her knowledge of human reproduction came a bit late: it took a year for her to realize that her husband was impotent. Shocked by her own ignorance, she researched and wrote Married Love *(1918), which eventually sold over one million copies.*

Having extolled the bliss of conjugal pleasure, she received sackfuls of letters from women telling her that this pleasure eluded them while they still feared successive pregnancies. The result was a book called Wise Parenthood, *which included diagrams of the reproductive organs and descriptions of available contraceptive devices. This was followed by the establishment of the Society for Constructive Birth Control and Racial Progress in 1921 and, in March of that year, the opening of the Mothers' Clinic in London, backed by such luminaries as H. G. Wells, Bertrand Russell and Arnold Bennett.*

final result in latex would fit snugly on to the neck of the womb, to be removed only during menstruation. In 1882, a German doctor named Hesse, using the pseudonym 'Mensinga', invented the diaphragm most commonly in use today – which Germaine Greer has described as "a rubber dinghy for spermicide".

ACCEPTING BIRTH CONTROL

In the 19th century, the contraceptive devices then available remained, for many, a dark, somehow illicit secret. An attempt to throw light on the subject was made by a New England doctor, Charles Knowlton. In 1832, when he published (anonymously) *The Fruits of Philosophy, or the Private Companion of Young Married People*, he was fined and imprisoned for publishing 'filth'. When a new edition was issued in England in 1877 by the free thinkers Charles Bradlaugh and Annie Besant, they were arrested for publishing contraceptive literature (categorized as obscene 20 years earlier). Within three months, 125,000 copies of the book had been sold.

At the time, however, the topic of birth control was becoming accepted in polite society. This was primarily due to the work of Thomas Malthus (1766–1834), an English economist who feared that the world's population would soon outstrip the food supply. His theories were seized on by the eugenists (*see p.67*), and the Malthusian League was founded in Britain in the 1860s; there were similar organizations in France and Germany. In the Netherlands, a Malthusian group opened the world's first birth control clinic in 1882, under the direction of Dr Aletta Jacobs, soon to be joined by about 30 others throughout Holland. It was Dr Jacobs' advocacy of the diaphragm that gave it its English nickname: 'Dutch cap'.

THE PILL

DEVELOPING AN ORAL CONTRACEPTIVE

"Welcome to the post-pill paradise ...." said a John Updike character

THE FIRST EXPERIMENTS into whether ovulation could be prevented in mammals by hormones (by injections of oestrogen) were carried out in the first decades of the 20th century by the Austrian physiologist Ludwig Haberlandt. However, obtaining adequate quantities of hormonal substances for research was impossible until an American organic chemist made a spectacular discovery.

In the early 1940s, Russell E. Marker, working in a laboratory rented from a friend, found that he could extract a substance called diosgenin from a yam that grew wild in the jungles near Veracruz, Mexico. When he subjected this to a series of simple processes, it was transformed chemically into the female sex hormone progesterone (or progestogen, as the synthesized variety became known). Within a year, he had made an enormous quantity – more than 6½lb (3kg). Marker formed a company, Syntex, in Mexico City to exploit his discovery, the first hormone to be produced from a vegetable source. However, in 1948, he abruptly abandoned the Company – and chemistry – and spent the next years, until his death in 1984, manufacturing copies of European silver antiques.

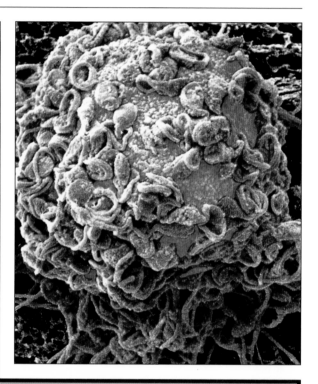

RIGHT *Human sperm (pale brown) mass round a human egg (pale pink). Only one sperm will succeed in its task and so create a new life.*

THE BULL AND THE PILL

Pincus's colleague John Rock, a devout Roman Catholic, had initially supported the research into what would become the pill in the hope that suppressing ovulation would cause a rebound effect in previously infertile women, enabling them to conceive. However, when concern about the pill increased within the Catholic Church, Rock stated that he championed it because it enabled women to stabilize their menstrual cycles completely, and so married couples could use Church-approved contraception – the 'safe period', or rhythm method – with confidence. Later, alarmed by the threat of world over-population as foreshadowed by Malthus's predictions (see p.147), he declared that the new therapy was a 'natural' contraceptive that Catholics could use in good conscience.

Rock's tussles with his conscience were in vain. In 1958, Pope Pius XII condemned the "deliberate intention and positive action taken by any means to deprive sexual union of its procreative potentiality". Four years later, Pope John XXIII called the Second Vatican Council to consider, among many other things, the Catholic Church's attitude towards birth control.

While the Council studied the question (and John was succeeded by Pope Paul VI), the Population Investigation

Committee in the UK carried out a marriage survey. They discovered that, in 1967/8, 80.5 per cent of British Catholics married between 1961 and 1965 were using birth control, and 30.2 per cent of the wives were taking the pill, nearly as many as non-Catholic women.

Finally, on 25 July 1968, Pope Paul issued his encyclical letter Humanae Vitae (On the Regulation of Birth). This unequivocally forbade the use of contraception except by 'natural' means (i.e. the 'safe period'), saying: "an act of mutual love which impairs the capacity to transmit life which God the Creator, through specific laws, has built into it, frustrates his design which constitutes the norms of marriage, and contradicts the will of the author of life". The encyclical created a storm: the Bishops of Chile, Shannon (Ireland) and Minnesota resigned, and American Cardinals McIntyre and O'Boyle threatened clergy with the extreme penalty of excommunication if they did not accept the Pope's doctrine unconditionally.

By 1973, an estimated 50 million women (of all denominations) were using the oral contraceptives marketed by 12 major drug companies. And for the first time – because hormone pills were drugs – the medical profession entered the arena of birth control.

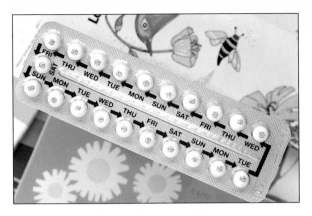

FROM YAMS TO PILLS

Meanwhile, Marker's colleagues, stunned by his sudden departure, continued his work. Two Syntex scientists, Carl Djerassi and George Rosenkranz, synthesized, respectively, the steroid cortisone and the male sex hormone testosterone from the same Mexican yam. Then, in 1951, Luis Miramontes, working under Djerassi's direction, managed to modify Marker's progestogen to form the compound norethisterone (norethindrone in the US), which was far more active than human progesterone when taken by mouth. This was sent for assessment to four researchers, including Gregory Pincus, a biologist at the Worcester Foundation for Experimental Biology in Massachusetts, who soon established that the substance inhibited ovulation.

At about the same time, in August 1953, Frank Colton of the Searle pharmaceutical company filed a patent for norethynodrel. This was very similar to norethisterone – in fact, it turned, more or less, into it after exposure to the stomach's hydrochloric acid.

Initially, Pincus was not interested in producing a method of birth control. However, the implications of his work were soon recognized by Margaret Sanger (see p.147), whom he had first met in 1950. She enlisted the help of wealthy Katharine McCormick, who arranged for Pincus and his collaborators – Worcester colleague Dr Min-chueh Chang, and John Rock, clinical professor of gynaecology at Harvard – to receive a grant of $115,000 for research into effective "hormonal birth control". From the first, the eugenic implications (i.e. birth restriction among the poor) were understood if not spelled out.

Pincus was also a consultant for Searle, and so, despite his work on the Syntex norethisterone, he chose the Searle compound for his research. It was first tried out on a small group of human volunteers in Boston, but conditions were hardly ideal: contraception was to remain illegal in Massachusetts until 1967. Then, in 1955, a large clinical trial was mounted among the poor of Rio Piedras, Puerto Rico.

The results were published in the *Science Journal* the following year. By 1957, norethynodrel had been approved by the US Food and Drug Administration as a 'menstrual regulator' and, two years later, as an oral contraceptive.

When Searle began mass production, they first removed 'impurities' in the drug. The resulting purer progestogen caused some women to suffer menstrual irregularity and breakthrough bleeding, and an unfortunate few became pregnant. Searle researchers urgently investigated the cause and found that the original compound had, in fact, contained just over one per cent of an oestrogen-type substance they

LEFT '*The pill*', *complete with 1960s packaging. At first, the pill contained a rather arbitrary amount of oestrogen, but high oestrogen levels were shown to cause side-effects, and the dose was reduced.*

called mestranol, which they quickly put back into the pills. So the oestrogen–progestogen combined contraceptive pill was only discovered by accident.

The amount of oestrogen contained in 'the pill' (as it was soon nicknamed) was based arbitrarily on the amount in the original compound. Because of the scientists' concern about unwanted pregnancies, the quantity was not increased gradually until the desired therapeutic effect was reached, as would normally happen in drug development – so women were seriously overdosed with oestrogen from the first.

By 1961, adverse side-effects were being reported – initially, thrombo-phlebitis, and later, migraine and jaundice. Then, in December 1969, came a bombshell: the UK Committee on the Safety of Medicines advised doctors to prescribe oral contraceptives with no more than 50 microgrammes of oestrogen, as higher doses had been shown to cause a higher incidence of thrombo-embolisms leading to potentially fatal heart attacks and strokes.

FROM STONES TO COPPER

The final weapon in the mechanical contraceptive arsenal was the intrauterine device (IUD), or 'coil', which prevents pregnancy by making the implantation of fertilized eggs impossible. IUDs have a long history: Arab camel drivers in biblical times would insert pea-size stones into the uteruses of their female camels; Hippocrates recommended inserting a hollow lead tube filled with mutton fat; and the Victorians had their 'stem pessaries'.

However, the first modern IUD – the 'thread pessary', made of silk – was invented by a German doctor in 1909. This was followed, in the 1920s, by the simple Graefenberg ring made of gold and silver, and later by devices consisting of plastic and, sometimes, copper, in a bewildering number of shapes: the Lippes Loop, the Copper 7 and T, the Birnberg Bow, the Dalkon Shield. This last, shaped like a crab louse, was the subject of multi-million-dollar lawsuits in the 1970s and 1980s, after it was shown to cause unacceptably high levels of pelvic infections and septic abortions.

BELOW *A Saf-T coil, one of a range of IUDs. Large plastic IUDs are rare nowadays, ones with copper being preferred.*

HAVING BABIES

THE RISE OF THE INTERVENTIONISTS

"An offspring is produced by a magician from a paralyzed birth canal"

AFTER WORLD WAR II, some pre-war developments in obstetrics, intended to make childbirth easier and improve the health of both mothers and babies, began to cause problems. Increasingly, technology came to the fore, often at the cost of medical staff and midwives losing their traditional skills, and eventually some doctors and some women found that they held opposing views on how child-birth should be conducted.

PAIN RELIEF

Spinal anaesthesia during childbirth had become more common, but it caused excruciating headaches for days after. These became much less of a problem with the development of epidural anaesthesia, in which an injection of local anaes-thetic is made into the epidural space near the spinal cord in the lower back. It virtually eliminates all sensation from that point down the rest of the body, but does not cross the placenta to affect the baby. By the mid-1970s, it was used fairly frequently for pain relief, and soon for women under-going elective caesarean section, allowing them to experience the births of their babies.

However, epidural anaesthesia requires the skills of an expert anaesthetist. In addition, women whose lower bodies are temporary paralyzed are unable to recognize the urge to push during the final stages of labour, resulting in a much higher incidence of forceps deliveries. "An offspring is produced by a magician from a paralyzed birth canal", as the British obstetrician Grantly Dick-Read (*see p.152*) described it. Indeed, the increasing use of epidural anaesthesia and drugs to dull pain tended to give even greater control of the birth process to the medical profession.

BELOW *Foetal monitoring allows doctors to detect foetal distress during labour and intervene — often too quickly, some say.*

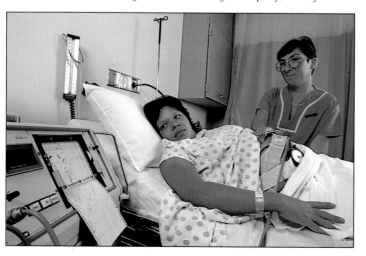

PROSTAGLANDINS

In 1969, a less dangerous alternative to oxytocin was announced. Thirty-five years earlier, the Swedish scientist Ulf von Euler (who was to win a Nobel prize for his work on nerve transmission in 1970) had discovered that a protein substance in human semen causes the smooth muscle of the uterus to contract. Because he thought this was produced by a man's prostate gland, he had named the substance prostaglandin, although it was later found that other tissues in the body produce it, including the lining of the uterus itself. In 1965, researchers at the Upjohn drug company devised a synthetic form, and it was this that was first used in the late 1960s by Dr S.S. Karim to induce labour. Since then, prostaglandin — as pessaries or cream, inserted into the vagina or cervix, and thus allowing a woman in labour to remain mobile — has become the preferred method of induction.

THE MECHANIZATION OF BIRTH

In the 1940s and 1950s, the focus was on medical interven-tion to preserve the health of the foetus — and not only that of the mother, as had always been the rationale in the past — and foetal monitoring machines rapidly appeared in hospital labour wards. While these were responsible for the saving of babies' lives, a survey in Britain in the early 1980s showed that many did not work properly.

With this new ability to detect foetal distress came an increase in the induction of labour. Some American hospitals still employed castor oil even into the late 1950s, but a number of other drugs were also tried, including quinine (with drastic results), sparteine and forms of oxytocin, the hormone first discovered by Henry Hallett Dale (*see p.102*) in 1906 and synthesized by French researchers in the 1950s.

Because different women require different amounts of oxytocin, a standardized dosage was impossible. Then, in the early 1960s, A.C. Turnbull and Anne Anderson in Cardiff developed an infusion pump that would gradually increase the oxytocin given to a woman as her uterine contractions increased in strength and frequency. However, the machine could only be used if women remained in bed, and the oxytocin-induced contractions were sometimes extremely strong, so that women usually needed powerful drugs to bear the pain. Research was later to show that foetal distress was quite common with high doses of oxytocin, and oxytocin inductions had a 10 to 20 per cent failure rate, necessitating caesarean sections.

BELOW *A caesarean section; with the mother having had either an epidural or general anaesthetic, the baby's head is delivered by forceps through cuts in the wall of the abdomen and uterus.*

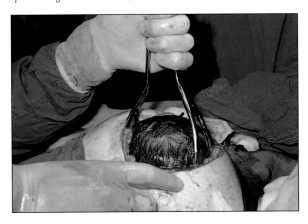

ACTIVE MANAGEMENT

At first, induction was reserved for cases in which there was real concern about the baby or when a baby was grossly overdue. However, a trend among medical staff to become increasingly reliant on foetal monitors opened up the possibility that a perfectly healthy baby could be prematurely delivered.

Monitoring allowed researchers to attempt to define what 'normal' labour is. In the 1950s, an American, Emanuel Friedman, published a series of computations taken from the average lengths of labour of women with varying obstetrical histories. From these figures, Friedman invented the 'partogram', a chart plotting the average rate of dilatation of the cervix and descent of a baby. This chart became gospel among many obstetricians, and if they felt a woman's labour varied in any way from this 'norm', she would be put on a drip to slow or speed it up.

The medical control of the birth process reached its apotheosis in Dublin, at the National Maternity Hospital. There obstetrician Kieran O'Driscoll instituted a regime he called (in the *British Medical Journal* in 1969) the 'active management of labour'. No labour was allowed to last longer than 12 hours: in a woman having a first baby, the amniotic sac was likely to be ruptured artificially one hour after a diagnosis of labour had been established; then an hour later, she would be given oxytocin intravenously. The system was inflexible and dogmatic. The administration of oxytocin was, according to Dr O'Driscoll, "a standard procedure, applied in all circumstances and by every member of staff", and after this began, it was impossible, he said, "for treatment to last longer than six hours".

A TIME OF CHANGE

To be fair to Dr O'Driscoll, it should be said that each of his patients was guaranteed a personal midwife to see her through her labour and delivery, and the rate of further medical intervention was low. However, the tide was begining to turn in favour of a more natural, relaxed approach to childbirth.

Perhaps the greatest proponent of oxytocin was the British obstetrician Professor Alex Turnbull, whose 1968 paper *The Induction of Labour* was immensely influential. But by 1976, he had recanted his former stance. Addressing a meeting of the British, Irish and Canadian medical associations, he stated: "The enthusiasm I have always felt for being able to induce or accelerate labour with efficiency when this was clearly indicated has never equated with enthusiasm for wholesale or 'routine' induction of labour simply because this had become feasible".

Professor Turnbull may have been influenced by a study of 39,864 pregnancies and births in Cardiff, Wales, published in the *British Medical Journal* in March 1976. Iain Chalmers and his colleagues could only conclude that, despite all the obstetrical intervention designed to improve matters, "a Cardiff woman ran the same risk of losing her baby in 1973 as in 1965 and her attendants have not witnessed a decline of perinatal mortality [deaths just before or just after birth] in the population that they serve".

Doctors and hospitals had succeeded in connecting normal pregnancy and childbirth with illness, "a feat", according to sociologist Ann Oakley, "which had to be accomplished if pregnancy was to be regarded in the future as a legitimate subject for medical discourse and treatment." But the major issue remained much as it had been in the 19th century (*see p.71*): who controlled pregnancy and childbirth – a medical profession dominated by men or women themselves?

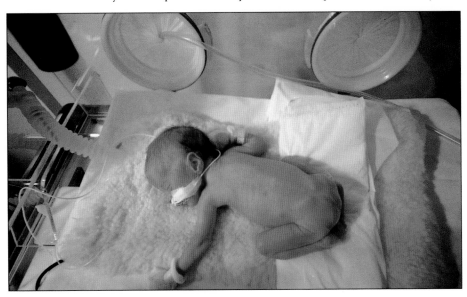

LEFT *One advance in the technology surrounding modern childbirth has saved millions of lives since its development. Here, a premature baby lies in a temperature-controlled incubator – it receives oxygen and nutrients through a tube to the nose and lies on sheepskin for warmth and comfort. Hand holes give the medical staff access, and allow parents to maintain contact with their child.*

In the 1940s, some babies in incubators mysteriously developed blindness. It was later discovered that this condition – retrolental fibroplasia – was caused by an excess of oxygen in the first few days of life.

NATURAL CHILDBIRTH

"...picture a crowd of men in white coats and horn-rimmed glasses ..."

IN THE FIRST DECADES of the 20th century, early feminists had fought hard for the right of every mother to receive pain relief during childbirth. By the 1960s, however, many women began to fight almost as fiercely to be free of the anaesthetics and analgesics of which their grandmothers had thought so highly, and instead advocated a return to more 'natural' birth practices.

CHILDBIRTH WITHOUT FEAR

But it was a man who first publicized the need for change. Grantly Dick-Read (1890–1959), a British obstetrician who for many years treated women from the slums of London, came to believe that the pain suffered during childbirth was, as likely as not, created by doctors and others.

As a child, he had become fascinated by natural history and, in particular, how different species were born. Later, when he practised as a doctor, he discovered that what came naturally for animals was not quite so easy for human females. He decided that this was because they had been made afraid of childbirth, and this fear caused muscular tension which, in turn, caused pain during labour – the 'fear–tension–pain syndrome'.

Dick-Read's answer was education, in the form of antenatal classes, and his books *Natural Childbirth* (1933) and *Childbirth without Fear* (1942) attempted to explain the process, to make it less frightening and to instil confidence. He railed against the "unforgiveable custom" of routinely anaesthetizing women during childbirth:

"I... picture a crowd of men in white coats and large horn-rimmed glasses, seeking fame and fortune searching for a weapon with which to protect all women from an enemy which in 95 per cent of cases did not exist, and their chosen method of protection was to risk the life of the woman and her baby by using the weapon upon them, not upon the enemy which they erroneously presumed to be present!".

However, Dick-Read never completely ruled out pain relief. If women were aware of what was happening to them, they would probably not need any, he said, but if they did, then something (usually gas-and-air) was ready to hand and in their control.

In 1956, the National Childbirth Trust was set up in Britain to bring Dick-Read's ideas to a wider audience and, with the help of National Health Service midwives and doctors, to put them into practice. Although the thought of 'childbirth without fear' appealed to many women in the US, the prevailing medical system – private rather than collective medicine, with few midwives – made achieving Dick-Read's aims almost impossible in that country.

CONCENTRATING THE MIND

American women turned instead to mind-over-body techniques espoused by various authorities across the Atlantic. From the Soviet Union (as it was then called) came news of 'psychoprophylaxis' – learning to ignore pain by concentrating on sensations elsewhere in the body – which was adopted there in 1951 as the official method of pain

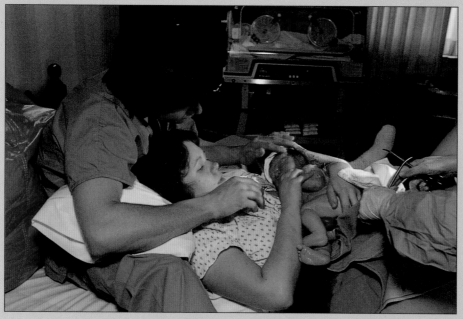

LEFT *A newly born baby rests in the arms of its mother at the Alternative Birthing Centre, at Memorial Hospital, Glendale, California. Such scenes are becoming increasingly common in Europe, where they are not considered particularly 'alternative'. American obstetric practice, however, tends to be somewhat more orthodox.*

relief in childbirth. Two doctors, Ferdinand Lamaze and Pierre Vellay, had been to the USSR to study the method and brought it enthusiastically back home to France. Lamaze's book *Painless Childbirth* (1956) detailed the two men's development of the Soviet idea, adding to it a system of rapid, shallow breathing to control contractions.

However, it was not until an American living in Paris, Marjorie Karmel, wrote about her experience of childbirth with the 'Lamaze method' in her book *Thank You, Dr Lamaze* that these ideas gained currency in the US. Karmel, physiotherapist Elizabeth Bing and Dr Benjamin Segal formed the American Society for Psychoprophylaxis in Obstetrics, a pressure group that tailored the Lamaze method to existing American medical practice.

LOOKING AFTER BABY

Trends in childbirth were changing: women were actively preparing for the births of their babies and actively participating in them. Now attention turned to the babies themselves.

In the mid-1960s, another French doctor, Frdrique Leboyer, of the Paris Faculty of Medicine, took to heart suggestions made earlier by the Italian educator Maria Montessori and others that the first impressions of a baby after birth were vital. In his book *Birth without Violence*, Leboyer described how birth should be a gentle experience, with lights dimmed and little noise – the baby being placed on the mother's stomach and massaged, and immersed in warm water to mimic the amniotic fluids it had just left.

LEFT *French obstetrician Dr Michael Odent achieved a certain notoriety in the world's newspapers when he was reported to have recommended underwater births. Unfairly so – in fact, women under his care occasionally delivered their babies while in a bathing pool to alleviate labour pains, in dimly lit, comfortable surroundings and in a position of their choice.*

Leboyer greatly influenced a fellow countryman, Michel Odent, who combined the techniques of both his mentor and Lamaze. At his unit at Pithiviers, south of Paris, Odent created a 'demedicalized' atmosphere: quiet, comfortably lit rooms bare of hospital equipment (although it was nearby if needed) but full of mattresses, cushions and even bathing pools. He encouraged women to adopt any position they wanted to deal with contractions and the birth, and found that even difficult births could be handled fairly easily. And pain relief was hardly ever needed.

The women's movement and rising consumerism ensured that many of these new techniques became established. By the 1980s, 'birth rooms' were being set up, birthing chairs had made a comeback, the importance of mother-baby bonding had been recognized and childbirth 'supporters' (usually fathers) were common.

DR SPOCK

As ideas about bringing children into the world were changing, those about raising them were also being revolutionized. In 1946, the American paediatrician Dr Benjamin McLane Spock published his **Common Sense Book of Baby and Child Care.** *In easily understood, often humorous language, he told parents to trust their instincts; to love and cuddle their children; and not worry too much about toilet-training and discipline. His book, based on Freudian psychoanalytic theory, directly contradicted the rigid authoritarian tomes of predecessors such as John B. Watson (see p. 121), and suited an affluent middle-class population tired of war and ready to relax and enjoy freedom.*

In the late 1960s, when protests against the Vietnam War reached their height, Dr Spock (himself strongly anti-war) came under fire from right-wing polemicists, such as Norman Vincent Peale and US Vice-President Spiro Agnew, who blamed his 'permissive' child-rearing advice for creating a generation of self-centred, undisciplined and even treasonous youth. However, much of their criticism was aimed at advice given in the first edition of Spock's book; he greatly modified his easy-going attitude in later editions.

Today, Dr Spock is criticized primarily for his assumption that all families contain both parents, that mothers stay home to look after their children, and that each child has his or her own bed in his or her own bedroom. Despite this, his practical suggestions for dealing with everyday problems and common illnesses have probably not been bettered.

ABOVE *Dr Spock's theories shaped a generation. Much criticized in the 1960s, his reputation has been rehabilitated.*

PROTECTING CHILDREN

IMMUNIZATION AND EARLY WARNING

Measles killed three-quarters of the population of the Faroe Islands

FOLLOWING WORLD WAR II, the health of children was generally better than at any other time in history. However, common childhood illnesses such as measles, mumps and rubella continued to damage some children, especially those in regions of the world previously untouched by these viruses, and others were crippled or killed by polio (*see pp.202–3*). In addition, babies were still being born with congenital and genetic conditions for which there had been no warning during pregnancy.

BELOW *A baby boy covered with the measles rash – in Africa,* *children still die from measles; in the West, a vaccine gives protection.*

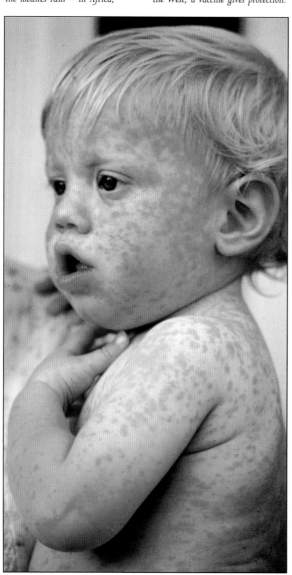

MEASLES AND MUMPS

People in the developed world took it for granted that every child would come down with mild cases of measles and mumps. However, in parts of Africa, 5 per cent of children with measles still die, and when it first appears it can be devastating. In the remote Faroe Islands, in the North Atlantic, three-quarters of the population caught the disease within six months of the first case in 1846, and many died; 29 years later, on the Pacific island of Fiji, the mortality rate was at least 20 per cent. Mumps was the leading cause of days lost by US forces during World War I, as well as a cause of male sterility and permanent brain damage.

During World War II, a remarkable man became involved in the search for vaccines. John Franklin Enders did not decide to devote his life to microbiology until his late twenties as a graduate student in literature at Harvard University. He eventually became Associate Professor of Bacteriology at Harvard, and, with two of his students – Thomas Huckle Weller and Frederick Chapman Robbins – went on to make an indelible mark on medical history.

When the US entered the war, Enders joined the armed forces commission on measles and mumps, both endemic among young recruits. With Joseph Stokes Jr, he isolated the mumps virus and grew it in monkeys, so leading to the development of a diagnostic skin test. They then created a vaccine of chemically inactivated virus, to be taken by soldiers shown to be susceptible to the disease. This first, effective and safe mumps vaccine unfortunately only gave short-term protection, but was eventually superceded by a live virus vaccine. A number of measles vaccines were also developed, but they caused severe side-effects.

GAMMA GLOBULIN

In the absence of a foolproof vaccine, those most at risk could be given temporary protection with injections of gamma globulin, the part of the blood that, in a person who has had a particular illness, contains the antibodies against it. In 1944, an American researcher, Edwin J. Cohn of Harvard, pioneered the process known as fractionation, in which gamma globulin is separated out from blood serum. The substance's first big success was in southern Greenland, in 1951, when measles erupted in the area for the first time. A record 99.9 per cent of the population (of all ages) was affected, but only 1.8 per cent died, because injections of gamma globulin decreased the severity of the disease and penicillin was used on those who developed complications.

Gamma globulin was eventually used to treat people at risk from hepatitis, polio and tetanus. It was also given to Rh-negative mothers (*see pp.92–3*) after they gave birth to Rh-positive babies, to prevent adverse reactions in their blood against incompatible blood cells.

MEASLES VACCINE

In 1946, Enders joined Weller and Robbins at the Children's Hospital in Boston, in order to grow viruses in animal tissues. By March 1948, Weller had grown mumps viruses in chicken-broth cultures, and by 1949, the team had managed to grow polio virus on human tissue.

Enders and his collaborators turned their attention back to the problem of eliminating side-effects from the measles vaccine, and worked closely with Dr Thomas Peebles. In 1954, he took throat washings and blood samples from a young Boston boy, David Edmonston, who had come down with measles, and the researchers seeded these into a human tissue culture, isolating the virus for the first time.

For three years, with the help of Yugoslav scientist Milan Milanovic, they passed the virus through tissues from birds, mice and monkeys until it no longer caused the illness in monkeys but did produce antibodies. In 1960, the 'Edmonston live measles virus vaccine' was ready for testing, and it was licensed in 1963. By 1974, it was reckoned to have saved 2400 lives in the US alone.

RUBELLA

For centuries, rubella (German measles) had been considered a mild, measles-like illness. Then, in 1940/41, there was an epidemic in Australia; in 1941, the ophthalmologist Norman McAlister Gregg reported 91 cases in which cataracts developed in infants whose mothers had rubella in pregnancy. Most of the babies also suffered other problems: deafness, heart disease, cerebral palsy and mental retardation. Gregg's report was almost completely overlooked, but interest grew when the war ended.

An Australian scientist, Frank Macfarlane Burnet, showed that gamma globulin injections would protect pregnant women exposed to rubella, and media campaigns led to 'German measles parties' for young girls, when it was hoped that an infected child would pass on the virus to her companions so all would be protected.

In 1960, the ten-year-old son of Thomas Weller, Ender's collaborator, developed a severe case of rubella, and there was an outbreak among army recruits at Fort Dix, New Jersey. Weller isolated the virus from a sample of his son's urine, and an army team led by Paul Parkman found it in throat washings taken from recruits.

Nothing more happened until the 1963/64 rubella epidemic in the US, one of the greatest in history. At least 20,000 unborn babies suffered brain damage, and the cost of treating them led the US Congress to pass laws making vaccination against childhood diseases a birthright. In 1966, Paul Parkman, with Harry Meyer Jr and Theodore C. Panos, developed a live rubella virus vaccine.

BELOW *Virus particles of the rubella virus: it can seriously affect children whose mothers were infected during pregnancy.*

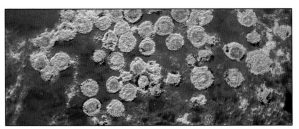

EARLY WARNINGS

Before the 50s, the type of damage caused by perinatal conditions could not be anticipated before the baby's birth. Then, in February 1952, the British doctor D.C.A. Bevis of St Mary's Hospital, in Manchester, published an article in the Lancet *that described a technique for discovering whether a pregnant Rh-negative woman's baby was suffering from haemolytic disease of the unborn (see pp.92–93). This was amniocentesis – the drawing out through a syringe of some of the amniotic fluid surrounding the unborn child. The test was later extended to suspected cases of spina bifida, Down's syndrome and other chromosomal and genetic abnormalities. One drawback was that amniocentesis is only possible after the 16th week of pregnancy.*

In 1949, the British researchers Murray Llewellyn Barr and Ewart George Bartram demonstrated that it was possible to sex every cell in the body by noting the presence (in females only) or absence of a small piece of chromatin at the edge of the nucleus. In 1983, a report in the Lancet *described a chorion biopsy – a technique similar to amniocentesis but which samples placental tissue and is able to be performed by the ninth week of pregnancy. This technique could establish the sex of a baby at risk of Duchenne muscular dystrophy, a sex-linked disease. Further advances in pre-diagnosis have been made in the use of ultrasound (see pp.168–9).*

ABOVE *A doctor performing an amniocentesis: a sample of amniotic fluid is taken from the womb (the needle is guided by ultrasound) and examined for abnormalities.*

HOPE FOR 'BLUE BABIES'

SURGICAL TREATMENT FOR CONGENITAL HEART DISEASE

A little girl hovered between life and death for two weeks ... but survived

ALTHOUGH THE FIRST DESCRIPTION of what came to be popularly called 'blue babies' was written in 1771, it was only in 1888 that the problem was universally recognized. Etienne-Louis Fallot, Professor of Anatomical Pathology at Marseilles, France, realized that the (usually fatal) condition some babies are born with has four components. First, the pulmonary valve between the heart and the pulmonary artery – through which blood should travel to pick up oxygen in the lungs – is narrowed. Second, the bottom right chamber of the heart, the right ventricle, becomes enlarged from having to pump blood through the narrowed opening. Third, the partition (septum) between the two sides of the heart is incomplete, and the baby has what is known as a 'hole in the heart', allowing oxygenated and deoxygenated blood to mix. Fourth, the aorta – which normally carries oxygenated blood to the rest of the body – is displaced so that it takes blood from both the left and right ventricles.

As a result of these four congenital defects – now known as the tetralogy of Fallot – the baby's body receives very little oxygen, and it becomes cyanosed: the skin has a bluish tinge, hence 'blue babies'. The situation worsens as the child grows, and until treatment became available, most died at a very young age.

A QUESTION OF PLUMBING

After being refused entry to Harvard and Boston University because she was a woman, Helen Taussig (1898–1986) entered Johns Hopkins Medical School in 1921. When she graduated, she became a physician at the paediatric cardiac clinic at the Harriet Lane Home, the Johns Hopkins' children's division. The speciality of paediatric cardiology was in its infancy, and, in 1938, Taussig visited Maude Abbot of Canada's McGill University, who, with the publication two years before of her *Atlas of Congenital Cardiac Disease*, had established her position as the world's foremost authority in this field – the result of 1000 dissections.

Helen Taussig became expert in diagnosis, following years of experimentation with fluoroscopy (an X-ray technique that can show organs in movement) and the study of electrocardiograms and palpation. But she felt helpless, for her diagnoses were usually not followed by any hope of a cure.

She found that some of her young patients with tetralogy of Fallot also had another congenital heart defect, called persistent ductus. In the womb, the unborn baby gets its oxygen supply from its mother. The oxygen bypasses the lungs through a duct called the *ductus arteriosus*, through which the blood (carrying oxygen received from the mother) passes directly from the pulmonary artery to the aorta. At birth, the *ductus* usually closes at the baby's first breath and the lungs take over, but in some children this remains open. If this is the only defect, the flow in the *ductus* is reversed

BELOW *Etienne-Louis Fallot (1850– 1911), Professor of Anatomical Pathology at* Marseilles, France, gave his name to the four-part syndrome that gives rise to 'blue babies'.

and the lungs begin to receive too much blood at too high a pressure, which can irreversibly damage them. However, Taussig noticed that patients who had both tetralogy and persistent ductus seemed to do better: in them, the *ductus* allowed blood to bypass the narrowed pulmonary valve and provided a better flow to the lungs.

The answer, then, seemed to be to build an artificial *ductus*, or shunt, in the tetralogy children. But Taussig was a physician, not a surgeon. In 1943, she turned to Alfred Blalock to come up with some answers to what was essentially a question of plumbing.

FROM ANIMALS TO HUMANS

The 44-year-old Blalock was then chairman of the Johns Hopkins Department of Surgery, and had done a great deal of work on methods of attaching blood vessels to each other. One area that he had studied was persistent *ductus*, and in experiments on dogs, he had diverted the subclavian artery, which carries most of the blood to the animal's foreleg, and connected it directly to the pulmonary artery.

Blalock was indebted to the work of his assistant, Vivian Thomas, a black man who had been forced to become a laboratory technician as a result of a lack of funding to attend university. It was Thomas who carried out 200 animal

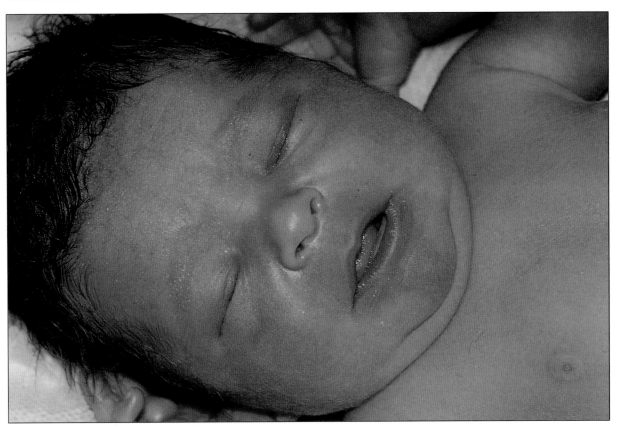

ABOVE *A blue baby – 'blue' refers to the colour of deoxygenated blood* *rather than the complexion, which is purple, especially round the lips.*

experiments – assisted by Blalock on only a few – until a method of attaching the subclavian artery to the pulmonary artery had been perfected.

The next step was to try the technique on a human subject, and, on 29 November 1944, 15-month-old Eileen Saxon was taken to the operating theatre. Weighing only 9.2lb (4.3kg), the child was near death. Blalock operated with Thomas close at hand to advise, and Taussig looked on, seeing her theories put to the test of practicality. Closely watched by the doctors, the little girl hovered between life and death for two weeks after the operation, her lungs collapsing repeatedly from the extra burden placed on them. But she slowly improved, and, on 25 January 1945, she was discharged from the hospital safe and sound.

After two more children had been operated on successfully, in February 1945 Blalock and Taussig published the results in the *Journal of the American Medical Association*. By the end of 1950, Blalock and his co-workers had performed a further 1034 operations, and the mortality rate had fallen from 20 to 5 per cent. In the meantime, Helen Taussig published her book *Congenital Malformations of the Heart* (1947), which became the bible of paediatric cardiology. What became known as the Blalock-Taussig operation helped thousands of children to hang on to life until the techniques of open-heart surgery could be developed to repair the very faults that threatened them (see pp.178-9).

Albert Blalock was elected to the National Academy of Sciences in 1945, and was fêted throughout the medical world. Helen Taussig, however, had to wait another 14 years before being appointed full professor at Johns Hopkins,

but she went on to become the first woman president of the American Heart Association and, finally, was herself elected to the National Academy of Sciences. Her investigation in 1962 into the horrendous damage caused by thalidomide (*see p.166*) in Germany, when presented to the American College of Physicians, was instrumental in having the drug permanently rejected by the US Food and Drug Administration.

Taussig retired from Johns Hopkins in July 1963, but used the money from a fellowship to do a follow-up of all the patients who had had a Blalock-Taussig operation between 1945 and 1950. Of the 779 patients for whom data was obtained by 1970, 685 had survived the postoperative period of two months, and 441 of these were still alive between 20 and 25 years later. Helen Taussig went on to investigate whether congenital heart defects in embryos might be a throw-back to a more primitive form of animal life. She was still hard at work just three days before her 88th birthday, when she was killed in a traffic accident.

LEFT *Dr. Helen Brooke Taussig, in 1967, who pioneered the procedure used to save the lives of blue babies and became the first woman president of the American Heart Association. Dr. Taussig died in a car accident, just a few days short of her 88th birthday.*

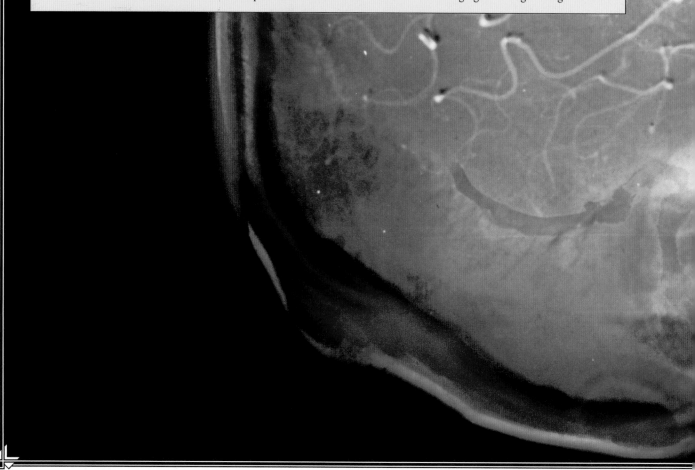

7 Medicine Since World War II – Advances in Science and Technology

By the second half of the 20th century, scientific research was very far from being an individual, amateur pursuit, as it had been in previous centuries. Vast amounts of money and a large dedicated team were needed to achieve progress, and generate what one British politician called "the white heat of technology". But the money was available, and in plenty, from the pharmaceutical companies and equipment manufacturers who had made healthy profits from previous discoveries.

The progress made as a result was extraordinary, much of it based on mathematics, physics and engineering. The development of computers allowed huge amounts of data to be assembled, collated and analyzed; later, too, computer imaging revolutionized diagnostic investigations, as doctors and scientists became able to peer into the body, tracking tracer chemicals through organs. Lasers played their part in surgery, as did fibre-optics, while newly discovered materials – some of them spin-offs from America's space exploration programme – led the way to practical kidney dialysis machines and successful hip replacements, which have given a new lease of life to millions all over the world.

Build up at the core of this white heat of technology was still the pristine fire of pure research. One of the most significant scientific advances since World War II, as far as medicine is concerned, has been the discovery of the structure of life itself: the double helix of the DNA molecule. Together with a new understanding of the processes and possibilities of immunity, this breakthrough has led the way to a whole range of probabilities for treatment of diseases through genetic engineering.

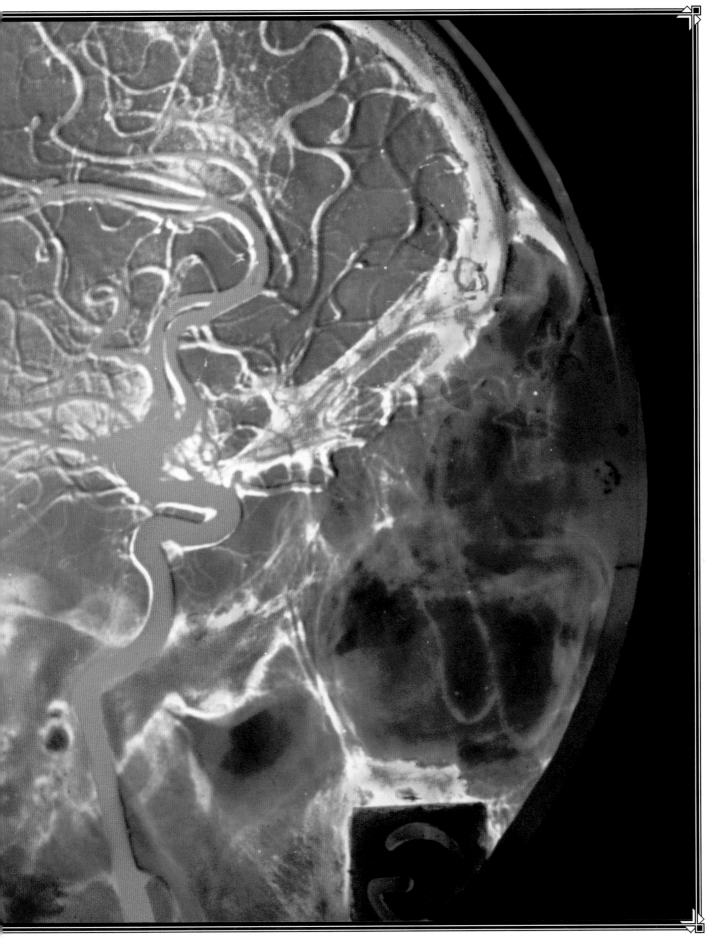

ABOVE *A false-colour X-ray angiograph of the arteries of the brain.*

THE STRUCTURE OF LIFE

THE DISCOVERY OF THE DNA DOUBLE HELIX

Two men — and one woman — worked out the basis of living tissue

THE WORK OF DARWIN AND MENDEL (*see pp.66-7*) had led to a theory of evolutionary change, but the causes of the changes that occur in species and are inherited to allow them to survive were not known. Although the final piece of the puzzle would fall into place in 1953, much research was needed before that could happen.

BELOW *The 46 human chromosomes, arranged in pairs — this is a female set; the pair at the bottom right is XX rather than the male XY.*

THE BIOCHEMISTRY OF INHERITANCE

In 1869, the Swiss biochemist Friedrich Miescher discovered that the same substance occurred in the nucleus of every cell of living tissue. He called this 'nuclein' (later changed to 'nucleic acid'). At the beginning of the 20th century, it was known that the nucleic acid molecule contained five distinct chemical bases: guanine (G), adenine (A), cytosine (C), thymine (T) and uracil (U). By the 1920s, two forms of nucleic acid had been identified: DNA (deoxyribonucleic

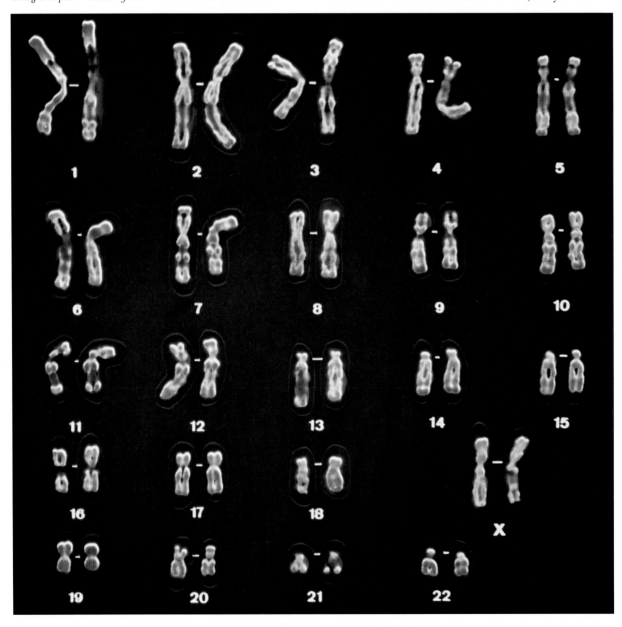

acid), which contains the GACT bases; and RNA (ribonucleic acid), with the GACU bases.

A Russian-born researcher, Phoebus Levene, envisaged a DNA structure that was simple and repetitive, and thus had no ability to hold or transmit information. It was known that chromosomes also contained protein, and until well into the 1940s, scientists believed that complex protein was the transmitter of inheritance, with uncomplicated DNA simply holding the protein together.

However, in 1928, a British medical officer, Frederick Griffith, published an important report. He had been working on two forms of the bacteria responsible for pneumonia: the S form was lethal when injected into mice; the R form was harmless. But when he killed S cells by heating them and added them to R cells, all the mice still died. Somehow the R cells had taken up the virulence from the S cells.

Oswald Avery, of the Rockefeller Institute, in New York, decided to find out what transforming substance did this. He and his team separated all the various chemical components that made up the bacteria, and through a process of elimination, they came to the conclusion, in 1944, that the virulence could only be transmitted via the S cells' DNA.

The final biochemical clue came from Erwin Chargaff, born in Vienna in 1905, who was working at Columbia University. When the Avery team published its results, Chargaff and his colleagues decided to devote themselves to discovering the chemistry of nucleic acids. And when it became clear that the four DNA bases were not in equal proportions, they knew that it was possible for a complicated code to be contained in DNA, much as the Morse code of only two elements (dot and dash) is able to transmit all the works ever written with the alphabet.

The Chargaff researchers did find that the amount of the bases G and A was the same as the amount of C and T, and that there was always the same amount of A as T, and the same amount of G as C. These 'Chargaff Ratios', published in 1950, were seen to be extremely important when the structure of DNA was finalized.

ENTER THE PHYSICISTS

In 1944, Erwin Schrödinger, one of the founders of quantum physics, published a little book called *What Is Life?*. In this, he described the unit responsible for heredity in purely molecular terms, and likened it to an 'aperiodic crystal'. Unlike a periodic crystal (e.g. a salt crystal), which is made up of an endlessly repeating unit in a regular pattern, an aperiodic crystal would have a structure obeying certain fundamental laws of physics but no repetition, so that it could hold an enormous amount of information in a code. This description, couched in terms familiar to them, entranced a number of physicists who previously had not worked on living matter – among them Maurice Wilkins, Francis Crick and James Watson.

Maurice Wilkins (1916–), who emigrated from New Zealand to Britain when he was six, had worked on the Manhattan Project during the war, but its ultimate result – the atomic bomb – disillusioned him and his interest turned towards biology. In 1950, as assistant director of the Medical Research Council's (MRC's) Biophysics Research Unit, at King's College, in London, he was given a sample of pure DNA. Cobbling together some war surplus radiography machine parts into X-ray diffraction equipment, he took

THE GENETIC CODE

From 1953, work was carried out to discover how the double chains of bases contained in DNA could represent a code that would, ultimately, produce a human being. It was soon found that chromosomes are made of genes, which are simply specific lengths of DNA, each containing about 1000 pairs of bases. The total DNA content of a human cell is about 2 metres long, and one millimetre of DNA contains about 5 million base pairs.

Biologists came up with what they call the 'central dogma': DNA makes RNA (ribonucleic acid), RNA makes proteins and proteins make everything else. When a double helix of DNA unzips, bases within the cell nucleus are attracted in a specific way to the unpaired bases in the DNA – as John Griffith (see over) had predicted, but with uracil (U) taking the place of thymine (T). This results in negative copies of DNA chains, and when the bases in these are joined by the appropriate bases, the RNA virtually matches the DNA. The RNA molecule passes through the cell's protein-synthesizing machinery to produce, first, amino acids, which in turn form proteins – the building blocks of life.

It is the order in which the bases occur on DNA that makes the genetic code. However, sometimes mistakes happen: one base may be substituted for another, a base might be lost, one might be added and so on. It is through these mistakes, or mutations, that evolutionary change occurs, but they are also responsible for genetic diseases.

pictures of the spotty patterns produced when the DNA was pulled out to form a thin fibre. While the spots suggested a helix (a spiral like a corkscrew), he lacked the expertise to interpret the X-ray data.

That expertise was provided by Rosalind Franklin (1920–58). Having worked on the structure of coal, she joined the team at King's in 1951 on the understanding she would take over the study of DNA from Wilkins. On arrival, she was less than pleased to find that he continued to be involved and even considered her a junior partner. There was excessive acrimony, and the atmosphere in the King's labs was hardly conducive to team work.

CRICK AND WATSON

In 1949, the physicist Francis Crick (1916–) joined the MRC's unit at Cambridge University as a research student. Two years later, he was joined by an American, James Watson (1928–), a former child prodigy who had entered the University of Chicago at the age of 15.

Watson was convinced that discovering the structure of DNA would be the next big breakthrough, and his enthusiasm infected Crick. Neither knew much biochemistry, but what they did have was a relationship that allowed them to bounce ideas off each other, and the ability to see the 'big picture' and meld together aspects of a number of different specialities to come up with something new.

No DNA research was possible without X-ray diffraction data, but Watson knew that a team at King's was working

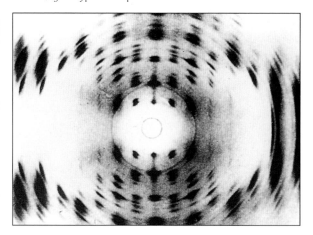

on just that. That team was led by Wilkins, a friend of Crick's, and the Cambridge duo soon realized that Wilkins found relief from his arguments with Rosalind Franklin by talking about DNA research with them.

In November 1951, Watson attended a colloquium at which Franklin presented her evidence that the DNA molecule was a helix with a phosphate-sugar backbone on the outside and the four bases tucked away inside. But he didn't take notes, and back at Cambridge, he and Crick built a model based on a theory by American chemist Linus Pauling that the structure comprised three helices. When Wilkins brought Franklin to see it, she showed how the model was hopelessly at odds with her X-ray data. Watson and Crick were so embarrassed that they abandoned DNA research for almost six months.

Then, in a casual conversation with John Griffith, a mathematician interested in biology (and nephew of Frederick Griffith), Crick learned that DNA's bases paired up, with A attracting T and G attracting C. This was vital in the later discovery of how DNA is able to replicate itself. Shortly after this, Crick was introduced to Erwin Chargaff, who described his 'Ratios' – which immediately explained Griffith's findings.

In January 1953, Peter Pauling, son of the eminent chemist, showed Watson a paper that his father was about to publish revealing the structure of DNA as a triple helix with phosphate backbones inside. Crick and Watson knew from their previous disaster that this had to be wrong, and agreed that they had just six weeks' grace to discover what the true structure was, before the Pauling paper was published.

Wilkins gave Watson (without her permission) a print of one of Franklin's best X-ray photographs of DNA, which told Watson that the structure might be a double helix. He and Crick began another model – a double helix but with the backbones on the inside and the bases sticking out. It was only when they compared this to Franklin's X-ray data that they realized how wrong they had been and changed the model so that the backbones were on the outside and the bases inside. The result looked like a twisted ladder, with the bases as the rungs, but it was another week or so before the two had assembled the bases in the right order.

The final, correct model of the DNA structure was completed on 7 March 1953. On 25 April, Crick and Watson published a short paper in *Nature* revealing their discovery. Rosalind Franklin never realized how much their model depended on her data – for one thing, she was never told that they had seen the all-important X-ray photograph beforehand.

In 1962, Crick, Watson and Wilkins were awarded the Nobel Prize for Physiology and Medicine. Rosalind Franklin had died of cancer four years earlier.

BREAKING THE CODES

There are up to 4000 human diseases caused by defective genes, and studies in the US indicate that as many as one baby in every 20 born alive may have a genetic disorder.

Sickle cell anaemia is the result of the substitution of a single wrong base, and up to 40 per cent of West Africans are carriers. Another disease caused by a single gene deficiency is cystic fibrosis, the most common such deficiency in Britain. On the other hand, the blood disorder thalassaemia – found around the Mediterranean, but also suffered by thousands of children in Thailand – can be due to any one of up to 40 different mutations. Finally, there are diseases caused by abnormal chromosomes, involving many genes – for example, Down's syndrome, in which a baby has three copies (instead of two) of chromosome 21.

Doctors have been able to screen unborn babies for genetic diseases by using amniocentesis and chorion biopsy (see p.155) to look for biochemical changes. Now, techniques are being developed to discover abnormalities in DNA itself. One is gene mapping, in which enzymes are used to cut up DNA so that particular genes can be compared with those of a healthy person to determine if there is a defect. Dr Fred Sanger, of Cambridge University, invented a manual method of deciphering DNA in 1977, but, since then, the Heidelberg team led by Wilhelm Ansorge has developed a computerized gene-reading machine.

In the mid-1980s, scientists embarked on a massive international project to identify every gene on the human 'genome' – the total of 100,000 genes carried within every human cell nucleus. James Watson headed the US end of this 'Human Genome Project'. By the early 1990s, researchers had labelled and decoded some 2000 genes.

In addition, researchers have been able to identify quite a number of genes responsible for specific diseases, including:

- Duchenne muscular dystrophy – gene discovered in 1986 by Tony Monaco and Louis Kunkel, of Harvard.
- Cystic fibrosis – gene located by Dr Francis Collins, of the University of Michigan, and Dr Lap-Chee Tsui, of Toronto.
- Cancer – the p53 gene responsible for an enzyme preventing tumour growth was found in 1979 by a British team led by David Lane, and by Dr Arnold Levine of Princeton; another gene, implicated in colon cancer, was found by Bert Vogelstein, of Johns Hopkins, in the early 1990s.
- Inherited high blood cholesterol levels (which usually lead to

heart disease) – gene discovered by Michael Brown and Joseph Goldstein, at the University of Texas.
- An inherited form of Alzheimer's disease – gene located by researchers at St Mary's Hospital, London, in 1991.
- Retinitis pigmentosa (inherited blindness) – gene found by David McConnell, Peter Humphries and Jane Farrar, of Trinity College, Dublin.

It will be some time before genetic engineering can tackle genetic disease head on. A start was made in 1980, when Martin Cline, of the University of California, unsuccessfully treated two thalassaemia patients by inserting a corrected version of a defective gene into their bone marrow. Ten years later, scientists at the National Institutes of Health in Bethesda, Maryland, injected white cells carrying a normal gene responsible for the production of adenosine deaminase (ADA), an enzyme vital to immunity, into a four-year-old girl; the replacement genes triggered production of ADA, but the cure was only temporary.

BELOW A young boy with the appearance characteristic of Down's syndrome (also called 'trisomy 21', for an extra chromosome 21). Down's can be detected in the foetus during pregnancy by amniocentesis, and a decision on termination made, but in the future genetic engineering may make the problem avoidable.

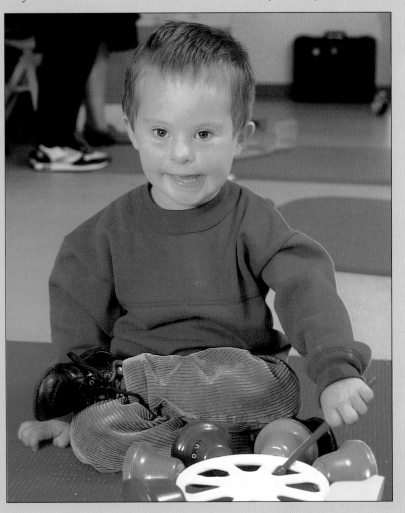

THE RISE OF PHARMACOLOGY

A NEW PANOPLY OF DRUGS

Side-effects led to a new concern about how and why drugs worked

EVEN BEFORE THE near-miraculous healing powers of penicillin *(see pp.136-7)* were fully demonstrated during World War II, investigators had proved there are many other natural sources of antibiotics besides the mould *Penicillium notatum*. However, it took years of dogged persistence by the biologist Selman Waksman (1888–1973) and his colleagues at Rutgers University to turn this theoretical general knowledge into specific practical effect.

Waksman, Russian-born but an American citizen, reasoned that if penicillin could destroy or inhibit more than 100 different disease-producing bacteria, other moulds or fungi might yield substances to combat diseases penicillin could not touch – among them, tuberculosis, meningitis and typhoid. His chosen candidates for testing were the streptomycetes, or ray fungi, and in particular the light grey *Streptomyces griseus* he had isolated and named. It was a difficult task. No two cultures of *S. griseus* have identical properties, and Waksman's team tested more than 10,000 of them before the breakthrough came. Then, as in Fleming's discovery of *P. notatum*, it contained an element of luck.

A CHICKEN'S THROAT

A poultry farmer whose chickens had been struck by a mysterious illness brought a hen to Rutgers' agricultural research station for examination. There, veterinarians noticed a white spot in the bird's throat, and scraped it to obtain material for analysis. The growth proved to be *S. griseus*, so as a matter of course it was passed to Waksman's team, who cultured it and then submitted it to the usual battery of experiments. Unlike the thousands of previous cultures, this

ABOVE *Dr Mildred C. Rebstock, of the Parke-Davis Pharmaceutical Company, in Detroit, featured on the cover of* The Illustrated London News *of 1949. Dr Rebstock was the first to synthesize chloromycetin – a wonderfully effective antibiotic later found to have fatal side-effects in very rare circumstances.*

LEFT *Streptomycin, first discovered by Waksman and his team in the scrapings from a chicken's throat, was soon manufactured under licence world-wide. Here, a technician works on the new wonder drug in the Nottingham, England, laboratories of Boots Ltd in 1946.*

ABOVE *A polarized light micro-graph of crystals of streptomycin:* *the drug was powerful and effective, but side-effects could be disturbing.*

one worked – rapidly destroying cocci, spirochetes and other germs, including the deadly tuberculosis bacterium.

Waksman and his team were jubilant. They ransacked the poultry run looking for soil samples, successfully seeking other examples of *S. griseus* with similar properties. Then, after tests on laboratory animals, they began clinical trials, with some spectacular triumphs. In one trial, streptomycin – as Waksman called the new substance – produced the first recorded cure of the previously fatal tuberculous meningitis. An outbreak of plague in India provided the opportunity to demonstrate streptomycin's power against one of humanity's oldest scourges – the antibiotic cut the death rate from 70 per cent to just 4 per cent in a matter of weeks. Within a year of streptomycin's discovery, US pharmaceutical companies were producing the world's second antibiotic on a mass scale. In 1952, Waksman received a Nobel prize.

ILL-EFFECTS OF A WONDER DRUG

Streptomycin swiftly proved itself capable of tackling a wide range of diseases not susceptible to penicillin or the sulphonamide drugs, adding a potent new weapon to the medical armoury. But although it appeared harmless in tests on laboratory rats, it created side-effects in the altogether more sensitive human body. In many cases they were mild and temporary, such as rashes, fever or inflammation around the site of the injection. In others, they were serious and permanent, with damage to hearing and balance, to the eyes, the kidney or the liver. Not only patients were affected – doctors and nurses handling streptomycin could absorb it through skin lesions or by inhalation.

The concern evoked by these side-effects led researchers to study closely the impact that streptomycin had on the physiology and biochemistry of the body. Though pharmacology was not a new science, it had been rather a hit-and-miss affair. Many drugs were used simply because they worked, without any real understanding of how or why, or of what their ancillary effects might be. Henceforth, research was to pay far greater attention to such questions.

In the case of streptomycin, researchers noticed that many of the unwanted symptoms resembled those produced by guanidine, a poisonous substance occurring in the body when enzymes released from injured tissues attack and break down protein. Sure enough, detailed analysis of the structure

THE CURSE OF TB

The discovery of streptomycin seemed to promise the final cure for tuberculosis (see pp.110-1). But while the antibiotic helped to alleviate or clear up many cases of the disease, many more – particularly those affecting the lungs – proved tenacious. The latter needed prolonged treatment with doses of streptomycin that increased several hundred fold in strength as the tubercle bacillus in the patient's body developed resistance. At first, the severe side-effects made this almost impossible. Even when the development of pantothenic streptomycin banished most of the side-effects, allowing patients to receive the drug constantly through intravenous drip infusion, the problem of increased resistance remained. TB victims who seemed well on the way to recovery would suddenly worsen and die.

From 1949, the Veteran's Administration in the US had begun to test TB treatments that used both streptomycin and para-aminosalicylic acid (PAS, or sodium aminosalicylate). This drug was shown to inhibit the tubercle bacillus, through a brilliant piece of applied logic by Sweden's Jorgen Lehmann, in 1943. Though PAS on its own was not nearly so effective as streptomycin, it slowed down the emergence of resistant strains of the bacillus, giving the antibiotic a better chance to work. The idea for combination therapy for TB had been born.

In 1951, a pharmaceutical company in West Germany and two others in the US independently discovered that the hydrazide salt of isonicotinic acid (isoniazid, as it came to be called) was successful against TB in animals. Given to humans by mouth, it produced few adverse reactions and appeared to be more effective than streptomycin, though not markedly more so than the combination of streptomycin and PAS. However, controlled trials by the US Public Health Service using streptomycin and isoniazid in tandem yielded dramatic results – 30 per cent of pulmonary TB patients showed improvement, against 18 per cent among those treated with the earlier pairing.

Doctors now had three specific anti-TB drugs where a few years earlier they had none. As TB bacilli developed resistance to one, the doctors could switch to another, varying the patterns of use and doses according to the progress of any given patient. Such treatment took time and painstaking monitoring – almost individualized pharmacology. By the early 1970s, another five antibiotics and three synthesized chemicals with anti-TB properties had been developed, greatly increasing the cure rate. Isoniazid had been shown to be effective, too, in preventing TB, paving the way for immunization campaigns that went a long way towards curtailing its ravages in developed countries.

of streptomycin revealed it contained two guanidine groups. Once those were removed, the toxic side-effects of streptomycin on human patients disappeared. Unfortunately, so did much of its antibiotic action.

THE THALIDOMIDE SCANDAL

In the 1950s, Wilhelm Kunz, a chemist at Chemie Grunenthal in West Germany, was experimenting with peptides (chains of amino acids) for use in antibiotics when he invented thalidomide. Noticing the similarity of its molecular structure to that of some sedatives, Kunz's colleague, Herbert Keller, suggested testing thalidomide for these properties.

It certainly was a sedative, but it also had no obvious side-effects and showed no toxic effects at any concentration. The company was convinced it had found the first safe sleeping pill.

Hailed as 'a major breakthrough', thalidomide was introduced in 1956 – over the next five years it would be marketed under 51 trade names and sold in 46 countries. However, reports of side-effects (giddiness, numbness, 'pins and needles', shivering) started to come in – culminating in 1961 with the realization by Dr William McBride, a consultant obstetrician in Sydney, Australia, that pregnant women who took thalidomide in early pregnancy were producing severely deformed children.

By the end of 1962, the drug had been withdrawn, but not before some 7500 'thalidomide children' had been born world-wide. Drug safety legislation followed: in the US, Estes Kefauver, who was presiding over a Senate Committee investigating the side-effects of drugs, was able to push an important Drugs Bill through Congress in 1962; in the UK, the scandal led to the setting up in 1964 of the Committee on Safety of Drugs – a voluntary body that reviewed all new drugs. Following the Medicines Act, in 1968, a regulatory body – the Committee on Safety of Medicines – was established.

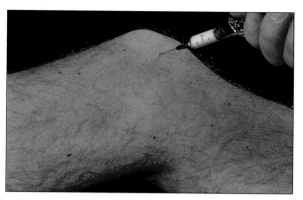

ABOVE *Injecting a knee joint with a corticosteroid to treat synovitis – inflammation of the interior lining of the joint. Since 1944, steroids have relieved pain and inflammation for millions, but at a price.*

good example. These fat-soluble compounds include the male and female sex hormones, adrenalin, cholesterol and vitamin D. They also include the body's own version of the heart stimulant digitalis, which occurs in the foxglove leaves administered by generations of herbalists.

The effects of digitalis had been known for a long time, and those of some other steroids became clear in the early 20th century. But chemists could not explain how they worked or emulate them artificially until a German, Heinrich Wieland, elucidated the structure of cholesterol in 1932. Chemists in several countries then found that other steroids share the same basic pattern of four linked carbon atoms to which hydrogen atoms are attached. There are thousands of possible arrangements and variations of these components, particularly with the addition of atoms of hydrogen, carbon and oxygen. And even a slight change in the chemical structure can alter the biological results.

During World War II, cortisone was a particular focus for research. Experiments with rats indicated its role in counteracting stress, and it was thought by both sides in the war to help in cases of battle fatigue. But the process of synthesizing it from cholesterol was extremely complicated. It was only in 1944 that a young American chemist, Lewis Sarrett, devised a process to make enough cortisone for medical use, obtaining it from the bile of cattle.

By then, the war was all but over and more peaceful applications were considered. At the Mayo Clinic, in the US, Philip Hench and Edward Kendall used cortisone in the treatment of rheumatoid arthritis, with what were said to be miraculous effects. The pair duly received a Nobel prize for their work, though cortisone and related drugs are now thought only to alleviate pain and disability in the middle stages of the disease, without affecting its progress. Possible side-effects, including raised blood pressure, diabetes and osteoporosis mean it can be administered only in carefully gauged quantities under strict medical control.

The inescapable conclusion was that streptomycin's power rested with its guanidines, which therefore had to be tamed rather than extracted. Experiments showed that this could be partially achieved by adding hydrogen, turning it into dihydrostreptomycin. However, it was not until 1953 that the true pharmacological solution to the problem began to emerge. First, researchers in Sweden demonstrated that doses of vitamin A minimized the damage done by streptomycin to the inner ear or kidneys. Then, German experts tested the drug in combination with pantothenic acid – an oily B-complex vitamin essential to cell growth, that protects mucous membranes against infection and nourishes the skin.

By enhancing the natural processes of the body, the pantothenic acid effectively neutralized most of the potential harm of the guanidines without diminishing streptomycin's antibiotic properties. The result not only made Waksman's drug far safer for general use, but it also opened the eyes of medical science to the close connection between the action of antibiotics and the metabolic role of vitamins.

PAIN-KILLING CORTISONE

The process of determining and taking into account the body's responses to a drug was a feature of the anti-TB campaign that had parallels in other areas of pharmaceutical research during the 1940s. The study of steroids provides a

RABBITS AND DOGS

Pharmacologists discovered that one of the physiological effects of cortisone is to depress the natural immune response protecting the body. Normally, medicine seeks to stimulate that response to help fight off disease. But in organ transplant surgery (*see pp.180-3*), the reverse applies: depressed immunity lessens the likelihood that the recipient's body will reject the transplant.

By the 1950s, cortisone was being used to help in skin grafts and kidney transplants. However, scientists such as William Dameshek, of Tufts University in the US, reasoned that if better suppressants could be found, a wider range of such operations could be carried out – for example, to replace bone marrow in victims of leukaemia. An early candidate was mercaptopurine, developed to combat cancer but also found to have suppressive properties in tests on rabbits.

But the drug had shortcomings. As a cytotoxin to inhibit cancer in humans, it was rapidly metabolized by the enzyme xanthine oxidase and lost its effect. And although it depressed normal cellular immunity in rabbits, it worked less well in experimental kidney transplants in dogs. Hundreds of similar drugs were prepared to see if mercaptopurine's performance in both respects could be improved. After extensive screening by George Hitchings and others, the variant azathioprine emerged as the most suitable in 1961.

Though azathioprine was equally effective as an immuno-suppressant, it could not match mercaptopurine as a cytotoxin. Hitchings took a different tack. Instead of looking for a mercaptopurine substitute that would be metabolized less easily, he searched for a substance that would block the action of metabolizing enzyme, xanthine oxidase. Among the vast array of synthetic purines screened earlier, he found one that slowed down the metabolism of mercaptopurine and improved the immunosuppression of azathioprine.

In the laboratory, the prospects looked good. Tested on leukaemia patients, the purine enabled the dosage of mercap-topurine to be reduced – but without any additional thera-peutic benefit. In that respect, Hitchings's pharmacological detective work had been a failure. Nevertheless, it was far from wasted. By inhibiting the action of xanthine oxidase, the purine reduced the levels of uric acid in the blood. That made it a valuable treatment for gout and kidney stones, which are caused by excessive deposits of uric acid salts. The drug was commercially marketed for that purpose from 1966, under the name allopurinol.

LEFT *Dr George Hitchings won a Nobel prize in 1988 in recognition of 40 years of brilliant research, mainly at the Burroughs-Wellcome Laboratories in the US.*

BELOW *Pharmaceutical production has come a long way since the days of the pestle and mortar – here, a technician operates a spray head used to coat tablets.*

THE BODY WITHIN

FROM ULTRASOUND TO NUCLEAR MAGNETIC RESONANCE

World War II submarine technology led to the first non-invasive technique

THE ADVENT OF HIGH-TECHNOLOGY diagnostics in the 1950s gradually transformed the doctor-patient relationship, making diagnosis in many instances far easier and more accurate – but also more mechanical and impersonal. Critics of the trend say it leads to practitioners concentrating on the quantifiable aspects of illness at the expense of the other, more qualitative elements, such as the patient's mental or emotional condition. That criticism has grown since the revival of interest in holistic medicine (*see pp.218-21; 240-1*). Those in favour argue that the new high-technology diagnostic techniques free doctors from mechanical chores, enabling them to spend more time considering their patients as entire human beings.

LOOKING INTO THE WOMB

A baby in the womb in some ways resembles a submerged submarine – and the similarity was not lost on Ian Donald when he became Professor of Midwifery at the University of Glasgow, Scotland, in the 1950s. Borrowing a technique developed by French, British and American scientists to detect enemy vessels and other objects underwater in wartime, Donald and his colleagues pioneered a new method of assessing the progress of a foetus through pregnancy.

Time was to prove it safer for that purpose than X-rays, which by the mid-1950s had been shown to increase the risk of leukaemia and other malignant diseases in later childhood.

The technique Donald adapted was known in the British navy as sonar. It relied on the fact that certain crystals, when subjected to an electric charge, emit sound waves at frequencies so high they cannot be heard by the human ear. These ultrasonic waves travel particularly well through water and similar fluids, sending back clear echoes when they encounter a solid object. The object's distance can be calculated simply from the time lapse between emission of the sound waves and their reception as echoes. More importantly, the echoes can be converted into visual signals displayed on a cathode-ray tube; variations in the echoes caused by different sound-reflective properties of different parts of the object compose a 'picture' of it on the screen.

Donald, like other medical pioneers of ultrasound in the US, Sweden and elsewhere, at first employed the technique to tackle problems unrelated to pregnancy. His earliest experiments, with an ultrasonic metal-flaw detector on loan

BELOW *The whole family views its new member in the ultrasound room of a US hospital – the left screen shows a foot; the right, an arm.*

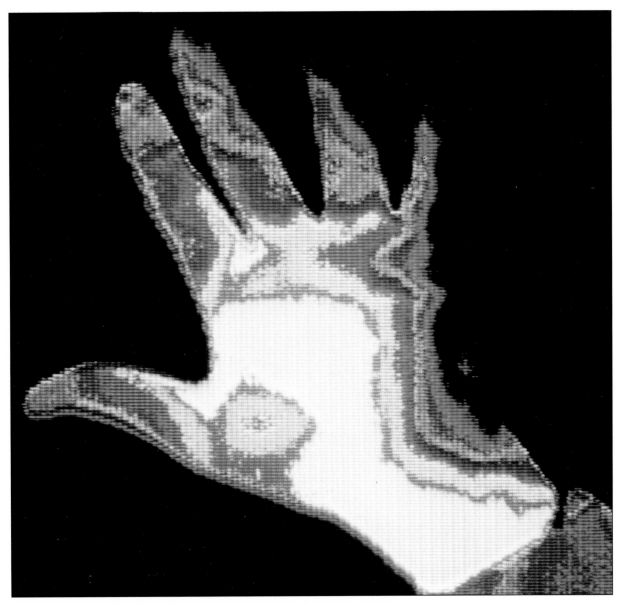

from a Glasgow engineering works, concentrated on demonstrating that different types of abdominal tumours give different echoes, and then on diagnosing the nature of tumours prior to surgery. But by 1957, he was using the technique to diagnose disorders of the foetus, and by 1963, he had applied it in more than 100 cases to establish the fact of pregnancy itself – all before 20 weeks and, in one instance, before nine weeks.

Many people, including Donald, expressed fears that in some circumstances ultrasound could prove as potentially harmful as X-rays to the foetus. But those doubts have largely been discounted in the light of experience and technical developmnent. Meanwhile, the use of computers to convert the sound signals into visual images has greatly improved their quality, so that the foetus can be monitored in minute detail for abnormalities.

WATCHING FOR HOT SPOTS

Because ultrasound quickly established itself in Britain and elsewhere as semi-routine in the management of pregnancy, it has become probably the most familiar of the high-

ABOVE *A thermographic picture of an arthritic hand, showing hot areas (red and yellow) round the joints of the thumb and fingers.*

technology diagnostic techniques developed since World War II. But there have been many others.

While Ian Donald and his colleagues were still refining their application of ultrasound in 1961, scientists at the Middlesex Hospital, in London, were working out the clinical requirements of thermography – a somewhat similar technique, but based on the infrared radiation found in heat rather than on sound waves.

Different parts of the body emit varying patterns of heat, measurable by the intensity of the infrared waves they contain. Using an infrared-sensitive camera and film, the patterns can be recorded and analysed to identify abnormalities. The sensitivity of the equipment is such that it can detect, record and analyse temperature differences between one and two degrees Celsius. Cancerous tumours, for example, are hotter than normal and show up on the film or screen as bright red 'hot spots'. Osteoarthritic joints, by contrast, are colder and may appear blue.

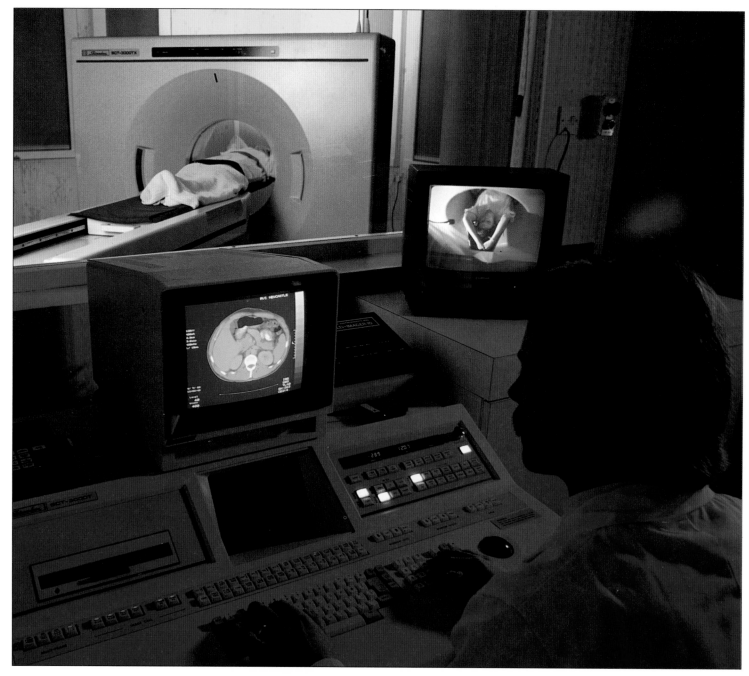

THREE-DIMENSIONAL X-RAYS

In 1967, G. N. Hounsfield, an engineer and computer expert working for the British company EMI, began work on a system that would build up a three-dimensional image of the body, or any organ within it. Such images, displayed on a screen, would be able determine the overall shape, together with details of length, breadth and depth, of a diseased area without the need for surgery.

The system, called computerized axial tomography, or CAT for short, feeds a series of narrow X-ray beams through the patient to produce detailed cross-sections, which are then processed by a computer to create a three-dimensional picture. The landscape of the picture is characterized by the varying density of the tissues being scanned. The denser a tissue is, the more of the X-ray beam it absorbs. Later refinements to the CAT scanner, for which Hounsfield

ABOVE A patient disappears into the maw of a CAT scanner, while a radiographer operates the scanner's computer terminal in the control room. The image on the screen is a view of the patient's abdomen.

shared the Nobel Prize for Medicine in 1979, enabled the computer to colour the scan according to tissue density.

The invention of the CAT scanner led to the development of other types, such as the PETT (positron emission transaxial tomography) scanner. This machine is used to diagnose and monitor brain disorders, but instead of scanning with X-rays it relies on radioactive emissions and enables doctors to study the brain actually at work. Patients are injected with mildly radioactive glucose. As the brain takes up the glucose, different areas take up varying amounts according to their energy needs and therefore their level of activity. These differing consumption levels can be monitored and analysed, allowing doctors to track down the distinctive patterns associated with mental illnesses, such as schizophrenia and dementia.

RESONATING ATOMS

An even more advanced method of producing pictures of what is going on inside the body is nuclear magnetic resonance imaging (NMR or MRI). This technique is based upon the principle that hydrogen atoms in the body resonate when energy from magnets is beamed at them. The phenomenon of magnetic resonance was first extensively analysed in 1946, in the US, but it was three decades before it began to be generally applied in medical diagnosis.

As with CAT scanners, the NMR machine enables doctors to display three-dimensional images of the body on a screen. Its main advantage over the CAT scanner, however, is that it does not involve radiation and can be used when X-rays might be considered harmful to the patient. NMR also allows the chemistry of the body's metabolism to be studied while it is actually taking place – the amount of a specific substance can be determined, without the need for laboratory analysis of tissue samples. Because of this ability to examine atoms and molecules, NMR has proved useful for monitoring the progress of such diseases as muscular dystrophy and operations involving organ transplants.

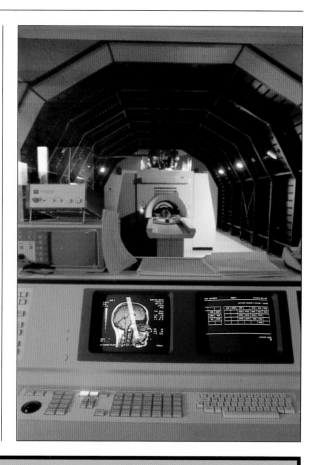

RIGHT *A patient undergoing an MRI brain scan lies in the coils of the scanner's magnets. The screen* *in the control room shows an image of the brain, with the spinal cord and grey and white matter visible.*

TUBES WITH A VIEW

Despite the technical advances in many forms of body scanning since Ian Donald's first clinical experiments with ultrasound, none of them can properly scrutinize certain conditions, such as stomach ulcers. In these instances, doctors look directly into the body by inserting an endoscope – an illuminated tube said to have been devised by Phillipe Bozzini of Frankfurt in 1806 – via the mouth or other orifice.

Bozzini's invention was developed and refined in various ways during the 19th and 20th centuries. But it entered the age of high technology only in the 1950s, when fully flexible fibre-optic instruments first appeared. In 1965, Professor Harold Hopkins, of Reading University, England, introduced a system of rod lenses that afforded a much clearer view than obtained when optics based on telescopes had been used.

Though several types of rigid endoscope are still in use, the most advanced kind consists of a narrow, flexible tube containing two smaller tubes – all of glass fibre. A beam of light is shot down one of the inner tubes to illuminate the area to be examined, while an eyepiece or camera is attached to the other tube. Some flexible endoscopes are equipped with microchip sensors to feed back data to a computer for analysis. They also play an important part in laser surgery, which was invented in 1963: a laser beam, directed along an optical fibre in the endoscope, burns off growths, such as tumours, or cauterizes ruptured blood vessels.

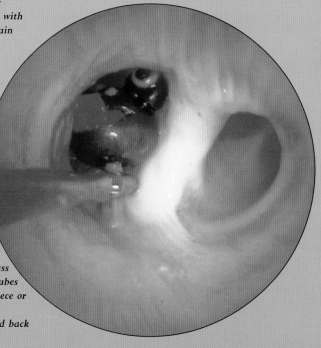

ABOVE *This remarkable endoscope photograph shows a martini stirrer stuck in the windpipe of a child who had been foolish enough to* *swallow it. Here endoscopy both identifies the position of the blockage and guides the surgeon as it is removed.*

MEDICAL TECHNOLOGY

FROM SAUSAGE CASINGS TO COMPUTERS

Twenty-three years of work saved the life of America's 'Heart Queen'

ADVANCES IN TECHNOLOGY since World War II have progressed far beyond anything the greatest visionary could have imagined. The following histories can only highlight a few of the many new machines and techniques that have so radically changed medicine.

THE KIDNEY DIALYSIS MACHINE

Human kidneys filter blood to remove impurities, which, if allowed to accumulate, can seriously damage the body. They do this in two stages: first, by coarse filtering through the glomeruli, knots of capillaries with very thin walls; and then, by fine filtering through the renal tubules.

As early as 1914, a team at Johns Hopkins, Baltimore, invented the first 'membrane vividiffusion apparatus' – or artificial kidney – for dogs. For their 'glomeruli', they used tubes made out of collodion (cellulose nitrate mixed with alcohol and ether), and ran arterial blood from a dog through them, keeping the blood liquid by adding hirudin, the anticoagulant made by leeches *(see p.139)*. When the tubes were bathed in a sterile water, the impurities in the blood would naturally cross over, through minute holes in the tubes, until the concentration of impurities was equal on both sides. This is 'dialysis': the separation of particles in a

liquid according to their ability to pass through a membrane into another liquid. The partly cleansed blood would then be returned to the dog's body.

The Johns Hopkins' animal experiments were largely forgotten by the scientific community, save by one man – Willem Kolff, of the Municipal Hospital at Kampen in the Netherlands. In 1943, during the Nazi occupation of that country, and in very difficult circumstances, he managed to construct a kidney dialysis machine for use by humans, but instead of collodion tubes, he used sausage casings.

Kolff's machine was later modified so that the blood passed through large, flat membranes made of cellophane, called 'Kil plates' after the Scandinavian doctor who invented them. But these were cumbersome, and were eventually replaced with more compact coils of flat cellophane tubing, a shape that ensures that the blood passes over the largest possible area of membrane. These dialysis membranes formerly had to be cleaned after each use, but they are now simply replaced, so greatly reducing the risk of infection.

At first, kidney machines were restricted to the treatment of patients with acute kidney failure or poisoning by drugs that could be removed through dialysis. The idea was to keep them alive long enough for their kidneys to recover or for the poison to be eliminated. Then, in the early 1960s, Belding Scribner, of the University of Washington, Seattle, began to treat patients with chronic kidney failure by giving them long-term and repeated dialysis.

This had been impossible in the past. The two tubes, or cannulae, carrying the blood from an artery to the dialysis machine and then returning it to a vein, would become blocked with clots. They would then have to be reinserted every few weeks at a different site, and soon no more suitable sites would remain. This problem was overcome by the introduction of cannulae made of Teflon-Silastic, a product of the US space programme, which were so smooth inside that clotting was far less likely.

From the start, kidney dialysis proved to be extremely expensive and doctors were faced with the terrible task of choosing which patients would benefit most from the treatment, with the rest under inevitable sentence of death. Scribner set up a committee to make these decisions, feeling that they were a matter for society, not doctors. He also began to look at ways to reduce the cost of dialysis, and to make the procedure fit better with the everyday lifestyles of his patients, instead of having them come into hospital twice a week for about 16 hours each time. In 1964, he arranged for two patients to begin dialysis at home, using a simplified and largely automated machine.

LEFT *A renal dialysis machine –* *replaces the function of the kidneys*
this example is for home use – *by clearing wastes from the blood.*

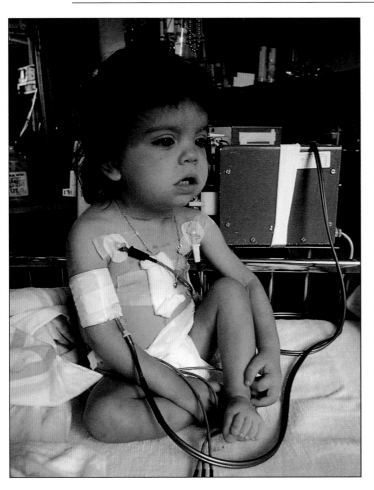

ABOVE *A young girl, suffering from diabetes insipidus, undergoes renal dialysis. The procedure is a life-saving one: the machine takes over the function of the damaged organ until a suitable kidney donor is found.*

Today, many kidney patients are taught home dialysis and manage to lead relatively normal lives. However, dialysis is not the ideal solution: patients become anaemic, are more prone to infection, especially from hepatitis B *(see p.201)*, and may suffer from severe depression. The best possible treatment for almost all kidney patients remains a kidney transplant *(see p.180)*.

THE HEART-LUNG MACHINE

Stopping the heart long enough for surgery to be carried out *(see pp.178-9)* was impossible until 1953. In some ways, the problems of developing the technology that would make this possible were similar to those faced by Willem Kolff, but instead of trying to discover ways of taking impurities out of the blood, researchers had to find a method of putting oxygen into it.

In October 1930, American surgeon John H. Gibbon, Jr was part of a team in Boston that operated on a woman, known now only as 'Edith S.', for the removal of a massive pulmonary embolism (a clot blocking the pulmonary artery carrying blood from the heart to the lungs). When she died, Gibbon resolved to devise a machine that would take over the work of the heart and lungs during surgery.

So began 23 years of work. Gibbon's first machine incorporated a hollow metal cylinder that revolved in a vertical position. On the inner surface of this, centrifugal force held a thin film of blood, on to which he blew oxygen as it moved from the top to the bottom of the cylinder. However, this method could not oxygenate enough blood fast enough, and Gibbon's mission seemed doomed until some of his associates came up with an idea. They covered the smooth inner surface of the cylinder with a wire screen to create turbulence in the blood film and a greater surface area, too. With this, they were were able to oxygenate eight to ten times more blood per minute – enough to support the life of an adult human.

LASERS IN MEDICINE

In 1917, Albert Einstein revealed his sole contribution to medicine: the principles of what would become the 'laser' (Light Amplification by Stimulated Emission of Radiation). From 1960, when the first machine was built, it would be known as 'a solution looking for a problem'. Hundreds of uses have since been found for it in industry, science and warfare, as well as in medicine – particularly in surgery, where lasers have the advantages of precision, painlessness and reduced risk of accident and infection.

The best known medical application is in eye surgery, where lasers are employed to repair detached retinas, destroy malignant tumours, remove cataracts and relieve glaucoma. Cancers of the intestines, spine, skin, lung and larynx are also attacked with lasers, and they can be used for 'tissue welding', when blood vessels are joined back together. One of the first ways they were used was in the removal of birthmarks known as 'port wine stains', and carbon-dioxide lasers have since been successful in obliterating tattoos.

An example of the addition of a very new technology to a very old healing method is laser acupuncture. A small

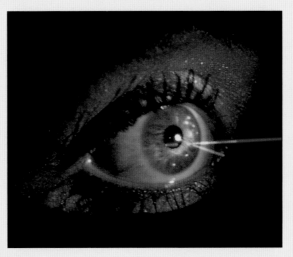

ABOVE *The development of laser technology has added a new dimension to the surgeon's repertoire. Here, a laser beam is passed through the pupil of a human eye during an operation.*

laser replaces the needles, and avoids the risk of infection from hepatitis B and AIDS.

TEST-TUBE BABIES

In the early 1960s, the British gynaecologist/obstetrician Patrick Steptoe had many women patients who were infertile due to blockage of their Fallopian tubes (through which their eggs should travel to meet sperm and, when fertilized, continue on into the uterus for implantation). He reckoned that this problem could be overcome if an egg were removed from an ovary – using a laparoscope, an instrument that he had pioneered – and fertilized with sperm, kept alive for a few days to ensure that an embryo was forming and then placed in the mother's uterus for normal development.

What Steptoe envisaged has become known as 'test-tube' fertilization. However, test-tubes were never used: the fertilization took place in shallow glass petri dishes, and the correct name for this technique is in vitro fertilization ('fertilization in glass'), or IVF.

A few years later, Steptoe began collaborating with Robert Edwards, a physiologist at Cambridge University, England, who had spent a great deal of time investigating laboratory fertilization. Edwards was able to recognize under the microscope the exact moment when human eggs are ripe and capable of being fertilized. In February 1969, he and Steptoe announced in Nature that they had achieved fertilization of 13 human eggs (out of a total of 56) outside the body for the first time.

Nine years later, in July 1978, Louise Brown was born at Oldham District Hospital, England, by caesarean section – the first 'test-tube baby'. Patrick Steptoe took her anaesthetized mother's womb out of the abdominal incision to show to the cameras the complete absence of Fallopian tubes. The newspaper rights to the story sold for £300,000 (about $500,000).

The media were ecstatic about IVF, and promoted it so heavily that many people (and not a few doctors) believed that it was the breakthrough for which all infertile women had been waiting. But, by May 1989, it was shown that only 10.1 per cent of all treatments in Britain produced live babies. According to Robert Winston, of London's Hammersmith Hospital and one of the world's leading experts on infertility, "IVF is still the most demanding, the most emotionally fraught, the most expensive and the least successful of all infertility treatments".

In 1983, another technique to overcome infertility was developed when Dr Tesarik and colleagues in Czecho-slovakia first transferred a mixture of egg and sperm into a woman's Fallopian tube to give them the best opportunity to fertilize. In August the following year, Ricardo Asch, of the University of Texas, reported the first pregnancy resulting from this GIFT (gamete intrafallopian transfer), as it was named.

But by the early 1990s, all forms of artificial fertilization were under scrutiny. First, large payments to surrogate mothers (who receive eggs and sperm from couples who cannot have their own children) were outlawed in some countries. The Roman Catholic Church pronounced against IVF (but not against GIFT). There was uproar when it was revealed, in 1992, that a 54-year-old Italian woman had been impregnated with a donor egg fertilized by her husband's sperm, and an American doctor was sentenced to ten years' in prison for having used his own sperm when artificially inseminating dozens of his female patients.

BELOW *After* in vitro *fertilization, the embryo is allowed to develop for a few days before being implanted in the mother's womb.*

Gibbon took his team's creation to Thomas Watson, President of IBM, whose engineers constructed a compact, portable apparatus. In the early 1950s, Gibbon began a series of animal experiments – creating heart defects and then correcting them – to perfect his surgical technique.

In 1952, he operated on his first human patient – a 15-month-old baby – who died shortly after the operation, from an incorrect pre-operative diagnosis, not from the procedure. His second patient was 18-year-old Cecilia Bavolek, who had a hole between two of the chambers of her heart. On 6 May 1953, Gibbons operated, connecting the girl to his heart–lung machine for 45 minutes – for 27 minutes, it was her sole source of circulation and respiration.

Cecilia Bavolek recovered completely, but her fame as the first successful heart–lung machine patient led to emotional turmoil. Pressed for interviews and public appearances, she changed her phone number and avoided all publicity. However, ten years after the operation, in 1963, she agreed to become the 'Heart Queen' for the American Heart Association and received an award from President Lyndon Johnson.

Further research was carried out on outside-the-body oxygenation, especially by Clarence Lillehei, at the University of Minnesota. In 1954, believing that Gibbon's

BELOW *One of the earliest heart-lung machines, from 1956, in use in theatre. Such machines made heart surgery possible.*

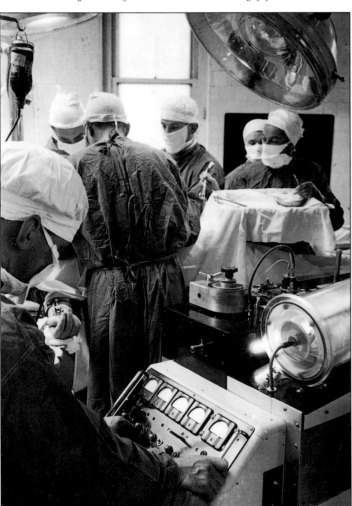

machine was not sufficiently developed, he operated on a child using one of its parents in place of the machine; the following year, he employed a dog lung as an oxygenator; and a few months after that, he devised a simple disposable plastic oxygenator – all with exceedingly good results.

COMPUTERS IN MEDICINE

In the mid-1950s, a few biomedical scientists began to use computers to analyze complicated data, but only a handful of doctors even considered their possibilities. Gradually, however, physicians became attracted to them because of the amount of information they could store in such a small space, and because they had the ability to retrieve information and establish complicated associations between data.

By 1960, over 1000 illnesses and about 200 symptoms had been ascribed to the cornea of the eye alone, and doctors could no longer remember everything to do with the body as a whole. In addition, more than 15,000 medical papers were being published annually – far too many for any one person to read, much less absorb. Into the breach stepped information technology companies, which developed computer programs that could index, abstract and search for relevant papers at the touch of a few buttons.

In 1959, a study of private medical practice in the US revealed that less than one fifth of doctors kept complete records of their patients. Each could deal with up to 4000 patients a year, and in hospitals, medical files could be over 100 pages long, with contributions from doctors, nurses and other medical staff. In the 1960s, doctors and experts from other branches of science banded together to exploit the full potential of computers in hands-on medicine.

Programs were developed to take medical histories from patients, with each answer determining the next question asked. The computers elicited at least as many – or even more – significant symptoms than doctors had, and many patients preferred them: using the computer allowed time for thinking, was less embarrassing and patients believed that they were saving their doctors' time. Despite this, some physicians found the questions somewhat limiting, and regretted the loss of all the information that could be gathered from body language. Computerized history-taking never took off.

The use of computers in more scientific ways was far more successful. In the mid-1950s, the Cytoanalyzer was invented, which scanned cells and transmitted data about them into a computer that could then distinguish between normal and abnormal cells. Another computer program enabled the electronic impulses generated by a scan of an X-ray to be converted into numbers, which could be then be compared to find any pathological conditions. In 1972, ten radiologists were pitted against a computer using this program, to find evidence of rheumatic heart disease in a number of X-rays. The computer won, with a 73 per cent accuracy rate compared to the radiologists' 62 per cent.

The American space race had its own impact on computers in medicine through the sophisticated equipment invented to monitor the physiological changes in monkeys and astronauts. As one commentator put it: "If monkeys 100 miles in the air can be monitored, there is no reason why patients cannot be monitored". Many of the monitors now commonplace in hospital wards and intensive care units, owe their conception to the US space programme.

HIP REPLACEMENT

THE SEARCH FOR A LOW-FRICTION SOLUTION

Surgical skill and materials technology combined to change millions of lives

THE STRIKING SUCCESS of total hip replacement ranks high on the list of significant medical advances during the last quarter of the 20th century. Its achievement is a perfect example of how surgical skills and developments in materials technology can combine to defeat disabling illness – in this instance, arthritis of the hip.

Many people think that appendicectomy (removal of the appendix) is a common operation – it is, but total hip replacement in the developed world is now far more common. Over 100,000 operations are performed each year in the US and a similar number in Europe. This staggering statistic means that, over the years, millions of people worldwide have had their lives transformed – an exhausting battle against pain and disability has been won and they can now walk freely and sleep all through the night.

'GORILLAS WITH SHAVEN ARMS'

The origins of modern orthopaedic skill are difficult to trace. An Australian anatomy professor, G. Eliott Smith, working in Cairo, has suggested that orthopaedics is at least 4500 years old – circumcision is thought to be the only surgical procedure to predate it. Smith has shown that the first orthopaedic procedure conducted by our ancestors involved placing wooden splints of bark, held in position with linen, on opposing sides of a broken bone.

The poor esteem with which those who treated bones were held by their contemporaries is reflected in the comment, still occasionally heard today, that orthopaedic surgeons are 'gorillas with shaven arms'. But the demographic fact that many people in the developed world (and increasingly so in the developing world) now live to a ripe old age has contributed to a change in this derogatory attitude. For many of the best scientific minds have turned their attention to what can be done to improve the quality of life for men and women who, because of arthritic hips, often spend the last 10 or 15 years of their lives bedridden and in terrible pain. The objective is now to ensure everybody is as independent as possible for as long as possible, thus reducing to a minimum the time they need intensive – and, therefore, costly – medical care before they die.

IVORY, STEEL AND PLASTIC

The earliest replacements of a joint were conducted around the turn of the 20th century. The French surgeon Louis Ollier performed 270 elbow replacements by the year of his death in 1900. In 1891, a German surgeon, Theodore Gluck, is said to have replaced a hip with an ivory ball-and-socket joint that he cemented and screwed into place. But it was unusual for surgeons to attempt to replace the hip because, in the normal course of events, each hip joint is subject to huge loadings – up to five times body weight is

normal. Replacement technology would simply not have been able to cope.

With the advent of acrylics, plastics and biologically inert materials before World War II, the idea of replacing the hip became feasible. Various orthopaedic surgeons, such as John Wiles, of London, attempted hip joint replacement, or arthroplasty of the hip. They either replaced the head of the femur with artificial materials, such as stainless steel, or lined the socket, or acetabulum, in which the ball of the femoral head sits and rotates during leg movement. But problems of materials, fixation and design of prostheses continued to thwart the most inventive surgeons in their attempts to create permanent hip repair.

The first step toward this goal was taken by US surgeon Marcus Smith-Petersen of Boston, Massachusetts, who developed a technique in which a loose-fitting and highly polished metal cup was placed between the femoral head, which had been reduced in size, and an enlarged acetabulum. But this proved mechanically unstable and led to eventual loss of mobility.

Then, in the 1950s, the French brothers J. Judet and R. Judet replaced the head of the femur with a polished plastic hemisphere attached to a spike – the spike was driven down the stump of the femur to fix the whole prosthesis in place. The Judet operation resulted in a more stable joint, but there were frictional problems that manifested as 'squeaks'

BELOW *A false-colour X-ray of an artificial hip – the steel shaft appears yellow against the yellow-blue of the thigh bone.*

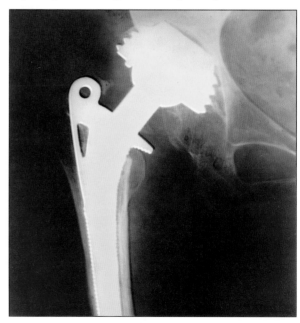

in the joint for the first few weeks. This friction resulted from the plastic rubbing against the bone of the acetabulum and even though the 'squeaks' stopped, the friction continued to strain the bond between the spike and the femoral neck.

But time and again, the replacement did not take, either because the cement did not properly bind the artificial material into its bodily location, or because the joint 'loosened'. A great deal of research has concentrated on trying to prevent this problem. Hundreds of different prostheses have been sampled and numerous surgical positions evaluated in an effort to discover the most mechanically advantageous arrangement and the one, therefore, that would be least likely to cause loosening.

MORE SLIPPERY THAN ICE

The turning point in total hip replacement came in 1960. John Charnley (1911–82), consultant orthopaedic surgeon to the Manchester Royal Infirmary, England, developed the technique for low-friction arthroplasty that has been the cornerstone of total hip replacements ever since. Announcing his new operation in the *Lancet,* in 1961, Charnley declared: "Neither surgeons nor engineers will ever make an artificial hip-joint which will last thirty years and at some time in this period enable the patient to play football". Charnley recognized the success of other methods but was aware that in nearly every case the hip replacement failed in the long term. His aim – and, ultimately, his achievement – was to "make this temporary success permanent".

Charnley, now known as 'the father of total hip replacement', was by training and inclination both engineer and orthopaedic surgeon. His low-friction arthroplasty involved using different materials for the two parts of the joint – the femoral head and acetabular cup. Friction between these two would be kept low if one was hard and the other was both soft and smooth. Charnley knew he could not mimic the lubrication of a normal animal joint, which he said was "rather more slippery than ice".

He replaced the femoral head with a mirror-finished, stainless steel prosthesis, which had a diameter of 0.88in

(22mm) – much smaller than normal but steel withstands the kind of loadings the femur has to experience better than other metals. For the acetabular cup, Charnley first chose polytetrafluoroethylene (PTFE, or Teflon as it became known when it was introduced as a non-stick lining to kitchen utensils after World War II). PTFE is a low-friction plastic but, as Charnley found out, it does not wear well. In 1962, he developed a cup made of high-density polythene, known as RCH 1000, which generated more friction but lasted up to a thousand times longer.

Finally, both the cup, which was deeply serrated on the outside, and the shaft of the prosthesis were bonded into position using an acrylic cement called methyl methacrylate. This produced an effective bond between the patient's own bone and the artificial joint and proved to be the best method of preventing loosening.

IMPROVED ASEPSIS

Besides loosening, the other great fear for surgeons is bone infection. The insertion of a foreign body such as a prosthesis into human tissues makes infection very likely, especially if it is close to bone and surrounded by inert cement. So infection was a common cause of failure in the early years of hip replacement. However, preventive use of antibiotics, to kill bacteria before they have had a chance to multiply in the tissues, has proved effective, and has reduced infection rates to below 2 per cent.

Theatre aseptic techniques have also improved. Hip replacement operations are routinely carried out in clean-air theatres, or tents. These micro-environments were pioneered by orthopaedic surgeons, led by John Charnley, and incorporate a uniflow system of air control – air is channelled in one direction over the patient's body in order to reduce the number of circulating bacteria. Moreover, former unhygienic practices have been abandoned. For example, it was once common for the surgeons to lob the very hot acrylic cement between themselves until such time as it had cooled sufficiently for the senior surgeon to hold it comfortably – it could then be placed within the patient's body without fear of burning the tissues.

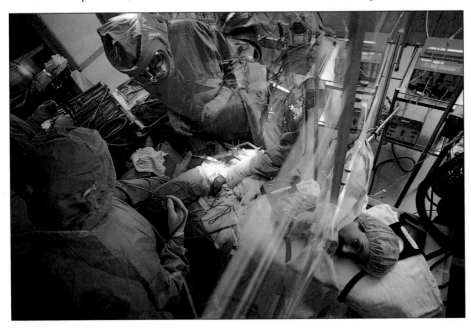

LEFT *Surgeons in a tent replace a hip joint that had been seriously damaged by rheumatoid arthritis. The patient, a young man, had requested that he stay conscious during the operation, in order to see exactly what was going on. However, the presence of a plexiglass screen effectively thwarted this ambition.*

GRAFTS AND TRANSPLANTS

FROM MAGIC TO MACHINERY

A 54-year-old man lived for 18 days with a 24-year-old woman's heart

IN THE THIRD CENTURY BC, a Chinese doctor, Pien Ch'iao, performed a startling, multi-organ swap on two soldiers he had anaesthetized with narcotic wine. Encouraged by his 'personal pixie' (who enabled Ch'iao to diagnose and treat patients), the doctor is said to have swapped several internal organs – hearts included. Legend also has it that when the soldiers finally came round three days later, they appeared to be in good shape.

A more reliable statement confirming the early practice of tissue transplantation was provided by the Roman doctor Celsus (*see p.21*). In *De Medicina*, he records that tissues had been successfully transplanted from one body to another. And, 150-odd years later, Galen (*see pp.22-3*) gave detailed instructions for the repair of facial defects by grafting.

Notwithstanding the early achievements of the Chinese, Romans and 'miracle workers', such as Cosmas and Damian (*see p.35*), the foundations for modern transplant surgery were laid in the United States at the start of the 20th century by surgeon Alexis Carrel (*see p.125*) and physiologist Charles Guthrie. Their successful blood vessel anastomosis operations, in which severed arteries or veins are surgically joined together, provided a springboard for all later transplant surgery. Carrel and Guthrie were able to show that not only were transplantations of tissues, organs and limbs clearly possible, but also – surprisingly – it was not necessary for nervous connections to exist for the transplant to function normally. At the time, much of the recognition for this work went to Carrel, while Guthrie's contribution received little attention.

DEFINING A TRANSPLANT

The term 'transplant' is a broad one. Organs, such as kidneys, and tissues, such as skin and bone marrow, may be removed from an animal and then replaced in the same body (an 'autotransplant' or 'replant') – though not necessarily in the anatomically correct position. Alternatively, they may be taken from one animal and transplanted into another of the

BELOW *A half-completed skin graft, following surgery to to remove a* *malignant melanoma – a virulent form of skin cancer.*

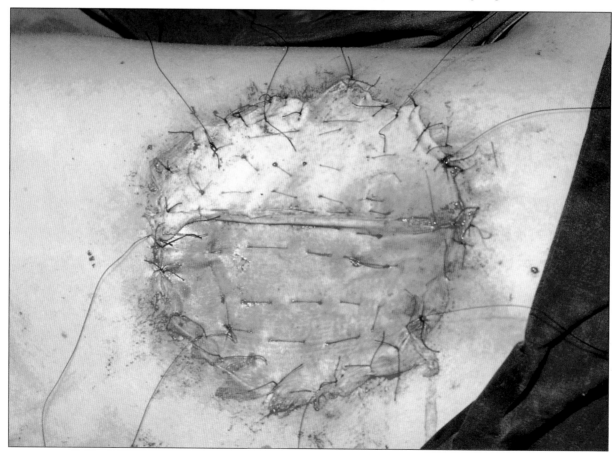

same species (a 'homotransplant'). When an organ or tissue is taken from an animal of one species and placed into the body of a different species, the process is known as a 'heterotransplant'.

For the next three decades, these transplant approaches were tackled again and again with varying degrees of success – and, some would say, unpleasantness. In 1905, Eduard Zirm performed the first successful corneal transplant in Olmutz, Moravia – the technique had to wait almost 50 years before it became popular worldwide. In 1912, Guthrie grafted the head of a puppy on to the neck of an adult dog, which lived for several hours after surgery. This experiment was repeated by Russian surgeon Vladimir Demikhov, 35 years later, and the puppy's head lived for 29 days. A Cleveland experiment by Robert J. White showed that a monkey's brain could be kept alive for a few hours, nurtured by the blood supply of another monkey.

But despite claims stretching back hundreds of years, the first successful replantation of a severed limb took place in Boston, in 1962. An accident had cost a 12-year-old boy his right arm, severed just below the shoulder. The boy and his arm were taken to Massachusetts General Hospital where the arm was packed in a solution of ice and salt and then grafted back onto its owner. A few months later, surgeons Ronald Malt and Charles McKhann completed their work when they reconnected the nerves. Within two years, the boy had virtually regained the full use of his arm and hand, to the point of being able to lift small weights.

THE PROBLEM OF REJECTION

The incompatibility between tissues and organs of different individuals seemed to dog the efforts of transplant pioneers. Autotransplants *(see p.138)* continued to be successful, but neither homotransplants nor heterotransplants could be made to work. It was as if the recipient's body rejected as foreign the donor tissue or organ. And this rejection was a direct result of the recipient's immune system attacking the transplant, as if bent on destroying it.

Charles Darwin's work on evolution and the origin of species, together with Gregor Mendel's laws of inheritance *(see pp.66-7)*, had transformed the scientific understanding of the differences between living things. After Karl Landsteiner published his studies into the human blood groups *(see pp. 92-3)*, it soon became clear that there were also crucial differences between the tissues, organs and even cells of individuals. Moreover, these differences caused incompatibilities: mixing blood from group A with blood from group O brought about clumping, or agglutination, of red blood cells as a result of the clash of differing antigens from each group.

An understanding of the process of rejection, and therefore ideas about ways to suppress it, started to crystallize as World War II was coming to an end. In 1945, US scientist Ray Owen announced that non-identical twin calves were able to tolerate cells transplanted between them, as if they had somehow 'inoculated' each other when they shared the same circulation in the womb.

Seizing on Owen's idea, and building on his long struggle to understand how humans react to viruses, vaccines and other foreign substances, Professor Macfarlane Burnet, from Melbourne, Australia, put forward a selective theory of immunology. Burnet proposed that the body's immune system is formed in the womb when, as a foetus, it 'learns'

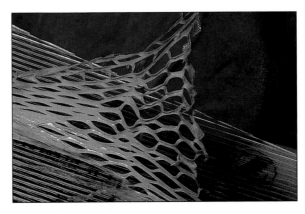

ABOVE *A close-up of a mesh skin graft, produced by rolling a section* *of skin through a meshing machine to create a hexagonal lattice.*

PROLONGING THE TRANSPLANT

The upsurge in pharmacological research following World War II (see pp.164-7) brought a wealth of chemicals into the medical armoury. Drugs to suppress the immunological responses of transplant recipients – other than for the transplants of corneas and cartilage, which did not suffer the same rejection problems – started to find their way into the operating theatre, raising hopes that successful transplants were just around the corner.

The first immunosuppressant was the steroid cortisone (see p.166), which was successfully used in 1951 to prolong the life of a skin homotransplant. Eight years later, immunological tolerance was induced with mercaptopurine and irradiation was used in Paris in the first successful kidney transplants between non-identical twins. In 1963, antilymphocytic serum (ALS) – a serum made from animal blood that had previously been injected with human lymphocytes – was shown to prolong transplant survival rates. The benefit of ALS was that it focused on suppressing rejection while leaving the body's defences against infection relatively untouched. But its drawback – the difficulty of knowing which batch was potent and which was not – gave it a hit-and-miss profile that outweighed its usefulness.

The anti-leukaemic drug, azathioprine (see p.167), in combination with steroids, soon became the standard means of suppressing rejection and prolonging a homotransplant. A more recent addition to the immunosuppressant armoury is cyclosporin, an antibiotic discovered in 1974 and in general use since 1983. It produces less harmful side-effects but, like all its predecessors, has a non-specific and indiscriminate action on the body's immune system. Immunosuppressants may prolong a transplant with varying degrees of success, but they cripple the body's ability to fight everyday bacteria, viruses and fungi. Transplant surgeons therefore have to weigh up the pros and cons of each case – the benefit of new tissues or organs versus drug side-effects combined with reduced immunity to infection.

to produce a whole alphabet of antibodies. The manufacture of any of these antibodies can be activated as and when the need to do so arises.

Proof for this line of thinking came from London University's Professor of Zoology, Peter Medawar, and his colleagues. Working with skin grafts, Medawar showed that if he gave an animal more than one graft from the same donor, then the second graft was rejected much more quickly than the first. He also showed that if the recipient was injected with leucocytes (white cells) from a prospective donor prior to grafting, then the graft's survival time was shortened. Because the skin and the leucocytes had shared common antigens, then the injection had conferred 'active immunity' against the graft.

Medawar and his team also experimented with the introduction of cells from a strain of brown mice into the foetus of a white strain to see if the prospects of a skin graft from the first to the second were improved. When the foetus was born, they grafted a patch of skin from the donor of the cells (skin is a notoriously hard tissue to graft permanently) on to its back. The skin graft 'took' without any problems and lasted longer than in normal conditions. As a result, Medawar proposed the theory of 'acquired immunological tolerance' – individuals exposed in the womb to cells of a prospective donor acquire an immunological tolerance to grafts and transplants from it.

For their respective contributions to the understanding of actively acquired immunity and acquired immunological tolerance, both Burnet and Medawar were awarded a Nobel prize for medicine in 1960. They had also given much-needed impetus to the search for ways to prolong the survival of transplanted tissues.

KIDNEYS AND LUNGS

Pride of place in the whole field of organ transplants has been occupied by the kidney. The organ is simple to remove and replace with a single artery-vein anastomosis, is easily tissue-typed, and the fact that everyone has two means that living donors can be used. Moreover, the advent of dialysis machines (see p.172) means there is back-up should a kidney transplant fail.

The first kidney heterotransplant is thought to have been performed in 1902 by the Austrian surgeon E. Ullmann, when he transferred a dog's kidney into a goat's neck. Then the development of the artificial kidney machine in the 1940s meant that many seriously ill patients could become fit enough for surgery to take place. In 1954, surgeons in Boston carried out the first successful kidney transplant from a living donor – a 24-year-old man, diseased in both kidneys and close to death, lived after receiving a healthy kidney from his identical twin brother.

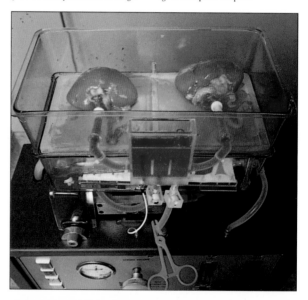

BELOW *Donor kidneys are preserved prior to transplantation in a life-support machine, at the University of Minneapolis Hospital.*

THE FIRST HUMAN HEART TRANSPLANT

An astonished world greeted Christiaan Barnard after he had carried out the first human heart transplant. Young, handsome and greatly talented, Barnard was known at Groote Schuur Hospital, Cape Town, for meticulous work that was comparable with the best in the world. Barnard had developed his surgical techniques for transplants with his brother Marius, after they had studied Norman Shumway's technique for nourishing the heart, and had been experimenting on dogs since 1964. They had found that in 90 per cent of the animals, the cooled and transplanted heart supported the circulation fairly successfully.

On 3 December 1967, a 24-year-old woman was admitted to Groote Schuur Hospital dying of head injuries sustained in a traffic accident. Louis Washkansky, who had suffered three heart attacks since 1959 and was now dying of intractable heart failure, had agreed to Barnard's proposal of a transplant and was only waiting for a suitable donor. The woman had compatible red-cell antigens and a

similar leucocyte antigen pattern to Washkansky. Barnard sensed the chance of a lifetime.

When Washkansky's chest was opened up it was clear that nothing short of a transplant could help. When a neurosurgeon reported that the woman's injuries were untreatable, her relatives gave their permission for her heart to be used. Just 3 hours, 12 minutes after the donor heart had arrived, the first human-to-human heart transplant was complete.

Washkansky's response to surgery and post-operative care (using corticosteroids, azathioprine and cobalt radiation) was quite remarkable; he lived for 18 days. Sadly, he contracted a lung infection that did not respond to treatment. The post-mortem recorded that death was due to extensive bilateral pneumonia – the heart had not been rejected, but instead maintained good circulation to the end.

LEFT *South African surgeon Christiaan Barnard pioneered heart transplant surgery.*

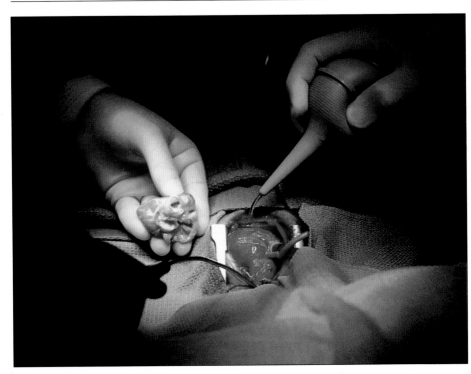

LEFT *This close-up of a heart transplant in a child shows the tiny defective heart – about the size of a walnut – held next to the transplanted heart. The patient, a six-year-old boy, was suffering from life-threatening heart defect.*

Progress in the transfer of either the liver or the lungs has been fitful since the 1950s, but such transplants are becoming relatively common. Following the news, in 1962, that Vladimir Demokhov had experimented on animal lung homotransplants some 15 years earlier, James Hardy, of the University of Mississippi Medical Centre, determined to attempt a human lung transplant. In June 1963, he transplanted the lung of a man who had died of a heart attack into that of a 58-year-old man dying of lung cancer and emphysema. The new lung immediately functioned well and continued to do so for 18 days until the patient died from a kidney complaint that was unconnected to the transplant.

THE HEART OF THE MATTER

Experiments to transplant the heart date back to those performed by Carrel and Guthrie in the early 1900s. In 1933, Frank Mann, of Georgetown University, Washington D.C., concluded from his own animal experiments that the heart behaved no differently to other organs in regard to heart transplants. In these early experiments, the heart had not been placed in its correct anatomical site but in some other location, usually in a pouch underneath the skin of the neck. But during the 1950s, moves were made to transplant a donor heart into the correct cavity, thereby completely replacing the function of the recipient's heart.

Transplanting the heart poses many problems apart from rejection. The donor organ must be completely healthy and untouched by the cause of the donor's death. And, because a heart will deteriorate within minutes of death and cannot be stored successfully for any length of time, it must be removed and transplanted with great speed, sometimes at the expense of full tissue-typing tests.

Norman Shumway, of Stanford University, California, made a major breakthrough in 1961 when he devised a vastly improved surgical technique to nourish the heart more efficiently. After surgery, Shumway used a machine to keep the recipient's circulation going until the new heart was ready to take it over. His experimental dogs lived for as long as 21 days, during which time they functioned normally – eventual death was due to organ rejection.

The first heart transplant in humans took place on 23 January 1964. When a 68-year-old man was admitted to the Mississippi Medical Centre with advanced heart disease, James Hardy put him on a heart-lung machine and prepared for the first heart transplant between humans – the donor was to be a young man suffering from irrecoverable brain damage. Yet, it was not to be – the prospective donor clung to life while the prospective recipient's heart suddenly failed. Hardy made the brave decision to use a chimpanzee's heart, believing it to be within the boundaries of ethics and morality. The heart functioned well after surgery, but was too small to cope (the patient was far heavier). Hardy implanted pacemakers in an effort to boost the heart's activity, but the patient died shortly after.

The press, which had been waiting to make the historic announcement, lost interest as soon as it found out that the donor was a monkey and not a human. It, and the world, had to wait almost four more years for the great event to happen: in Cape Town, in 1967, South African surgeon Christiaan Barnard and his team transplanted the heart of a 24-year-old woman into the body of 54-year-old Louis Washkansky (*see box*).

Heart transplants soon became all the rage – increasing media coverage prompted new funding, and widespread research improved technical expertise. By 1984, there were 29 centres in the US capable of carrying out heart transplants – approximately 300 were performed, and of the patients who received new hearts, 75 per cent lived for at least a year and almost two thirds survived for five years. However, questions still remain about the enormous costs and relative benefits of heart transplants – many people would prefer to see the money diverted to other areas of the health services where a much larger number of patients can receive treatment and care.

TREATING THE HEART

FROM ASPIRIN TO ARTIFICIAL HEARTS

Nuclear fuel now keeps hearts beating for as long as 20 years

HEART DISEASE has been called a 'lifestyle' disease because many experts believe it is caused by the poor diet, lack of exercise, excessive stress or smoking that characterize everyday life for millions in the West. But while research into prevention continues (*see pp.216–7*), much has been achieved in correcting disorders of the heart.

CIRCUS TRICKS

In the summer of 1929, a 25-year-old German medical student, Werner Forssmann, arrived at a small Red Cross hospital in Eberswalde to begin clinical instruction in surgery. In July, despite being forbidden to experiment by his surgeon mentor, he inserted a catheter into his own arm, slid it 26in (65cm) up a vein and then walked to the X-ray department. After kicking the shins of a friend who tried to stop him, he had a photograph taken of the catheter, the tip of which he had pushed into the right atrium of his heart.

Publication of Forssmann's research caused a brief media sensation. When he applied for a lectureship in Berlin, the German surgeon Ferdinand Sauerbruch hissed: "You might lecture in a circus about your little tricks, but never in a respectable German university!" Despite this, Forssmann experimented again, in 1931, creating the first angiogram by injecting a radio-opaque substance through a catheter into his heart. Thereafter, he sank into obscurity.

His work did not: it was read by two American researchers, André Cournand and Dickinson Richards. In 1936, they began a series of animal experiments to discover the changes in the concentrations of oxygen and carbon dioxide in the blood inside the heart; and, in 1940, they performed their first catheterization on a patient.

The innovative techniques of these three scientists – who received a Nobel prize in 1956 – eventually became routine

BELOW *Surgeons perform a cardiac catheterization – the catheter is put into the groin, and guided by X-ray imaging to the coronary arteries.*

in the diagnosis of heart disease. In 1947, catheterization was used to study congenital heart disease, and 12 years later, X-rays of individual coronary arteries became possible. In addition, the pressure in each of the heart's chambers could now be measured.

Catheterization also came into play in the treatment of heart disease. The inner lining of coronary arteries (which, if blocked, can cause heart attacks) can be scoured in a technique known as endarterectomy. In 1967, New York heart surgeon Sol Sobel refined this technique by injecting a powerful jet of carbon dioxide gas into an artery via a hypodermic syringe. Three years earlier, angioplasty had been invented by the Swiss doctor Andreas Grünzig: a tiny balloon is inserted into a constricted artery via a catheter and inflated, thereby clearing a path for blood flow.

NEW HEARTS FOR OLD

The same thinking that went into the development of replacement valves eventually resulted in attempts to develop an effective artificial heart. Willem Kolff (see pp.172–5) began researching into this in the US, and, in 1957, he implanted his first model into a dog. It survived some 90 minutes.

In 1970, Robert Jarvik, of the University of Utah, devised the Jarvik-7: made of a polyurethane biomer and glass-fibre fabric, it operated on compressed air and was first tested on calves, whose mean survival was 66 days. The cause of their deaths was the artificial hearts' inability to grow with the animals.

On 2 December 1982, Dr William de Vries implanted the device for the first time in a human – Barney Clarke,

a 61-year-old dentist, who survived 112 days. After that, about 90 Jarviks were given to patients around the world. An American, William Schroeder, who received his in 1986, survived the longest: 20 months. However, before he died, the world became privy to his suffering, and controversy raged. Finally, at the end of 1989, artificial heart surgery was banned in the US.

Since then, other devices have become available that perform some of the same functions though are not artificial hearts. In 1989, Dr. Richard K. Wampler's 'Hemopump' appeared, a miniature turbine that can take over from cardiac muscle on a temporary basis, and in 1990, the US firm Novacor announced the development of a heart assistance device that could be implanted.

KEEPING THE BEAT

The heart has its own electrical system, which regulates the rate and timing of each heartbeat. If it goes wrong, the result can be 'heart block', or arrhythmia – the beat is too slow to meet the demands of exercise, and the heart can stop.

At first, artificial cardiac pacemakers were external, with batteries connected to the heart by a wire running through a vein. These were satisfactory for a short period in hospital, but not for permanent use. The first internal pacemaker was constructed by Rune Elmqvist in 1958, and implanted by the Swedish doctor Åke Senning two years later.

These early models, with a matchbox-sized power source implanted under the skin, used mercury-zinc batteries, lasting only two or three years. Then, in 1973, a lithium-iodide fuel cell was developed in Canada, which could last for at least six years. And, in the early 1980s, the pacemaker became computerized – a tiny microprocessor alerted the generator when the heart's rhythm became erratic. In 1986, the German firm Biotronik developed a programmed pacemaker based on blood temperature, which indicates a person's activity. Finally, in 1988, a 47-year-old man was fitted with the first double-pulse nuclear pacemaker, with a tiny pastille of plutonium and believed to have a life of at least 20 years.

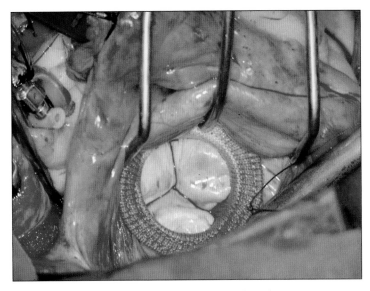

ABOVE *Open heart surgery, showing an artificial heart valve (in this case, the tricuspid valve), made from the membrane of a pig's brain, being implanted in a human patient. American surgeons tend to prefer the use of plastic and metal valves, rather than animal ones.*

SCALPELS AND PILLS

Following the pioneering work of the 'blue baby' team (*see pp.156–7*), new diagnostic techniques and the heart-lung machine (*see pp.172–5*) made open heart surgery possible. The first operations were to correct congenital heart defects, such as coarctation (narrowing) of the aorta, and atrial and ventricular septal defects ('holes in the heart').

The heart valves control the direction and flow of blood through the organ; when one or more of these become blocked, the heart works less efficiently. In the past, rheumatic heart disease was common, as was one of its consequences – mitral stenosis, the thickening of the mitral valve. In 1948, surgeons would open the valve simply by inserting a finger into it. Later, however, it was realized that the best answer was simply to replace failing valves with artificial ones.

In 1952, US surgeon Charles A. Hufnagel inserted a plastic valve into the descending part of the aorta in the chest, to take over from a diseased aortic heart valve. Three years later, surgeons started to replace failed valves with ones taken from human cadavers. Since then, this branch of replacement surgery has split into two schools: those who prefer plastic and metal valves (mainly the Americans), and those who plump for animal (usually pig) valves.

Of the synthetic variety, the first popular model was the Starr-Edwards ball valve, used in 1960 and designed by the US heart specialist Albert Starr and the aircraft engineer M. L. Edwards. A number of other designs have since been tried, not always with great success. In some, blood clots tended to form; in others, the lining of the heart grew to block the valve opening; and in still others, turbulence was created,   leading to destruction of red blood cells.

Blocked arteries in the limbs had been replaced since the 1950s, but not until 1967 were the coronary arteries tackled. In that year, Rene Favaloro, a cardiovascular surgeon at the Cleveland Clinic, Ohio, inaugurated the coronary bypass operation: he 'bypassed' an occluded artery by grafting on a section of healthy vein from the patient's leg above and below the blockage.

Innovation was not only seen in surgery; drugs had their place, too. In the 1960s, Sir James Black developed beta-blockers, which block the action of the sympathetic nervous system on the heart, so reducing its workload. Originally prescribed for angina pain, they were later given to reduce blood pressure and stabilize the heartbeat; drug companies carried out much publicized tests on ski jumpers and racing car drivers to show that they did not impair performance. However, by 1974, side-effects had begun to appear. Eraldin, marketed in Britain, was linked with deafness, peritonitis, pleurisy and damaged sight: some 20 people went blind and 18 fatalities were linked to the drug. While beta-blockers still have a place in the treatment of heart disease, their dangers are now much better understood – for instance, sudden withdrawal can lead to heart attacks.

Two drugs known for their blood-thinning abilities – streptokinase, developed in the 1960s, and aspirin (*see p.49*) – have been much more successful. In March 1988, following trials involving more than 17,000 patients at 400 hospitals in 16 countries, it was announced that, if streptokinase is given within a few hours of a heart attack, and followed by low maintenance doses of aspirin, deaths are reduced by 40 per cent.

In the same year, the results of the American Physicians' Health Study – begun in 1983 and involving 22,000 US doctors – showed that 325mg of aspirin taken on alternate days reduced the risk of heart attack by 47 per cent. This finding was later backed up by Richard Peto and his team at Oxford University, England, who analyzed the results of 215 trials involving over 100,000 participants. But they recommended a daily dose of only 75mg.

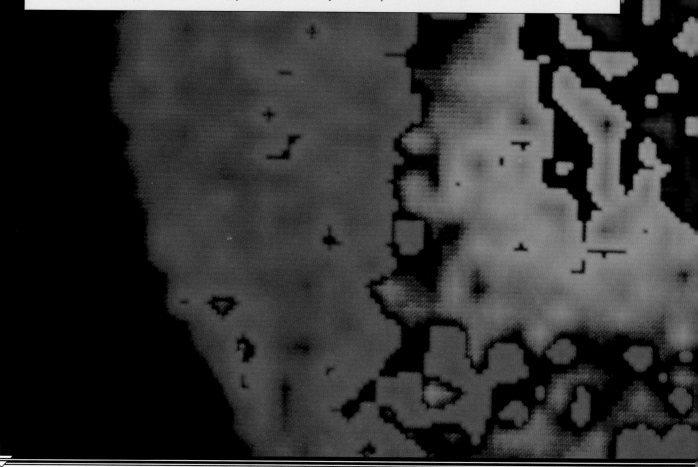

8 Medicine Since World War II – Breakdowns and Breakthroughs

Sophisticated though modern medicine may be, it still has its shares of failures, as well as successes. And, for a time, one can be mistaken for the other – until the side-effects of a particular treatment become clear.

This chapter takes a look at some specific examples of medicine in action over the last 50-odd years. The development of the first true tranquillizer, for example, allowed some schizophrenics to live relatively normal lives in the community; but some tranquillizers, once prescribed freely, have proved addictive, dangerous and destructive to family relationships. Two undeniable success stories, though, have been the treatment of Parkinson's disease with L-dopa and vaccination against polio build up.

Another, though less obvious, success story has been that of sexual therapy. Sex has been a joy to most and a misery for some since human beings first walked on Earth. But it was not until about 45 years ago that medical science made any serious attempt first to understand human sexual behaviour, then to devise a therapy for those with sexual dysfunction.

The story of the fight against cancer is by no means so clear cut. There have been successes, true – 70 per cent of children with the commonest form of leukaemia now survive; and Wilm's tumour, affecting the kidney, is fatal in only about 20 per cent of cases. Nevertheless, science still awaits the breakthrough in the treatment of cancer, though there are high hopes for the future.

There are hopes, too, that a cure will be found for AIDS, the new scourge of the world. But, at the moment, work goes on – in the attempt to understand the disease process fully, as well as to find a cure for it.

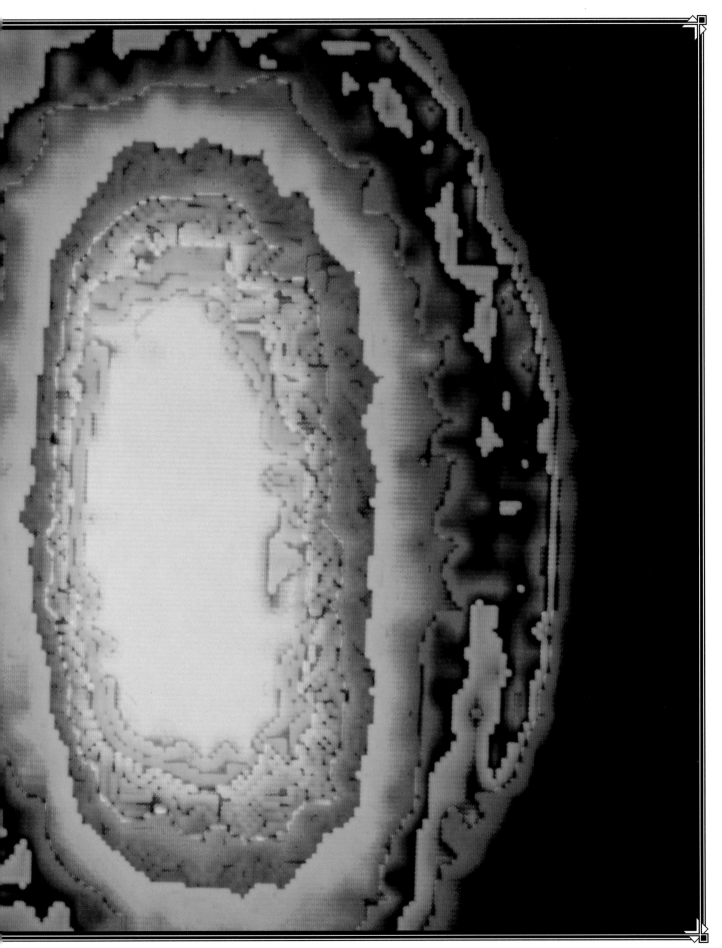

ABOVE *A scan of radio-isotopic gas in a pair of lungs shows the left lung cancerous and the right lung healthy.*

MENTAL ILLNESS

NEW DRUGS, NEW THEORIES

Theories about how animals hibernate led to the first true tranquillizer

THREE-AND-A-HALF YEARS as a prisoner of the Japanese during World War II gave Australian physician and psychiatrist John F. J. Cade (1912–80) ample opportunity to observe serious mental disorders among his fellow captives. The experience convinced him that mental illnesses such as manic depression and schizophrenia have a physiological cause – a view that accorded more with traditional medical science than with the newer theories of psychiatry and psychoanalysis (*see pp.118-21*). Specifically, Cade conjectured that the mania seen in manic depression might be the result of an excessive level of some substance in the body, while severe depression might occur when the level was unusually low. However, he had no idea what this substance might be.

BELOW *A still from* One Flew Over the Cuckoo's Nest (1975), *a film that revealed the shocking side of mental illness.*

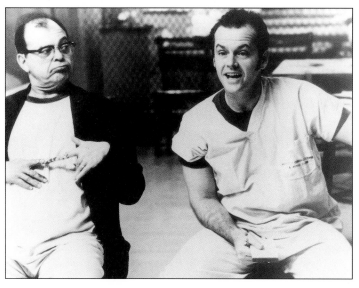

After the war, in 1946, Cade took up a psychiatric post at the Repatriation Hospital on the outskirts of Melbourne, Australia, and started a series of rough-and-ready experiments on guinea pigs. First, he injected some of the animals with urine from psychotic patients and others with urine from people in normal mental health. From the results, Cade concluded that, while injections of any human urine would eventually kill a guinea pig, urine from those suffering from manic-depressive illness killed them more quickly.

The toxic agent in the urine was soon identified as urea. Cade suspected that fluctuating levels of this substance might be related to mental disturbance. This proved to be a blind alley, so he examined the part played in the experiments by uric acid, another substance present in urine. Uric acid does not dissolve easily in water, so for his comparative tests

Cade used the most soluble compound of uric acid he could obtain – lithium urate – and struck medical gold. The presence of lithium made the urea less toxic and, when tested on its own, rendered the usually highly strung guinea pigs placid and docile for an hour or two. By an apparent accident (although he always insisted it was the product of logic), Cade had hit on a new method of calming patients who suffered from a severe mental disturbance.

For nearly a century, lithium had been used medically in the treatment of gout, and it is disputed whether Cade was, in fact, the first person to notice its possible application to mental illness. But the Australian was certainly the first to conduct formal clinical trials of lithium in the management of mental illness, after taking it in various forms himself to check its safety. The results, published in 1949, were impressive. Ten patients suffering from various types of mania became calm and tractable when lithium carbonate was administered regularly. Six schizophrenics showed reductions in restlessness and noisiness, although other symptoms, such as hallucinations, seemed unaffected. Only three patients, all of whom suffered from chronic depression, failed to show any improvement.

Cade's personal case notes show he was well aware that lithium treatment can have damaging side-effects on the digestive and nervous systems – possibly fatal ones if the amounts of the chemical in the blood are not carefully monitored (one of his original patients had died of lithium poisoning in 1950). But in his published work, he tended to play down such matters – from worthy motives. For he believed that, in most circumstances and under proper control, the lithium's benefits outweighed its dangers.

The one question Cade was unable to answer was how lithium achieved its effects. He suggested that it was a trace element whose presence in small quantities in the body was essential to health, and whose deficiency produced psychosis. Neither he nor subsequent researchers could prove this, but that did not prevent lithium carbonate therapy from becoming standard treatment for manic-depression sufferers.

THE AGE OF THE TRANQUILLIZER

John Cade's work on lithium was, in its time, the culmination of more than a century of research and experiment into chemical methods of calming people who suffer from mental disorders. These methods began with potassium bromide, first used in the 1830s; this was followed by chloral and paraldehyde, and then the barbiturates that were developed from 1903. But these and other substances had drawbacks. Bromide, for example, accumulated in the body to produce a kind of intoxication that could be far worse than the original condition. As for barbiturates, they were addictive and overdoses could be fatal.

BELOW *A scan of a schizophrenic's brain shows reduced levels of a* radioactive tracer of protein synthesis (red) in the frontal lobes.

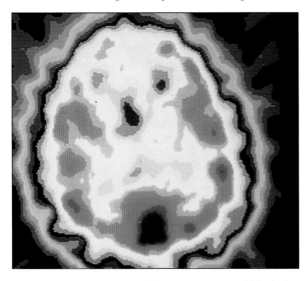

More importantly, none of the treatments available before the 1950s really tackled the symptoms of severe mental illness, such as delusions, hallucinations and chronic mood disorders. Even lithium failed to help treat people suffering from schizophrenia and deep depression. But while the psychiatric world focused its attention on Cade's discoveries, the breakthrough was to come from another branch of medicine. It was not the result of research into mental health, but a by-product of new methods of surgery.

Surgeons had long been concerned about the physical shock to patients who had undergone otherwise successful major operations. In many cases, this delayed recovery and was sometimes fatal. Scientists reasoned that the effects of shock would be reduced if the body's metabolism could be slowed down during surgery, in the same way that it slows automatically in hibernating cold-blooded animals. Among those carrying out research in this area was the Rhone-Poulenc drug company in France. In 1950, researchers there produced a substance that did the trick – chlorpromazine, a derivative of the drug phenothiazine, which was synthesized in 1883 to treat mental illness and is still used today.

The potential for chlorpromazine outside the operating theatre was not lost on its inventors. Within two years, it had been tested (in combination with other drugs as well as on its own) on manic and schizophrenic patients in France and elsewhere. The researchers Delay and Deniker demonstrated that it not only relieved manic excitement and aggression in schizophrenics, as earlier drugs had done, but it also reduced delusions and hallucinations, thereby greatly improving the contact between psychiatrist and patient.

Delay and Deniker described chlorpromazine's action as 'neuroleptic' (working on the nerve cells). It was the first true tranquillizer, and the results achieved with it stimulated pharmaceutical companies around the world into a frenzy of research to devise similar products of their own. The outcome is today's huge array of custom-made drugs for the treatment of mental disorders of all types and severity – from such widely taken pills as diazepam (Valium) and chlordiazepoxide (Librium) to flupenthixol, which through long-lasting injections allows some schizophrenics to live relatively normal lives in the community.

PHYSICAL OR PSYCHOLOGICAL CAUSE?

While spectacular progress was taking place in the development of drug treatments, arguments over the causes of mental disorders became increasingly bitter. Cade and the British neurologist Sir Henry Miller, among others, insisted on the importance of physiological factors; some doctors believed that the disorders were rooted in psychological or social disturbances. The second group included the British psychiatrist R. D. Laing (1927–89), proponent of the theory that schizophrenia stems from family pressures during childhood, which force individuals to conform to behaviour unsuitable for them.

Both factions could produce evidence to support their contentions. The work of the psychoanalysts suggested that the strain of everyday living affected mental health, a view later reinforced by studies of stress (see pp.220-1). Conversely, research by the American psychiatrist Franz Kallman showed that there is a hereditary element in schizophrenia.

A working compromise evolved among many practical psychiatrists, to the effect that neuroses, such as anxiety and phobias, are the result of psychosocial pressures, and psychoses are organic brain diseases. As the US professor Thomas Szasz pointed out, neither logic nor experience justified this simplistic division, but it was a useful yardstick against which to measure other theories.

A more convincing attempt at reconciling the two views of mental disorders – and of schizophrenia in particular – was made by another American professor, Ian Stevenson, in 1957. He accepted that heredity can predispose to schizophrenia, that it is accompanied by profound changes in the body, and that it can be improved, if not cured, by drug treatment. However, he argued that psychological stress often triggers the onset of the disorder, and that psychotherapy may be successful in treating it. Stevenson reasoned that stress may cause the release of a substance into the blood and produce schizophrenia in people whose brain cells might be abnormally susceptible to it. To effect a full cure, he suggested, it would not be enough to suppress this: the patient must also be taught to master stress itself.

Like Cade, Stevenson had no idea what the substance might be. Hundreds of candidates have been put forward, including adrenaline or one of the chemical messengers in the brain. None has yet been conclusively proved responsible, though 'breakthroughs' have frequently been claimed. When the real one finally occurs (and few scientists doubt it eventually will), this will resolve one of the most contentious issues in modern medicine.

RIGHT *British psychiatrist R. D. Laing theorized that schizophrenia is the result of pressures to conform during childhood.*

PARKINSON'S DISEASE

Overcoming the tremors of the 'shaking palsy'

IN 1817, JAMES PARKINSON, a 62-year-old family doctor in the East End of London, wrote a monograph entitled *Essay on the Shaking Palsy*. Parkinson's essay became a classic of medical literature: his exact description of the symptoms and the evolution of an illness that had been in existence since biblical times needs little revision today – indeed, the illness was named after him. Prior to Parkinson's description, any form of muscular disorder or paralysis had been referred to as a 'palsy'. This, in effect, grouped together all manner of tremors which resulted from conditions such as aging, nervous disorders and alcohol abuse.

Parkinson's disease is characterized by three main symptoms – a tremor in one or more limbs, a stiffness of the muscles and a slowness as well as difficulty in initiating movement. The symptoms of the disease vary according to the individual, but in most sufferers one symptom predominates over the others. The tremor is most often visible in

BELOW *An elderly woman in a typical Parkinsonian pose: rigid, stooping, shuffling and with a set, expressionless face.*

one or more limbs on one side of the body. It is more obvious when the sufferer is resting or feeling especially nervous or tired. The tremor disappears during sleep and decreases in severity (or may disappear altogether) when the affected limb is used.

The 'shaking palsy' became known as paralysis agitans (because of the symptoms) before becoming the eponymous Parkinson's disease. In his description, Parkinson pointed out that the tremor was a symptom of a disease and not a disease in its own right. The tremor was due neither to paralysis nor to weakness, but, paradoxically, to an extreme slowness of movement. Sometimes, this tremor could be so severe as to "not only shake the bed-hangings but even the floor and sashes of the room".

THE SEARCH FOR A CURE

Parkinson's disease develops when a small group of nerve cells in the brain fails to function normally. The location of these cells was not established until the 1950s, when the *substantia nigra*, a deeply pigmented layer of grey matter in the midbrain, was clearly implicated in the disease. After the identity of a new neurotransmitter, dopamine, was discovered, and it was found to be present in the *substantia nigra* and basal ganglia cells of the brain in large amounts, the search for a cure hotted up.

At this time, scientists also discovered a side-effect of the new neuroleptic drugs, reserpine and the phenothiazines: they seemed to produce the symptoms of Parkinson's disease. And since these drugs were known to interfere with the action or storage of dopamine at nerve endings, it was thought that there was a direct link between dopamine and Parkinson's disease. For some reason, the cells in the *substantia nigra* of Parkinson sufferers were not producing enough dopamine to transmit signals to other brain cells and thereby initiate muscular movement.

In 1961, trials using levodopa (L-dopa), a chemical which enables the body to synthesize dopamine, began in Vienna and Montreal. The results showed clearly that L-dopa enabled the affected brain cells to begin making dopamine once more, therefore alleviating many symptoms, especially the slowness and difficulty in initiating movement. In 1967, George Cotzias and others led the way with the introduction of L-dopa therapy.

AWAKENINGS

Hailed as a new wonder drug, L-dopa gave hope to thousands of sufferers of Parkinson's disease, many of whom had undergone surgery of their neural pathways during the 1950s and 1960s. Sufferers who had been confined to bed for years could walk, while others found relief from the

ABOVE *British neurologist Dr Oliver Sacks gave L-dopa to* encephalitis *lethargica patients. They awoke from their sleep – but only for a time.*

ABOVE *A still from* Awakenings *– starring Robin Williams and Robert De Niro – the film version of Oliver Sacks' famous book.*

rigidity and pain of their characteristic posture. Despite several side-effects, such as nausea, occasional vomiting and reduced appetite, all Parkinson sufferers who turned to L-dopa found their quality of life greatly improved.

Parkinson sufferers were not the only beneficiaries of the new wonder drug. At the end of World War I, a disease called *encephalitis lethargica* appeared in the Western world, apparently linked to the influenza pandemic at that time (*see p.109*). The disease frequently caused death through a kind of brain fever, but its survivors were left with a condition known as post-encephalitic parkinsonism. The British neurologist Oliver Sacks treated such patients, many of whom had been suffering a kind of sleeping sickness for about 40 years. In his book, *Awakenings (1973)*, he writes that they were "as insubstantial as ghosts and as passive as zombies".

Dr Sacks administered L-dopa to a number of these 'sleepy sickness' patients in the Mount Carmel Hospital, New York, and watched enthralled as the drug awakened them. Many responded extraordinarily well – speaking, walking and gradually becoming normal once more. But, as time wore on, the disease could only be kept in abeyance by taking larger and larger doses of L-dopa. Side-effects, such as sudden, involuntary movements of the limbs and grimacing caused by twitching of the muscles of the face, started to take over the hapless patients. Eventually, the side-effects outweighed the advantages and the post-encephalitic patients sadly returned to their sleeping state.

Throughout the 1970s and 1980s, a great deal was learned about the best ways to use L-dopa as a treatment for Parkinson's disease. Initially, the drug is given in small doses and, when the side-effects begin to emerge, the dosage is moderated or temporarily halted, according to the individual reactions of the patient. In many cases, L-dopa is administered in conjunction with other drugs, such as selegiline (which prevents the breakdown of dopamine).

EXPERIMENTS WITH TRANSPLANTS

In 1981, a novel treatment using adrenal autographs was developed at the Karolinska Institute, in Stockholm. Several patients underwent operations in which part of the centre of their adrenal gland, which contains dopamine-producing cells, was transplanted into the affected part of their brain. The treatment did reduce the rigidity of the patient's muscles but the improvement was short-lived, and the patients returned to their original medication.

A more radical – and controversial – treatment involves implanting tiny amounts of nerve tissue from the brain of a foetus into the damaged area of a Parkinson sufferer's brain – the theory being that the normal cells in the foetal brain will relieve some of the symptoms by causing an increase in the secretion of dopamine. In March 1988, Betty Knight became the first recipient of a foetal cell implant in the UK, in an operation performed by Professor Hitchcock, in Birmingham. And in 1990, Dr O. Lindvall from Sweden reported the successful treatment of a severe Parkinson sufferer using a implant of foetal cells.

Despite the obvious controversy over foetal cell implants, not least because of the abortion laws in various countries, pioneering work has been carried out in Sweden and Mexico under rigorously controlled conditions. However, there is as yet no guarantee of success in these operations.

Current medical research into the disease also concentrates on early diagnosis and the implications of a genetic factor. It has also come to light that chemicals, such as the neurotoxin methylphenyltetrahydropyridine (MPTP), play a part in creating a Parkinsonian-like syndrome. Experiments in the mid-1980s showed that MPTP selectively destroys nerve cells in the *substantia nigra*. And in the early 1990s, a small number of young people in the US contracted Parkinson's disease after taking drugs such as heroin, which have been contaminated with MPTP.

THE ENIGMA OF PAIN

PAIN PATHWAYS TO PAIN CLINICS

"... flickering, quivering, pulsing, throbbing, beating, pounding ..."

IN THE 1640S, THE FRENCH PHILOSOPHER Descartes came up with the concept of the 'pain pathway', a straightforward channel from the skin (where the painful stimulus is applied) to the brain (where the pain is felt). He likened this system to the way a church bell is rung: "by pulling at one end of a rope, one makes to strike at the same instant a bell which hangs at the other end".

Over the centuries, research seemed to add credibility to Descartes' theory. In 1894-5, the German physician Max von Frey carried out a series of experiments. He first ascertained the places on the body sensitive to cold and warmth. Then, by attaching a pin to a spring, he gauged the pressure necessary to produce a pin prick, and he mapped out these 'pain spots' all over the body. Finally, he repeated this exercise using pieces of wood to which two-inch horse-tail hairs had been glued, so he could map 'touch spots'. He then matched his maps of these four types of 'spots' to the presence of four specialized structures in the skin, which he called 'receptors'.

When other researchers later located nerves running between the receptors and the brain, the 'specificity theory' was born: a specific sensation is picked up by a specific receptor, which sends impulses along a specific nerve to a specific part of the brain. Surgeons used the theory as the basis for operations to terminate chronic pain by cutting through the nerves along which the pain impulses had allegedly been travelling.

However, these operations were never very successful: patients still felt pain but could no longer locate it, and, in their distress, a number committed suicide. Trying to resolve this problem, scientists then examined the structure

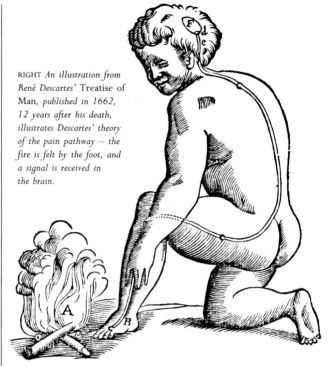

RIGHT *An illustration from René Descartes'* Treatise of Man, *published in 1662, 12 years after his death, illustrates Descartes' theory of the pain pathway – the fire is felt by the foot, and a signal is received in the brain.*

of the skin, but could find no correlation between the presence of temperature spots and von Frey's receptors, and no one has been able to link a specific nerve fibre to a specific sensation.

It was soon realized that how much – and, indeed, if – pain is felt is dependent on a variety of factors. For example,

---

MEASURING PAIN

Lt-Col. Beecher's study into the pain experienced by wounded soldiers (see p.191) emphasized the importance of measuring pain, which is a very subjective experience. A variety of methods were devised to try to do this.

The American researchers James Hardy and Harold Woolf developed a machine called a 'pain thermometer', also known as a 'dolorimeter', to gauge pain thresholds (the point at which pain is first felt) and pain tolerance (how much pain a person can bear). They found that the majority of skin abrasions and toothaches caused the least pain, while some labour pains, the passing of kidney stones and the pressure of a burning cigarette against the skin caused the most.

Ronald Melzack and his colleague at McGill University, Professor Tolgerson, invented the McGill–Melzack Pain

Questionnaire, comprising 20 groups of words that variously describe how a pain feels and what effect it has on the patient. For instance, group 1 gives the following choices: "flickering, quivering, pulsing, throbbing, beating, pounding". In 1981, Melzack and other researchers published the results of using the questionnaire; labour pain turned out to be the most severe.

The simplest method of measuring pain was devised by British rheumatologist Edward Huskisson. His Visual Analogue Scale (VAS) consists of a vertical line, at the bottom of which is marked 'No pain' and, at the top, 'Worst possible pain you can imagine'. Patients mark the level at which they feel their pain to be, and examination of a series of these self-assessments gives a good indication of the progress of pain and any treatment.

amputees frequently suffer pain from a 'phantom limb', which, of course, would have no pain receptors; and wounded soldiers often do not feel much pain initially despite suffering horrendous injuries. Thus, a person's psychological make-up and his or her central nervous system must both come into play in the perception of pain.

GATE CONTROL

Until the mid-1960s, pain researchers fell into two camps: those who held to the specificity theory; and a new group that believed that all the sensory receptors produced a variety of signals that were transmitted directly to the brain, which then decided which signals were to signify pain and which were not.

In the 1950s, a Canadian psychophysiologist, Ronald Melzack, and a British neuroanatomist, Patrick Wall, were both working at the Massachusetts Institute of Technology when they began talking about the physical and psychological aspects of pain. The result of these conversations was the 1965 publication of their 'gate theory'.

Two types of nerve fibres and part of the spinal cord are intimately involved in the perception of pain, although the exact mechanism is still not completely understood. It seems that, when the skin is damaged, thin C fibres carry only pain signals to the spinal cord for forwarding to the brain, and the thicker A-beta fibres carry non-pain signals. However, the A-beta fibres can transmit faster and, in the spinal cord, are able to block some of the pain signals carried by the C fibres. This blocking is Melzack and Wall's 'gate'.

Even very young children know the benefit of 'rubbing it better'. By massaging an injured part, the A-beta fibres are activated and block the transmission of at least some of the painful impulses. This is not all: the sensation of pain can also be enhanced or inhibited by signals from the brain.

IMPERVIOUS TO PAIN

During the Battle of Anzio, in January–May 1944, Lt-Col. Henry Beecher, of the US Army Medical Corps, was astounded to find that many terribly wounded men seemed to feel little pain from their injuries, yet yelped if a corpsman gave a clumsy injection. When Beecher published his observations of 215 soldiers in 1946, he admitted finding the results puzzling: 32.1 per cent had claimed to feel no pain; 25.6 per cent, slight pain; 18.6 per cent, moderate pain; 23.7 per cent, great pain. Yet when he compared the soldiers with civilians injured badly in accidents, he found that the latter suffered far more pain.

Beecher concluded that the difference lay in what the wound actually meant to the individual. For the soldiers, it meant the end of hardship and the threat of death; for the civilians, it was just the beginning of disaster. What went on before the injury was important, too: the soldiers – like atheletes before a competition – were 'psyched up', full of adrenaline in preparation for the basic 'fight or flight' response; the civilians were hurt suddenly, out of the blue.

In the 1950s, Beecher and others in Boston made another discovery: that if patients in great pain were unknowingly given a placebo – a substance with no pain-killing properties – about 35 per cent reported marked relief from pain. This 'placebo effect' seems to have been due to the optimistic encouragement the patients received, similar in effect to the 'suggestion' given during hypnosis.

LEFT *A patient using a transcutaneous electrical nerve stimulation (TENS) device to relieve the pain of recurrent headaches. A small current, produced by the portable power pack, is passed through the skin between two electrodes contained in the bandage round the head. In some, though not all, patients, the current blocks the transmission of pain impulses.*

TREATING PAIN

Many of the drugs commonly used to treat pain – from aspirin to anaesthetics – had been discovered by the end of the 19th century (*see pp.46-9*). The explanation of pain transmission provided by the gate control theory also explained how less orthodox methods of pain relief worked.

Closing the 'gate' partially or completely at the spinal cord could be the way acupuncture (*see pp.222-3*) relieves pain: stimulating an area in some way related to the painful part could block the transmission of pain impulses. The same is true for transcutaneous electrical nerve stimulation (TENS), in which a small electric current is passed through the skin between two electrodes. This was invented by scientists to reproduce artificially the benefits of 'rubbing it better', and is said to relieve pain in about 10 per cent of those who try it. Closing the 'gate' via the brain is the rationale behind such methods as hypnosis, meditation and techniques involving distraction and counselling.

Over the decades, researchers began to realize that there should be different treatments for acute and chronic pain. Although an acute pain may hurt more than a chronic one, it is the prospect of the latter continuing that leads to anxiety, depression and despair – and so to feeling more pain.

In 1946, the American anaesthetist John Bonica founded the first pain clinic in Seattle, Washington, bringing together different specialists – from surgeons to psychiatrists – to investigate the causes and treatment of chronic pain. Today, patients at thousands of pain clinics in the US and the rest of the world receive drug therapy and acupuncture, learn relaxation techniques and exercise regimes, retrain themselves in various life skills and take part in counselling sessions. While the actual reduction in their pain may be minimal, taking control of their lives enables them to cope with it much better.

BELOW *A physiotherapist adjusts the frequency and amplitude of electrical impulses produced by a TENS device while treating nerve damage.*

THE SEX RESEARCHERS

FROM HAVELOCK ELLIS TO MASTERS & JOHNSON

17,500 interviews were condemned as "dirty words on fences"

INTEREST IN SEX is as old as humanity, but objective research into it was, for centuries, severely limited by religious and moralistic strictures. In fact, it was not until the late 19th century that sex research truly began.

HAVELOCK ELLIS

Until he was 59, Dr Henry Havelock Ellis (1859–1939) suffered an inability to enjoy full sexual relations with the women he loved. This divorce between love and sexual response – very characteristic of Victorian England – was exacerbated by numerous tracts condemning masturbation and other so-called 'evil' practices.

Despite his handicap, Ellis was able to shed his sexual inhibitions when it came to intellectual theory. He and his wife agreed to an 'open' marriage, and both had numerous extramarital affairs (even though Ellis's, including one with American birth control advocate Margaret Sanger, were less than complete). And this 'openness' informs his masterwork – the seven-volume *Studies in the Psychology of Sex*, published between 1896 and 1928.

Ellis collected hundreds of case histories – from friends and patients and, later, from his readers – which he used to illustrate one of his primary theses: that, in sex, there is a very wide range of variation within the limits of what can be considered 'normal'. His conclusions were several: sexual behaviour and sexual responses begin well before puberty; masturbation is common among both males and females; boys reach their sexual peak before girls; homosexuality and heterosexuality are present in varying degrees in most people. His findings about women were little short of revolutionary: their supposed lack of sexual desire was a Victorian myth; the orgasm is very similar in both men and women; and frigidity in women can be traced back to repression of their sexuality in early life and to a lack of technique in their men.

Through what he learned and his own experience, Ellis became a campaigner – for sex education for the young, equal rights for women, liberalization of the divorce laws, birth control, and legalization of homosexual acts between consenting adults.

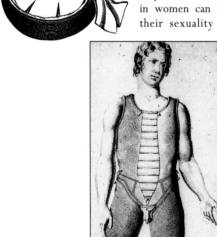

LEFT *19th-century attitudes towards sex led to the invention of these bizarre devices to prevent masturbation – they may also have caused sexual difficulties in later life.*

SEX AS DISEASE

Another book, published in Germany in 1886, achieved almost instant popularity and has remained in print ever since, even though its author's views were diametrically opposed to Ellis's.

In *Psychopathia Sexualis*, Richard von Krafft-Ebing (1840–1902) maintained that any sexual practice varying from the traditional Victorian norm was part of a loathsome disease. He, too, collected case histories – some from defendants in criminal courts where, as Professor of Psychiatry at Strasburg, he often acted as an expert witness. Most of the case histories deal with fetishism, homosexuality, sadism or masochism, and contain pseudo-scientific comments on 'hereditary taint' and 'moral degeneracy'. They are so arranged that stories of 'lust murder' invite confusion with innocent fetishism or even love bites. The professor, who himself seems to have completely rejected sexuality, blamed all 'deviations' on masturbation.

FROM SEX RESEARCH TO SEX THERAPY

From the end of the 19th century, and particularly after World War I, social mores – and especially attitudes towards sex – changed slowly but radically. The extent to which they had was discovered by Alfred Kinsey and his team (*see box*), and it was in the newly liberal atmosphere that followed in Kinsey's wake that William H. Masters (1915–) and Virginia E. Johnson (1925–) undertook their scientific investigation into how the body responds sexually.

From 1948, as Masters, a gynaecologist at Washington University in St Louis, Missouri, began research into hormone replacement therapy (HRT), he became interested in studying the physiology of sex in the same way that others had investigated blood circulation and digestion. In 1954, he launched his study, using prostitutes as experimental subjects in laboratory observations. A few years later, he was ready to recruit 'respectable' men and women, and to help him, he hired the psychologist Virginia Johnson.

The two researchers persuaded 694 individuals (including 276 married couples) to participate. They ranged in age from 18 to 89: most were well educated and the vast majority were white. The only qualification required was that they could achieve orgasm through both masturbation and sexual intercourse.

These individuals were wired up to machines recording heart and breathing rates, were observed by the researchers and filmed, and the women were asked to undertake 'artificial coition' with a transparent probe. The most important finding from all this laboratory work was that both men and women experience a cycle of physical responses to erotic stimulation, which can be divided into four phases: excitement, plateau, orgasm and resolution. In 1966, Masters and

KINSEY'S QUESTIONS

Although Alfred C. Kinsey (1894–1956) obtained a degree in psychology, he later turned to zoology and spent 17 years studying gall wasps, one of the few species that reproduce asexually. In 1937, when he was asked to teach a new marriage course at Indiana University, he discovered that there was virtually no statistically valid research on sexual behaviour. He began to rectify this immediately, asking his students a list of some 400 questions.

It was just the beginning. Kinsey obtained research grants from, among others, the Rockefeller Foundation; engaged the services of more researchers; and, in 1942, founded the Institute of Sex Research to administer the mammoth project. By 1956, the year Kinsey died, he and

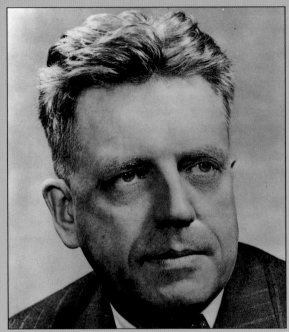

ABOVE Dr Alfred Kinsey, in June 1952 – his meticulously researched books on male and female sexual behaviour shocked America.

his associates had carried out 17,500 two-hour interviews, mainly among whites, but at almost every level of US society: small towns, city slums, gay bars, YMCAs, schools, prisons, hospitals and so on.

Their interviewing technique was to become the basis of all market research. They remained friendly, interested but detached, and (promising complete confidentiality) obtained most of their information by framing their questions as "When did you first start doing [a particular sexual activity]"? Their questions – eventually totalling 521 – ranged across nine main headings: social and economic data; marital histories; sex education; physical data; nocturnal sex dreams; masturbation; heterosexual history; homosexual history; and animal contacts.

The results – published in Sexual Behavior in the Human Male (1948) and Sexual Behavior in the Human Female (1953) – surprised America. Now it was known that only between 2 and 10 per cent of women could be called 'frigid', and whether women did experience orgasm was directly related to their level of sexual experience in their youth. As for men, 86 per cent had sex before marriage, 50 per cent had extramarital affairs and 37 per cent had engaged in homosexual behaviour involving orgasm. In addition, the Kinsey reports revealed strong differences in sexual behaviour between social classes.

When Human Male was published, it caused a furore. Princeton University's president compared it to "the work of small boys writing dirty words on fences". Kinsey was accused of attacking the family and of aiding communism. And shortly after publication, the Rockefeller Foundation withdrew its grant. Kinsey soldiered on, but after publishing Human Female, his health deteriorated, due to overwork, the pressure of criticism and worries about research funding. He died of a heart attack in 1956.

In its obituary, Time magazine stated, "No single event did more for open discussion of sex than the Kinsey Report", and later studies revealed a liberalizing of attitudes. However, controversy continues to surround Alfred Kinsey and his work to this day.

Johnson published their results in *Human Sexual Response*, which sold more than 300,000 copies in the US alone.

In 1959, they also launched a two-week therapy programme designed to help couples with sexual problems. In all, 790 people took part, all of whom began their therapy with three days of intensive history-taking. Masters

LEFT William Masters and Virginia Johnson were proud that only three divorces occurred among their patients. However, in 1971,

Masters married the already divorced Johnson; in the early 1990s, the two world-famous sex researchers were divorced themselves.

and Johnson found, as Ellis and Kinsey had, that the major cause of female sexual inadequacy was being brought up in the belief that sex was dirty and shameful, but the researchers also discovered that the same held true for men.

However, rather than working through this psychological disorder, they detoured round it by having their couples focus on carefully controlled erotic sensation. This 'sensate focus', and other techniques they taught, were a great success. The failure rate was just 18 per cent, and in a five-year follow-up, they discovered that only 5.1 per cent of their patients had relapsed, and there had been only three divorces. When Masters and Johnson published their results in *Human Sexual Inadequacy* in 1970, they marked a distinct shift from straight research towards therapy.

FIGHTING CANCER

FROM COCKTAILS TO CURES

Bacteria, viruses, irritations and chemical toxins have all been blamed

ALL LIVING THINGS – plants as well as animals – can suffer from cancer, a disease that arises through uncontrolled cell division. The word 'cancer' comes from *karcinos*, the Greek word for crab, and was first used by Hippocrates and other ancient Greek physicians to describe a tumour or swelling with 'fingers', or channels, spreading outwards. This accurately describes an untreated breast tumour – at that time the most commonly recognized cancer – where the outer skin becomes hardened and the channels of cancerous cells with enlarged veins spread out over the breast, causing a deep, gnawing pain.

IMBALANCE OF BILE OR INFLAMMATION

The ancient Greeks (*see pp.18–9*) recognized cancer in many forms, but whether these included non-cancerous ulcers and carbuncles is not known. They believed that cancers were due to an imbalance in the four humours, with an excess of black bile being produced in the spleen. Galen (*see pp.22–3*) thought that cancer could also be caused when too much blood circulated through the body as the result of inflammation.

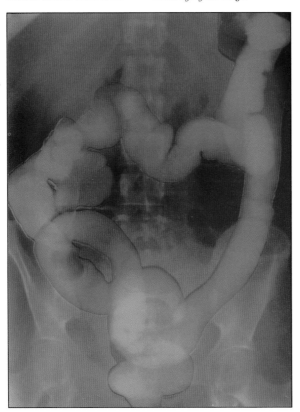

BELOW *A false-colour X-ray of the abdomen shows a cancer in the* ascending colon: the oval shadow on the left of the image.

Throughout the Renaissance, different forms of cancer were described – John of Arderne described a rectal carcinoma in the 14th century but considered it "nothing more than a hidden cancer". Antonio Benivieni (1443–1502), an early pathologist, described stomach cancer and, during an autopsy, the Swiss pathologist, Felix Plater (1536–1614), discovered a large tumour in the brain of a knight who had been behaving peculiarly prior to his death.

After the Swedish scientist Olof Rudbeck discovered the lymph glands, in 1652, scientists pointed to lymph as a factor in the cause of cancer. Previously, Hieronymous Fabricius (1537–1619), Professor of Anatomy at Padua, Italy, had postulated that the lymphatic involvement in breast cancer (*see pp.198-9*) necessitated the removal of the lymph nodes in mastectomies – and he produced a specialized tool to carry out the procedure.

Until late in the 18th century, the idea that cancer followed from inflammation due to an imbalance was secure. Then, John Hunter (*see p.41*) formulated the idea that a blastema (embryonic tissue) was the basic building block for the repair of the structures of the body, but that under certain conditions it could initiate destructive growth. Soon after, Marie François Xavier Bichat (1771–1802), a French anatomist from the Jura, started to consider complex organs as a function of their elementary tissues, and, in his lectures, declared that all tissues were capable of independent growth and that cancer was an overgrowth of tissue. Bichat's ideas led to the notion that a rebel part of a blastema caused the growth to turn malignant.

THE CELLULAR LEVEL

In the 19th century, Matthias Jakob Schleiden (1804–1881), a German botanist, discovered that plants were composed of cells and, in 1831, observed a plant cell nucleus. By chance, Schleiden met Theodor Schwann (1810–82), a German anatomist and physiologist, at dinner one evening and told him of his observations. Schwann later confirmed that animals, too, were composed of cells with a nucleus. An improved microscope invented by J. J. Lister (*see p.52*) enabled scientists to see tumour cells and their nuclei. Together with Johannes Mueller (1801–1858), a German physiologist, Schwann propounded the cellular theory, though their idea that the nucleus was responsible for cell division fell on deaf ears. Rudolf Virchow (*see p.65*), a student of Mueller, extended their work to explain that cells were the basic unit in tumours and that their continued division was the reason for tumour growth.

The man who coined the word 'chromosome', Wilhelm Waldeyer-Hartz (1836–1921), published two papers on the genesis and pathology of cancer – the first modern description of the disease. Waldeyer-Hartz wrote that cancer formed

RIGHT *A bone scan of the spine and ribs shows metastases (secondary tumours) from prostatic cancer as pink and white areas in the spine.*

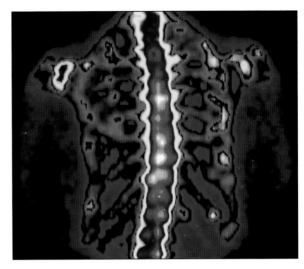

initially from a normal cell and grew by uncontrolled cell division; a metastasis, or malignant secondary tumour, formed when a cancer cell migrated from its original site to another via the blood, lymph or interstitial fluids. He suggested that data about cancers could not be generalized and indicated a cure would be possible if the disease was detected at an early enough stage. This idea was to be of great value when radiotherapy and, later, chemotherapy were added to surgery as possible treatments.

Bacteria, viruses, mechanical irritations and chemical toxins have all been blamed as the primary cause of cancer, almost as soon as they were discovered. But scientists now realize that there is no single external agent that causes every cancer. Different cancers are linked with different agents: for example, sunlight with skin cancer; smoking with lung cancer; hepatitis B with liver cancer; Epstein-Barr virus with lymphoma (cancer of the lymphatic system); arsenic with skin cancer; asbestos with mesothelioma (cancer of the lining of the lungs); uranium and radiation with leukaemia (cancer of the bone marrow and white blood cells). Viruses are now thought to be responsible for about 15 per cent of all cancers.

COMING TO GRIPS WITH CANCER

Both the ancient Greeks and Galen thought that all cancer treatment was palliative (unless surgery could remove the whole mass). The belief that there was no cure largely held true until the 20th century, with a few exceptions, such as Paracelsus (*see pp.36–7*), who recommended a mixture of the doctrines of signs, and antimony, and the eugenists (*see p.67*), who suggested breeding control and quarantine to isolate and eliminate the 'carriers' of the disease.

The first specialist cancer hospital was built in 1740, in Rheims, France, from funds donated by the canon of the cathedral in an attempt to isolate the disease he thought was contagious. In 1791, the brewer, Samuel Whitbread (1720–96), endowed a cancer ward at the Middlesex

NEW HOPE FOR CHILDREN

Leukaemia, a term coined by Rudolf Virchow (see p.65) to describe cancer of the white blood cells produced by the bone marrow, is the most common cancer in children, though more adults are diagnosed as having it than children. Treatment has advanced rapidly since the 1940s, when leukaemia proved rapidly fatal. Sidney Farber, at the Children's Hospital in Boston, Massachusetts, noticed that children given folic acid to help their leukaemia, not only failed to improve, but actually worsened. In 1947, the first anti-folate drug, aminopterin, was developed and this proved successful in causing a remission – though only for a limited time. Farber decided that it was important to keep children on a maintenance dose until resistance to the drug developed. In so doing, he was able to prolong the life of many sufferers for up to a year – and a few were cured. In 1952, other anti-leukaemic drugs, such as purinethol and methotrexate, were developed, beginning the era of combination therapy for leukaemia. And in 1956, the steroid cortisone (see p.166) was combined with either of the other two to increase the number and length of remissions.

Donald Pinkel, a former associate of Farber, was a medical director in Memphis, Tennessee, when in 1962 he pioneered a three-stage total therapy for children with leukaemia. This involved regular doses of anti-leukaemic drugs for up to three years, followed by radiotherapy to kill leukaemic cells in the brain (where drugs are less effective), then steroids and vincristine (a drug extracted from the Madagascan periwinkle) to limit the damage to body tissues. By the late 1960s, doctors found that, by using the drugs in different combinations, there was less chance of the cancer cells becoming resistant. This multi-faceted approach to treatment has resulted in a remarkable improvement in survival rates and now 70 per cent of children with the commonest form of leukaemia survive.

Sufferers from chronic myeloid leukaemia, a rare form of the disease, were given new hope in 1992 with the announcement by Michael Dexter, Professor of Experimental Haematology at the Christie Hospital, Manchester, UK, that his team had developed a new gene transplant technique. This involves a blood transfusion in which a genetically engineered virus introduces and spreads so-called 'healing genes' to all parts of the patient's body.

BELOW *The cancer drug vincris-tine is extracted from Catharanthus roseus, the Madagascan (rosy) periwinkle for leukaemia treatment.*

Hospital, London, for research purposes. In 1827, William Marsden opened a dispensary for the poor in London which soon became The Royal Free and Cancer Hospital. The word 'Free' denoted that no letter of recommendation was required to enter the hospital – the rule for most of the other hospitals at that time.

The idea to establish a research institute that would look into the cause, nature and treatment of cancer was the brainchild of Sir Henry Morris (1844–1926), a leading surgeon and head of the Middlesex cancer department in London. Funded by private individuals and controlled by the royal colleges, the Cancer Research Fund was founded on 4 July 1902, with Morris as secretary. The title 'Imperial' was added in 1904 when the then Prince of Wales (later, King George V) became the first President of the fund.

Dr E. F. Bashford (1873–1923), who became the first director and spokesman for the fund at the age of 29, organized the first scheme of research. When the Post Office, in 1904, refused to transport tumour samples – "as cancer is an infectious disease the transmission of specimens was dangerous both to the public and to postal officials"– Bashford replied that "No analogy exists between cancer and any known form of infectious or contagious disease".

Cancer is often considered a 20th-century disease and is the second major cause of death after circulatory diseases in the industrialized world. After the first international classification of causes of death was established in 1900, cancer appeared on death certificates with increasing frequency. But it is suspected that previously many people who died of old age may well have had undetected cancer. As cancer is primarily a disease of late middle age and old age – with some exceptions such as Wilms' disease (kidney tumours in children) and leukaemia – a longer life expectancy means more people die of cancer than before. In 1850, the average life expectancy was around 45 years – it had been lower – and stands, in 1992, at around 72 years for men and 77 years for women. Moreover, cancer figures are higher, in industrialized nations particularly, because of the increased exposure to carcinogenic substances, such as asbestos, coal-tar fumes, carbon polymers (plastics, adhesives, lacquers), certain food dyes and pesticides.

COCKTAILS AND CURES

Treatment for cancer has developed tremendously in the 20th century. Many treatments are now a 'cocktail' of surgery, radiotherapy and chemotherapy, each being specifically devised for the individual and the stage of progression of the cancer. The first 'cocktails' were prepared during the

1960s, in order to increase the effectiveness of treatment and also to reduce side-effects. The 1980s saw the first attempts to classify cancers by degrees of their severity.

Surgery has improved with increased awareness of the need for early detection. Successful breakthroughs in medical technology (see pp.172-5), such as CAT scans, ultrasound and MRI scans, have brought great advances in early detection, resulting in fewer 'open and see' operations and more precise surgical intervention. Isotope scanning, where a radioactive material is selectively taken up by normal cells but not by cancer cells, has contributed to the accurate pinpointing of tumours. Another technique involves monoclonal antibodies – specifically cloned antibodies produced by lymphocytes to recognize foreign material on a cell wall,

ABOVE *A brain scan reveals a slow-growing large tumour (purple), with a calcified (yellow) lining. Such tumours can suddenly turn malignant.*

CANCER OF THE PROSTATE GLAND

In 1896, following the discovery that removal of the ovaries sometimes caused a regression in breast cancer (see pp.198–9), it was postulated that there may be a connection between the cancer and hormones. In 1939, Charles Brenton Huggins, while Professor of Surgery at Chicago, found that cancer cells as well as the prostate gland were stimulated by the male hormones (androgens). Two years later, he suggested that removal of the testes causes a regression in prostatic cancer. (The fact that eunuchs do not succumb to the disease seems to bear this out.) Huggins shared a Nobel prize in 1966 for his work in cancer research, and in particular for his hormonal treatment of prostatic cancer.

As a result of Huggins' work, oestrogen and anti-androgens are now given to patients with prostatic cancer, often effectively. Prostatic cancer is only slightly less common than breast cancer, but screening is just taking off – in 1989, during a Prostate Cancer Awareness Week in the US, some 15,000 men were screened. Studies show that although 40 per cent of men aged 65 or over may have a small prostatic cancer, only about 4 per cent will develop the symptoms of clinical prostatic cancer over the subsequent 15 years.

stick to it and destroy it. First developed in the 1970s, these antibodies can be tagged with radioactive isotopes, so that when they search out and bind to the cancer cells they provide a radioactive profile for scanners to detect.

Surgery remains the first treatment of choice for many cancers, such as colorectal and bowel cancers, as well as some types of lung, ovarian, stomach, testicular and uterine cancers. Surgery has also been successful with a single metastasis in the liver or kidney, early melanoma (skin cancer) and Wilms' disease. A major success has been in cone biopsies (the removal of small pieces of tissue for examination by a pathologist) for early cervical cancers, which at the beginning of the 20th century were a major cause of death in women and is now curable, if detected early enough.

No longer equated with the intrusive scalpel, surgery has moved on to include non-invasive methods, such as cryosurgery using ultra-low temperatures, laser surgery, and chemosurgery using zinc chloride paste for skin cancers, which have become increasingly common with the modern desire for a tan. In Australia and New Zealand, for example, malignant melanoma – the most virulent and dangerous of the three skin cancers – is the commonest form of cancer affecting young adults.

Radiotherapy has progressed significantly from the achievements of Pierre and Marie Curie (see pp.128–9). When the radium they discovered was found to be extremely hazardous, it was replaced by cobalt 60, still the most commonly used radiation source today. The early problems of the fragile X-ray machine, where only 15 per cent of the skin dose reached further than 6in (15cm) into the body, therefore requiring the patient to receive vast doses to reach a deep cancer, have been overcome by the linear accelerator in use today. Developed in the 1960s, this produces 'hard' electron beams that can penetrate to deep areas, such as the pelvis and bone without damaging the skin and without scattering into the surrounding tissues.

Chemotherapy, the use of drugs to destroy cells, started in 1865 when potassium arsenite was used to treat leukaemia. With Paul Ehrlich's discovery of Salvarsan (see pp.100–1), many were convinced that a drug could be found that would zoom in and destroy cancer cells, leaving the normal cells untouched. Unfortunately, this has not as yet proved to be true. Of the hundreds and thousands of compounds tried and tested by the pharmaceutical companies this century, only about 40 are in clinical use.

ANTI-CANCER TOXINS

Until the interferons, a group of proteins produced by the body during certain illnesses, were discovered in 1956 by scientists at the National Institute for Medical Research in London, there was little progress in the search for an effective anti-cancer toxin. Interferons stimulate the body's defences, inhibit cell division and are toxic to certain cells. Produced from genetically engineered bacteria, interferons are now used successfully to treat various cancers, including hairy cell leukaemia, and are helpful in others, such as malignant melanoma and AIDs-related Karposi's sarcoma.

Another naturally produced group of proteins involved in the immune response is the interleukins, discovered in the 1980s; clinical trials started in 1986. In 1980, Dr. Stephen Rosenberg found that, with immune cells, one of the interleukins activated killer cells (called LAK cells) and that these slowed lung and liver metastasis in animals.

But new developments in the science and technology of medicine (see p.230) give reason to hope that cancer will, in the future, be both avoidable and treatable.

Techniques such as gene replacement therapy, as well as an ever-increasing sophistication in pharmocology, may make cancer a killer of the past.

BELOW *An osteosarcoma, or bone tumour, just above the knee of a 17-* *year-old girl. Such tumours are most common in children and young adults.*

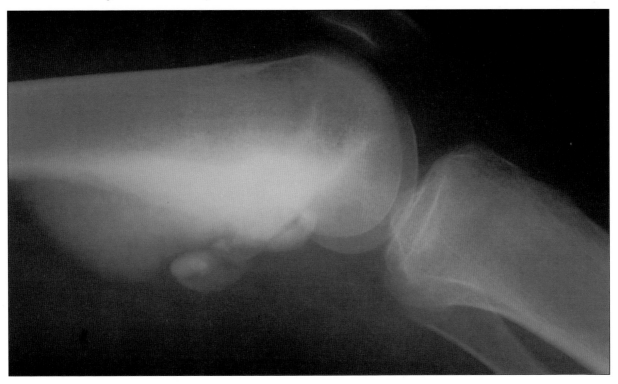

WOMEN AND CANCER

From breast removal to detection, lumpectomy and treatment

Breast cancer remains the most common form of the disease in women, killing hundreds of thousands every year. Yet, despite decades of experimentation and research, both its treatment and its detection remain controversial.

FROM RADICAL SURGERY TO LUMPECTOMY

William Halsted's radical mastectomy (removal of breast, lymph nodes and chest muscles) of the 1890s (*see pp.90-1*) relied on two untested suppositions: first, that breast cancer remains in the breast for some time before spreading; and, second, that the lymphatic system is relatively separate from blood vessels, and thus the removal of lymph nodes creates a barrier to the passage of cancer cells.

The 'treatment of choice' became the modified radical mastectomy developed by British surgeon P. H. Patey. This operation retained the chest muscles, and was followed by X-ray treatment. In fact, the first 30 years of the 20th century comprise the only period in the history of breast cancer when there has been any consensus on treatment.

In 1937, Geoffrey Keynes, of St Bartholomew's Hospital, London, became the first to claim satisfactory results with the simple removal of breast tumours (what came to be called 'lumpectomies'), followed by radiation. Before these findings made an impact, however, there was increasing discontent with the reigning surgical treatments, especially

ABOVE *Rembrandt's* Bathsheba at Her Toilet *shows evidence of* breast cancer in the deformation of the left breast, below the armpit.

after World War II, when it was realized that the success rate of the Halsted operation had been overestimated.

Cancer surgeons became polarized: in the 1940s and 1950s, some advocated a 'supraradical' mastectomy, even more mutilating than Halsted's; others, such as French radiologist François Baclesse and his co-workers at the Curie Foundation in Paris, championed lumpectomy. Between 1937 and 1953, the Baclesse team treated 100 women in the earlier stages of the disease: the results were comparable with those achieved through orthodox methods, but with vastly improved quality of life for their patients. In 1963, Hugh Auchincloss, of Columbia University, stated that extensive surgical intervention only persisted because of tradition, training and "personal prejudice tinged with emotion".

By the 1970s, researchers had realized that breast tumours could not be pulled out by their roots like weeds. They found that, by the time breast cancer was diagnosed, most, if not all, patients had cancer elsewhere in their bodies; surgery did not 'cure' the cancer, but the immune systems of some patients probably did. They also discovered that the lymphatic system and bloodstream are so intertwined that they cannot be separated, so removing lymph nodes to prevent cancer spread was useless.

The statistics agreed. In 1975, a World Health Organization survey showed that, in the previous 75 years, not only had deaths from breast cancer failed to decline, but they may have actually increased. A 1985 study, carried out by the National Surgical Adjuvant Breast Project in the US and Canada, concluded that the same percentages of women

DES DAUGHTERS

In 1938, Charles Dodds synthesized a hormone called diethylstilboestrol, or DES. From 1943 to 1959, it was prescribed to nearly six million (mainly American) women with a history of miscarriage.

In 1969, two Americans – the gynaecologist Arthur Herbst and the pathologist Robert Scully – noticed an unusually high rate of clear-cell adenocarcinoma, a rare type of vaginal cancer, in the teenage daughters of women who had been given DES in the first 17 weeks of pregnancy. A study carried out in 1971, by David Poskanzer, confirmed that the link existed, and, by 1986, about 350 cases had been discovered in the US – some 4 in every 1000 'DES daughters'.

The hormone was also found to have caused abnormalities in the reproductive tracts of these daughters, as well as difficulties in conceiving and carrying babies to term. In addition, sons were more likely to suffer from genital abnormalities, and the mothers themselves also ran an increased risk of developing breast cancer.

with cancers of varying spreads remained alive after ten years whatever their treatment. Today, an increasing number of women with breast cancer are treated with lumpectomy, usually followed by radiotherapy. Following work in France in the 1960s, the radiotherapy may now take the form of implants – 12 to 16 plastic tubes containing radioactive iridium wire – left in place for three or four days.

The first true breakthrough in the battle against breast cancer came in January 1992, in a study by British researcher Richard Peto, published in the *Lancet*. Involving 75,000 women world-wide, it showed that 10 per cent of those under 50 with early breast cancer survived ten years longer if, in addition to surgery and radiation, they took tamoxifen, an anti-oestrogen drug available since 1971 but only commonly used·since about 1989. A further 5 per cent gained ten years' survival if they also received cancer chemotherapy.

In the early 1990s, tamoxifen was also given to women before surgery, because of its capacity to shrink tumours by up to 90 per cent, and the possibility that it may 'sterilize' them and prevent their spread. In addition, researchers were excited by the prospect of giving the drug as a preventive to healthy women with a family history of breast cancer.

BELOW *A mammogram is the most effective breast cancer detector – here,*   *one shows a small, round white cancerous tumour at the centre.*

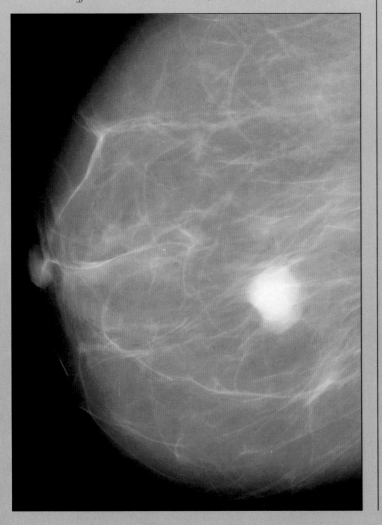

LOOKING FOR LUMPS

The new treatments for breast cancer depend for their success on the early detection of breast tumours, and a great deal of effort and money has been invested since the 1960s.

One possible method (other than self-examination, or manual palpation) was thermography (*see pp.168-9*), which measures minute temperature variations. Although cancers are warmer than other body tissues, it was realized by the late 1970s that, in breast thermography, about 30 per cent of small cancerous tumours are missed and benign ones often register as 'hot'.

The most successful detection method so far is mammography, the X-ray examination of the breasts. It gained acceptance after 1962, when a Houston, Texas, radiologist, Robert Egan, published his conclusions: it was superior to manual palpation in detecting early cancer.

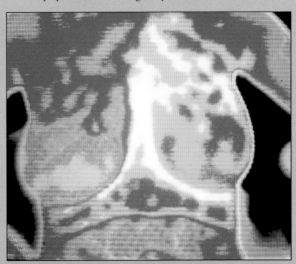

ABOVE *Although this thermogram*   *on the right of the image, some*
shows a 'hot' (i.e. cancerous) area   *small cancers can be missed.*

A number of major studies were then carried out. One was the Breast Cancer Detection Demonstration Project, undertaken in 1973 by the American Cancer Society and National Cancer Institute and involving 280,000 women. Of all the cancers detected, 90 per cent were found by mammography, and this led to revised recommendations: women should be screened every one to two years over the age of 40, and annually after 50. In 1987, the British government agreed to fund a breast cancer screening programme, with every woman between the ages of 50 and 64 being invited to have a mammogram every three years.

MORE HOPE FOR OTHER CANCERS

The news is much better for women suffering other forms of female cancers. In the US, deaths from uterine cancer have decreased by more than 70 per cent since the 1930s (even though incidence has increased markedly since the 1940s). With screening tests, such as the Pap smear (*see p.114*), the early detection – and virtual 100 per cent cure – of cervical cancer has become a possibility (though screening has thus afar had little effect on death rates). Tests for ovarian cancer – called the 'silent killer' because of its lack of early symptoms – are in an advanced stage of development.

EMERGING VIRUSES

OLD DISEASES IN NEW SETTINGS

Giving children pieces of corpses' brains brought a disease to life

SINCE WORLD WAR II, medicine has been surprised by a number of unknown, lethal diseases. Some feared that these were caused by microbes that were either brand new or newly evolved, and against which medicine had few, if any, defences. However, research has suggested different reasons for the emergence of these 'new' infections.

PROGRESS AND DISEASE

In 1967, 31 researchers at Marburg, in Germany, became ill with very high fevers and severe haemorrhaging, and seven of them died. Eventually scientists traced the disease to direct contact with blood or tissue from a batch of African green monkeys from Uganda, used for experiments. The first recognized outbreak in Africa itself of what had come to be called 'Marburg disease' occurred in 1975.

In 1969, another 'new' disease was discovered. When an American worker at a mission hospital in the small town of Lassa, in Nigeria, developed a very high fever, she was flown to the US for further treatment and study. There, the illness spread to those investigating the mystery virus, and some of them died. Epidemics of this 'Lassa fever' subsequently occurred in West Africa.

In 1976, two severe and virtually simultaneous epidemics of haemorrhagic fever devastated parts of Sudan and Zaïre, resulting in at least 300 deaths – at one Sudanese hospital, 76 of the staff became ill and 41 died. The illness looked suspiciously like Marburg disease, and when the virus was isolated from a sample taken from a patient (who lived near the Ebola river in Zaïre) and examined under the microscope, it appeared almost identical to that causing Marburg. However, animal studies showed that immunity to Marburg did not confer immunity to the new Ebola disease, and thus the viruses, though related, had to be different.

Other previously unknown diseases have since emerged, named after the places where they were first identified: Junin in Argentina, Orapuche in Brazil, Hantaan in Korea, Rift Valley in East Africa. For a long time, no one knew why these diseases had erupted, but eventually the picture became clearer. The viruses are not, in fact, new. Neither are they new mutations: they are old viruses in new clothes.

For instance, Lassa fever is now one of the leading causes of disease in eastern Sierra Leone – it was here, in the 1950s, that a new diamond mining industry started, bringing people into the forest and into contact with the rodents known to

---

STOPPING THE SPREAD OF HEPATITIS B

Hepatitis B (serum hepatitis) is spread by contact with infectious blood or through sexual contact. Its primary symptom is liver inflammation, often leading to damage and, frequently, to liver failure. In addition, a chronic carrier of the hepatitis B virus has a 270 times greater chance of contracting liver cancer than other people. In 1967, Baruch Blumberg developed a test that could reveal the presence of the virus in the blood, work for which he shared the 1976 Nobel Prize for Medicine with Gajdusek.

Hepatitis B is one of the greatest global health problems, affecting millions of people in Asia and Africa. With the birth of the gay liberation movement in the US,

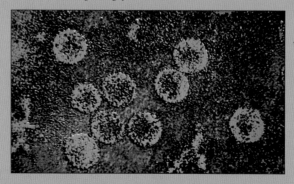

in 1969, and the resulting changes in sexual lifestyles, it also became endemic within the gay community: in New York City alone, more than 50 per cent of gay men showed evidence of the disease.

By 1974, a vaccine had been developed in the US, using sterilized viral particles from the blood serum of carriers. During the next four years, the Polish-born epidemiologist Wolf Szmuness, a refugee from both the Nazis and the Soviets, undertook a series of population studies to find out the best group on which to carry out a double-blind trial of the vaccine. The New York gay community was ideal, and in 1978-9, working with the Gay Men's Health Project, Szmuness and his team screened over 10,000 men to find 1083 volunteers, who were then injected with vaccine made from the serum of 300 carrier volunteers.

By June 1980, the results were in. Of the 160 volunteers who had developed hepatitis B during the trial, all had been given the placebo, not the vaccine, which, when all the statistics were available, proved to be 92.3 per cent effective. And the trial itself had been shown to be the most complex and impeccable in the history of medicine. Sadly, Szmuness died of lung cancer two years later.

LEFT *The hepatitis B virus – the disease still affects millions in Asia* *and Africa, but there is now an effective vaccine.*

BELOW *The Ebola virus appeared suddenly in Africa in 1976; it is similar to the Marburg virus which killed German researchers in 1967.*

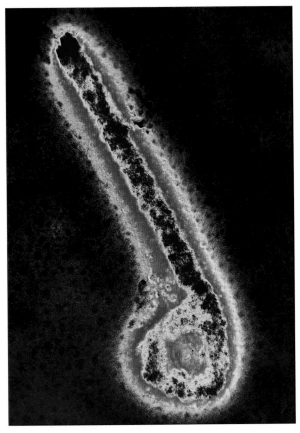

carry the Lassa fever virus. Shortly before Rift Valley disease emerged in Egypt, in 1977, the Aswan Dam provided an enormous inland lake for the disease-carrying mosquitoes to breed. As for Ebola disease, it was probably able to spread in a remote part of Zaïre because of the building of a hospital, where one of the practices was the sharing of needles. AIDS, too, has swept parts of Africa because of population shifts away from rural areas into overcrowded cities (*see pp.204-7*); it is now reckoned that one of the HIV viruses has been around for at least a century.

THE MYSTERY OF KURU

Another disease – later found to be caused by a change of lifestyle – decimated the Fore tribe of New Guinea, then under Australian control. In 1953, a patrol officer reported that many women and children were shivering and shaking until, after 18 months or so, they became paralyzed and died. The Fore named the disease 'kuru' – 'to shiver or tremble with cold or fear' – and blamed it on sorcery.

The ebullient American research scientist D. Carleton Gajdusek (1923–) was passing through New Guinea in March 1957 when he heard about the kuru epidemic. After a brief investigation, he decided to stay on, and somehow persuaded the National Institutes of Health (NIH) in the US and the Australian authorities to support him. He began learning the native languages and compiling family histories of the victims. By August, he had uncovered more than 500 deaths and 150 active cases in a total population of 15,000. The cause remained a mystery: nothing showed up in any of the samples he sent to Australia and the US, there was no

evidence of case-to-case transmission, and poisoning and dietary deficiency were both ruled out.

Through his research among the Fore – during which he walked more than 1000 miles – Gajdusek found that no European had contracted kuru; Fore Indians who had left the area could still develop it; and Fore women could spread it to other communities by passing it on to their children. Because of this, there seemed to be a complicated genetic basis for the disease, and as a result, in July 1960, the Australian government passed the first 'genetic law' in history, placing the Fore in quarantine. (This proved impossible to police and was quietly dropped.)

Meanwhile, in 1959, the British veterinary scientist W. J. Hadlow stated in a letter to the *Lancet* that the symptoms of kuru were remarkably similar to those of scrapie in sheep, a disease known for over 250 years. He suggested that the kuru scientists transmit the disease to an animal in the same way that had been done with scrapie: by injecting suspensions of brain tissue from a kuru victim into an animal and then waiting – for possibly as long as two years or more.

In 1962, Gajdusek returned to New Guinea and, in the most difficult of conditions, obtained 16 brains from kuru victims and sent them to NIH, where suspensions were injected into chimpanzees. In late 1965, when the animals began to fall ill, it was certain that kuru was a transmissible, infectious disease caused by a previously unknown 'slow virus', with an incredibly long incubation period. Gajdusek shared a Nobel prize in 1976 for his work on kuru.

The final mystery of kuru was cleared up by anthropologists Robert Glasse and Shirley Lindenbaum, who studied the Fore in 1961-2. They found that the women had begun to cannibalize their dead in about 1915, learning about it from a neighbouring tribe. Very few of the men tried it; the practice was almost exclusively carried out by the women, who would give tidbits (including brain tissue) to their sons and daughters. Thus the disease would be transmitted and would reveal itself between two years and two decades later. Once cannibalism was outlawed, the incidence of the disease declined until, today, there are only a handful of new cases.

As well as testing chimpanzees with kuru, the NIH scientists also injected some with brain tissue from victims of other chronic central nervous system diseases. Those injected with tissue from a person who had died of the rare Creutzfeld-Jakob disease (CJD), which results in early senile dementia, also became ill and died. CJD, too, had to be caused by a slow virus.

BELOW *The Fore people of New Guinea were decimated by kuru in the early 1950s: the cause was some 40 years of cannibalism.*

POLIOMYELITIS

THE SALK AND SABIN VACCINES

The way was opened by $1,370,000 and 30,000 monkeys

BY THE LATE 1940s, doctors knew that the polio virus was transmitted via faeces, and that, in crowded communities in under-developed countries, it would infect the under-threes who rarely, if ever, contracted the paralysing form of the disease. However, in developed nations, with increased hygiene and more rigorous toilet training, the virus bypassed the very young and, instead, struck schoolchildren and young adults, sometimes with devastating effects. Polio epidemics were thus, ironically, the result of public health measures.

John Enders, Thomas Weller and Frederick Robbins had, by 1949, succeeded in growing the virus on human and animal tissue (see p.155), for which they were awarded the Nobel prize in 1954. From 1949, the US National Foundation for Infantile Paralysis (NFIP) funded a huge research project at four universities, aiming to classify the different strains of the polio virus. By 1951 – and 30,000 monkeys and $1.37 million later – the programme had established that there were three recognizable families of the virus, and the way was open for serious research into a vaccine.

THE SALK VACCINE

Jonas Salk (1914–) of the University of Pittsburgh had been involved in the NFIP classification project, and had developed formalin-inactivated influenza vaccines during World War II. He now started work on a formalin-killed polio vaccine (against all three strains), always mindful of the previous disaster with this type of vaccine (see pp.108-9).

BELOW An electron micrograph of polio virus particles – polio attacked more than 30,000 people in America in 1950.

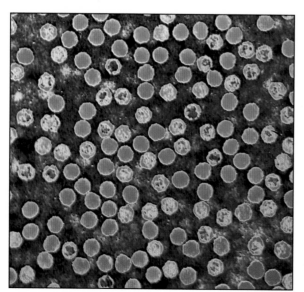

Salk decided his vaccine was ready for testing on selected groups of children, including his three sons. "When you inoculate children with a polio vaccine," he commented, "you don't sleep well for two or three months." The results, he reported to the NFIP, were encouraging but "should not be interpreted to indicate that a practical vaccine is now at hand".

The NFIP immunization committee begged to differ and, in January 1953, voted to proceed with a mass trial, despite the fact that both John Enders and Jonas Salk disagreed. Covering 217 areas in 44 states and testing some 1.8 million schoolchildren at a cost of $7.5 million, the polio vaccine trial of 1954 was the largest single clinical trial in history. The results were impressive: the vaccine caused children to produce antibodies against all three strains of polio; there were 50 per cent fewer polio cases in areas where vaccinations had been carried out; and not one child contracted the disease after being vaccinated. All over the US, church bells rang and factory sirens sounded when the news was announced early in 1955.

However, the final report after the trial did point out that, while the Salk vaccine was 90 per cent or more effective against polio types II and III, it was only 60–70 per cent effective against type I. In addition, the vaccine had to be injected and followed up with regular booster shots.

Within weeks, the stockpile of 10 million doses of Salk vaccine was released. In April 1955, after 400,000 children had been inoculated, reports from California and Idaho revealed that the vaccine had induced paralytic polio in 204 adults and children, 11 of whom had died. California's health department ordered that a tainted batch of vaccine be taken off the market. By 7 May 1955, four million doses had been dispensed among America's young. By November, the Center for Disease Control in Atlanta was able to announce that "the decline in attack rates for naturally acquired paralytic cases had been from two to five times greater among vaccinated children than among the unvaccinated".

THE SABIN VACCINE

Salk's vaccine did not confer permanent immunity and it was not wholly effective against polio type I. Russian-born virologist Albert Sabin (1906–) of the University of Cincinnati believed that a vaccine made from live virus whose virulence had been eliminated would be far more effective, would give permanent immunity and could be taken by mouth.

Although he and others soon produced such vaccines, the abrasive Sabin – unlike the charming Salk – could not gain the backing of the NFIP immunization committee which was deeply committed to the forthcoming mass trial of Salk's vaccine. The resulting rift between the lay and scientific members of the committee led to talk of the scientists

THE TALE OF SISTER KENNY

One of the most remarkable – and controversial – figures in the history of polio was Elizabeth Kenny (1886–1952), who first started treating polio victims in 1910. Working in the isolation of the Australian bush, and unaware of the accepted procedures for treating the disease, Sister Kenny developed her own method that emphasized the importance of continually exercising the affected limbs. During the acute stage, she would apply warm compresses to aching muscles and keep them passively exercised. This was followed up in later stages by intensive exercise of the muscles to 're-educate' them into mobility.

Established polio specialists recommended immobilizing the affected limbs in splints to ensure complete rest, but Sister Kenny was convinced this orthodox regime would exacerbate the problems of paralysis and further atrophy the muscles. Her disagreements with the medical establishment attracted much publicity and criticism, but she held firmly to her beliefs and eventually succeeded in winning her critics over and shifting the emphasis of aftercare from rest to muscle re-education.

Funding for her polio treatment programme became a casualty of the controversy, however, and so the Sister Kenny Foundation was set up by her supporters in 1945. Although this gave her independence, the political struggles involved in keeping it going made huge demands upon her time and prevented her from working on the wards.

BELOW *Jonas Salk (1914-), inventor of the first polio vaccine,* which went into mass production in 1954, but required booster shots.

resigning *en masse*. Eventually, in December 1954, the NFIP granted Sabin funds to continue his work but would not support mass trials.

Between 1957 and 1959, Sabin's live virus vaccine was tested elsewhere in the world - in Mexico, Holland, Britain, Sweden, Singapore, Czechoslovakia and the USSR. The NFIP committee praised the potential of the vaccine, but still refused to recommend mass trials in the US. It took another three years of mass trials before, in August 1961, Sabin's vaccine against type I polio was licensed for manufacture and marketing in the US. The type II vaccine followed three months later, and finally, in March 1962, his trivalent (effective against all three types) oral vaccine became available. Taken on a sugar cube or in a spoonful of syrup – eminently preferable to a syringe – the Sabin vaccine has now largely replaced the Salk variety.

BELOW *Sabin vaccine is usually given on a sugar cube.*

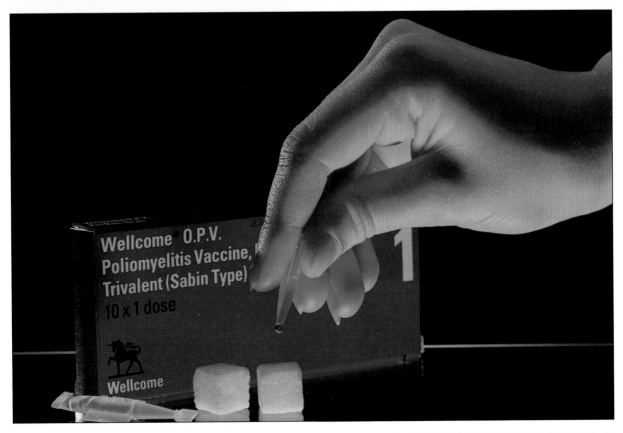

THE SCOURGE OF AIDS

THE NATURAL HISTORY OF A SERIAL KILLER

The WHO forecast that 15 million would be infected by 1995

IN THE SUMMER OF 1981, the Centers for Disease Control, a federally run monitoring organization in the US, published details of a mysterious outbreak of illness in San Francisco. Five men in the city had been diagnosed as suffering from *Pneumocystis carinii*, a deadly type of pneumonia so rare that a single case occurring without obvious cause would have been noteworthy, let alone several in the same place at the same time. The CDC was duty-

bound to look for any factor linking them. It found one and duly emphasized it in its report: each of the five victims was homosexual. The document went on to speculate that their illnesses could have some connection with their way of life or sexual contacts.

BELOW *A model of HIV shows a nucleus surrounded by protein and* *enveloped in a spherical membrane studded with protein and antigens.*

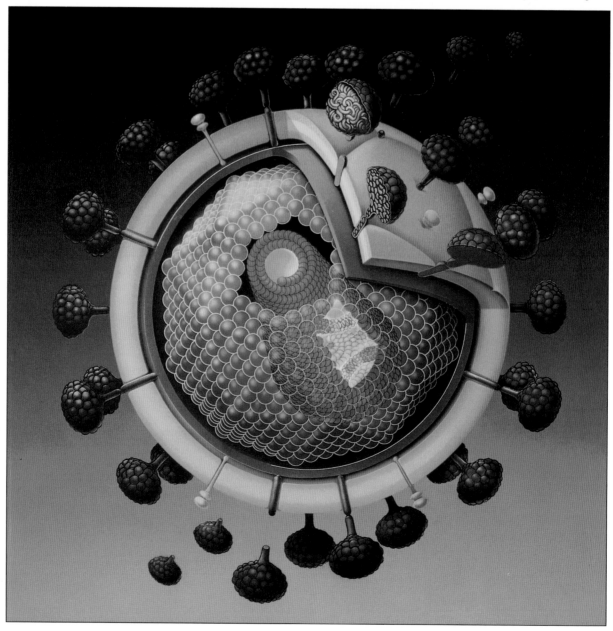

Publication of the CDC's findings unleashed a wave of similar accounts from physicians in San Francisco, Los Angeles and New York, indicating a spreading pattern of unusual disorders among homosexual males. The disorders took many forms, but all of them implied a potentially fatal breakdown in the patient's immune system, the complex mechanism by which the body fights invasions of harmful organisms. Some disorders, such as the pneumocystis pneumonia, had previously been identified only in people whose immune systems were known to have been damaged or suppressed, for example by drugs used to facilitate acceptance of transplanted organs. Other disorders were relatively common, but they failed to respond to treatments that would ward them off in otherwise healthy people, and progressed to become life-threatening.

US experts studying the phenomenon at first called it 'Gay-Related Immune Disease' (GRID), though they soon realized it was not confined entirely to gay men. Within a few months of the CDC report, cases had been diagnosed among intravenous drug users, blood transfusion recipients, haemophiliacs and others, of both sexes, all ages and varied sexual preferences. In recognition of that and the various forms in which the condition manifested itself, it was redesignated 'Acquired Immuno-Deficiency Syndrome' (AIDS).

Almost from the beginning, scientists suspected AIDS was caused by a virus capable of being transmitted from one person to another. Intense efforts were made to identify it and, by early 1984, a French team under Luc Montagnier had succeeded, establishing that the virus deactivated the immune system by destroying white blood cells. The organism was eventually named the Human Immuno-Deficiency Virus (HIV). Shortly after its discovery, French and US researchers devised a test to indicate its presence before any overt symptoms appear.

Thus far, the story is a triumph in medical history. In less than three years, a previously unknown disease had been identified, the immediate cause found and a technique developed to help identify people who may be carrying it.

THE DEADLY VIRUS

Studies of the AIDS virus indicated that it is transmitted when infected blood, semen or vaginal fluid enters the body, but probably not in other ways. To that extent, and because the virus is delicate, it is not highly contagious by comparison, for example, with influenza or even hepatitis B. Other discoveries were less reassuring.

Scientists showed that HIV, once contracted, can lie dormant in the body for perhaps up to 20 years, during which the carrier appears entirely healthy or suffers disorders, such as fevers, night sweats and shingles, bearing no ostensible relation to AIDS. Because of this dormancy, and the difficulties in many cases of ascertaining when infection took place, it was not possible to forecast accurately how many carriers would develop AIDS. Nor was it possible to predict when, if at all, a carrier would develop the disease. Predicting the course of any individual case of HIV infection was complicated further by the many forms AIDS could take. In the mid-1980s, scientists found that AIDS could emerge not only in 'opportunistic' disorders such as pneumocystis pneumonia, but also that it sometimes affected the central nervous system. In these cases, the disease could lead to meningitis,

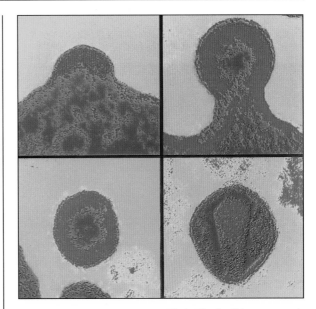

ABOVE *An HIV virus emerges as a bud from the surface of a white blood cell* (TOP LEFT & TOP RIGHT). *The bud breaks off* (BOTTOM LEFT) *and reorganizes itself into a mature virus* (BOTTOM RIGHT).

encephalopathy and dementia, and would usually result in death within three years.

THE SPREAD OF AIDS

As if the nature of AIDS was not formidable enough, it was soon shown to be present in many parts of the globe, though no one could say where it originated. By mid-1986, some 21,000 cases had been diagnosed world-wide, of which more than half were in the US, with the rest spread mainly among the countries of Europe and central Africa. At that point, one third to one half had proved fatal. But experts feared the figures were only the tip of an iceberg, estimating that up to 500,000 people could have the lesser disorders that might or might not be a prelude to AIDS itself – the so-called Aids-Related Complex (ARC) – and that up to 2 million could be carrying HIV while showing no symptoms. On that basis they predicted AIDS would become a pandemic, an epidemic that sweeps the world. The hunt for protection and cure was stepped up.

But there were major difficulties. HIV changes its form more than 1000 times faster than most influenza viruses, leading scientists to describe attempts to develop a vaccine against it as "trying to hit a moving target". A cure looked even more elusive, because most treatments for infectious diseases rely, at least in part, on support from the body's immune system, precisely the target the virus attacks. So, as both the threat posed by AIDS and the fact that science was unlikely to remove it quickly became fully apparent, measures had to be taken to slow down the rate at which it was spreading.

Some of these measures were medically straightforward once the danger had been recognized. The HIV screening of blood donors and the heat-treatment of blood products used by haemophiliacs, for example, became standard practice in many countries, though only after thousands of cases of infection by such routes had already occurred. Other approaches to prevention were more complex, involving social and psychological factors, as well as medical ones.

BELOW *The personal tragedies caused by AIDS have found expression in 'AIDS Quilts'. Embroidered* *cloth squares, celebrating individuals lost to the disease, keep their memories alive and raise awareness.*

REDUCING THE RISKS

In the US and Europe, two groups of the population were deemed, from statistics available in the mid-1980s, to be most at risk of HIV infection as a result of their behaviour patterns. These included males engaging in intimate homosexual activity, particularly anal intercourse, with its opportunities for blood and semen to mingle, and intravenous drug abusers injecting themselves with non-sterile, often shared, needles. Male homosexuals were by far the more vulnerable, according to the figures; they accounted for nearly three quarters of known AIDS cases in the US and nine out of ten cases in Britain in 1985-86. Drug abusers made up about one third of AIDS cases in New York, but a much lower proportion across the US as a whole and less than 1 per cent in Britain.

The two groups were therefore the main targets for health education campaigns and related measures to combat the spread of AIDS. In the main, these were instigated by the groups themselves, whose lead was followed by governments as public concern mounted. The message of the campaigns was simple – the avoidance of risk. In the case of homosexuals and bisexuals, that entailed a panoply of measures grouped together under the name of 'safe sex', among them greater care in the choice of sexual partners and the use of condoms as prophylactics. Among drug abusers, the dangers of sharing needles were stressed.

To be effective, the campaigns had to be blunt about the seriousness of AIDS and the way in which it is spread. Inevitably, this bluntness increased public anxiety over the condition and also reinforced prejudices held by many against the high-risk groups. Controversies arose over such issues as general testing for the presence of HIV, needle-exchange programmes for drug abusers, nursing facilities for AIDS patients and the employment rights of people known to be HIV-positive – all of which continue to simmer.

The early portrayal of AIDS in some quarters as a 'gay plague', based on US and European statistics, was to some extent given the lie by an analysis of its distribution in central Africa, where approximately equal numbers of men and women were found to have fallen victim. This fact,

which has still not been adequately explained, confirmed that HIV can be passed on by heterosexual, as well as homosexual, activities, and that the same 'safe sex' rules apply in reducing the risk. However, because of the targeting of the initial health campaigns in developed countries, the public was slower in coming to awareness of that. One result, in the US, was that the number of women infected through heterosexual activities grew steadily as a proportion of the total number of AIDS cases. Between January 1989 and mid-1991, 55 per cent of AIDS cases registered in the US were women, of whom one third had contracted the syndrome through sex.

BELOW *Promoting AIDS awareness is especially urgent in Kinshasa,* *Zaïre, where 7 per cent of the population may carry the HIV virus.*

DOES HIV = AIDS?

In the early 1990s, fundamental questions arose concerning the true cause of AIDS and the role that HIV plays in the spread of the disease. The orthodox line – that HIV causes AIDS – has been disputed by almost 50 scientists, among them Peter Duesberg, Professor of Molecular and Cell Biology at the University of California, Berkeley, who was the first to map the genetic structure of many of the retroviruses – the family of viruses to which the HIV virus belongs.

The dissenters are asking that the scientific community re-evaluates all the evidence, implements new, far-reaching epidemiological surveys and re-examines the immunological implications of AIDS. They maintain that HIV is not a new virus and does not necessarily lead to AIDS. They further believe that concentrating on HIV research directs resources from equally promising avenues.

Their wish is to promote a new concept of AIDS that is based on the belief that, instead of HIV being responsible for killing the cells of the immune system, AIDS sufferers fall victim to a process in which the cells turn upon themselves. It is in this context that HIV, when combined with as-yet-unknown 'co-factors' brought on by high-risk situations (such as drug abuse and multiple blood transfusions) that can affect the immune system, may be linked to the development of AIDS.

However, many eminent scientists – including those representing government health departments in both the UK and the US – strongly dispute this.

TOWARDS CONTAINMENT

By 1991, intensive research around the world had not succeeded in producing a vaccine to give universal protection against AIDS, much less a cure, though no fewer than 11 were in the process of being tested on humans and more

ABOVE *Babies with AIDS are cared for at a home in New York state. Babies that are HIV-positive at birth may lose the antibodies (received from their mothers) as they grow, but others develop AIDS and may die by the age of four.*

BELOW *Information about HIV and AIDS is an important weapon in the fight against the spread of the disease. At the forefront of this fight in the UK is the Terrence Higgins Trust, founded in the early 1980s in memory of the first person to die of AIDS there.*

were being tried on animals. Scientists of the World Health Organization (WHO) forecast that, by 1995, 15 million adults would be infected with HIV, and that by the end of the decade AIDS would probably kill up to 1 million people annually. Many of these deaths would be children who had contracted the disease in the womb and most deaths would occur in the developing nations of Asia, Africa and elsewhere. In Asia, in particular, an explosion in intravenous drug abuse would be partly to blame.

In Western countries, however, there are signs that AIDS might be approaching its peak. According to WHO, most HIV infections there had been contracted in the first half of the 1980s, and the incidence of infection had tailed off as the extensive health education campaigns began to make their mark. Judged by this criterion, the high point for AIDS cases and deaths in the industrialized world would be reached in the mid-1990s.

Some experts disputed this conclusion. They argued it was derived from figures distorted by the health-management of HIV-positive and AIDS patients in the West, prolonging their lives though not, in the last resort, curing them. Such treatment falls into two broad categories. The first involves the use of drugs such as AZT, DDI and DDC in an attempt to delay a transition from latent infection to AIDS itself. Their efficacy is still being evaluated.

The second category is to use standard treatments, some of them 40 or more years old, to treat the disorders to which AIDS patients are vulnerable, such as pneumocystis pneumonia or the brain infection toxoplasmosis. However, the drugs used in both approaches can cause adverse reactions in some individuals. So alongside the quest for protection and cure, the search for better ways of managing AIDS continues.

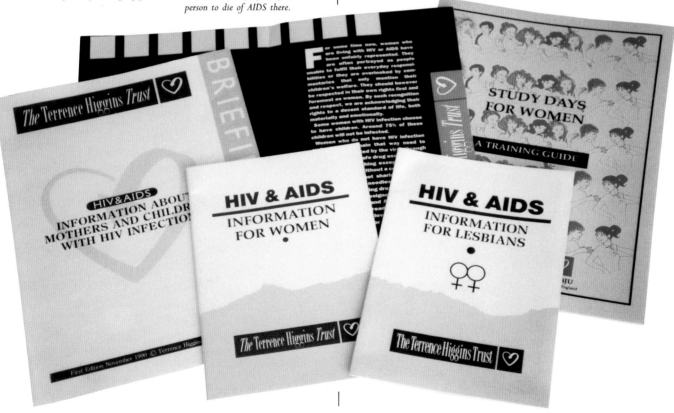

9 Ancient and Modern Approaches

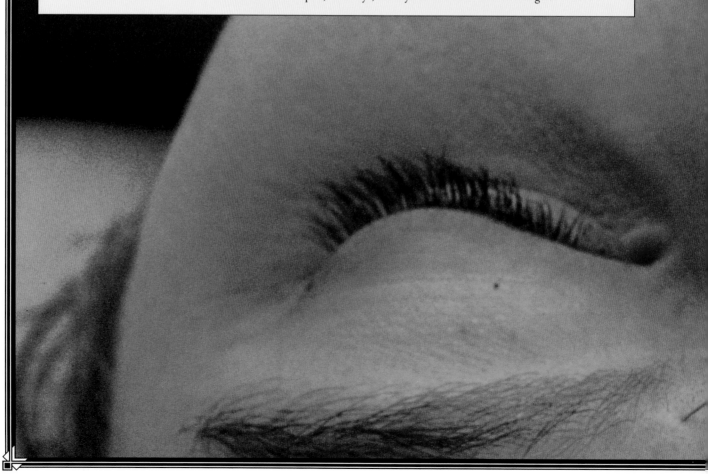

One of the paradoxes of modern medicine is that much of what can be done to cure diseases, rather than ameliorate their symptoms, only applies to acute conditions, not to chronic ones. As a result, large numbers of the general public have turned to other therapies: those of alternative, or complementary, medicine – some of them ancient, some of them more recent in inspiration and development – hoping that these will provide the cure that conventional medicine currently cannot promise with conviction.

And so techniques as diverse as acupuncture, shiatsu, meditation, osteopathy, chiropractic, herbalism and biofeedback have become popular throughout the Western world (some of them have always been routine in Asia). As conventional medicine has evaluated the techniques,

some have become generally accepted – and taken into the fold of medicine under the name of 'complementary' techniques – while others are still considered to be extremely dubious.

Parallel to this movement, there has been a general shift in medical perceptions towards the idea that preventive medicine is the most effective medicine of all. So many diseases, the argument goes, are avoidable, if people receive adequate health education and sufficient resources are available to fund public health programmes. To date, the results of programmes to deliver these have been both encouraging and frustrating: diseases such as smallpox can be eradicated; millions of lives can be saved if people can be persuaded not to smoke, and to take responsibility for their personal health. But the limiting factors are, as always, money and the will to make changes.

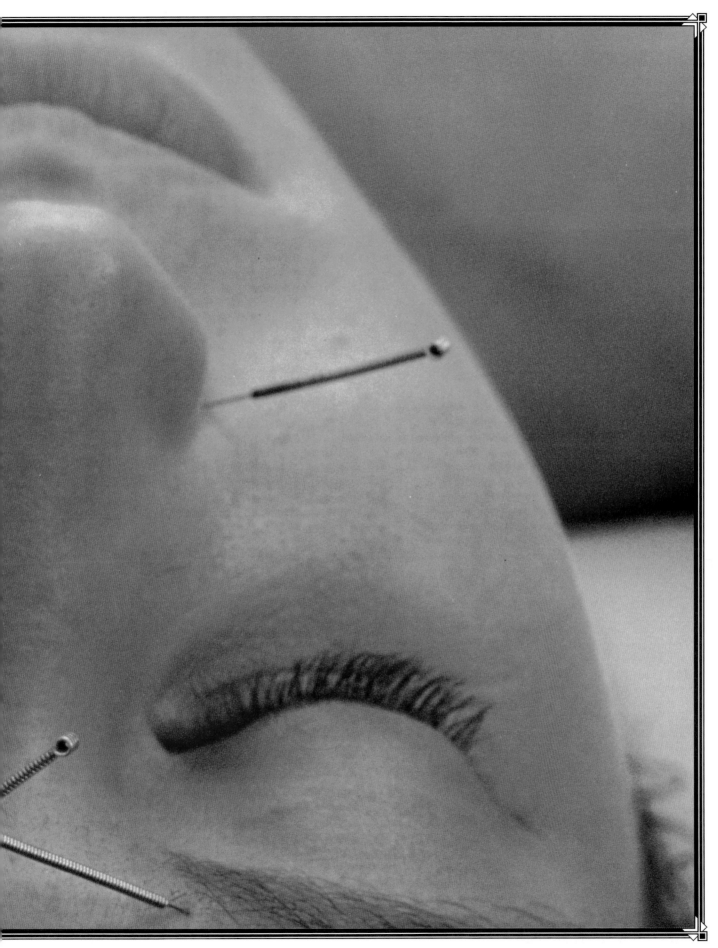

ABOVE *Acupuncture needles stimulate acupoints on the meridians for the large intestine and bladder.*

INTERNATIONAL ACTION

VACCINATION, RURAL HOSPITALS AND WAR WORK

Primary health care is to deliver 'health for all by the year 2000'

FROM THE END OF WORLD WAR II, those trying to improve health on a global scale could be divided into two camps: those who would enter a country in a blitz of immunizations and other treatments and then disappear; and those who concentrated on building up local health infrastructures to provide preventive medicine. Both approaches had their successes – and their failures – and it was gradually realized that both were necessary, in tandem.

Tackling the appalling health of the world's poor was an uphill struggle. While immunization helped, its benefits were frequently outweighed by the results of environmental and lifestyle changes, and by natural catastrophes and war. But, though most of these were the partial responsibility of governments and financial institutions – many of which have yet to address them fully, much less deal with them – there has been a measure of progress towards alleviating humanity's burden of disease.

'HEALTH FOR ALL'

Before the war, the most important work in the field of world health was carried out by the Rockefeller Foundation. Established in 1913, by the ruthless American industrialist and latter-day philanthropist John D. Rockefeller, its programmes included attacks on yellow fever and malaria.

BELOW *A doctor takes primary health care into the field, as recommended by the World Health Organization. Here, a nomadic tribeswoman is* examined in Pakistan: *TB is still a problem where a nomadic lifestyle can allow an untreated case to spread the disease.*

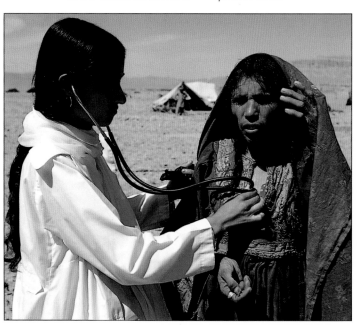

In 1948, the United Nations set up the World Health Organization (WHO), based in Geneva, with one sole purpose: "the attainment by all peoples of the highest possible level of health". To achieve this, it performs a wide variety of functions: carrying out research, maintaining records of notifiable diseases, standardizing international medical nomenclature, providing aid in emergencies and to prevent accidents (in 1963, it gave Saudi Arabia ice factories to deal with heat stroke during the annual pilgrimage to Mecca), improving housing and living conditions, and ameliorating maternal and child health.

Through the years, WHO has carried out 'blitzes' against certain diseases. Its greatest success was without doubt the eradication of smallpox (*see pp.212–3*), and in the 1950s, with the Rockefeller Foundation and Unicef (the UN's children's agency), it was also able to reduce sharply the incidence of yaws in South-east Asia. However, there were defeats, too. In 1965, in its first worldwide campaign, an attempt was made to eradicate malaria, using DDT (*see p.95*). However, it proved impossible to spray every pool of water and mangrove swamp, and then the mosquitoes became resistant to the insecticide. Meanwhile, the old control methods – drugs, mosquito nets and draining stagnant pools – had vanished, and research programmes and laboratories had closed. When the resistant mosquitoes returned, thousands of people died.

This disaster greatly affected the way WHO acted from then on. Research was again emphasized and, most importantly, heavy reliance was placed on establishing grassroots health networks, which could maintain any work carried out by WHO. Out of this came, in April 1977, the decision to try collectively to achieve 'health for all by the year 2000', and the method chosen was primary health care.

In September 1978, an international conference, convened jointly by WHO and Unicef and meeting in Alma Ata, Kazakhstan, determined exactly what primary health care involved:

- health education.
- adequate food supplies and proper nutrition.
- safe water and basic sanitation.
- maternal and child health care, including family planning.
- prevention and control of local endemic diseases.
- immunization against the major infectious diseases.
- treatment of common diseases and injuries.
- provision of essential drugs.

The 'Alma Ata Declaration', signed by 134 member countries, also emphasized the need for self-reliance and self-determination.

In the same year, WHO set up a diarrhoeal disease control programme to combat the illnesses that resulted every year in the deaths of at least 4 million children,

LEFT *A 'barefoot doctor' administers a Heaf Test (see p.111) to a child in Zaïre, Central Africa, in order to determine whether vaccination against TB is needed.*

'Barefoot doctors', trained to carry out simple procedures and deal with specific diseases, have revolutionized health care in underdeveloped countries.

primarily from dehydration. It promoted the idea of rehydrating children with a simple fluid containing sodium, potassium and sugar, which could be made up by parents. By 1988, some 100 countries had launched their own programmes, and 25 per cent of all diarrhoeal episodes were being treated with rehydration 'salts'. It was also found that diarrhoeal disease control also protects against cholera.

In March 1984, WHO and Unicef set up the 'Task Force for Child Survival', with the aim of giving every child a healthy headstart in life. In part, this was to be achieved by immunizing 80 per cent of the world's children by 1990. The campaign – dubbed the 'planned miracle' – involved over 100 developing countries, but, despite massive effort and investment, the goal was not achieved. Nevertheless, millions of children were immunized, and their plight was firmly placed on the world's political agenda. And, as a result of WHO's 'Health for all' effort, between 1960 and 1988, the number of countries in which 20 per cent or more of children die before the age of five has been halved.

FRONTLINE DOCTORS

While agencies such as WHO attempt to improve the world's general health, there are others who leap in to save lives in times of war and natural disaster. Two of these are the International Red Cross and Medicins sans Frontières.

The Red Cross, founded in 1864 and the active arm of the Geneva Convention, now comprises over 100 national societies (called the 'Red Crescent' in Muslim countries) and an international headquarters in Geneva. As well as helping in times of natural catastrophe – earthquakes, floods, epidemics – it is perhaps best known for its war work: arranging exchanges of sick and wounded soldiers, aiding prisoners-of-war, and caring for refugees. It received the Nobel Peace Prize in 1917 and 1944 in recognition of its efforts in the two world wars. However, it has had to remain strictly neutral to do this sort of work.

Neutrality is the last thing that Medicins sans Frontières (MSF, 'Doctors without Frontiers') is concerned with, having its roots in the Paris demonstrations of 1968. A small group of politically active French doctors went with the Red Cross to Nigeria during the Biafran war (1967–70); appalled by the brutality and suffering they found – at least one million Biafrans died of starvation – they spoke out, thus breaking their oath of neutrality with the Red Cross. The doctors then went to East Pakistan (now Bangladesh) in 1970, when cyclones killed 500,000 in floods, and the following year, MSF was founded.

Today, MSF is the world's largest volunteer medical relief agency. Based in France, there is now a European network and, in 1991, a branch was opened in New York. Volunteer doctors, nurses and other medical staff – all working for a pittance in horrific and dangerous conditions – come primarily from France, but also from the US, Britain, Belgium, Argentina, Iran and elsewhere.

Like Amnesty International, MSF sees itself as bearing witness for victims. In 1985, it was the only relief agency to protest against the Ethiopian government's 'relocation programme', which meant simply removing people to labour camps and led to the deaths of 250,000. As a result, MSF was ordered out of the country. In 1991, the organization also relayed the news of extraordinary hardships in Somalia when the media were concentrating on the Gulf War. And, in the same year, it was the first to tell of the devastation of the Kurds wreaked by the government of Iraq; within 24 hours, MSF was chosen by the European Community as its principle partner in the distribution of $25 million in aid.

BELOW *Clearly identified for their own protection, International Red Cross workers tend a casualty in war-torn Lebanon.*

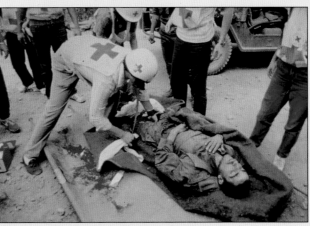

SMALLPOX

A race against time to wipe out a scourge of millions

IT MAY WELL BE that a few decades into the next century scientists will know how to hold the aging process at bay. But there will be one sure indicator of middle and old age: a curiously indented blemish on the upper arm, which marks its possessor as having been born before 1976. That small, barely visible vaccination scar will serve as a living reminder of a disease whose epidemics and pandemics changed the course of history time and time again, and spread untold suffering equally among the highest and the lowliest. Today's children are not to be so marked, for smallpox has now been eradicated from the face of the earth – the very first time that an entire disease has been eliminated by human intervention.

MASS VACCINATION

In 1966, after a number of unsuccessful attempts, the World Health Organization (*see pp.210-1*) voted for a ten-year mass vaccination campaign to eradicate smallpox once and for all. Even at that time, 10–15 million people in 33 countries caught smallpox every year, and 2 million of them died.

The multi-national WHO team, led by an American, Dr Donald Henderson, eventually comprised 50 full-time medical workers and 600 on short-term contracts, all of whom were allocated to the various parts of the world where smallpox raged virtually unchecked. Providence was very much on their side. Areas that, before the campaign, had been cut off politically from the outside world, opened their doors for just the right amount of time – before slamming shut again. In this way, Iran, Uganda and Afghanistan could be cleared of the disease. Elsewhere – in Nigeria, for example, embroiled as it was in the Biafran war, and in Ethiopia under Haile Selassie – delicate diplomatic

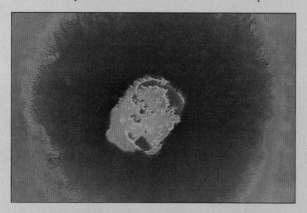

ABOVE Variola major, *once the scourge of nations, is confined to two high-security, WHO-inspected laboratories in the US and the* former Soviet Union. In 1993, *these are due to be destroyed, resulting in the total extinction of the virus from this planet.*

relations (both official and behind the scenes) had to be established before the WHO teams could go in.

The medical workers had to endure all manner of hardship, frustration and, sometimes, much worse: one was killed by an arrow, another had his head opened with a cleaver and a third was kidnapped by Ethiopian rebels. This last, a Brazilian doctor, refused to leave, once he had been released, until he had vaccinated all his captors.

Gradually, the outer limits of the disease shrank away from the Americas, Africa and the Middle East to centre on India and what was then the divided country of West and East Pakistan. By 1971, smallpox had been eliminated from both parts of the latter. But within months, Pakistan was rent by civil war, and in December 1971, the new nation of Bangladesh was born out of what had been East Pakistan.

During the hostilities, 10 million people had fled to refugee camps in India, where smallpox suddenly reappeared. When this was discovered – by an employee of the Centers for Disease Control in Atlanta, Georgia, who just happened to see the signs of smallpox on the faces of refugees in a television news film – medical teams were hurried to the affected camp. But when they arrived they discovered that the refugees had already been transported back to Bangladesh, where they had fanned out in all directions.

EPIDEMIC IN BANGLADESH

The disease took rapid hold: in the capital of Dhaka, 800 people were catching smallpox every day. The WHO response was to form surveillance teams; these located the focal points of the disease, which were then isolated so that the chain of transmission could be cut. From work done in Nigeria and West Pakistan, it was known that it was only necessary to vaccinate a percentage of a population for a campaign to be successful – so long as that percentage was very carefully chosen. Nevertheless, the vaccination of even a small percentage of Bangladesh's population of 75 million still represented an awesome task.

So health workers spread across the country, concentrating on markets, ferry docks, bus and railway stations – anywhere, in fact, where people gathered. The technique was simple: health workers would hold up a picture of a baby with smallpox and ask: "Do you know anyone who looks like this?". On one occasion in Dhaka, photographs accompanied by the "Do you know..." slogan painted in red, white and blue, were fastened to both sides of an elephant in order to attract the maximum attention.

As the campaign continued and success seemed to be in sight, the pace of vaccinations quickened. Some of the methods used, though, and the mechanics of locating and isolating victims, were less than diplomatic. Some people refused to be vaccinated because of religious belief, or from fear, apathy or ignorance, and the teams often had to chase individuals and search under houses and in fields for those who had hidden. Later, gentler tactics were used, with teams staying in villages overnight and seeking the cooperation of the residents.

The WHO people and their colleagues worked 20 hours a day, every day, living in the field, rarely washing properly and sleeping where and eating what they could. And yet all these privations seemed worthwhile, as the noose around the disease was gradually drawn tighter. A total of 12,000 Bengali workers had been co-opted, and in one survey, 89 per cent of all the homes in the country – about 12 million of them – were visited in only nine days, as the workers searched for new outbreaks.

In October 1974, it was predicted that smallpox would be eradicated in two months. But then the River Brahmaputra flooded, tens of thousands of people ran for higher ground, and famine and disease struck. By January 1975, the smallpox in Bangladesh was as rife as ever.

The teams were mobilized yet again, racing in boats, cars, motorcycles, trains and even carts to get to any village with a smallpox case. Then the disease struck Dhaka. Over 200,000 people went into or out of the city each day, so massively increasing the likelihood that the disease would spread. The team isolated the shanty area that seemed the focus of the outbreak, congratulating themselves on their success. Then, one morning, the team found the shanties had been bulldozed, on the orders of the president, who felt they were an eyesore on the route from the airport. The residents, many incubating smallpox, had scattered.

On 9 December 1979, the WHO issued a proud declaration to the world's press, ABOVE; after a 13-year campaign, the world was free of smallpox.

The health workers carried on, against seemingly impossible odds, but helped by a government edict that those not allowing themselves to be vaccinated would face imprisonment. By mid-September 1975, it seemed that they were winning, and two months later they were able to celebrate a famous victory. WHO issued a press release, the fact that Bangladesh was free of smallpox made headlines around the world, the workers in Dhaka held a party – and then a cable arrived from Bhola island in the Ganges delta, saying that one case had been reported.

By steamer, motorboat and Land Rover, the smallpox workers sped to the small village of Kuralia. There they found a three-year-old girl, Rahima Banu. She was the last person to catch smallpox by ordinary transmission.

But poor Rahima was not the last person to catch smallpox. That fatal honour fell to Janet Parker, a British photographer. In 1978, she was working one floor above a research laboratory in Birmingham when the virus escaped through the ventilation system. She caught the disease and died. Today, the smallpox virus exists in only two WHO-inspected, high-security laboratories in Atlanta and Moscow. All the rest of the world's stocks have been destroyed.

The ambitions of the World Health Organization have not been decreased by its achievement in eradicating smallpox. Using many of the techniques developed during the smallpox campaign, it is currently attempting to eradicate major childhood diseases worldwide. These diseases – measles, whooping cough, diphtheria, polio, tuberculosis and tetanus – cause the deaths of millions of children every year.

THE FINAL VICTIM

The last person in the world to catch smallpox (Variola major) by ordinary transmission was a three-year-old, malnourished Indian girl called Rahima Banu, who fell victim to the deadly virus on 16 October 1975. A massive effort by WHO workers succeeded in saving Rahima's life and ensuring that the outbreak did not spread.

PREVENTIVE MEDICINE

THE LIFESTYLE APPROACH TO PROPHYLAXIS

Exercise, diet and monitoring saved 300,000 a year in America

BY THE MIDDLE OF THE 20th century, medical science had notched up triumph after triumph in its efforts to prevent, as well as cure, disease. However, the preventive successes almost all involved specific prophylactics against specific disorders, from malaria to poliomyelitis. Around 100 years had elapsed since a more general breakthrough had been achieved – improvements in public health wrought by better sanitation and nutrition.

Events were poised to change, however. As they did, the term 'preventive medicine' broadened its meaning to encompass not only specific prophylaxis, but all the inter-related measures that can help to prolong the span of human life and keep it disease-free. Because many of these entail choices by people about the way they lead their lives, this broader prevention is sometimes called the 'lifestyle' approach.

The approach has many roots. Particularly significant was medicine's developing struggle against heart disease and lung cancer. The latter disease was rampant in much of the Western world by the 1950s – once contracted, it was almost always quickly fatal, resisting both the surgeon's knife and drug therapy. In Britain alone, deaths from lung cancer rose, in the half century from 1918, from 15 per million of population to 900 per million.

SUSPECT SMOKE

Doctors in Britain, the US and elsewhere noted the growing incidence of lung cancer soon after World War I, but they paid little attention to its causes until well into the 1930s. Then, some experts suggested it must be due to an external factor, such as vehicle exhaust fumes – or the smoking of tobacco. The first major medical paper proposing a link between smoking and lung cancer was published by Dr F. H. Muller in Germany in 1939.

By 1951, two surveys had appeared to confirm Muller's hypothesis. One, conducted by doctors from Washington University, in the US, showed that out of 650 men with lung cancer, 95 per cent had been smokers for 25 years or more. The other survey, by Richard Doll and Austin Bradford Hill in Britain, found that in a large sample of hospital patients, virtually all those with lung cancer were cigarette smokers; far fewer sufferers from other diseases, including other cancers, had ever touched tobacco.

In 1956, Doll and Hill published the results of a subsequent five-year study of the smoking habits of 40,000 medical practitioners. The study, which concentrated primarily on participants over the age of 35, showed that lung cancer deaths among doctors who were heavy cigarette smokers (25 or more a day) were more than 20 times higher than those among participants who had never consistently smoked. In addition, more than twice as many moderate cigarette smokers (15 to 24 a day) than light smokers (1 to 14 a day) had died of the disease.

The study unleashed a storm of controversy. The main criticism from the medical profession was that it did not

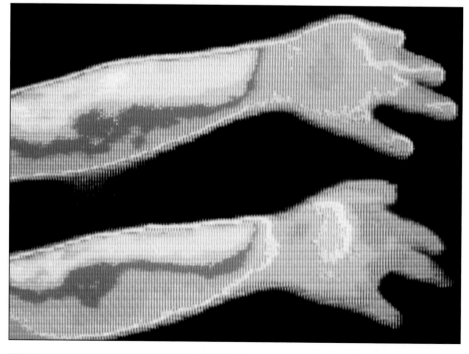

LEFT *A thermogram of a person's hand and arm before smoking a cigarette* (TOP): *the hottest point on the heat scale is white; it then goes down through yellow, red, pink and light blue to dark blue, the coldest point. A thermogram of the same person's arm taken after smoking a cigarette* (BOTTOM) *shows a drop in temperature in the hands, indicating that peripheral blood circulation is affected.*

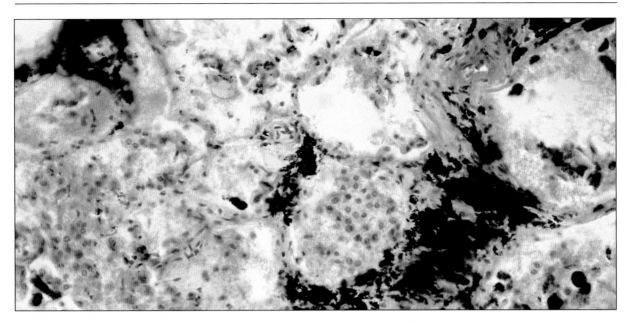

identify the precise cause of lung cancer, nor even whether that cause lay in the tobacco or the smoke. Statisticians, such as Britain's Sir Ronald Fisher, pointed out that, as most cigarette smokers do not die of lung cancer, no direct cause-and-effect relationship had been established. At the University of London, psychologist Hans Eysenck weighed in with a study indicating a statistically significant connection between the extrovert type of personality and proneness to lung cancer. Nevertheless, by 1962, Britain's Royal College of Physicians was declaring unequivocally that smoking 'causes' lung cancer. In 1964, following large-scale investigations carried out since 1953, the US Surgeon-General's Advisory Committee took the same line.

Coincidentally, the numbers of British doctors who smoked fell by 50 per cent in the period between 1951 and 1964. Many started encouraging their patients to follow suit. Their reasoning, based on the maxims 'better safe than sorry' and 'prevention is better than cure', laid the foundations for preventive medicine in its broad lifestyle sense. This attitude appeared increasingly justified, morally and socially if not truly scientifically, as the connections became clearer between smoking and other potentially fatal diseases, such as bronchitis and circulatory disorders (*see box p.216*).

GOVERNMENTS ACT – SLOWLY

The authority of such organizations as the Royal College of Physicians, the Surgeon-General's Committee and, in 1970, the World Health Organization could not be ignored by governments. But, in trying to curtail smoking on public health grounds, the politicians faced powerful countervailing pressure – the clout of tobacco companies, the huge tax revenues from tobacco sales, and employment problems in both consumer countries and producer nations.

The process of weaning the public from tobacco moved slowly, and as much as possible with the cooperation of the tobacco manufacturers. Britain, for example, banned television advertising of cigarettes in 1965, and in 1971 secured an agreement from the industry that all cigarette packets and printed advertising should carry a government health warning. In the US, too, health warnings were introduced on cigarette packs.

ABOVE *A smoker's lung, with carbon particles (black) from smoke; white cells attack them, and fibrous tissue forms in response to irritation.*

Meanwhile, research was increased to try to isolate any possible cancer-causing agent in tobacco, much of it quietly funded by the manufacturers. A British medical committee, initially including nominees of tobacco firms, looked at ways of measuring the tar and nicotine levels in cigarettes – the first tar/nicotine 'league table' of available brands was published in 1973. Tar was a prime suspect as a carcinogen, but careful analysis later showed that those cancer-producing agents in tobacco are not in themselves enough to account for the link with the disease.

The slow pace of action to eliminate smoking as a health hazard since Doll and Hill's initial study in 1951 has frustrated many of the world's medical bodies, as well as the growing number of lay, anti-smoking organizations. In some countries, public and privately funded preventive campaigns have been organized on a massive scale, targeted both at the high-risk middle-aged groups and at young people to prevent them from starting to smoke. Legal and voluntary restrictions on smoking in public places and at work have multiplied, notably since the appearance in the late 1980s of data (since disputed) suggesting that exposure to other people's tobacco may in itself cause disease.

However, the effectiveness of the preventive approach has been modest. By the early 1990s, 50 million Americans (nearly one quarter of the entire population, including children) were still regular smokers, and federal experts put the death rate from smoking-related diseases at 1000 a day. It was estimated that fewer than 4 per cent of US smokers succeed in giving up the habit unassisted. Even with the whole panoply of therapies, such as behaviour modification and hypnosis, and aids, such as nicotine gum and nicotine skin patches, three out of four would-be non-smokers are back on the weed within six months of trying to quit.

AFFAIRS OF THE HEART

The startling rise in lung cancer deaths this century was as nothing compared with the spread of coronary heart disorders in the affluent Western world. As recently as

1892, the most eminent doctor of his day, Sir William Osler, could describe coronary disease as "relatively rare" in Britain and the US, having seen only a few dozen cases in his long career. But less than two decades later, coronary disorders accounted for some 12 per cent of all deaths in advanced nations. By 1970, that proportion had doubled.

In the 1980s, in many Western countries, the figure reached 30 per cent – making coronary disease the biggest single killer of the age, ahead of all forms of cancer. Furthermore, for every two people who died from a coronary attack, another three suffered one, but survived thanks to prolonged and increasingly expensive medical care. This huge upsurge prompted tens of thousands of medical studies, such as the comprehensive and long-running Framingham Heart Study in the US, started in 1948 (*see box*).

In essence, both coronary heart disease and strokes are the result of atherosclerosis, in which fatty substances in the blood are deposited in patches, or plaques, on the walls of arteries, narrowing them and thus increasing blood pressure. Pieces of a plaque may break off and create a blockage, or embolism, elsewhere. Alternatively, the plaque may initiate a bloodclot, causing thrombosis. Both the embolism and the thrombosis may be fatal.

The build-up of fatty deposits begins in childhood and continues throughout life. At least part of the 20th-century rise in coronary deaths could be attributed to greater longevity. Whereas in 1900 one in every three Westerners

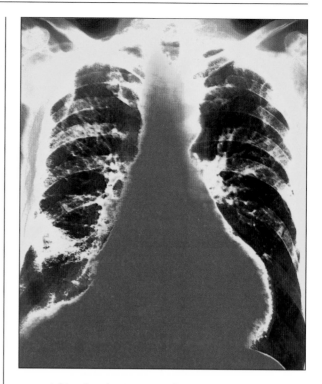

ABOVE *A false-colour chest X-ray shows a heart enlarged as a result of abnormally high blood pressure, with probable arteriosclerosis.*

THE FRAMINGHAM HEART STUDY

Extensive, long-term monitoring of more than 5000 men and women in Framingham, Massachusetts, underlined the sharp changes in US patterns of ill-health between the 1950s and the 1980s – notably the decline in cardiovascular disease among middle-aged males. The study, set up in 1948 by experts from the New England Research Institute in Massachusetts, closely followed the medical histories of the participants for some 40 years.

As part of the investigation, 1700 men were classed in three groups according to whether they would fall into the 50-59 age bracket at the start of 1950, 1960 or 1970. Each group was monitored for the ten years following the respective base dates. When all the data was finally assessed, deaths from heart and circulatory disorders in the 1970 group were found to be 43 per cent lower than in the 1950 group, and 37 per cent lower than in the 1960 group. The onset of cardiovascular disease among those who had been free from it as each group came under scrutiny also dropped signifi-cantly – from 190 per thousand in the 1950 participants to 154 per thousand in the 1970 group.

The researchers – Pamela Sytkowski, William Kannel and Ralph D'Agostino – were cautious in attributing causes for the decline in heart deaths. A lower incidence of

disease, greater medical success in averting deaths from heart disorders and a combination of primary and secondary prevention were all cited as possible factors.

However, the report clearly indicated that lifestyle changes had played some part. The 1970 group had lower average cholesterol levels and lower average systolic blood pressure than the 1950 group. Fewer of them smoked —34 per cent against 56 per cent. In addition, those in the 1970 group who were diagnosed as having blood pressure problems received medication; no one in the 1950 group received similar treatment. The researchers suggested that the improvements in such risk factors had a greater impact in cutting deaths from, rather than reducing the incidence of, heart disease.

Another outcome of the Framingham Study was the first clear statistical evidence that cigarette smoking may make a significant contribution to the risk of strokes in men under 65 and women over that age. Nevertheless, the study showed that high blood pressure is a more readily identifi-able factor – doubling the incidence of strokes, irrespective of sex or smoking habits.

LEFT *A treadmill test on a child, part of the 40-year Framingham Study.*

could expect to survive to age 70, by 1970 the figure had improved to better than one in two. But longer life was by no means the only explanation.

A MATTER OF DIET

The main component of arterial plaques, at least in their early stages, is cholesterol – the steroid first observed in gallstones in the 19th century and extensively analysed by Heinrich Wieland in the 1930s (see p.166). It is manufactured naturally in the liver, and is supplemented in the diet by such foodstuffs as egg yolks and fat-rich meats. By the 1950s, scientists in Britain, the US and elsewhere had started to postulate a connection between eating habits and a risk of heart attack.

Ample circumstantial evidence supported their view. Coronary disease was far more prevalent in countries where animal fats played a large part in diet, and less common in nations where they did not, such as the Mediterranean region. Within the 'high-risk' countries, the wealthy appeared statistically more prone than poorer people, for whom high-fat foods were a relatively rare luxury.

Not all experts were convinced. Some argued that emotional stress was the dominant cause, pointing out that those who were apparently the most vulnerable were also ambitious, striving types. And this was in marked contrast to people such as southern Italian peasants, among whom coronary attacks were uncommon. The only fact on which the two camps agreed was that, as heart disease tends to run in families, heredity must also play a role.

Public debate raged through the following decades. The theory of stress as a single main cause gradually lost ground as the nature of stress was gradually unveiled (see pp.220-1) and the circumstantial evidence for a dietary connection grew. The average Japanese lifestyle, for example, is just as stressful as that in the West, yet the Japanese suffer far fewer coronary attacks. This fact was attributed to the preponderance of fish and vegetables in the Japanese diet – a fact underlined by the discovery that Japanese living in the US and adopting American eating habits developed US levels of coronary disease. By contrast, Finnish lumberjacks, who ostensibly led a low-stress, outdoor life with plenty of exercise, had one of the highest incidences of coronary deaths of any population in the world – and their diet was dripping with animal fats.

It was not until the 1980s that scientists from the University of Southern California came up with definite proof that a large reduction in blood cholesterol levels can slow or even reverse the arterial fatty deposits contributing to high blood pressure and coronary disease. In 1985, Michael Brown and Joseph Goldstein of the University of Texas won the Nobel prize for their work in discovering how cholesterol is transported to and from the liver, enabling the manufacture of drugs to control cholesterol levels. But showing that lowering blood cholesterol slows heart disease is not the same as proving that lowering dietary cholesterol has the same effect; many scientists maintain that this has still not been achieved, despite a number of studies.

THE AMERICAN WAY

While researchers and experts still argued the precise interplay of the factors leading to coronary disease, many family doctors and well-informed members of the US public

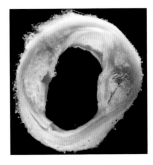

LEFT *A section through the aorta, the main artery of the body, showing the build-up of fatty plaque (atheroma) and the resultant hardening and thickening of the aortic wall.*

had, by the 1970s, drawn their own conclusions. As with smoking, it boiled down to prevention being better than cure.

Undoubtedly, the health campaigns of such organizations as the American Heart Association played a part in raising awareness. But the general shift in lifestyles that began in the 1960s and fostered a new interest in holistic approaches to medicine (see pp.218-21) made a vital contribution.

Lifestyle changes were already apparent in the Framingham Study's 1970 group, whose cholesterol levels and fondness for cigarettes were far lower than those of their counterparts of 20 years before. Across the broader spectrum, sales of such foods as vegetable oils that contain the polyunsaturated fats said to decrease total blood cholesterol were rising at the expense of fatty meats and dairy products. Exercise as a means of combating stress, improving blood circulation and keeping trim boomed as never before. For their part, doctors monitored blood pressure more closely than they had done in the past; the advent of new drugs also meant they could control it better.

As a result of all these preventive measures, the frequency of coronary heart disease in the US dropped by about half between 1970 and 1990, representing a reduction in deaths of around 300,000 a year. Moreover, there was a substantial decline in strokes. But the improvements were not spread evenly across the population. College graduates and the professional classes proved to be more receptive to preventive advice than the poor and less well-educated – an ironic reversal from the time when coronary disorders were found almost entirely among the well-to-do.

Nor was the US experience widely emulated elsewhere. In Britain, for example, male deaths from coronary disease remain proportionately 10 times higher than those in Japan and half as high again as those in US, despite the best persuasive efforts of the public health authorities to reduce intakes of the saturated fats linked with cholesterol.

BELOW *Low-cholesterol, high-fibre foods can help reduce blood* cholesterol levels, in conjunction with stress control and exercise.

RETURN OF THE HOLISTIC

FROM CYNICISM TO ACCEPTANCE

"Obscurantist mysticism … striking flints to light the gas fire"

PHILOSOPHERS COINED THE WORD 'holism' in the 20th century. However, the idea it expresses – that the whole is greater than the sum of its parts – is very old indeed. As applied to human well-being, it appears in the teachings of Pythagoras and Hippocrates, the Indian Ayurveda and many other ancient healing systems that assert true health is attained only when body, mind, emotions and spirit are all in proper balance. As Western science from the time of the Renaissance concentrated more and more on specific treatments to cope with specific manifestations of bodily disorders, the holistic approach to health care was first overshadowed and eventually largely overlooked. Its revival in Western societies began as they moved into economic recovery after World War I.

Many factors contributed to the return of the holistic. One was the reaction of young people in the US and elsewhere against a culture they saw as materialistic, sterile and, with its development of the atomic bomb, frightening. Rejection of that culture led the 'Beats' of the 1950s, and the 'Hippies' and 'Flower Children' of the 1960s, to look for alternatives. Eastern philosophies and religions such as Buddhism were a source of inspiration, with their emphasis on the roles of meditation, exercise and diet in inner development and all-round health.

ORTHODOXY REAPPRAISED

By itself, the flirtation of some young people with Eastern mysticism would not have influenced Western medical conventions. But the latter were already facing something of a reappraisal. While orthodox medical science had delivered magnificent successes against a whole range of disorders, it had achieved little real progress in curing others – cancers and hay fever, for example. At the same time, there was growing public concern about the side-effects of prescribed drugs, the validity of certain surgical operations, and the soaring costs of medical treatment. Questions were being asked, too, about the effects on health of chemicals employed in the growing and preparation of foodstuffs. And, in the light of emerging research findings into the links between cigarette smoking and lung cancer or between diet and coronary disease, more attention than ever was being paid to the preventive role of medicine.

This climate of reassessment translated into a new readiness to explore unorthodox therapies, not only among

ABOVE *Traditional cures on sale on a holy mountain in Sichuan, China, where such remedies – many of them strange to Western eyes – have never lost their popularity.*

RIGHT *Massage is a growth area in complementary medicine. Here, the back of the patient's neck is being 'hacked' – the aim is to relax muscles and improve the circulation.*

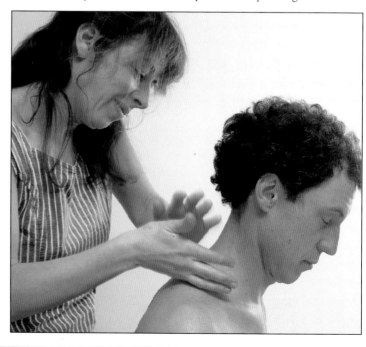

those espousing alternative lifestyles, but among the much larger group of people whom orthodox medicine had disappointed in one respect or another. Gradually, also, it evoked curiosity among sections of the medical profession.

A PANOPLY OF THERAPIES

At the height of their self-confidence in the l9th and early 20th centuries, orthodox Western physicians tried to stamp out most forms of medical treatment other than their own. In much of Europe, the law was already on their side, based on the premise that anything not specifically permitted is forbidden. It was, therefore, fairly easy for the medical establishments in such nations as France, Germany, Italy and Spain to ensure that few of the therapists of whom they disapproved secured permission to practice.

In Britain, the US and other countries with an Anglo-Saxon legal heritage, the situation was more complex. British doctors failed in 1858 to win an outright ban in law on their unorthodox rivals, so they made their own rules stating that any of their number referring patients to non-recognized therapists would in effect be disbarred. In the US, most states adopted legislation defining unorthodox therapies as the practice of medicine and therefore the preserve of qualified physicians, though there were some exemptions and waivers.

Despite such restrictions, and numerous court actions brought against unconventional practitioners, the forces of orthodoxy did not win total victory anywhere. Traditional herbal medicine, some of which had in any case been taken up as conventional treatment, survived. So did other folk therapies, such as bone-setting, later to evolve into chiropractic and osteopathy. Faith and related types of healing with their biblical pedigree were not readily susceptible to the framers of earthly rules. And a few qualified physicians themselves practised unorthodox techniques: notably hypnosis, homoeopathy, manipulative therapies, naturopathy, herbalism and, eventually, acupuncture (see pp.222-3).

So when the upsurge of public interest in unconventional forms of medicine began in the 1960s, a large residue remained. Its legality depended on what the therapy was, who was giving it and where the therapist and patient were located. In Britain, for example, various quirks of fate, including support from the Royal family, had preserved homoeopathy as a recognized method of treatment available on the National Health Service. In Germany, nature cures and hydrotherapy had for many years enjoyed special status.

Furthermore, even while orthodox attempts at suppression were at their height, brand new types of unconventional diagnosis and therapy were constantly appearing. To improve their prospects of acceptance, most of the newcomers claimed some sort of scientific basis, though few succeeded in impressing conventional scientists. One, however, came to be widely accepted as a valuable aid: this was biofeedback (see p.220), pioneered by Joe Kamiya in the US from 1958.

RELENTING A LITTLE

As more people flocked to practitioners of both old and new unorthodox medicine, orthodox physicians were, for the most part, predictably stuffy. "Obscurantist mysticism" was the verdict in 1978 of the British polymath Dr Jonathan Miller on many traditional folk therapies, and he likened the revival of interest in them to "striking flints to light the gas fire". However, even the most unbending of the orthodox

BELOW *Reflexologists believe that many diseases can be treated by foot massage, since, they say, meridians connect all parts of the body to the feet. Anatomists disagree, and reflexology is considered an alternative, rather than complementary, therapy.*

were forced to give ground a little in the face of the enthusiastic support of public opinion.

Thus, between 1983 and 1986, the staid British Medical Association (BMA), cajoled by Prince Charles as its president, conducted a lengthy inquiry into unorthodox medicine. The resulting report was not encouraging for supporters of the therapies, virtually all of which were damned as unscientific. But the tone of much of the document was so dismissive that it was open to charges of vested interest, and the debate it engendered ensured that many forms of unorthodox medicine received even wider publicity than they had enjoyed before.

Meanwhile, out of the public gaze and despite the pronouncements of their leaders in the BMA, British medical students and doctors were expressing interest in learning more about the subject. Surveys conducted in Britain in the early 1980s showed, for example, that around 75 per cent of a sample of 145 general practitioners sometimes referred patients to unconventional therapists and half believed treatments such as hypnosis and acupuncture should be generally available on the National Health Service. Nine out of ten in a sample of 86 students thought unorthodox therapies should feature in their training. Furthermore, a growing number were actually qualifying in unconventional techniques, so that by 1988 around 2,000 British doctors were skilled in one or

ORGONE THERAPY

When Sigmund Freud lectured to the brilliant Austrian medical student Wilhelm Reich, he little knew what extraordinary theories his pupil would devise in later life. In 1934, Reich came up with the concept of a fundamental unit of life, called the 'bion'; after moving to the US, in the 1940s, he claimed to have discovered the basic life force. Called 'orgone', he said it was orgasmic energy. To store this force, he built an 'orgone box', claiming that almost any disease could be cured by 'bioenergetics', which meant the patient staying in the box for a time. Hounded by the authorities and the press, Reich died in prison in 1957 at the age of 60.

BIOFEEDBACK

Experiments undertaken on both animals and humans from the late 1950s showed that responses are not entirely involuntary, but may to some extent be modified by training. Much of the early work with human subjects was carried out in the US by Joe Kamiya, who demonstrated, through biofeedback techniques of instant response-monitoring, that people can learn to stimulate their brain's output of alpha rhythms, associated with feelings of relaxation and well-being. Significantly, the processes involved in learning were precisely those forming part of many unorthodox therapies, such as breathing exercises and meditation.

ABOVE *A patient learns to relax with the help of biofeedback monitoring.*

more of them. Similar trends were starting to develop in other western countries.

The aim of practitioners referring patients to unorthodox therapists, or acquiring the skills for themselves, was to harness resources additional to those of orthodox medicine. In doing so, they effectively made judgments about which alternatives they believed to have merit, and in which disorders those might help best. This corpus of treatments and conditions is sometimes referred to as 'complementary medicine', to distinguish it from the broader range of unorthodox therapies, though the dividing line is a source of contention *(see pp.240-1)*.

The combination of orthodox and complementary medicine, with an element of health education, is now termed 'holistic' in a slight shift from that word's original meaning. However, since many of the complementary techniques have their roots in holism, it is not inaccurate. And many of the disorders against which the holistic approach is most widely used appear connected to the patient's entire way of life – an idea familiar to ancient pioneers of holism.

ROLE OF THE COMPLEMENTARY

The disorders that drew people, including medical professionals, to explore unorthodox therapies in increasing numbers from the 1960s varied widely in nature and seriousness. Among the most common were degenerative diseases of the body cells and the circulatory, nervous and musculo-skeletal systems, chronic infections, allergies, migraines, insomnia, long-term debility, anxiety and depression. Some, like cancers and heart disease, could be fatal. Others, such as arthritis and rheumatism, were not intrinsically life-threatening, but could cause near-permanent misery. Others again – for example, hay fever and similar allergies – were merely occasional inconveniences.

Despite their disparities, they mostly shared certain features. They were chronic conditions, which orthodox medicine in the mid-20th century could alleviate but rarely cure outright. In many cases, the alleviations produced ill-effects or reduced the sufferer's quality of life.

Unorthodox therapies stressed that the disorders were not the product of a single cause, but of an accumulation of factors – inherited predispositions, the individual's whole way of life, including such factors as diet, and mental, emotional or spiritual states. A similar theme, in fact, also ran through many long-established unconventional therapies of Western origin, such as homoeopathy, chiropractic and osteopathy. A significant aspect of all these therapies was the time and effort spent in diagnosis, designed to identify everything with a bearing on the disease. By contrast, orthodox diagnostic sessions were often short, technical affairs.

Many people who consulted unorthodox practitioners did so only after orthodox treatments had failed to help them. This tendency largely shaped the pattern of disorders unorthodox medicine was called on to treat. There was one major exception, perhaps a legacy of the old rural bone-setting tradition. Sufferers from musculo-skeletal disorders seem to have been readier than others to use unconventional therapy as a first port of call, to the benefit of chiropractors and osteopaths.

Evidence was starting to emerge that suggested aspects of unorthodox medicine were worth further, specific scientific study. And as science started to analyze this evidence, more conventional physicians began borrowing from the most promising areas of the unconventional.

BELOW *A herbalist dispenses dried marigolds. Widely used in India and the Far East, herbalism has had limited appeal in the West.*

SCIENCE CATCHES UP

Anyone reaching back into the history of orthodox medicine could trace in it many of the components of the major unconventional therapies. The concepts of hereditary predispositions to disease, mental and emotional contributions to ill-health and environmental factors were well known. Even the lengthy and wide-ranging diagnostic sessions were, in a sense, an extension of the established principle that merely talking about their disorders to a sympathetic listener can make patients feel better. The debate on unorthodox medicine (*see pp.218-9*) that began in the 1960s served to refocus attention on all such matters.

American and other research into degenerative heart disease and the roles played in it by high blood pressure, unhealthy diet and lack of exercise, provided probably the biggest single vindication of a holistic approach to therapy. But many other studies contributed to wider acceptance that some unorthodox forms of medicine had, wittingly or unwittingly, hit on scientific truths. The most intriguing investigations concerned the interplay between mind and body.

The fact that mental pressures such as fear produce physical responses, including changes in heart rate and breathing patterns, had long been observed, and some connections had been made between sustained subjection to pressure and obvious physical disorders, for example in the stereotype of the harassed businessman with his gastric ulcer. Postwar developments in technology allowed more of these so-called involuntary responses, such as variations in the

BELOW *A 46-year-old man undergoes a stress test on a treadmill.*   *Sensors attached to his chest monitor heart changes.*

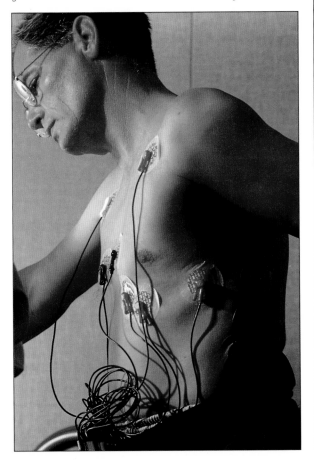

brain waves and in the electrical resistance of the skin, to be identified and measured. The results were convincing.

Other experimental findings suggested that the range of disorders whose onset and development are influenced by mental pressure extends far beyond the executive's ulcer. They encompass degenerative heart disease, cancers, rheumatism and chronic infections – in short, most of those against which orthodox medicine had achieved little. A pioneer in that field of research was Professor Hans Selye of Montreal. In 1976, he published his work *The Stress of Life*, postulating the now widely accepted view of psychological factors in physical disease.

DEADLY STRESS

The term 'stress', borrowed from engineering, denotes the changes caused in the body when the senses and mind perceive a threat or challenge, real or imagined, physical or mental. The mechanism, triggered by the release of hormones into the bloodstream and electrical impulses into the nervous system, is essentially protective. It prepares the body to meet the challenge or flee from it ('fight or flight') with a host of reactions, including heightened awareness, increased heart and breathing rates, raised blood pressure and alterations to muscles and digestion.

In the normal course of events, stress develops in three stages, from initial arousal to full physical and mental alert. At any stage, once the perceived challenge is removed, surmounted or escaped, the stress should dissipate, allowing the body to return to a balanced, calm and relaxed inner state. As long as this pattern holds, stress is not only harmless, but often positively beneficial; without it, human life would be stripped of all feelings of achievement, excitement or joy, as well as of fear or anxiety.

However, as Selye and others showed, modern living disrupts the pattern for many people. The fight-or-flight response originally evolved in animals and humans to cope with situations that were usually quickly and clearly resolved, with the stress discharged in physical activity. But in modern societies, the causes of stress are more likely to be emotional or mental than physical, and incapable – because of social constraints – of being dealt with physically. In many cases, too, they are sustained or cumulative. One result is to keep the body in a permanent state of partial fight-or-flight readiness, in which it neither lapses back into complete relaxation nor moves beyond full alert to achieve release.

Selye's experiments were among the first to demonstrate that the application of negative, unpleasant stress to laboratory animals over sustained periods could induce in them some of the irreparable disorders increasingly plaguing humanity, such as ulcers, heart disease and damage to the immune system. It also became clear that, beyond a certain point, the body loses its capacity to return fully to normal once the causes of sustained stress are removed. Individuals have a certain tolerance to stress, according to its degree, nature and persistence – now called the 'elastic limit'.

Such discoveries underlined the importance in preventing or combating disease of 'stress management', ways of minimizing negative stress or ensuring its discharge through exercise, as well as for promoting the relaxation that is the opposite side of the coin. Here, many unorthodox therapies and techniques such as yoga had a headstart, and could be respectably annexed to orthodoxy in the name of holism.

THE ACUPUNCTURE PUZZLE

JUSTIFYING AN ANCIENT TRADITION

The 'runners' high' may help explain how a centuries-old technique works

A T THE END OF THE 1960s, the People's Republic of China entered an era of political rapprochement with the US after two decades of mutual hostility. The event that marked its new relationship was a highly publicized visit to China by US President Richard Nixon in 1972. This stimulated interest among Western nations in all things Chinese – including the ancient medical technique of acupuncture *(see p.16)*, which in Mao's China had more than one million practitioners.

Delegations following in Nixon's wake gave impressive accounts of operations and treatments by acupuncturists, using needles made of silver alloy, stainless steel and other metals whose tips were carefully and precisely inserted into some of 365 or more 'acupoints' on their patients' skins. According to Chinese medical philosophy, the needles allow energy (*chi*) to enter or leave the body, improving or sustaining health or diminishing pain.

Acupuncture and the related Japanese technique of shiatsu (which uses finger pressure instead of needles) had long been known to a small coterie of medical people and others in the West. But now, along with other forms of complementary medicine, acupuncture became a topic for debate, investigation and experiment on a much wider scale.

SIFTING THE CLAIMS

The wildest claims made for acupuncture in the early 1970s were soon discarded. Even its staunchest advocates speedily admitted it was of little direct value or unsuitable in many types of disorders: severe infections; broken bones; cancers; heart ailments; motor neurone disease; and muscular dystrophy. They also conceded that certain types of patient, such as the very young and the very old or weak, are not suited to acupuncture treatment involving needles, though the acupoints on their skins can be stimulated by finger pressure or some other means.

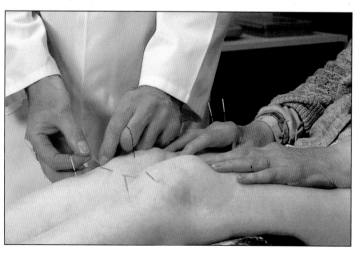

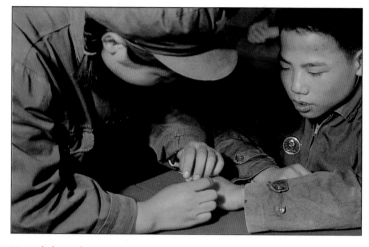

BELOW *China is thought to have some one million acupuncturists.* Here one of them treats a child at a school for deaf mutes.

Nevertheless, there remained a long list of both mental and physical conditions in which, according its supporters, acupuncture was beneficial – from anxiety and depression to arthritis and haemorrhoids. In 1973, the Royal Society of Medicine in Britain published a survey of 642 cases treated by acupuncture, involving nine categories of disorders. Overall, the study classified 37 per cent of the patients as "cured or much improved" after acupuncture, while the remainder showed no change.

The highest proportion of 'cures' – for more than half of the patients in each case – were achieved for migraine, asthma and dysmenorrhoea (menstrual pain). The lowest success rates, with more than one third of patients showing no change at all, were for dysmenorrhoea (again), peptic ulcers and indigestion, general psychiatric conditions, impotence and frigidity. Nine out of ten of those with muscular aches and pains, four out of five hay fever sufferers and three out of four of those with arthritis in its various forms, registered some improvement.

The results of this and similar studies proved very little one way or the other in the strict terms of Western medical science. Even so, the number of orthodox practitioners offering acupuncture as an adjunct to conventional treatment began to grow to the point at which, by about 1980, there were several hundred of them in the US and several thousand in Europe. In countries such as India and Sri Lanka, where forms of acupuncture had already played a part in their medical tradition, interest spread more rapidly, as it did in the Soviet Union.

LEFT *As an alternative to steroids, an acupuncturist applies needles to* both the knees and hands of an arthritis sufferer.

Mainstream Western research involving acupuncture came to concentrate largely on its apparent capacity to alleviate pain, though there were forays into other areas, too. One was the use of a staple or pin in the earlobe to combat nicotine and other drug addictions, with, at best, mixed results. Gradually, various theories evolved that go at least partway to explaining how acupuncture may achieve its effects.

HOW DOES ACUPUNCTURE WORK?

The traditional Chinese belief in acupuncture rests on the assumption that *chi* energy is carried through the body, to and from vital organs, along a series of pathways called meridians. At the acupoints, where the meridians are closest to the surface of the skin, skilled acupuncturists can adjust the energy flow to maintain or restore balance. To date, there is no direct proof that the meridians exist.

Western scientists encountering acupuncture attributed its results to hypnosis or suggestion, and a number of facts seemed to bear this out. Acupuncturists admitted that there are some people, perhaps one in three or four, on whom the technique just does not work. Furthermore, the success rates of acupuncture in China, even when rigorously measured, were higher than in the West, possibly indicating that it worked better with the Chinese because their culture and tradition gave them greater faith.

Against these arguments, advocates of acupuncture claimed to have used it with success on animals, which would not be expected to react to suggestion. They also pointed out that, in China, acupuncture treatment is part of a whole regimen of diet, exercise and other therapies, all geared to balancing *yin* and *yang*, which is not so widely true in the West.

A more specific theory tying in with acupuncture's role in relieving pain had emerged in the mid-1960s, several years before the upsurge of popular interest in the subject. In the 'gate control' theory of Ronald Melzack and Patrick Wall (*see pp.190-1*), stimulation by acupuncture or shiatsu could act as the 'gate', blocking pain signals at the spinal cord. (But, this does not fully explain how the techniques apparently succeed with chronic pain as in arthritis.)

In addition, close examination of acupoints has revealed that many are located where nerves emerge from the deep tissues towards the skin, or where a particular muscle's nerve enters that muscle. Finally, it has been found that 71 per cent of acupoints correspond to 'trigger points' — areas on the skin that become tender in certain diseases, such as the referred pain felt in the shoulder from liver disease.

In the 1970s, scientists investigating the central nervous system hit on another possible explanation for acupuncture's effects. They discovered that drugs such as morphine and heroin achieve their effects by acting on special receptors in the brain and spinal cord. Logically, they reasoned, the receptors would not exist unless the body produced similar substances, relieving pain in the sick and increasing feelings of well-being in the healthy. In 1973, these substances, called endorphins, were isolated and identified.

Endorphins are now said to be responsible for the delay in feeling pain experienced by many victims of serious injury, including people hurt while engaged in sports. Some suggest that acupuncture and related techniques may achieve their effects by stimulating the release of endorphins and other chemical messengers. The connection is far from being fully proved, but the research goes on — not least because the prize is a safe, non-addictive way of killing pain.

ABOVE *A cast of the head and shoulders showing a traditional Chinese acupuncture chart, with meridians and acupoints indicated.*

BELOW *Acupuncture needles are placed in the acupoints on the face for the bladder and large intestine meridians, to treat hay fever.*

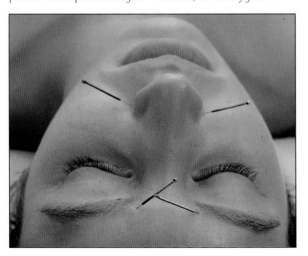

THE QUEST FOR ENDORPHINS

Once it was suspected in the 1970s that the human body produced its own natural version of the painkilling drug morphine, the race to find it was on. Researchers in Britain, the US and Sweden led the field, and a team from Scotland's Aberdeen University, under Professor Hans Kosterlitz and Dr John Hughes, won. In 1973, they discovered two substances in the brain and spinal cord that fitted the bill. The names given to them were cumbersome — methionine-encephalin and leucine-encephalin.

Many more were soon identified, and they were collectively labelled endorphins, a contraction of words meaning 'morphine originating within the organism'. One of them is 100 times more powerful as a painkiller than morphine itself.

No one is entirely sure how endorphins work or what stimulates the body to release them. But they are credited with creating the 'runner's high' — the near-addictive feelings of euphoria experienced after prolonged, vigorous exercise — as well as with painkilling properties. Researchers also claim they are released into the brain after acupuncture and similar techniques.

10 Into the Future

*F*or this, the last chapter of A HISTORY OF MEDICINE, we asked a number of distinguished doctors and scientists to give us their ideas of how medicine might develop in the next 30 years.

This was a tall order. So many different factors are involved: the effect of ever-increasing, ever-aging populations; the influence of growing industrialization and decreasing physical and financial resources in underdeveloped countries; the effects of recently realized pollution in developed ones – all may lead to the emergence of new health problems. How, too, can one forecast what new scientific and technological breakthroughs might be just around the corner, laden with the promise of extraordinary and unimagined cures? After all, it would have been difficult to imagine, 30 years ago, that we would today treat kidney transplants as routine; and that we would be able to cure some diseases through the implantation of genetic material.

Nevertheless, forecasting the future has a fascination all of its own, even if – as in this case – it is based on future developments of existing knowledge and techniques.

Some of the prognostications for the future are gloomy; some are full of hope. Only the reality of the scientific, medical, social, political and environmental progress of humankind will show who is right and who is wrong.

ABOVE The Inner Self, *by Oscar Burrel.*

DISEASES OF THE FUTURE

by DR NICOLA McCLURE MBBS

Family Doctor, Principal in General Practice, London

WHEN I LEFT MEDICAL SCHOOL, in the mid-1970s, it seemed that most of the great medical mysteries were, if not solved, well on the way to becoming so. It seemed inconceivable that major new diseases would or could be identified – all that remained was a search for cures and a tendency for sets of symptoms previously thought to be disparate to be sorted into unified, clearly described and attributable syndromes. And yet, almost 20 years on, the world has changed in such a way that it is impossible to be certain about the medical problems that will confront humanity in the future.

For me, one of the biggest changes over those 20 years has been the emergence of AIDS – but that is probably because I work in West London, an area that has the highest incidence of AIDS in Britain. Opinions vary about how long AIDS – or, at least, HIV – has been with us (*see p.206*). But could another virus sweep through the world to create similar devastation, in the same way as the series of plagues of the Middle Ages?

There are some reasons for believing that one could. New diseases appear to result from new living conditions – both social and environmental. Viruses can mutate into other forms, closely related but with different effects (HIV seems to have done so several times), and mutations occur for a variety of reasons, including both chemical influences (possibly from pollution) and the body's immunological responses. Some long-dormant viruses can be brought to life by changes in social behaviour, too – for example, the kuru virus of New Guinea (*see p.201*), which was triggered by the adoption of ritualistic cannibalism.

A more extreme, but not completely stupid, theory to explain the emergence of new viruses in the future might draw on nature's own methods of population control. In some species – rats, for example – overcrowding causes females to become infertile; very serious overcrowding leads to serious aggression, and, ultimately, cannibalism. Lemmings, too, may have their own way of controlling population increases: they 'commit suicide' by leaping off cliffs. But the common vole may provide a better parallel for the human population explosion that is forecast over the next 30 years: these small rodents have three-year cycles of population explosions, after which a parasitic worm in the brain cuts vole numbers back to size.

A WORLD OF POLLUTANTS

Industrial chemicals may, possibly, lead to the mutation of viruses, but it is much more likely that they will cause a whole range of physical problems, both acute and chronic.

BELOW *A flask of nuclear waste debris, waiting to be transported by rail from the Three Mile Island nuclear plant near Harrisburg, Pennsylvania. The plant was severely damaged in an accident in 1979; the cleaning-up operation may take as long as 40 years.*

RIGHT *Two technicians in protective clothing monitor radiation levels following the accident at Chernobyl, Ukraine, in April 1986.*

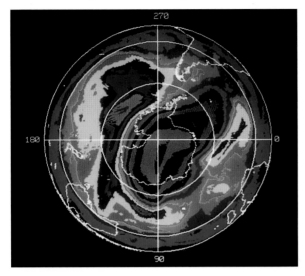

There are many reasons for this, particularly the problem of the disintegrating Eastern bloc. It seems that the old Soviet regime ignored the effect on both the environment and the health of people of industrial pollution. Today, it is difficult to pick up a magazine in the West without reading some new horror story of conditions behind the old Iron Curtain.

One recent report in Britain's *Observer* newspaper, of a claim by Yablokov, a Russian politician, had it that 20 per cent of Russians lived in what could be termed an ecological disaster zone, and that another 35 to 40 per cent lived in an 'ecologically unfavourable' zone; the result of this, he claimed, was that the average life expectancy was between five and seven years less than in the industrial West – because of extraordinarily high levels of industrial pollution, unthinking working practices, and terrifying levels of radiation let loose in the countryside. Since, Yablokov claimed, Russia would have to spend twice the amount of its gross national product in 1991 over the next 20 years to correct the problem, it seems that little improvement will be made. Add to that the facts that the previous infrastructure of the Eastern bloc no longer exists, but that a large number of near-obsolete and inadequately maintained nuclear power stations do; throw in the consideration that some sheep in Wales and the land in some of Scandinavia still bear the mark of the fall-out from Chernobyl, making the problem extremely relevant to Western Europe; and the calculation becomes terrifying.

So we can expect a large number of new diseases, about whose nature we can barely even speculate, due to industrial pollution. We may also experience an increase in forms of cancer from low-level radiation, as well as a number of new variants on existing systemic diseases. And as underdeveloped countries become more and more industrialized, the problem can only become worse.

INDUSTRIALIZATION AND THE THIRD WORLD

One of the major health stories of the last century has been the way in which a number of industrial advances, generated in the attempt to service a consumer boom, have been successively shown to be either life-threatening or damaging to the environment. Asbestos seemed the ideal insulating material – but it causes cancer; pesticides increase agricultural production – but some also cause birth defects, among other problems; aerosol sprays and the first refrigerators were a boon – but they helped deplete the ozone layer, and so may have caused skin cancers, and their effects will increasingly do so in the future. And what will be the effects of the equivalent consumer godsends of the 1990s, by the time we reach 2020? The answer is that nobody really knows, for such substances do not go through the same exhaustive tests as drugs (and even some drugs pass the tests but fail in practice); some scientists argue that, since testing of new substances on animals is being reduced, for moral reasons, the risk is increasing.

One thing, though, is certain: the problems of industrialization will become worse – and worst of all in countries presently said to be underdeveloped. Such countries need industry desperately, in order to survive and to feed their ever-increasing populations (the birth rates in Africa, the Middle East and Far East increase exponentially each year). The need will be so extreme, and the effective labour force – already massively reduced in Africa by AIDS – so inadequate, that scrupulous safety standards may well of necessity go by the board.

Under such pressures, underdeveloped countries will have few resources available to counter the diseases that travel hand-in-hand with a lack of public health funding and overcrowding: cholera, dysentery, tuberculosis and typhus. Recent outbreaks of cholera in South America are an ominous pointer to the future. Antibiotics on their own do not provide the long-term solution, because bacteria have a nasty habit of developing new strains that are resistant to the antibiotics used. (Sheffield University, in Britain, now has a database of new strains of bacteria, with the antibiotic to which they are resistant noted; it is becoming bigger and bigger.) The only answer is an increase in the resources directed to health education, public health schemes and improved sanitation. But where these resources are to come from is still a matter of argument.

FINANCIAL OPTIONS

Ultimately, it all comes down to money. Medicine has been remarkably successful at dealing with acute disease. The result is that the developed countries have an ever-aging population: simply, far fewer people die young from acute problems. The majority live longer and longer, eventually to die from chronic degenerative problems: Alzheimer's disease (only recognized after I qualified); motor neurone disease; emphysema; chronic bronchitis; and so on. Chronic disease costs more money in nursing and care, and the declining birth rate in the West means that fewer and fewer carers are available; the explosion in possibilities for increasingly expensive treatments of acute disease reduces the financial options even further.

Sometimes – but not too often – I feel very grateful that I will have retired by 2020; and even more grateful that I am a doctor, not a politician.

PREVENTION

by PROFESSOR MICHAEL CONNOR BSC MD FRCP

Professor of Medical Genetics and Director of the West of Scotland Regional Genetics Service, Duncan Guthrie Institute, Glasgow

ALL DISEASES ARE CAUSED by genetic or environmental factors that act singly or in combination. Public health programmes in many countries have already led to a striking reduction in environmental causes, such as malnutrition and infections, with a consequent rise in the proportion of illnesses with a genetic contribution. Prevention of such diseases, which have either a major or minor genetic contribution, now poses a key problem for medical science.

CLONING OF HUMAN GENES

Perhaps the single most important development in tackling this problem will be the laboratory isolation and cloning of all human genes. Currently, just over 1000 of our estimated

BELOW *A scientist examines the sequence of DNA components on a light box, before finding out which genes are present in the sample.*

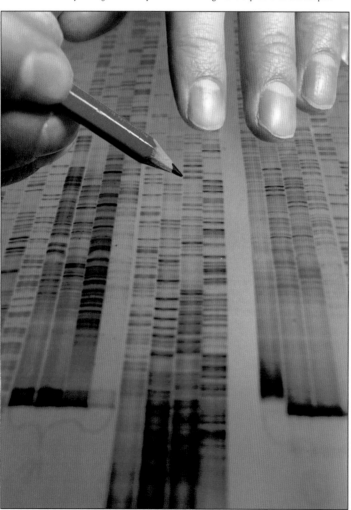

total of 100,000 genes have been cloned, yet this small fraction of the total has already produced significant clinical benefits in the treatment of some of the commonest genetic disorders that arise from faults in one or both members of a pair of genes (single gene disorders).

Cystic fibrosis provides a good example of this, for it is now possible to track the faulty genes within a family, detect couples at risk with certainty and, if the couple wish, give a reliable diagnosis of whether the child will be affected before birth. The same approach could also be applied to population screening to detect which person in every 20 carries a faulty gene for cystic fibrosis – if the procedure was accepted and widely introduced, the frequency of this condition could be markedly reduced.

DNA diagnosis is now also the mainstay of genetic management for other common single gene disorders, including sex-linked muscular dystrophy, myotonic dystrophy, fragile X syndrome, sickle cell disease, thalassaemias and Huntington's disease, and will apply to every single gene disorder once the appropriate genes are cloned. The cloning of each gene also allows a detailed analysis of its protein product and, in turn, opens up prospects for treatment of a particular condition. This can be achieved either by genetic engineering – the laboratory production and replacement of the missing protein, for example in haemophilia; or by supplemention gene therapy – giving the patient normal copies of the faulty gene, as, for example, in a case of immune deficiency due to the defective enzyme adenosine deaminase *(see p.163)*.

LINKS WITH CANCER

Some single gene disorders can cause cancer, and their study has already provided invaluable insight into the mechanisms underlying the commoner, non-inherited cancers. Cloning of the appropriate genes will allow identification of families in which the condition is inherited, and provide appropriate screening for early diagnosis in family members at risk. In the non-inherited cancers, a knowledge of the cascade of genetic faults that accompanies the progression of malignancy will lead to accurate prognosis at different stages and influence the choice of therapy for each patient; it may also be possible to screen accessible tissues for evidence of any pre-malignant genetic changes. Moreover, it will also become feasible to identify the environmental factors that induce or interact with the genetic changes, and to determine if some individuals are more susceptible than others to particular carcinogens. The frequency of certain cancers could then be reduced if susceptible individuals took action to avoid their specific carcinogens.

This idea of genetic prediction of individuals at particular risk of developing disease is expected to extend to other common disorders of adulthood, including premature vascular disease, diabetes, arthritis, depression and schizophrenia. In each disorder, genetic or environmental factors alone are insufficient to cause disease and so identification of genetically predisposed individuals, together with targeted avoidance of specific environmental factors, could prevent disease.

SCREENING BEFORE BIRTH

Some genetic disorders, though, cannot be predicted prior to conception, and in such cases screening for affected pregnancies is likely to remain the mainstay of management. Analysis of maternal blood during pregnancy has already allowed a doubling of the detection rate for serious chromosomal abnormalities, including Down's syndrome, as compared with offering antenatal diagnoses on the basis of maternal age alone. Some major congenital malformations, most notably spina bifida, can also be detected by maternal blood tests, while routine introduction of detailed ultrasound scanning would lead to antenatal diagnosis of a wide range of other malformations. Further development of these and other approaches to pregnancy screening are to be expected.

All of these developments have the potential to reduce the burden of disease with a genetic contribution, with

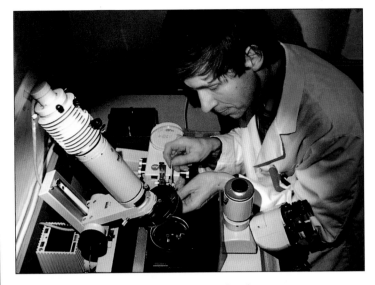

consequent benefits for the families concerned and society in general, but each development needs wide public debate of the issues involved. Scientific possibility need not become clinical practice, and it should always be borne in mind that genetic disease merely represents the extremes of normal human diversity without which evolution could not occur.

BELOW *A light microscope is used to facilitate the micro-manipulation* *of DNA. The genetic material is contained in the petri dish.*

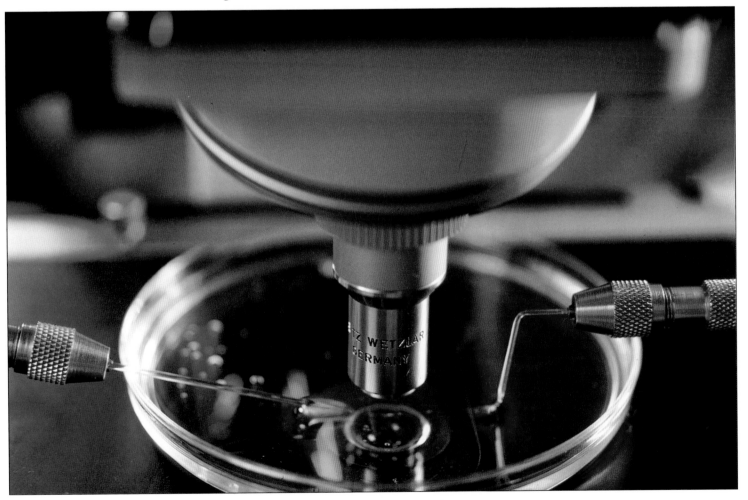

DIAGNOSIS

by DR BILL LEES FRCR

Consultant Radiologist, The Middlesex Hospital, London

WITHIN A FEW YEARS of Wilhelm Röntgen's discovery of X-rays (*see pp.126-7*), all the basic principles and concepts of medical radiography had been established. It was not until the early 1970s, almost 80 years later, that a new generation of imaging techniques, such as ultrasound scanning and X-ray computed axial tomography (CAT scanning), made any significant impact on medical diagnosis.

These new imaging methods all shared a common feature: scanning. Each scanner, however rudimentary or sophisticated, interrogates the body, piece by piece, taking large numbers of individual measurements from which images are generated by a process of mathematical reconstruction. The early computers used for this purpose were slow, often relying upon analogue components to achieve practicable speeds. The astonishing developments in all scanning techniques during the 1980s have been due mainly to the application of greater computer power.

BELOW *A 3-D computer generated image of an 18-week-old foetus:* such computer images have revolutionized diagnostic techniques.

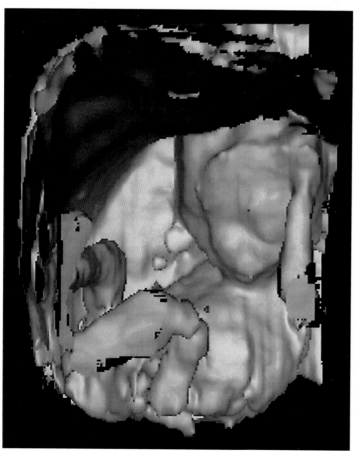

THE PROSPECTS FOR ULTRASOUND

The first ultrasound machines were manufactured in the early 1950s (*see p.168*), often using war surplus radar equipment that was modified to use sound waves and produced blips and traces on primitive oscilloscope screens.

The present generation of ultrasound scanners can produce two-dimensional slice information at high speed to track moving structures, such as valves within the heart. The scanners can record and illustrate subtle changes in the density of soft tissues whilst simultaneously mapping blood flow in full colour over the whole field of the moving image.

Ultrasound transducers have been made in many hundreds of specialized forms for external scanning of particular organs and for insertion into body cavities. Recently, probes have been miniaturized down to 1 millimetre in size, and mounted in catheters for use in conjunction with endoscopes and surgical instruments. They can even be used within the coronary arteries of the heart.

This evolutionary process has diffused ultrasound into every area of medicine, and, with the advent of portable machines, it now routinely takes its imaging power to the bedside, the clinic and the operating theatre. On average, 25 per cent of the imaging undertaken in a UK hospital will involve ultrasound. This figure is rising, and is expected to reach the 40 per cent already attained by some hospitals.

The safety of ultrasound, and its lack of ionizing radiation, has made it the pre-eminent imaging tool in obstetrics and gynaecology, but its uses are far wider than this. For example, Doppler scanning provides data on rates of blood flow, helping vascular surgeons detect changes in the diameter of blood vessels. The technique makes use of the Doppler effect, familiar to all those who have heard the changing pitch of an emergency vehicle's siren as it approaches and then recedes. Other areas in which ultrasound is likely to be increasingly employed in the future include gastro-enterology, scanning of the prostate gland and the delivery of treatment in neonatal heart and brain surgery.

CAT SCANNING

The earliest CAT scanners (*see p.170*) were slow and clumsy, barely capable of producing two image slices per minute. The latest machines, which employ continuously rotating gantries and table movements, scan in a spiral fashion and sweep an interrogating X-ray beam through a volume of tissue to produce up to 30 slices in 30 seconds. Such high-speed scanning methods can freeze the motion of most of the body's parts, so mapping the passage of an intravenously injected contrast agent through blood vessels and into the substance of organs and tumours.

Although CAT scanning is at present enjoying a fair amount of popularity, the radiation burden it imposes on

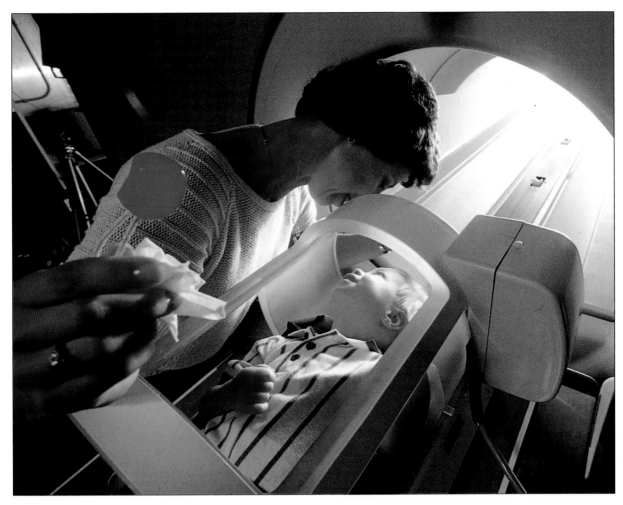

ABOVE *A toddler lies outside an MRI scanner with his mother, prior to being scanned in the investigation of a congenital heart defect. In this case, a series of conventional two-dimensional MRI scans were assembled by computer to give 3-D images of the heart.*

BELOW *A series of false-colour 3-D images of the heart of the child (ABOVE), looking from the foot to the head. The thin horizontal line (TOP LEFT) is a tiny left ventricle; while the left and right atria are only separated by a thin strand of tissue.*

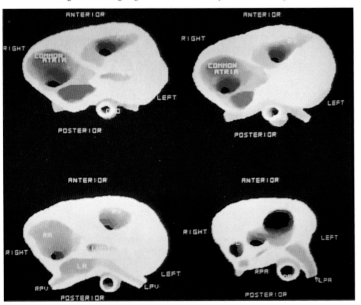

patients is relatively high, particularly in paediatric cases. As a result, the technique is expected to decline as other methods take over, but it will remain the standard technique for the study of the lungs and abdominal organs.

MAGNETIC RESONANCE IMAGING

Interrogating a patient with special sequences of radio pulses in a strong magnetic field can provide images of the distribution of water and its chemical environment within the body. This magnetic resonance imaging (MRI) technique (*see p.171*) is ideal for picturing parts of the body that do not move, such as the head. It has revolutionized the diagnosis of neurological disorders, is having an enormous impact on orthopaedic and musculo-skeletal imaging and proves invaluable when viewing liver tumours.

Most MRI machines use superconducting magnets of enormous size and power to generate the necessary strength of magnetic field. However, the technique has its limitations, because of the trade-off between data and dose: the longer a patient is scanned, the more data is acquired but the greater the radiation burden imposed. Despite this drawback, an enormous investment in research and development, coupled with imaginative new ideas, continues to improve the quality and speed of image acquisition. This effort makes it likely that the technique will be adapted for use in new areas, such as imaging blood vessels, and it is generally accepted that MRI will gradually improve until smaller and cheaper systems are widely available.

THE NEW CONCEPT OF THE MEDICAL IMAGE

Computerization of conventional X-rays has initiated the era of digital radiography, which is gradually replacing the existing technologies of analogue components and silver-based film. The subsequent loss of resolution is outweighed by the enormous advantages inherent in digital X-rays, especially the potential to reduce by a large measure the dose of radiation delivered to the patient. As a result, conventional X-ray film will become obsolete, giving way to digital images that can be viewed on high-resolution (2000 line) computer screens. While this concept is feasible, it remains expensive and impractical for day-to-day diagnosis.

The impact of computing has changed our concept of what constitutes an image. Once, an image was a physical entity, a pattern of shadows on a piece of film. Now, it is more likely to exist as a pattern of numbers held within a computer as a three- or many-dimensional model of the patient that can be manipulated and displayed in many different ways. Increasingly, imaging devices will be networked and their output electronically stored and distributed, potentially accessible anywhere in a country's health service.

The enormous computer power now available allows us to extract more and more usable information from an image data set. We can already generate three-dimensional models of a patient and interact with them in the workstation to improve our perception of complex anatomy and of spatial relationships. We can simulate and rehearse critical surgical procedures. We can generate output in CAD (computer-aided design) and CAM (computer-aided manufacture) form, producing solid models for templates to manufacture tailored prostheses and other implantable devices. Three-dimensional

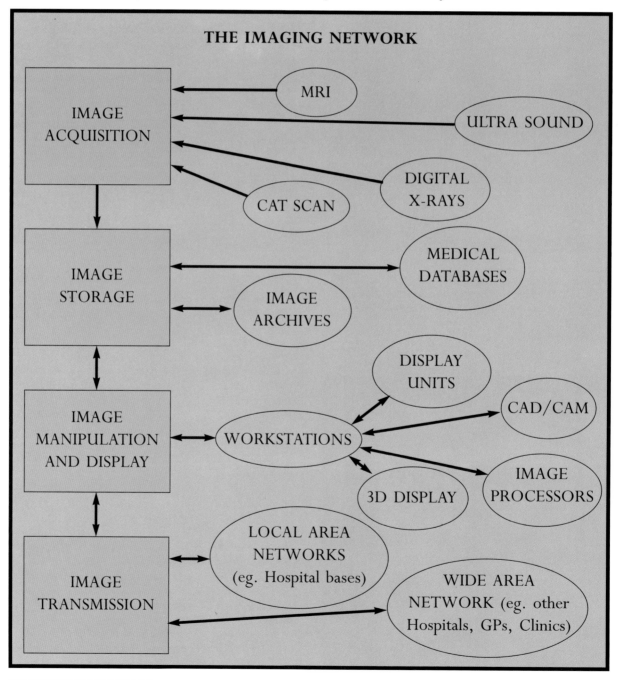

THE IMAGING NETWORK

imaging workstations can also be transformed into simulators and other training aids. The intelligence built into the hardware means that radiologists, except those at the leading edge, will be operating user-friendly equipment and will need to be well-versed in the details of human anatomy and disease to carry out their work.

Image data sets acquired from different scanning devices can be 'registered' or fused within the workstation to produce multi-modality images that can reveal more detail of the body's internal structure. This process can be taken further to control the delivery of treatment. The workstation can 'register' the patient, surgical instruments and images into one multi-dimensional space, thereafter to control and direct needles, laser fibres and even robotic surgical instru-

ABOVE *Modern diagnostic techniques involve an awe-inspiring array of technology. Here, medical images are being transferred via the RNIS* *system: a commercial network, run by* France Telecom, *that transfers sound, images and data on the same line from hospital to hospital.*

ments with precision under the remote control of the surgeon and radiologist.

Imaging laboratories are developing all these techniques so that, by the early 21st century, they will be commonplace. New forms of energy, and new computing tools, such as artificial intelligence and mathematical modelling, will yield more information without the burden of radiation. These will enhance the diagnostic and treatment capabilities of the radiologist and surgeon without affecting patient relationships.

REPAIRING THE BODY

by PROFESSOR DR HERO VAN URK MD PHD

Head of Vascular Surgery, University Hospital, Rotterdam, The Netherlands

First used in 1985, the term 'minimally invasive surgery' describes a complex of developments, all of which are directed towards making surgery less invasive to the patient's body. To a large extent, the practice of such surgery is a genuine alternative to conventional surgery, but in instances where no appropriate surgical treatment previously existed, it represents an entirely new technique – for example, laser treatment for port wine stains.

A general tendency to limit the negative effects of extensive surgical procedures – in the past, 'big surgeons' made 'big incisions' – has been favoured by the simultaneous development of two ranges of diagnostic and therapeutic procedures. New imaging techniques (*see p.168–71*), such as ultrasound, computerized axial tomography (CAT scanning), magnetic resonance imaging (MRI scanning) and single photon emission computed tomography, have transformed the field of diagnostic procedures. They are starting to be employed on a wide scale and will be even more readily available in the near future.

The introduction of endoscopes and associated instruments and tools, including the use of laser energy to replace the surgical scalpel (*see p.173*), represent the kind of therapeutics that has played such a major role in the furtherance of minimally invasive surgery. The therapeutics often go hand in hand with the newer imaging techniques. For example, CAT scans and ultrasound are used in guiding needle biopsies, while at the same time identifying and characterizing the lesion under investigation. Abdominal abscesses and pancreatic pseudo-cysts can be therapeutically drained by needle punctures guided by ultrasound.

The general feeling that a large surgical scar was no longer something to be proud of, and the growing consciousness that many of the complications and detrimental side-effects of open surgery could be avoided by performing smaller operations or 'button hole' operations with equal effectiveness, have created a climate in which these new developments have not only been welcomed by the public, but also by the political and governmental authorities, who have provided active endorsement.

FLEXIBLE AND STEERABLE
The historical use of endoscopes (*see p.171*) dates back to 1853 with the development of the first workable endoscopic instrument for visualizing the urethra and urinary bladder. For over a century, endoscopes were introduced only

BELOW *A surgeon uses a laparoscope (a type of endoscope)* *inserted through the abdominal wall to examine the organs within.*

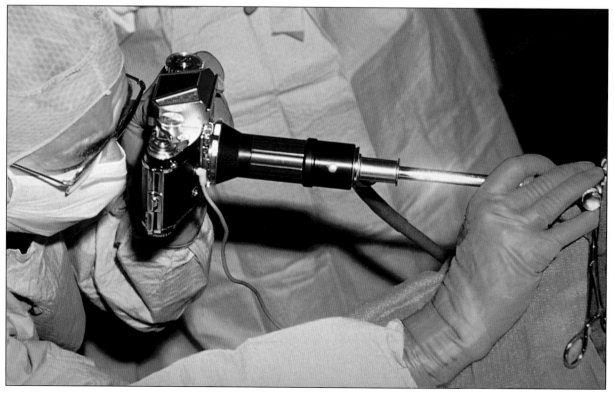

through the natural orifices of the body, such as the mouth, the anus and vagina. Rigid endoscopes, mounted with a light source, were substituted by semi-rigid 'scopes, later to be replaced by flexible fibre-optic endoscopes.

Extra channels were soon included in the instruments, thereby providing the means to inflate an organ for better viewing, to flush water for irrigation, or to replace blood when using an angioscope in a blood vessel. 'Working channels' were also created for the passage of miniature instruments, forceps, snares, coagulation devices and fibre systems so that laser energy for the removal of tumours or atherosclerotic lesions could be conducted.

The materials used in flexible and steerable endoscopes are usually vulnerable, resulting in a limited lifespan for these instruments and a need for costly repairs. Ingenious and imaginative manufacturers have solved this problem – and continue to refine their solutions – by providing disposable instruments or spare parts for the various 'scopes.

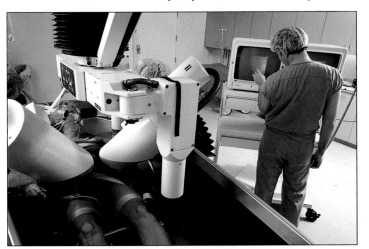

ABOVE *A patient's kidney stones are broken into smaller pieces, which can be passed in the urine, by ultrasound waves in lithotripsy.*

Percutaneous (through the skin) procedures have now been developed, both for diagnostic and – increasingly – for therapeutic purposes. For example, percutaneous transluminal (coronary) angioplasty, or PT(C)A for short, is established as a standard procedure in vascular conditions, possibly to be replaced by lasers, drills and cutting and vibrating tools.

Custom-built steel or hard plastic tubes, called stents, can be inserted, under angioscopic or ultrasound guidance, to prevent the collapse of blood vessels and ducts. Such a procedure improves the long-term results of percutaneous catheter operations. Self-expanding stents, shunts, or even vascular prostheses can now be introduced through the skin or by minimal surgical exploration.

Extra-corporeal shock wave lithotripsy (ESWL) was introduced in the early 1980s to treat urinary tract stones, and is now the treatment of choice for this disease. Shock waves are beamed from outside the body so that the stones break up into tiny pieces and are more easily passed. Now this example of completely non-invasive therapy is starting to become the treatment of choice for bile stones and pancreatic duct stones. Other applications of this treatment procedure are being tested in experimental studies – for example, ESWL appears to be surprisingly effective in the treatment of non-union after bone fractures. In the future,

it may be feasible as a pretreatment of heavily calcified atherosclerotic lesions in arteries – in order to allow balloon angioplasty (expanding blood vessels) in situations that seem not to be amenable for state-of-the-art catheter passage.

INCREASED DEMAND

Strangely enough, technical development is more advanced than clinical application. Many of the new devices have not been produced as a result of a clinical need, but rather as a result of technical pioneering. Such catheter procedures as PT(C)A can replace coronary bypass surgery, and carry the promise of lowering the costs of health care in this area by reducing the length of hospital stay and the employment of expensive hospital equipment. In the future, recovery from percutaneous procedures will be faster, allowing an early return to normal professional activity and so a saving of potentially an enormous amount of money.

However, there is another side of the coin. The ease and allegedly low risks pertaining to catheter procedures and other forms of minimally invasive surgery have created an increased demand amongst consumers – the patients.

The cost-effectiveness of these procedures has not been fully investigated in randomized controlled trials, and safety has not always been tested in reliable programmes. Definitions for efficacy and success rate are lacking in most instances, and long-term follow-up is not yet available for newer techniques. Some of these procedures, such as laser-angioplasty, became quickly fashionable and were clinically introduced long before their efficacy could be reliably demonstrated Consequently, several machines have – not surprisingly – disappeared from the medical armoury just as fast as they arrived.

Although considerable scepticism is both needed and healthy when forecasting the future, several of the new treatment methods have demonstrated their value beyond any doubt and are here to stay. Over-enthusiastic application of technical gadgets, however, may lead to disappointment for the patient and the doctor, and should be avoided. In general, it seems clear that minimally invasive surgery is a definite trend for the future and that many new and exciting developments in this field can be expected, both in this century and the next.

BELOW *A surgeon uses a flexible endoscope to direct an argon laser at blood vessels in the abdomen to control bleeding. Another doctor (RIGHT) follows the procedure, observing through a second eyepiece.*

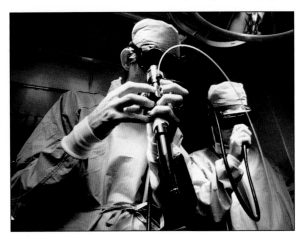

HELPING THE BODY

by PROFESSOR JAMES MOWBRAY MBBCH FRCP

Professor of Immunopathology, St Mary's Hospital Medical School, London

THE FIRST SCIENTISTS TO NOTE the importance of immuno-logical processes in the body's control of infection were Louis Pasteur and Robert Koch *(see pp.56–9)*. Immunity was deemed to be fundamentally good, with a primary role of protecting the body against all infectious agents. After scientists began to understand its role in transplant rejection and the control of tumours, immunity was considered good in prophylaxis and cure. And so matters stood, until the 1960s.

Then Sir Macfarlane Burnet, the Australian scientist and Nobel prizewinner, put the cat among the pigeons by suggesting that immunity was often a 'bad thing', and might cause a group of disorders later to be called 'auto-immune' – that is, the result of the body reacting against itself. The idea generated enormous excitement and research: first, into the identification of antibodies that were auto-reactive; then into investigating cellular immune reactions that might also damage the body. It was soon realized that the auto-reactive antibodies acted as messengers in the control system of the body's immunity. Known as 'anti-idiotypic antibodies', these then became the focus of interest.

A further advance came when it was realized that the control of different groups of white cells (lymphocytes) required the transmission of messages from one cell to another. One of the first of these messengers, the 'macrophage immobilizing factor' (MIF), was found to immobilize phagocytic cells at the antigen site. At the same time, haematologists were also identifying proteins, known as growth factors, that controlled the proliferation of different cell types in bone marrow. Similar growth factors were also identified for lymphocytes, and given a variety of names – of which the most common is interleukin 2 (IL-2). This is released at certain sites in response to a particular antigen, and can increase the growth rate of the cells involved.

BELOW *Grown as a result of IL-2, a lymphokine-activated natural killer (LANAK) cell (yellow) attacks a cancer cell (red).*

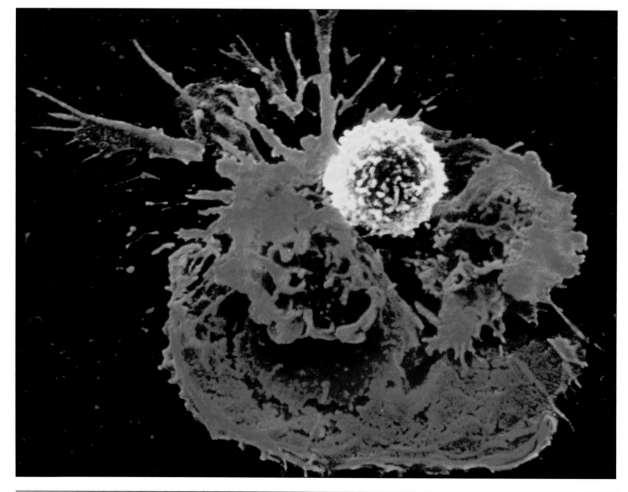

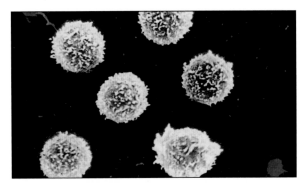

ABOVE *A scientist checks cell cultures of lymphocytes, which have* *been doped with interleukin 2, for possible contamination.*

ABOVE *A group of 'killer' T-lymphocytes – these recognize* *antigens on viruses and bacteria and release enzymes to kill them.*

The small proteins that carry messages from cell to cell are now called, generically, cytokines. The cells have receptors on their surface, to which cytokines can bind, the effects depending on the nature of the cytokine and the type of the receptor: one cytokine may bind to one receptor and stimulate the cell; a related cytokine may bind to the same receptor and block it, preventing stimulation by other cytokines. But the second cytokine may bind to a different receptor, perhaps on another cell, and cause stimulation.

And this is where we stand in 1992. When theoretical immunology began to explode with ideas, in the 1960s, it was hoped that a vast number of clinical applications would stem directly from the research. But such applications have been slow to come, partly because the workers in their ivory towers did not know which derangements of the immune system would present as diseases in clinical medicine. Instead, scientists invented theoretical derangements of the system, and then tried to assign diseases, which superficially resembled them, to the derangements. However, the need to control the immune response to allow transplanted organs to survive led to attempts in the 1980s to produce some order out of the chaos that typified the early 1970s.

THE WAY FORWARD

So where do we go from here? There is still a great deal to learn about how the controlling networks operate – those produced by antibodies, by the differential actions of cytokines, and by the variation in antigens. What clinical uses can we expect to see developed from the theoretical understanding of a vastly complex system that involves many cell types and tens of thousands of antibody specificities?

Organ transplants inspired much of the development that led to the clinical application of modern immunology. Today, kidney transplants are so routine that the tens of thousands that take place each year evoke minimal interest; bone marrow transplants are routine in, for example, the treatment of leukaemia; and heart transplants are the treatment of choice for some conditions.

But one transplant method has so far only seen limited use – that of genetic material. Although genetic engineering is evolving as a treatment of some genetic diseases, there are some disorders in which it may be easier – and preferable – to transplant whole tissues containing the healthy gene instead of using vectors to carry it. I was involved in some very early attempts to overcome rare disorders of lysosomal tissues; we grafted cells from normal HLA-identical siblings into children with a mutated enzyme gene. This type of procedure has a considerable future if the appropriate cells can be grown in tissue culture and rejection is prevented, either by using compatible family donors to supply the cells, or by immunosuppression with drugs such as cyclosporin.

About 10 per cent of Britain's population suffers from disorders, such as rheumatoid arthritis, which have an immunological basis. Despite drugs to control inflammation and inhibit some antibody responses, these diseases remain troublesome. However, agents that block the activation pathways will probably be developed once the mechanisms behind such diseases are understood. The drugs will probably be either natural cytokines or genetically engineered ones, which may have more potent blocking or stimulating effects.

MONOCLONAL ANTIBODIES

In 1984, Dr Cesar Milstein and his team at Cambridge University won a Nobel prize for their work on the development of monoclonal antibodies. Since then, it has become possible to make antibodies to exact specifications for particular cell shapes. These antibodies can detect particular antigens on the surface of cells, and so bind to a specific set of cells – or even to a set in a particular stage of activation. This means that monoclonal antibodies can be used to target cytotoxic drugs to tumour cells with particular markers.

Furthermore, the presence of viral antigens on the surface of infected cells means that it should be possible to detect and eliminate the cells, and theoretical systems exist to do this. Practical developments of them may lead to the successful treatment of some of the viral infections which evade the normal immune responses; they may, too, provide a means by which people exposed to an infectious agent can be passively protected before their own immune systems have had time to react. It is likely that monoclonal antibodies will be used much more widely for this purpose than naturally occurring antibodies produced by infection or by the immunization of humans or laboratory animals.

Over the last 20 years, immunology has crept into almost every area of medicine, largely because its techniques are the best way to assay hormones and drugs. The widespread use of monoclonal antibodies in analytical work means that they will play a much greater role in screening and diagnosis over the next ten years. The techniques of immunology and molecular biology will take over much of the labour-intensive, and often rather inaccurate, laboratory methods of today. And for this reason alone, an understanding of the processes and, especially, the methods of immunology will be an essential requirement for those working in health care.

THE SEARCH FOR CURES

by PROFESSOR KAROL SIKORA MA MB PHD FRCR FRCP

Professor of Oncology, The Hammersmith Hospital, London

THE FIRST DISEASES SUFFERED by humanity prompted a search for cures that, thousands of years later, is still not over. Various cancers, multiple sclerosis, AIDS and even the common cold are just some of the many disorders that have eluded all attempts by medical science to elicit a cure. As in the Renaissance and the Enlightenment (*see p.32*), the 20th century brought hope that every disease would be conquered: by new drugs, vaccines or some other therapy. Unfortunately, this goal has not yet been achieved – but the hope remains that technological and scientific breakthroughs will lead to a new range of medical and scientific triumphs over the next 30 years.

In the environmentally conscious 1990s, multinational companies are finally coming to realize that a storehouse of medicinal drugs awaits them in the dwindling gene pools of botanically rich habitats around the world. The success of two such drugs will no doubt act as a beacon in the search for more: vincristine, from the Madagascan periwinkle (*see p.195*), has helped in the fight against leukaemia; and taxol, from the bark of the endangered Pacific yew tree, is used to reduce tumours in both breast and ovarian cancer. Nevertheless, the remorseless routine of devising, researching and testing new drugs, whether natural or synthetic, continues in many pharmacology and pharmaceutical laboratories around the world.

CONTROLLING CELL GROWTH

Much of current research into the prevention (*see p.228*) and cure of diseases is focused at the genetic level. The bold enterprise of the international Human Genome Project to identify every human gene by the year 2006 (*see p.163*) indicates the scale of the effort being made to come to grips with disease. With spin-offs from this project likely to bring results at any time, there is a good chance that progress towards curing some of the 4000 diseases believed to have a hereditary factor is just round the corner. Moreover, increased knowledge about our genes will give greater understanding of the molecular basis of normal and abnormal growth – and especially of how cell proteins and ribonucleic acid (RNA) are synthesized under the control of the DNA template (*see pp.160–3*) of our genes. Advances in such knowledge will almost certainly improve diagnostic and therapeutic procedures as we enter the next millennium.

The discovery and identification of genes that lead to the synthesis of growth-control molecules is expected to revolutionize the production of anti-cancer agents over the next few decades. Drugs, such as antisense, that selectively inhibit the synthesis of RNA from a DNA template, may be used to change the activity of selected genes – to switch them on and off – and to prevent tumours from turning malignant.

Progress is also likely in the future in another area of cancer management: methods of blocking the growth of new blood vessels (angiogenesis – a normal and vital process when wounds are healing) in order to prevent tumours from spreading. Two potential methods exist: obstructing the vessels by injecting tiny plugs, known as starch microspheres; and the use of drugs to inhibit the production of substances called angiogenesis factors in the area involved.

SELECTIVE TARGETING

One way of helping the body to help itself might be to modify the genetic basis of immunity – a technique known as genetic immunomodulation. When genes that control the synthesis of cytokines (*see p.236*) are introduced into cancer cells or lymphocytes, they trigger an immune response that is cytotoxic: tumour or other diseased cells are killed.

At present, these cytokines produce unwanted side-effects because they are not yet sufficiently selective to prevent healthy cells from being killed. Methods to improve selectivity include the use of chemically modified anti-cancer drugs that remain non-toxic until they reach their target site: when they are in place, they are activated either by light (photoactivation), by monoclonal antibodies, or by enzymes.

LEFT *A technician monitors the purification of monoclonal antibodies as contaminating proteins are removed by ion exchange chromatography: one of the final steps of a complex process.*

Until now, photoactivation has only been possible in the case of superficial skin tumours. Now, however, the advent of lasers, fibre-optic systems and *in vitro* blood separation techniques means that photochemotherapy will have a much wider application in the future.

Selectivity has proved the keyword in the search for other cures. Monoclonal antibodies (MAbs) lock on and bind to features on the surface of cells (*see p.237*). The features are a kind of cellular fingerprint, different cells having different sets. Scientists have already started to identify these features – both normal and abnormal – and as their chemical profiles are mapped, so relevant MAbs can be created. They can now be produced in sufficient quantities to be used for some diagnostic purposes – pregnancy tests, for example, and the microscopic study of diseased tissue. It seems likely that monoclonal antibodies will be used for clinical purposes in the not too distant future.

One example of a clinical application might, for instance, be the treatment of multiple sclerosis. This is an auto-immune disease in which lymphocytes lose their normal defensive role and turn against the brain and the nervous system. The prospect that a MAb can eventually be found that will lock on to a feature of these lymphocytes, and prevent them destroying nervous tissue, is not beyond the bounds of possibility. In another effort to employ chemical-specific MAbs, scientists have tried to turn them into drug carriers: by attaching a particular drug to MAbs, they can be sure that the drug will end up exactly on target, and not reach any unwanted areas. Ricin, a plant poison, has already been used in this way, with some success, in the treatment of lymphomas and leukaemia. In the future, it should be possible to attach an increasing number of drugs to MAbs, and so target particular sites throughout the body.

ENLISTING VIRUSES AND BACTERIA

Just as MAbs can lock on to specific features on a cell's surface, so harmless viruses might be employed to enter a cell and deliver cytotoxic drugs. A characteristic of diseased cells is that they often synthesize quantities of RNA that are absent from, and not vital to, healthy cells. Virally directed drugs may, in theory, be targeted specifically at the diseased cells: the viruses would recognize the RNA and release cytotoxic drugs at the site.

One harmless group of viruses has already been employed in the battles against disease: the bacteriophages, which attack and destroy disease-producing bacteria, particularly in the intestinal tract. Using such viruses has proved successful in animals, and in certain diseases in humans. In the future, they could prove extremely effective against such diseases as dysentery and cholera. The advantage of bacteriophages over antibiotics is two-fold: first, bacteria seem, as yet, unable to develop resistance; second, the bacteriophages stay even after the bacteria have been destroyed, giving a degree of immunity to re-infection.

In the 1980s, biotechnologists started to enlist the help of harmless bacteria to produce specific chemicals, such as insulin and interferon and later, genes and drugs. Biotechnology itself is not new – makers of wine, beer and yogurt have exploited bacteria and yeast for centuries. But once scientists discovered how to insert a gene into a single-celled organism, such as a bacterium, genetic engineering could begin in earnest. After genetic material has been

inserted, bacteria grow quickly in fermentation tanks, producing a large quantity of the gene required. This can then be filtered out and used in gene therapy. At present, only bacteria can be used in this way, because other cells will not multiply unless fixed to something firm. In the future, though, it may be possible to grow animal and even human cells on tiny beads or drops of oil to enable gene transplants to take a more direct route to diseased cells.

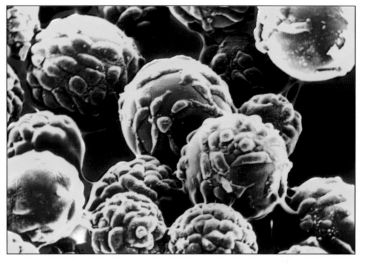

ABOVE *Culture cells after 48 hours of growth on microcarrier beads – beads offer a much larger area than that available in a petri dish.*

BELOW *Human hybridoma cells, the result of a fusion between a lymphocyte and a tumour cell, can produce highly specific antibodies.*

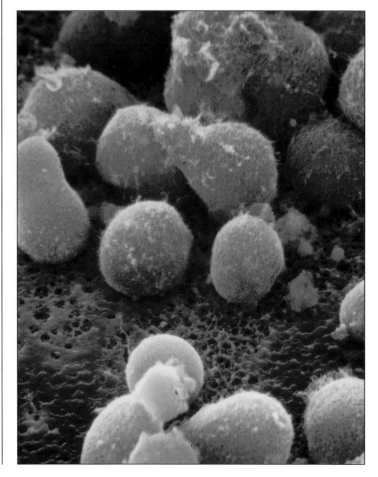

COMPLEMENTARY MEDICINE

by DR PATRICK PIETRONI FRCGP MRCP DCH

Founder member and former Chairman of the British Holistic Medical Association

IN 1982, THE CONSUMER MAGAZINE *WHICH?* – conducted a major survey and identified a total of 30,000 complementary practitioners of one kind or another in the UK. Subsequent developments have suggested a growth of 10 per cent a year, which would make the figure nearer 50,000. The survey of almost 2000 readers found that one in seven had visited a complementary therapist in the preceding year. A survey undertaken by MORI in 1989 showed that 74 per cent of the sample surveyed (1826 adults) would like to see some form of complementary medicine (*see pp.218–221*) introduced into Britain's National Health Service.

Interest amongst family doctors (known as GPs in the UK) has increased in the last ten years. A 1982 survey found a positive attitude towards complementary medicine in 86 out of 100 GP trainees and a 1986 survey of 200 GPs in the Avon District of England found that 38 per cent had received some additional training in one form of complementary therapy.

Clinical outcome and research papers in several areas of complementary therapy now find a place in orthodox medical journals and it is no longer possible to maintain the traditional medical stance that referring patients to complementary therapists is unethical. The pressure for including some form of complementary therapy within the UK health service will continue to increase. In 1991, a Bill before Parliament recommending the recognition and registration of osteopathy was introduced, but the subsequent election in April 1992 delayed its successful passage.

THE CHALLENGE TO THE MEDICAL PROFESSION

Practitioners of complementary medicine in the UK practise under Common Law, and are, as yet, not subject to any statutory regulatory body. As a result of both its popularity and its growth, complementary medicine is unlikely to retain this status. Initially, the European Commission chose to adopt a neutral position regarding complementary medicine, referring all questions related to practice to the jurisdiction of the individual member states. Indeed, when the European Court of Justice passed judgment on a specific case regarding the practice of osteopathy by a non-medically qualified practitioner, it ruled that:

"In the absence of harmonization at the community level in relation to activities relating solely to the practice of medicine, Article 52 of the EC treaty does not preclude a member state from reserving a paramedical activity, such as in particular, osteopathy, exclusively to those holding the qualification of doctor of medicine."

The same ruling was given to the practice of acupuncture in February 1991.

It is therefore clear that the centuries' old battle between doctors and their complementary counterparts (whether they

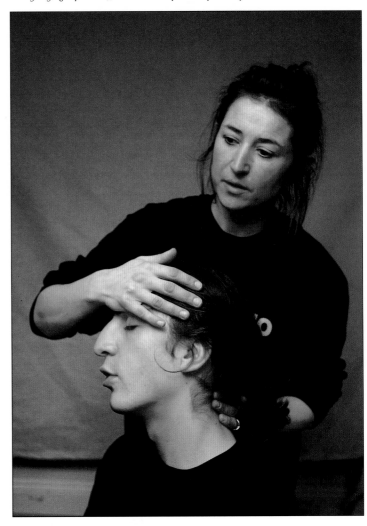

BELOW *In shiatsu (the Japanese word for 'finger pressured), the* hands are used to stimulate acupuncture pressure points.

are alternative, traditional, folk or natural) will continue and the powerful medical lobby will do all it can to restrict and protect its monopoly. But it is doubtful whether it will be successful, for it is not only the complementary therapists who are challenging the control of the medical profession. Nurse practitioners who now have the freedom to prescribe, midwives who retain the right to work independently of the obstetrician, pharmacists who establish 'surgeries' for minor self-limiting conditions, all provide examples of how the power of the medical profession is being eroded.

For complementary therapists, the major area of debate will be whether they practise within the primary health care field and challenge the role of GPs, or whether they accept

BELOW *British and American doctors now refer patients to osteopaths as a matter of routine. Here, one is treating a nodule of nerve or muscle tissue with thumb pressure, having moved the shoulder blade away.*

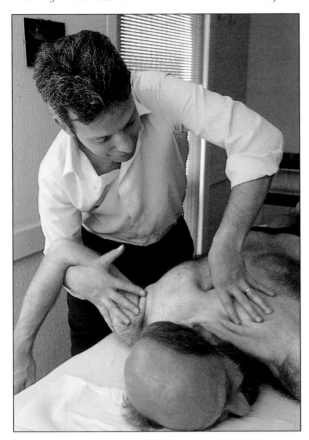

the role of 'specialist'. Many examples of co-operation between GPs and complementary therapists exist within the UK, and in several centres GPs refer freely to osteopaths, herbal practitioners, homoeopaths and massage therapists.

The reorganization of the NHS in 1990, which introduced 'market' and commercial factors into the relationship between doctor and patient, will further facilitate the integration of complementary medicine. Fund-holding GPs who are able to manage their own budgets are quickly appreciating that having the services of an osteopath or massage therapist within their health centre not only reduces the drug bill but allows them to refer far less frequently to expensive orthopaedic services. The move away from 'high-tech' medicine, which is experienced as being impersonal, costly and dangerous, is linked to the move towards complementary therapies, which are seen as being personal, low cost and low risk.

Western medicine has, by and large, been a male preserve practising so-called 'masculine' interventions (drugs, surgery, radiotherapy). As a result of major social changes in the relationships between men and women, and influenced by the feminist movement, medicine has gradually adopted a more 'female' perspective (increase in woman doctors, increasing influence of the nursing profession) and many so-called 'gentle', or 'feminine', therapies have come to the fore (counselling, massage, aromatherapy). Complementary medicine has been linked to this more gentle approach to health care and is expected to continue to gain in popularity and prestige.

THE AMERICAN PERSPECTIVE

In the US, the alternative medical system has met with the same hostility from orthodox medicine as it has in Europe. However, both the School of Chiropractic and the School of Osteopathy are fully recognized and insurance claims for treatment are accepted by both Blue Cross and Blue Shield. There are about 45,000 practising chiropractors and 14 accredited schools offering a full, five-year academic programme. Similar degrees can be obtained in osteopathy, and there have been developments regarding the training of naturopaths and homoeopaths that are further advanced than Europe.

The attraction of alternative therapies in the US is partly a result of the high cost of modern, orthodox medicine but also, as in Europe, reflects a wish for 'whole-person medicine'. In a recent *Time/CNN* poll, some 62 per cent of Americans who had never sought alternative medicine said they would do so if conventional treatment failed; and 84 per cent of those who had visited alternative therapists said they would make further visits.

Many popular books written in the US have helped to encourage the myriad of 'mind-body therapies', which aim to reverse disease processes and encourage 'balance' and 'harmony' within the individual. Books such as *Love Your Own Cancer* and *The Anatomy of an Illness* have helped to support the view that positive-thinking techniques, together with creative visualization, are alternative forms of managing cancer and, more recently, AIDS.

The medical establishment in the US is far more critical of these approaches than is the case in the UK, but the growth of interest in all forms of alternative therapies, although patchy, is much greater. There are 1800 therapists practising biofeedback (*see p.221*); hypnotherapy is very popular amongst trained psychologists and most of the serious research into it is being conducted in the US.

The new speciality of psycho-neuro-immunology (PNI) has flourished and become eminently respectable: it focuses on how behaviour, lifestyle, mood and attitude affect bodily processes, including the endocrine, autonomic and immune systems. If alternative therapies are to gain a scientific respectability, it will almost certainly be as a result of research work undertaken in this new speciality.

BELOW *Customers relax at a 'brain tune-up' session at the 'Universe of You' clinic, in California. Coloured lights soothe the eyes and the sounds of waves flood the ears, to aid new-age meditation.*

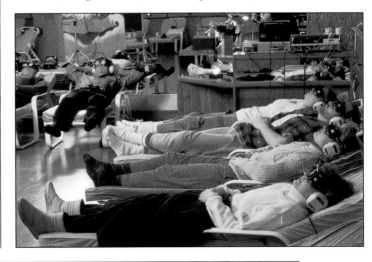

MIND AND BODY

by DR COSMO HALLSTRÖM MD MRCP FRCPSYCH DPM

Consultant Psychiatrist, Charing Cross Hospital, London

BIOLOGICAL PSYCHIATRY will undoubtedly see major advances and successes over the next 30 years. The mapping of the human genome (*see p.163*) is expected to locate and define the genetic abnormalities that underlie genetic syndromes, such as Huntington's chorea, and more complex conditions, such as schizophrenia and manic depressive psychosis. The protein defects involved in these disorders will be isolated and treatments developed to identify and correct the abnormalities before they are expressed during life, or even before birth.

Refinements and developments in brain-imaging will supersede current techniques. In particular, developments in MRI scanning (*see pp.230-3*) should result in simultaneous high resolution structural and functional images, providing serial images over brief periods of time. From these we will understand more about the organizational, structural and metabolic abnormalities underlying mental illness. Development of brain electrical activity mapping (BEAM) should also delineate more precisely the functional aspects of the brain through sophisticated use of computerized electroencephalography, again showing abnormalities of mental activity and organization.

DRUGS AND THE MIND

Psychopharmacology is poised to make extraordinary advances. By refining current therapeutic avenues, drugs will be safer and more pleasant to take, thereby improving the compliance of the patient. (At present, this lack of compliance is a barrier to ensuring effective long-term treatment and prophylaxis.) Moreover, a curtailment of side-effects will enable medication to be taken in proper and effective doses – this can be a major problem with anti-depressants, which are often given at sub-therapeutic doses because the side-effects are intolerable.

The benzodiazepines (minor tranquillizers) are due for a new lease of life as we increase our understanding of their positive, negative and selective actions at the receptor level of nerve pathways. For example, we know that the classic drug diazepam (Valium), as well as having anti-anxiety actions, is also an anti-convulsant and can impair memory as well as potentiating alcohol. Some new benzodiazepines can cause extreme anxiety and trigger fits, while others of greater interest can enhance memory and block the intoxicating effects of alcohol.

Nootropics are substances that are said to act like a tonic – without actually doing anything in particular, they seem able to promote health and offer protection against stress. Already gaining in popularity in Japan and other parts of the Far East, nootropics will emerge as agents that have little intrinsic activity of their own, but protect the individual against noxious environmental stimuli. These agents may, for

BELOW *BEAM scans of an epileptic show an abnormal spike of electrical activity deep in the brain,* to the right of centre: a magenta patch in the vertical scan (TOP); orange-pink in the lateral (BELOW).

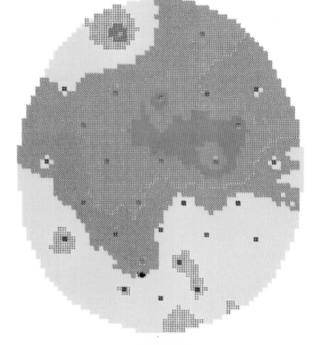

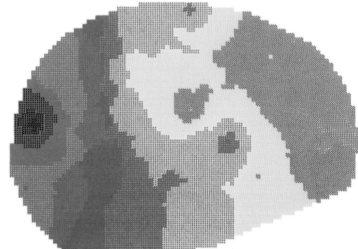

example, delay the process of aging and reduce the effects of disease processes on the individual.

Many other drugs are being developed with novel modes of action, offering real hopes for a different spectrum of activity and greater therapeutic efficacy. Although some will fail to live up to their promise, others will undoubtedly succeed, resulting in treatments that should correct the fundamental defects causing mental illness.

UNDERSTANDING DEMENTIA

With the ever-increasing age of our population, senile dementia of the Alzheimer type will become more common and important. Again, a greater understanding of the pathological nature of this condition will be reached, resulting in earlier detection and treatments that can arrest the process of the disease. The drug Ondansetron, acting at the receptor level, has demonstrated significant improvements in age-associated memory impairment – an example of the many cognitive enhancers under development.

Greater emphasis will be placed on earlier diagnosis and long-term prophylaxis of disorders throughout the spectrum of psychiatric illness (from anxiety through depression to schizophrenia) as the chronic nature of these conditions is fully recognized. In addition, there will be a significant development in our understanding of the biological mechanisms underlying social and psychological disorders, such as dependence on alcohol and drugs. Also in the pipeline are drugs to improve the treatment of withdrawal symptoms and to reduce the compulsions that lead to relapses.

DEVELOPMENTS IN SOCIAL PSYCHIATRY

Significant organizational changes are predicted within psychiatry, which is ultimately a psycho-social discipline. The shift from institutional to community care will gain momentum as more mental hospitals are closed, and the community and social agencies will be required to absorb the hundreds of thousands of individuals who would in previous times have resided in long-term mental institutions.

This shift is expected to throw up many challenges and result in both positive and negative effects. Innovative community care projects will develop, providing more humane and personalized residential facilities for patients nearer their original communities. 'Normalization' (where an individual is encouraged to live as near a normal existence as possible within the level of his or her disabilities) will result in significant improvements in the quality of life for many patients with serious long-term psychiatric problems. Unfortunately, many patients could fail to adapt if their disabilities are underestimated. These individuals will place a heavy burden on the community and will be found languishing inappropriately in prisons or joining the ranks of the homeless, sleeping rough in shop doorways.

To cope with the required housing schemes, paramedical and untrained staff will, increasingly, have to be employed, giving the initial appearance of saving money but in reality jeopardizing the quality and levels of care. As a result, new models of care, together with more appropriate and effective mental health legislation will be needed.

The increased social and financial cost of providing a comprehensive, community-based, mental health service, together with the realization that not all mental illness can be cured, is very likely to result in a reversal of the trend – a return to institutional care on a smaller, more personal level than has hitherto been seen.

ADVANCES IN PSYCHOTHERAPY

Psychotherapy is likely to move away from its roots in classic psychiatry, where its contribution will not be valued as a

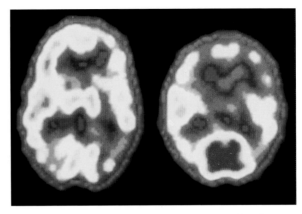

ABOVE *An axial PET scan of a normal brain* (LEFT), *compared with a schizophrenic's brain. Radioisotope tracers have been used to show increased glucose metabolism as a red area in the abnormal brain.*

treatment of severe depression and schizophrenia, and adopt an increased role in primary care. Counselling will be in greater demand and more available, too, as people grow richer and become more concerned about their overall well-being. Psychotherapy will become more directed towards brief focal therapy rather than classic long-term psychoanalysis, which will be restricted to introspective individuals and those undergoing training.

The future for psychotherapy is expected to be in helping those with physical illnesses understand the psychological roots of their symptoms. Currently, many patients come to family doctors and specialists with physical symptoms, when clearly these are an expression of an underlying psychological conflict, or at least are aggravated by one.

Progress in cognitive behavioural techniques, especially in the field of anxiety management, will lead to therapies designed to reduce the psychological stresses that precipitate episodes of major psychiatric illness, such as schizophrenia.

QUESTIONS OF COST

As treatments become more expensive, plans are certain to be devised to improve the quality of life for the individual patient with maximum cost-effectiveness. Patients, insisting on their rights as consumers, will turn increasingly to legal action to gain compensation for adverse side-effects of drugs and for negligence among practitioners. As a counter-measure, defensive psychiatry is bound to develop.

Conflicts over expenditure will persist between those who work towards finding a cure for different conditions, and so sacrifice the present for the hope of a long-term future improvement, and those preoccupied with treating serious mental illnesses in the present circumstances, which are far from ideal.

Significant – almost quantum – leaps in our understanding of the causes of major mental illnesses, their treatment and care are undoubtedly just around the corner. The past has demonstrated that these leaps are usually – despite questions of cost and expenditure – unplanned and poorly predicted, but when they occur they have revolutionary effects. Such leaps are followed by a prolonged period of therapeutic refinement and a period of consolidation. But, in the final analysis, it is impossible to predict where and when the next breakthrough will come, since effort is not necessarily rewarded by success.

COPING WITH DEATH

by DR ROBERT TWYCROSS MA DM FRCP

*Macmillan Clinical Reader in Palliative Medicine, University of Oxford;
and Consultant Physician, Sir Michael Sobell House,
Churchill Hospital, Oxford*

"HE WHO PRETENDS to look on death without fear lies. All men are afraid of dying, this is the great law of sentient beings, without which the entire human species would soon be destroyed."

These words, of the 18th-century French philosopher, Jean-Jacques Rousseau, will be as true in the year 2020 as they were when first published 200 years ago, and the challenge of coping with death will essentially be unchanged. In general, society will still be focused on youth, physical vitality and material profit. On the other hand, the impact of the hospice (palliative care) movement will be even greater.

CARE OF THE WHOLE PERSON

As a result of the controversy over the dalliance by the Dutch with euthanasia in the 1990s – a social experiment which rapidly got out of hand – and following the establishment of a chair in palliative medicine in every medical school in Britain, the selection and training of medical students is expected to be radically different. Stimulated by recommendations from the Council of Europe and by the inclusion of palliative care education as one of the goals of the 'Europe Against Cancer' programme, doctors and other health-care professionals will be competent in the skills of communication and of psychological assessment. No longer will non-physical aspects of care be peripheral: 'add-on' extras for the enthusiast. Care of the whole person will be the new orthodoxy, demanding carers who have the ability both to think and to act in a multi-dimensional way within a multi-professional team.

Despite advances in cancer detection and treatment, the incidence of cancer in 2020 will be much as today: one in three will develop a cancer at some point in their lives and one in four will eventually die from it. These statistics will represent an improvement, however, on the situation in the early part of the 21st century, when the impact on the population of cigarette smoking and of aging is expected to peak. Then, for several years, more than two in five will develop cancer and a correspondingly higher proportion will die.

BELOW *The increasing life expectancy of men and women in developed countries means that a network of supportive care – as provided at this old people's home – will become of prime importance.*

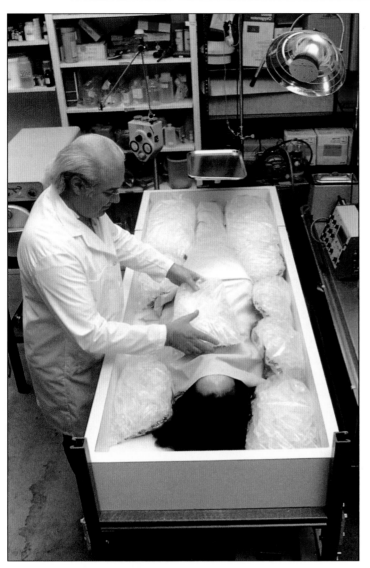

ABOVE *Some present-day terminal patients may be cured by the medicine of the future: here, a clinically dead patient is frozen in 'suspended animation' at the Trans Time Clinic, California.*

'A SAFE PLACE TO SUFFER'

Thankfully, expertise in pain and symptom control will have long reached the point at which patients can expect to be almost free of physical pain. The fear of an agonizing death will be a thing of the past. But no longer distracted and exhausted by unrelieved pain, patients will have time and energy to reflect on their approaching death. Then, as now, few will do this with equilibrium. Most will defend themselves psychologically in a variety of ways – some by a persistent denial of reality. The majority, as now, will have periods of emotional turmoil as they seek to integrate what is happening to them into their personal world. The hospice will continue to be a 'safe place to suffer'.

"They need to know that their turmoil and distress is a sign that they are making a major adjustment, and not that they are going mad, for the fear of madness is even greater than the fear of death", said Dr A. Stedeford, in *Palliative Medicine*, in 1987. Faced with this, the carers will need to learn, as now, the skill of remaining alongside people in their personal Gethsemane. As one doctor put it:

"Slowly, I learn about the importance of powerlessness. I experience it in my own life and I live with it in my work. The secret is not be afraid of it – not to run away. The dying know we are not God .... All they ask is that we do not desert them".

Fortunately, with the expected introduction of an HIV vaccine before the turn of the century, AIDS should have been consigned to the chapter on conquered diseases in the history books, alongside smallpox. The situation in relation to Alzheimer's disease will still be bad, however, partly because of the increased numbers of over-80s. Though, here too, there will be hope because of advances in neuropharmacology, and the worst cases will be relatively few.

THE SURFACE AND THE DEEP

To cope with the continuing need for supportive care, a network of hospices for people with Alzheimer's and related degenerative disorders will have been established. Like the older cancer-oriented hospices, these, too, will concentrate on home care with specialist community nurses working alongside the primary health-care team. The hub of the Alzheimer hospices will similarly be the day centre, with 'back-up' inpatient beds for respite admissions and for longer-term care for those worst affected.

Both types of hospice will acknowledge and respond to two levels of experience – the surface and the deep, the conscious and the unconscious, the tangible and the intangible. Inevitably, the focus will be on healing and not cure: the enhancement of 'right-relatedness' (i.e. harmony) with self, neighbour, environment and Maker. Activities that facilitate the crossing from the surface to the deep levels of experience will be part of all hospice programmes – creative activity, such as poetry, art, crafts, etc., as well as music, massage, reminiscence and relaxation. The emphasis will be on the search for meaning, of making sense of the suffering. Even in 2020, suffering will be an inevitable, ineradicable and integral part of the human experience. And, even in 2020, words spoken by a bereaved husband in the late 20th century will still express the terrible paradox:

"I think my wife learnt more of our love during those dreadful months than she did at any other time, and we of hers too .... The suffering of a long and terminal illness is not all waste. Nothing that creates such tenderness can be all waste. As a destroyer, cancer is second to none. But it is also a healer; or an agent of healing".

BELOW *Specialized care in hospices will mean that physical pain as death approaches will become a thing of the past.*

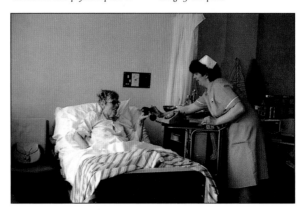

INDEX

Page numbers in *italic* indicate an illustration on a page separate from its text; page numbers in **bold** indicate a boxed entry.

ACKNOWLEDGEMENTS

Bayer AG 49, 51, 95 (right); **Bridgeman Art Library** 24, 30, 36 (right), 42, 82 (left), 84 (top), 89 (bottom), 117 (top); **National Portrait Gallery** 84 (bottom); **British Library** 41 (top), 43 (left), 47, 52 (right), 53 (left); **British Museum, Courtesy of the Trustees** 8/9, 10 (top), 14 (left), 14 (right), 15 *Dr Dominique Collon*, 19 (left); **British Red Cross** 211 (bottom); **Christies, South Kensington** 53 (right); **Columbia Pictures** 189 (right); **Commonwealth Institute** 201 (bottom) *John R. Leach*; **Format** 241 (top); **Frank Spooner Pictures** 206 (left), 206 (right) *Pascal Maitre/Gamma*, 207 (top) *Mike Okoniewski/Liaison USA*, 245 *Kermani/Liaison USA*; **Allen Furbeck** 189 (top left); **Dr Cosmo Hallstrom** 242; **Heather Angel** 21 (left), 195 (bottom); **Hulton Deutsch** 19 (right), 20, 23, 25 (top), 26, 27, 37, 39, 66 (right), 74 (right), 74 (bottom), 75, 77 (right), 78, 81 (bottom), 82 (right), 83, 85 (bottom), 88, 93, 94 (right), 109 (top), 110 (right), 111 (left), 115, 119, 131, 135 (bottom), 138 (right), 139 (top), 140/141, 142, 147, 153 (bottom), 164 (bottom), 180 (bottom), 193 (top); 69, 90, 91, 101 (top), 102 (right), 105 (left), 109 (right), 147 (left) *Bettman*; **The Hutchison Library** 10 (bottom), 151 (bottom), 210, 211 (top), 222 (top); 218 (left) *Melanie Friends*; **The Illustrated London News Picture Library** 164 (top); **The Imperial War Museum** 123 (top), 130 (top), 132/133, 134, 135 (top), 138 (left), 143; **Dr Bill Lees** 230; **Magnum Photos** 216 (bottom) *Stuart Franklin*; **Mary Evans Picture Library** 35 (right), 38 (top), 43 (right), 43 (bottom), 56, 57, 59, 73, 79 (left), 79 (right), 80 (left), 81 (top), 85 (top), 120 (top), 128; **MGM-UA** 186; **National Medical Slide Bank** 188; **Popperfoto** 157 (bottom) *Reuter*, 187 (bottom), 193 (bottom); **Royal College of Surgeons** 76; **St Bartholomews Hospital** 22 (top), 48; 32/33 *Department of Medical Illustrations*; **Sally & Richard Greenhill** 240, 244, 245 (bottom); **Science Museum** 12 (right), 71 (left), 116, 124 (left), 127 (middle), 169.

Science Photo Library 38 (bottom), 54 (right), 65, 67, 71 (bottom), 103, 106, 117, 122, 123 (bottom), 129 (top), 184/185, 194, 199 (right), 200, 214, 216 (top); 218 (right), 220 (bottom) *Paul Biddle*; 208/209, 219, 222 (bottom), 223 (bottom) *Paul Biddle/Tim Malyon*; 111 (right), 151 (top) *Biophoto Associates*; 136 *Martin Bond*; 94 (left), 96 *Dr Tony Brain*; 171 (top) *BSIP Boncharlat*; 50 *Dr Jeremy Burgess*; 224/225 *Oscar Burriel/Latin Stock*; 187 (top) *CEA-Orsay/CNRI*; 25 (bottom) 40, 60, 64, 100, 101 (right), 120 (bottom), 125 (left) *Jean-Loup Charmet*; 92, 97 (top), 99, 107 (top), 107 (right), 108, 110 (left), 130 (bottom), 158/159, 160, 176, 195 (top) *CNRI*; 61 *CNRI Rhone Merieux*; 191 (bottom) *Martin Dohrn*; 201 (top), 202 *A.B. Dowsett*; 54 (left) *John Durham*; 170 *Simon Fraser*; 182 *Simon Fraser/Freeman Hospital, Newcastle-Upon-Tyne*; 197 *Simon Fraser/RVI, Newcastle-Upon-Tyne*; 154 *Lowell Georgia*; 204 *Graphico*; 127 (top) *David Grossman*; 149 (top) *Adam Hart-Davis*; 238 *James King-Holmes, Celltech Ltd*; 233 *Ivaldi, Jerrican*; 199 (left) *Kings College Hospital, Breast Screening Unit, London*; 98 (top) *Kings College School of Medicine, Department of Surgery, London*; 217 (top) *Richard Kirby, David Spears*; 6/7, 34, 196 *Mehau Kulyk*; 183 *David Leah*; 98 (right) *Francis Leroy, Biocosmos*; 234 *Charles Lightdale*; 212 *London School of Hygiene and Tropical Medicine*; 217 (bottom) *Andrew McCleneghan*; 155 (right), 167 (top), 220 (top), 221 *Will & Deni McIntyre*; 124 (right) *D. McMullen*; 125 (right); 162 (bottom), 203 (top), 241 (bottom) *Peter Menzel*; 104 (bottom), 215 *Astrid & Hans-Frieder Michler*; 95 (left) *Moredun Animal Health Ltd*; 173 (top), 174, 180 (top), 191 (top), 229 (bottom) *Hank Morgan*; 150 *Larry Mulvehill*; 227 *NASA*; 18 *National Library of Medicine*; 97 (bottom) *National Medical Library*; 139 (bottom) *Joseph Nettis*; 205 *NIBSC*; 149 (bottom) *Robert Noonan*; 129 (bottom); 226 (bottom) *Novosti*; 105 (right) *Dr L. Orci, University of Geneva*; 165 *David Parker*; 144/145 *Petit Format/Nestle*; 229 (top), 237 (left) *Philippe Plailly*; 172 *Chris Priest*; 236, 237 (right) *J.C. Revy*; 89 (top), 113 (right), 157 (top), 166 *St Bartholomew's Hospital*; 137 (left), 137 (right) *St Mary's Hospital Medical School*; 112, 148 *David Scharf*; 162 (top right) *Science Source*; 102 (top left), 113 (bottom) *Secchi, Lecacque, Roussel, UCLAF, CNRI*; 239 (bottom) *Professor Karol Sikora*; 235 (left) *SIU*; 228 *Sinclair Stammers*; 178, 179 *James Stevenson*; 155 (left), 239 (top) *Tektoff-RM-CNRI*; 203 (bottom) *Sheila Terry*; 167 (bottom) *Geoff Tompkinson*; 12 (left), 168, 171 (bottom), 173 (bottom), 177, 181, 226 (top), 231, 235 (right) *Alexander Tsiaras*; 152 *Tom Tucker*; 243 *US National Institute of Health*; 46 *Van Bucher*; 72 *US National Library of Medicine*; 223 (top) *World View/Igno Cuypers*; 163 *Hattie Young*.

Sigmund Freud Copyrights/Freud Museum, London 118; **Tate Gallery** 86/87; **Terrence Higgins Trust** 207 (bottom); **Topham Picture Source** 153 (top); **University of Pennsylvania School of Medicine, Philadelphia** 44/45; **Weidenfeld & Nicholson Archives** 162 (top left) *A.C. Barrington-Brown*; **Wellcome Institute, London** 11, 13, 16, 17 (left), 17 (right), 21 (right), 22 (left), 28, 29, 31, 35 (left), 36 (left), 41 (bottom), 52 (left), 55, 58, 66 (left), 68, 70, 77 (left), 80 (right), 98 (left), 104 (top), 114, 122 (top), 126, 146, 156, 190, 192; **World Health Organisation** 213 (top), 213 (bottom) *Dr D. Tarantolf*.

Morgan Samuel Editions would particularly like to thank the following for their contributions to the creation of this book:

Claire and Stuart Brown; Pat Cairns; Andy Clarke and Julia Kamlish of the Science Photo Library; Dick Cliff-Atkins of Lablink; Sam Garst and Tynan of Pre-Press Ltd, London; Professor G.W. Hanks; Dr John Ingles; Dr Anna Kuroska; Per and Peter Saugman of Blackwell Scientific Publishing, Oxford; William Schupbach and Catherine Draycott of the Wellcome Institute for the History of Medicine, London; Mr John Shepherd; Ian Shepphard; Maxwell Summerhayes; Paul Valerio and Catherine Pearce of Toppan (London); Dr Jonathan Waxmann; Emma Worth.

The Publisher would like to thank Nicola Perryman for listening to him talk about this project for eight years, and for encouraging him; and Thomas Perryman.